Ring the Dinner Bell

Morley's warning came not a moment too soon as the entire upper section of the apartment *folded* inwards, like a multitude of avalanches coming together. An explosion of paper erupted from the walls as something ghastly and vaporous pushed itself through, sloughing brick and plaster dust in its wake.

Loose pages glued themselves to its form, a nightmarish arrangement of clockwork limbs, membranous insectile anatomy, and a sinuous, feral quality common to the leaner wolfhounds. Oliver backed away in horror from the thing as it thrashed in the grip of the constricting apotropaic symbols Morley had etched there.

Its edges were defined by the paper, yet even they were inconstant and ever-shifting. The beast's jaws spread and black, vaporous breath issued forth like swamp gas. It was ancient, this thing, ancient and eternally hungry, an apex predator from the dawn of time against whom no distance or span of time was too great to cross in search of prey…

Dweller in the Deep

Book Three of the Dark Waters Trilogy
by Graham McNeill

For Matthew Churchill, Magnum Innominandum.

© 2014 by Fantasy Flight Publishing, Inc.
All rights reserved.
Paperback edition published in 2014.
Printed in the United States of America.

Cover illustration by Lino Drieghe.

This is a work of fiction. The characters, incidents, and dialogue are
drawn from the author's imagination and are not to be construed as real.
Any resemblance to actual events or persons, living or dead, is entirely coincidental.

ISBN: 978-1-61661-713-4

Arkham Horror, Fantasy Flight Games, and the FFG logo are registered trademarks of
Fantasy Flight Publishing, Inc. All associated characters, character names, and distinctive likenesses
in *Dweller in the Deep* are trademarks owned by Fantasy Flight Publishing, Inc.

No part of this publication may be reproduced, stored in a retrieval system,
or transmitted in any form or by any means, electronic, mechanical, photocopying,
recording, or otherwise, without the prior permission of the publishers.

Fantasy Flight Publishing, Inc.
1995 West County Road B2
Roseville, MN 55113
USA

Find out more about Fantasy Flight Games
and our many exciting worlds at

www.FantasyFlightGames.com

If you purchased this book without a cover, you should be aware that this book is stolen property. It was
reported as "unsold and destroyed" to the publisher, and neither the author nor the publisher has received
any payment for this "stripped book."

Dweller in the Deep

PROLOGUE

Nothing, George Gammell Angell had decided long ago, stirred the heart of a Providence man like the sight of his hometown from the water. The ferry carrying him back to Providence had set out from Newport several hours ago, but as far as George was now concerned, every second spent at sea was a second too long.

Hideous secrets uncovered in the latter years of his life and the horrors he had witnessed aboard the rotted hulk of the *Persephone* in Kingsport's mist-haunted waters had soured any pleasure he might previously have taken in the slap of the sea on the ship's hull or the rolling sway of its onward motion.

George stood at the starboard rail of the chugging ferry as it bullied its way through the heavy swells of Narranganset Bay, staring out over the rambling colonial townhouses of East Providence with a look of wistful longing. Like great Rome of antiquity, Providence was built on seven hills, a comparison President Faunce of Brown University was never shy of reminding his staff in faculty meetings when he perceived standards were slipping.

George's own modest dwelling on Williams Street stood at the top of a precipitous climb from the wharfs, and his researches had taken him from its comforting warmth for too long. Though this visit promised to be just as brief as the last, there was still something uplifting in returning to any place that had earned the name *home.*

A freezing November wind cut across the bay, and George's long, woolen coat was pulled tightly about his ninety-two year old frame. A fleece-lined deerstalker was pulled down over his ears, and his careworn features were canyoned by lines of age and unwished-for knowledge.

George was alone on the forward deck, the weather too inclement for his few fellow travelers, and he took pleasure in the solitude. The ferry was almost entirely empty. Only a few passengers were making their way back to the mainland: a studious looking young man, a drunken husband and wife who argued constantly, and a few burly nautical types of indeterminate heritage.

The wealthy elite of America summered in Newport's great mansions, but the brief social season had long since passed and the likes of the Astors and the Vanderbilts had returned to the fashionable parlors of New York, where thick walls and intransigent doormen kept the cold and unwashed at bay.

A boisterous wave struck the ferry's hull, the cold spray stinging George's face and causing him to almost lose his grip on the tin lockbox held tight to his chest. The contents of the box were more valuable than any Texan oilman's fortune, more dangerous than any anarchist's bomb and more hateful than anything penned by Donatien François or von Juntz.

They were also what had driven George to make the unseasonable crossing to Newport.

For the briefest moment, George was tempted to release his grip on the box, to let its contents fall into the ocean and be erased from the sight of Man. Perhaps it would be better for the ink to run, the words to be obliterated and the paper to disintegrate than allow such knowledge to exist a moment longer. The temptation passed, and George clamped down on his flight of fantasy, knowing it to be the result of a momentary weakness brought on by soul-sick weariness.

The box contained George's most important revelations pertaining to the damnable Cthulhu cult, and had until this morning resided in a safe held in the Harrison Room of Newport's Redwood Library and Athenaeum on Bellevue Avenue. Upon his arrival in Providence, George had swiftly returned home to obtain a change of clothes and the key to the box. Wasting no time at all, he had hurried downhill to the docks and boarded a ferry to Newport.

A cab had taken him to the Grecian-fronted library, where he had met with its curator, Lavinia Shrewsbury, the younger sister of Miskatonic's celebrated—and currently *in absentia*—anthropologist, Laban Shrewsbury. George first met Lavinia when Laban was visiting Providence in 1910 to take part in a symposium on the ritual customs of primitive cultures, and had brought his sister to dinner one night.

Despite her tender years, Lavinia had proven to be a vivacious, well-rounded woman with an enquiring mind and studious demeanor. She had enthusiastically taken part in the discussions surrounding her brother's proposed plan to journey overseas to study the myth cycles of Pacific islanders, and George had maintained a semi-regular correspondence with Miss Shrewsbury over the years. A mutual respect existed between them, comparable to that of a proud father and devoted daughter.

Before traveling north to investigate the host of bones washed up on Kingsport's beaches, George had deposited the box of his findings with Lavinia, together with strict instructions that it be passed to his grandnephew, Francis Wayland Thurston, in the event of his death. Though reluctant to be custodian of such a morbid instruction, Lavinia had nevertheless agreed and secured the box in the library's safe.

Her relief at seeing George this morning had been tempered by the manic urgency in his demeanor and the haunted shadows under his eyes. With little time for small talk, George had answered Lavinia's polite inquiries on his recent trip to Kingsport with vague platitudes. The truth of that venture had left scars deep enough on the venerable professor's mind. He had no wish to relive the treachery and horror unleashed on the *Persephone*'s rotted deck nor recall the hideous beasts that murdered the crew of the *Nicodemus*.

George had accepted the return of the lockbox, thanked Lavinia profusely, and taken his waiting cab back to the wharfs to board the next ferry to Providence.

Another swell struck the ferry and George shook himself from his reverie. He checked his watch. Quarter to three in the afternoon, and the sky was already bearing down on the world. George felt a tightness in his chest that was partly the compound exhaustion of his recent adventures and partly the pressing weight of the knowledge contained in the box. He found it difficult to remember a time when he had been ignorant of the true face of the world, a time when his only concerns had been lecturing, faculty politics and the social upheavals following the Great War.

It had been the grotesque clay bas-relief brought to him by Henry Wilcox that led George to uncover knowledge of the most hideous kind. The disturbed young sculptor's ravings, together with the testimony of an Inspector of Police from New Orleans named John Legrasse, had led George to knowledge of the existence of a dreadful cult.

This cult worshipped a monstrous alien being known as Cthulhu, an ancient star god imprisoned in deathless slumber beneath Earth's ocean for millions of years and whose lunatic followers sought to see restored to his throne on Earth. It was now a matter of supreme urgency that he gather what few possessions he might need to formulate a plan of action.

The ferry's horn sounded, a mournful bray that echoed from the quayside buildings and made George jump in surprise. His heart leapt with fright and he fought to calm his jangling nerves. He looked to the approaching wharfs as waiting dockers stood ready with heavy ropes and a wood-framed gangway. His fellow travelers emerged from the ferry's shuttered interior. The husband and wife stood apart, distanced by an unresolved argument, while the rough-looking nautical types gathered like brooding conspirators and the studious young man scribbled in a leather-bound notebook.

Ropes were thrown over the gunwale and the engines cut as the boat gently bumped against the quay. The horn sounded again and one of the ferry's crewmen unlocked the gate in the port rail as the dockside crew rolled the gangway into place.

"Providence, final stop," said the crewman. "Next sailing, thirty minutes."

George allowed the bickering couple to disembark, faintly amused by the banality of their squabbles when the fate of the world hung in the balance. He made to step onto the gangway, but a swarthy man in a heavy woolen sweater and seaman's cap jostled him aside.

George started to form a rebuke, but the man—a native of some exotic kingdom near the equator by the cut of him—met his reproachful gaze with one of sullen menace. George stepped back as the man and his equally surly companions made their way to shore and began climbing into the queer dark courts that lined the streets leading from the waterfront.

George shook his head as the studious young man approached him, his notebook tucked into a wide pocket at his hip.

"A brutish lot," he said. "Not even an apology or an excuse me."

"Quite," agreed George. "Though I am disinclined to seek redress."

The young man gestured to the gangway and said, "After you, sir."

George nodded his thanks and descended the gangway, holding tight to the handrail as it gently swayed with the rise and fall of the moored boat. He paused on the quayside as the young man followed after him, grateful to be on *terra firma* once again.

"Do you reside in Providence?" asked the young man.

"I do," answered George, pointing to a shortcut uphill he knew well. "On Williams Street."

"You have a steep climb ahead of you," said the young man.

"One I have made many times before," George reassured him. "And yourself? Do you call Providence home?"

The young man smiled. "Indeed I do, but I intend to take a taxi to my destination. I find I have not the constitution for strenuous exercise. Childhood illness, you understand."

George nodded and put out a hand and said, "A pleasure to meet you…"

"Howard," replied the young man, shaking the proffered hand.

"George Gammell Angell," replied George.

"A pleasure," said Howard, setting off toward a line of waiting cabs. "Enjoy your climb."

George watched Howard go, and girded his loins for the precipitous climb to his home. He had walked this route many times before, it was true, but as he lifted his gaze to the far summit of the hill, he was reminded of his somber dreams in Kingsport. The darkly threatening men from the ferry had disappeared into the warren of streets, and George shook off a lingering unease as he set off.

No matter what lay ahead, it was good to be home.

Part One
Generation, 1926

Dark clouds hung over Arkham Asylum, a brooding reflection of Oliver Grayson's mood as he drove up the rough gravel drive to the main entrance. Situated beneath the central tower of the building, the doors to the asylum were heavy dark wood, more akin to something found in the wall of a Colonial-era fort. Every angle and every element of the asylum's design appeared specifically crafted to intimidate approaching mortals, reminding them that but for the slenderest margins of sanity, they too might become an inmate.

But Oliver had learned too much of the world and its secrets to fear any man-made architecture or be intimidated by its brutal geometry. He had traveled to grim underworlds and realms where dreams and reality were one and the same. The work of human architects no longer held any awe for him.

Yet even Oliver's newfound indifference to the works of Man could not fail to recall the terrible times he had visited this abode of the damned with fear in his heart. Its shadowed corridors, hung with feverish artwork of madmen and staffed by warders who had become little better than jailers, were still places that spoke to the fearful parts of Oliver's psyche.

He shook off such grim thoughts as he guided his wheezing car to the main entrance. Its wheels crunched to a halt and he engaged the hand brake, pausing to retrieve his hat and briefcase from the back seat. He buttoned up his coat before opening the car's door. Autumn had well and truly broken, and a Massachusetts winter had closed on Arkham with a vengeance. Temperatures had plummeted and cold winds borne from the Atlantic blew through the town like cold whips on flesh.

Oliver stepped from his car and hurried to the asylum's entrance, pressing down on his hat as the wind threatened to tear it from his head. His face was wet by the time he reached the door, and he took a moment to peer through the rain to look for any sign that he was observed. It seemed reasonable that Alexander might expect him to make an approach to Henry Cartwright, but if any of the treacherous bastard's allies were watching, Oliver couldn't see them.

"Where's Gabriel Stone when you need him?" muttered Oliver. He would have dearly liked the tough, no-nonsense Pinkerton man at his side. Handy with his fists and a gun, Gabriel would be welcome company right about now.

Realizing he was prevaricating, Oliver planted an authoritative knock on the door. The sound echoed within like a peal of thunder in a cave, and moments later the click of footsteps across a tiled floor came from the other side. He stepped back as the door opened, and a tall nurse with pale skin, dark eyes and hair worn in a tight bun opened the door. Despite his earlier conviction, Oliver was thrown off balance by the sight of this nurse. She had, at one and the same time, a dreadful familiarity and a sense of otherworldliness that made Oliver just a little uneasy. It felt as though he had seen her many times in many places, but could remember none of them precisely.

"Professor Grayson," she said, and Oliver's sense of unease was dispelled by her husky tones. "This way. Dr. Hardstrom's been expecting you."

"I should say so," said Oliver, harsher than he intended.

He followed the nurse into the building, its interior scarcely less gloomy than its exterior. The lights were dim in the heart of the asylum, but here they were stark and bright, as if to deliberately contrast with its bleak purpose. The nurse took up position behind a reception desk and lifted the mouthpiece of a telephone to her ruby-red lips. She spoke softly and nodded in response to whatever she was hearing from the earpiece pressed tightly to the side of her head.

She smiled at Oliver and said, "Dr. Hardstrom will be along directly."

"Thank you," said Oliver.

The nurse nodded and set the earpiece back on its cradle before turning her attention to an opened file on the desk. Oliver caught a glimpse of a name written on the evaluation sheet. Thomas Olney. The name meant nothing to Oliver, but he wondered what terrible sights he might have seen to have been brought to Arkham for an evaluation.

Oliver made a slow circuit of the vestibule as the nurse placed another call. The floor's herringbone pattern of black and white tiles, combined with the iron bars and sepulchral paintings on the walls appeared designed to sap the willpower of any visitor. He paused by one striking painting, a depiction of a liveried biplane taking off from a long runway. Emblazoned with the emblem of Varney Air Lines, Oliver realized it was an airmail plane, one of the new developments in transcontinental mail.

A letter could travel from New York to San Francisco in less than a day and a half, and the speed of such communication astounded Oliver. How long, he wondered, would it take for even that swiftness to be superseded?

"The patients often unwittingly give us a glimpse into their troubled minds with their paintings," said a voice behind Oliver, and he turned to see Dr. Hardstrom. Monroe, the sullen orderly Oliver had long suspected of being no more than a bully, stood at Hardstrom's shoulder, but he avoided Oliver's gaze.

Hardstrom nodded toward the painting of the biplane. "For example, it's not hard to read the symbolism of this one."

"Freedom? The desire to take flight?" said Oliver. "Not surprising, really."

"Very good," replied Hardstrom, his tone ever so slightly patronizing.

Hardstrom was the head of Arkham Asylum, a somewhat unctuous man who might once have viewed his lofty position as one of a crusading healer, but who had since found himself reduced to the level of caretaker. The madnesses of the inmates were too strange and too deep-rooted to ever be cured, and thus Arkham had become a repository of very peculiar strains of insanity, ones that would confound even the scandalous Austrian.

Yet it was the *restored* sanity of one inmate in particular that had brought Oliver to the asylum.

"Dr. Hardstrom," said Oliver. "I have been more than patient, but I demand that you allow me to see Henry."

"I understand," said Hardstrom, gesturing in the direction of his office, "but perhaps we might discuss Henry's apparent lucidity in private?"

Oliver heard the doctor's emphasis on the word *apparent*, and was not about to allow Hardstrom the home turf advantage.

He shook his head. "No, I want you to take me to him right now."

"Please, Professor Grayson, you must understand that while it's true that Henry is no longer in a catatonic state, he is still highly agitated."

"I'm not surprised," retorted Oliver. "If I awoke and found I had been kept in this dungeon for three years, I would be pretty damn agitated."

"You misunderstand, what I mean is—"

"Trust me," interrupted Oliver. "I believe I know more of the true nature of Henry's condition than you. Just as I know that the madness that afflicted him has now passed."

Oliver took a step toward Hardstrom, his limited stock of patience now worn thin.

"I want to see Henry, and you're going to get your goddamn jailer here to take me to him. This isn't a request."

Hardstrom looked Oliver in the eye, and he saw the good doctor register the wealth of hideous experience and damnable knowledge in his gaze. Hardstrom was no stranger to the demented and the bizarre, but his learning was limited to observation of those afflicted by the kinds of things Oliver had witnessed firsthand. That knowledge was writ large in Oliver's face, his features wearing his years before their time.

Hardstrom nodded and turned to the orderly at his side.

"Monroe, take Professor Grayson to Henry Cartwright's room, if you please."

* * *

Henry Cartwright had been a patient at Arkham Asylum for three years, following a series of senseless arson attacks around the town. A professor of previously unimpeachable credentials, Henry had been found raving in Arkham's streets, his body scorched and smeared with ash. It had taken the judge no time at all to decide he was a lunatic and confine him to the bleak walls of the asylum.

And for those three years, Henry had languished in states ranging from vegetative to raving, from apathetic to comatose. Oliver had sat by his bed and read to him every week: *The Great Gatsby*, the Thorndyke mysteries and, of course, the fantastic adventures of his beloved Jules Verne. He had no idea whether those words had helped his friend in his madness, but it was not in him to do less.

Monroe silently led Oliver through the corridors of the asylum, unlocking its iron-barred doors and locking them again in their wake. They passed no one else en route, and Oliver paid no mind to the paintings on the walls or the lingering scent of disinfectant soap scrubbed into the walls and floor.

At length they arrived at a heavy door marked with Henry's name and Monroe opened it with a key from a jangling ring at his belt. He pulled the door and stood aside.

Oliver stepped into the room—it was difficult not to think of it as anything other than a cell—to see Henry Cartwright sitting on the edge of his bed with a book in his lap. Oliver smiled to see it was Fitzgerald's *The Beautiful and the Damned*. Henry's left hand held the book open, while his right turned a glassy blue figurine depicting a familiar star-shaped symbol around like a good luck talisman. Oliver remembered seeing Henry clutching it tight while seated at Luke Robinson's table in the Dreamlands. It surprised him that it had returned with Henry, but then what did he really know of that wondrous realm?

Henry looked up as the door closed, and his face broke out in a beaming smile of welcome that made everything Oliver had endured to bring his friend back to the world worthwhile.

"Oliver, good God, but you are a sight for sore eyes," said Henry.

Oliver extended his hand, but Henry threw down his book and rose to meet him with his arms open. The two men embraced, and Oliver felt tears prick at the corners of his eyes. Oliver stepped back and the two men regarded one another with a look that spoke of shared experiences and a heartfelt friendship.

"You look well," said Oliver, and Henry laughed.

"I'm as skinny as a hobo's dog, and just as hungry," said Henry, patting the concave arch of his stomach. "The slop they serve here isn't fit for pigs."

"Don't worry about the food," replied Oliver. "I'll take you for a prime rib steak at Aunt Lucy's as soon as we get you out of here. I've spoken to some legal fellows at the university, and now that you're completely lucid again, they seem to think there's an excellent chance we can get Hardstrom to end this ridiculous incarceration forthwith."

"Thank heavens for that," said Henry, his ebullient manner turning abruptly serious. "I've spent altogether far too long here already, though I suspect Hardstrom will not easily be persuaded to see me released."

"Damn Hardstrom," said Oliver. "You can't stay here, and come hell or high water, I'll see you're freed."

Henry sat back on his bed and placed the blue figurine in the breast pocket of his shirt as he gestured Oliver to take a seat on the stool opposite.

"My release will be most welcome," said Henry. "But I believe we have graver concerns than my liberty, yes?"

"Debatable," said Oliver. "Alexander has betrayed us and we need you out of here."

"Dash it all," snapped Henry. "If only I'd been coherent enough in the Dreamlands to realize what you were telling me, I could have warned you there and then. How bad is it?"

"It's worse than you can imagine, my dear friend," said Oliver.

And Oliver reacquainted Henry with all that had befallen him since being drawn into the web of Alexander's deception—the ghoul murders in Arkham and the strange silver sphere Finn Edwards had obtained from the insectoid monstrosities. He told Henry of how Gabriel Stone, Rex Murphy, and Minnie Klein had each in their own way become part of the horror that had ended with the mysterious burning down of the AQA Frat House.

"I think I can shed some light on that," said Henry. "I believe I may have inadvertently called that fire down from the heavens."

"You? How is that possible?"

Henry's fingers laced together, as though wringing his hands in guilt. His breath came in shallow hikes and he wouldn't look Oliver in the eye.

"You must understand that I remember little of my time here, just horrible fragments of nightmares stitched together in ways that make no sense. I…I think…that night…a dreadful apparition appeared to me and forced me to speak the words I had been deceived into saying so many years ago…the words that saw me brought to this place as a prisoner."

"You weren't yourself, Henry," said Oliver. "You mustn't hold yourself responsible. In any case, that fire wiped out the nest of the damned ghoulish creatures."

"And destroyed any evidence of Alexander's involvement," spat Henry.

Oliver reached out and placed a hand on Henry's shoulder. There was no meat to the man, and his bones felt like sharp-edged kindling.

"Perhaps that was his intent, but it destroyed the last of the monsters."

"Don't be so certain, Oliver," said Henry. "What did Alexander tell you of Château-Thierry? Did he tell you how he and I found that damnable catacomb chamber the German shelling had unearthed? Did he tell you of the books belonging to the Comte D'Erlette?"

"He did, but his account of what happened there must now be called into question. He told us that some of the men went mad with what they read. He told me that you delved too deeply and called the fire of the Old Ones down upon the enemy. God forgive me, but he said you were the one who became obsessed with bringing the knowledge back to the States. I'm sorry, Henry, but we took him at his word…"

"Perfectly understandable, Oliver," said Henry with a kindly smile. "Given Alexander's devilish charisma and my abode in an asylum, it would be hard not to take the veracity of his tale at face value. Swap his and my names around and, for the most part, the story is true."

"The best lies are those built around a kernel of truth, I suppose."

Henry nodded. "It was a bad business at that Frenchy's castle, and I wish I'd had the gumption to stop Alexander, but we were set to be overrun and the Kaiser's men weren't about to give quarter to the men who'd bloodied them so many times over the past few days. The things we saw in that cellar…"

Henry lapsed into silence, but Oliver did not press him to continue. From his talks with William Hillshore, he understood enough of soldiers' traumatic memories to know that the horrors of war could only be drawn out slowly. His English psychiatrist friend taught at the Jesuit College in San Francisco, but also worked at the Presidio in the treatment of American soldiers who had returned from the war suffering from shell-shock.

Henry took a deep breath and his fists were clenched in his lap.

"Alexander brought fire from the sky and burned the German soldiers to death without mercy. I can still picture him, standing on the battlements and laughing as he brought columns of flame down on the enemy. Battalions of men burned to ash, tanks reduced to molten slag, and an entire landscape burned black as far as the eye could see.

I understand war, Oliver, I've been there and I've seen friends die. I've killed men too, but I took no pleasure in it. For a long time after I came home I would see some of their faces when I slept. But Alexander…? He reveled in the slaughter. He couldn't wait to wield that power again."

"At Belleau Wood?" asked Oliver.

"Just so, my dear friend, just so," agreed Henry. "But it didn't end there. I began to hear stories circulating about him and his men. Tales of butchery and mutilations. His unit gained a terrible reputation, one that bore all the hallmarks of the books belonging to the damned Comte. Before I could investigate the truth of the stories, I was wounded and sent back to the States. And that was the last I heard of Alexander Templeton until he sought a position at Miskatonic."

"Do you think he knew you held tenure there?"

"He must have done," said Henry. "Alexander was never one to chose a course of action without due consideration of every outcome."

"But why come here when he knew you would certainly oppose his appointment?"

"It is this place, Oliver," said Henry. "You must have felt it? There is cosmological significance to Arkham, a confluence of alignments that draw the mystical, the unholy and the macabre. In such a place, it was a matter of utmost simplicity for Alexander to remove me from his schemes."

Oliver nodded in agreement. He still felt foolish at having failed to recognize that the very enemy he sought to defeat was at his side all along. But Alexander had fooled everyone from the students on up to the Dean of the University. A moment of silence fell between the two old friends, until Henry sat up straight.

"Continue with your tale, Oliver," he said. "Tell me everything."

So Oliver told Henry how their researches had uncovered evidence of a terrible artifact known as the Eye of Infinite Stars. Oliver shuddered as he recounted how he had read passages from the dread *Necronomicon*, a damned book rightly kept under lock and key by Miskatonic's head librarian, that told how the Eye could twist the light of the heavens into a blasphemous alignment of stars that would herald the awakening of the Great Old One himself.

Further researches had led Oliver and Alexander to believe that the crystal lay forgotten in the hold of a merchantman sunk in Kingsport Bay during the Revolutionary War. Already preparing to travel, Oliver had been called upon by the Kingsport authorities to aid in the identification of a host of bones washed up on the shoreline. Henry's eyes widened as Oliver told him that these bones belonged to the missing Yopasi, the selfsame tribal group that Oliver had been researching in the South Pacific and who had been presumed dead in the wake of their island's virtual destruction.

Professor George Gammell Angell entered proceedings at this point, and Henry smiled at the mention of that venerable scholar, a man whose expertise he himself had sought on more than one occasion over the years. From here, the tale grew ever more fantastical, as Oliver recounted how Luke Robinson had arrived in Kingsport seeking his help to reunite Henry's dreaming mind with his body. Oliver, Rex Murphy, and Luke had climbed the titanic crag of Kingsport Head and journeyed into a realm of dreams beyond the wall of sleep, the realm in which Henry had been kept prisoner.

"Luke is a good man, one of the best," said Henry. "He took me in and crossed worlds to help me. I don't know many individuals who would have done that for a stranger."

"I spent only a short time in the Dreamlands, but I believe that land brings out the best in most of us," said Oliver, remembering how he and Rex had appeared to one another in that miraculous place. "Or perhaps it brings how we *wish* we were to the fore."

"I think you might be right, Oliver, and it saddens me that I shall never see Luke again. I fear he will not venture back to the waking world and I am forever denied entry to the Dreamlands."

Though it had been the only way to extricate Henry from the Dreamlands, Oliver still felt a flush of guilt at thrusting the dream knife into his friend's chest. To die in the Dreamlands was to hurl a drifting soul back to its body, but ensured it could never again breach the walls between the waking world and the realm of dreams.

"When you plunged that dagger home I opened my eyes in this room," said Henry. "I remembered everything in an instant. The fog that had kept me wrapped in its confounded amnesiac hold dissipated, and I knew all that you had spoken of, everything that had transpired in my time here. I tried to warn you, to get these damned fools keeping me here to send word to you of Alexander's true colors."

"It wouldn't have mattered," said Oliver. "No sooner had we returned from the Dreamlands than we put to sea in an attempt to retrieve the Eye of Infinite Stars."

That fateful voyage out to the decaying, waterlogged hulk of the *Persephone* still made Oliver shudder as he recalled the moment he understood that Alexander had betrayed them. Worse even than the undersea beasts sent to murder them, worse than the nightmarish sight of the winged horror that carried Alexander to safety, and worse than the thought of drowning in the freezing waters of the bay—betrayal left the deepest scar.

Just as the *Persephone* had been on the verge of sinking for the second time, a celestial White Ship, crewed by the keeper of the North Point Lighthouse and a silent steersman had hove to out of the mist and borne them to safety atop Kingsport Head.

Here, the last of Oliver's tale unfolded as he spoke of the brief, but violent encounter with Charles Warren, a dying man who sought to storm the Dreamlands. Oliver did not know what transformations that miraculous place would have worked on such a debased creature, but knew it could only have brought terror to a land that had its own fair share of monsters.

"Good God, man!" cried Henry. "Charles Warren? He was the worst of Alexander's cronies during the war. The vile things that man was capable of do not bear repeating, but let me assure you that you were lucky to have survived that encounter, for he was a man of savage rages and unnatural hungers."

"Cannibalism?" said Oliver, disturbed that such a notion was no longer as surprising to him at it would have been only a few scant weeks ago.

"He devoured the living and the dead," said Henry with a shudder. "Charles was always a violent, unstable man, but when Alexander showed him what was in those books it opened a door that unleashed the very worst of Humankind's bestial nature."

"Well, there's no need to worry about him now," said Oliver. "He is dead."

"Are you sure?"

"Absolutely," said Oliver. "He fell from Kingsport Head, beset by all manner of horrors conjured by the man who lives at its summit."

"But you're sure he's dead?" pressed Henry, and Oliver saw Henry was close to panic at the thought of Charles Warren's continued existence.

"Without a doubt," Oliver assured him.

* * *

"Get up," said the voice, imperious and impossible to disobey.

He wanted to make the voice happy, because there was something in the way the words were said that made it clear its being unhappy would result in dire consequences. He wanted to move, he really did, but no part of his body seemed able to respond.

Where was he?

Who was he?

He remembered nothing before the voice had spoken to him, or whether there had even been a before. Had the voice brought him into existence? It seemed preposterous that a voice could achieve such miracles, but this was no ordinary voice. It had the echoing cadences of sounds no mortal tongue ever ought to form, of blasphemous words not meant for the ears of Man.

If any voice could bring life from lifelessness, it was this one.

His body felt as if it was folded up, concertinaed like a doll whose limbs were twisted underneath it. He felt broken up inside. He could actually *feel* splintered nubs of bone piercing his rotten-meat organs and the fragments of splintered ribs within his chest. His perforated lungs billowed and flapped with fetid air as a dead heart pumped sluggish fluid around his body that wasn't blood, but something oily and caustic.

He heard the cries of circling sea birds.

Their cries were hungry; they were angry at being denied their decaying banquet.

He tried to speak, but all that came out was wet, sopping gurgle. His jaw flapped loose and his vocal chords felt like swollen ropes in his throat. He tried to open his eyes, but the lids were gummed shut, sticky with coppery residue. Even through closed eyes, the brightness of a pale light was painful, lancing into his skull like hot knives. It felt as though he were looking right at the sun. Milky tears oozed over his cheeks, adding another layer of sedimentary gunk on his eyelids.

"Come on, get up," said the voice again. "West's fluids aren't perfect, but they're good enough for the likes of you."

The voice was familiar. He knew it. He knew the speaker, and he had once loved him.

He felt reluctant hands on his body, straightening legs and unfolding arms from the misshapen angles in which they had been lying. Neither his arms nor his legs could move, but he sensed that was about to change. Whatever dark elixir had been pumped into his body was even now filling his limbs with strength. The darkest creation of forbidden alchemy, distilled by a lunatic visionary whose life-giving arts had ultimately doomed him.

Flesh consigned to the carrion creatures by the natural order of the world was re-energized and invigorated. Electrochemical reactions that no earthly scientist would recognize were taking place in the pulped matter of his brain. Sense returned and with it a heaving gulp of rebirth as an obscene parody of life was exhaled into him.

He sat upright, jagged rocks still embedded in his spine and scapula. Stagnant matter drooled from the base of his cracked skull. He reached up and wiped his hands across his eyes, scraping away a reservoir of whitish mucus, layers of dirt and pools of sticky blood. His eyelids came loose, flapping over his cheeks. He tore them off like flaking scabs.

His vision was blurred in one eye, non-existent in the other.

He tried to communicate this, but only ragged grunts emerged from his mouth.

With one hand, less an extremity capable of manipulation, more a broken, useless feeler, he touched his face. The skin was swollen and torn by a ferocious impact, coated in a sticky residue. He probed the edges of his eye sockets, finding one empty and glutinous, the other bulging and distended with fluid buildup.

He pushed himself to his feet as the black ichor continued to circulate, sustaining what should be descending into decay. His body felt strong, powerful, and he reveled in the sensation of having cheated the eaters of the dead from their feast.

His one eye still hurt, though he saw it was night. Light from the low-slung crescent of a mist-shawled moon shone down upon him. A poor illumination, but enough to see the man who stood before him.

Tall and broad-shouldered, the man wore a long robe of red with a hood pushed back over his shoulders. One arm seemed twisted at an unnatural angle, but his vision was too indistinct and the sepulchral gloom too complete for him to be sure. The man's hair was dark, and though everything else was blurred, he saw the power in his eyes.

This was a man who could keep the dissolution of flesh at bay, a man who could drown the world. This was a man whose very existence demanded unquestioning service. He nodded, though no question had been asked, and looked up at the wheeling sea birds as they returned to nests on the sheer rock behind him. The cliff thrust to the clouds, its summit lost in the mist, but what he could see was surely thousands of feet high.

The brittle cracking of bone shards gradually re-knitting in his battered flesh told him that he'd fallen from that cliff. The scavenged meat of his body was black and blue, red and raw, but in defiance of all natural laws, he was…*alive?*

Strange, iridescent powder coated his body and rivulets of black fluid dribbled from the gashes and tears in his skin. Despite the ruination of his form, he felt powerful and lethal, as though all mortal frailties were behind him and he had evolved to a new plateau of existence.

The man saw this understanding and nodded, satisfied at his perversion of nature.

"Welcome back, Charles," said Alexander Templeton.

Chapter Two

In his line of work, Rex Murphy had gotten to know more than a few cops, and of all the jobs they hated the most, bringing news of a loved one's death was one of their least favorite things. Right up there with pulling floaters from the docks and cleaning human waste from the drunk tank.

What Rex had to deliver wasn't news of a death, the opposite in fact, but he didn't think it'd be any easier to hear. He'd stood outside the limestone-faced mansion house in Boston's Beacon Hill for an hour, smoking cigarette after cigarette and debating what to say that wouldn't make him sound like a lunatic to whoever opened the door.

The buildings around the square were a mix of Federal and Greek Revival styles, but here and there he saw examples of American Gothic and a few newer apartments that he felt sure had been vehemently opposed by the Mount Vernon Proprietors. He knew he was stalling by pretending to admire the surrounding architecture, but he'd never been good at this kind of thing.

He smiled to himself.

This kind of thing…

When had he *ever* done "this kind of thing"?

At least the rain had stopped. Rex was more used to standing in the rain to get his stories. It was a wonder he'd never caught pneumonia.

Ever since that gypsy broad in Romania had shouted that string of unintelligible curses at him, he'd grown used to expecting previously sunny days to suddenly turn sour, sure-fire sources to give him the bum's rush, or gold-dust copy to get lost on the way to the printers.

But ever since that night in Kingsport when he'd dreamed of Minnie and woken to burn the picture of the fiery sky, it felt like the world had decided to cut him a break. Ladies smiled at him like he was a prize catch, waiters and bartenders stopped ignoring him, and even Harvey Gedney had let up on him.

His editor at the *Arkham Advertiser* was a decent sort; harsh but fair, and he already had more than enough reason to throw Rex out the door. After all, Rex had given Harvey plenty of rope, but after filing stories about the attack on the Kingsport Congregational Hospital and the ghostly ships sighted in the bay, all was forgiven and he was the newspaper's new golden boy.

This task wasn't newspaper business, it was a debt of honor to a friend. A man he didn't expect to see any time soon, but who'd entrusted him with this task. After what Luke Robinson had done for them, this was the least Rex could do. He felt for the yellowed envelope in his pocket and took a deep breath.

"Now or never, Rex, my man," he said.

He stubbed out his last cigarette and straightened his glasses. He'd worn his best suit on the train from Arkham to Boston, but like everything he owned, it had more or less instantly transformed into something that looked like he'd slept in. Rex stepped off the curb and crossed the cobbled street, wincing in pain as he was forced to dodge a couple of Model T's and a cart hauling a load of coal.

His arm still hurt like hell from the vicious bite he'd taken on the *Persephone*, and his ribs would always bear the angry scars of that frog-faced undersea monster's claws. He shuddered as he thought of that mist-shrouded night on the ocean, then wished he hadn't as his stitches pulled tight enough to make his eyes water.

Rex took a moment to compose himself and pulled out the envelope to check the address, though he knew fine well he'd come to the right place.

"Hell, the old gal's probably upped sticks and moved on by now," said Rex, but he knew that wouldn't be the case. He put the letter back in his pocket and knocked on the door. Eventually he heard approaching footsteps and was mildly surprised when a handsome, middle-aged man in a crisp Brooks Brothers suit opened the door instead of a butler in a penguin suit.

Wall Street broker, thought Rex. Or a lawyer.

Neither occupation particularly endeared the man to him.

"Can I help you?" asked the man, instantly taking in Rex's rumpled clothing and lived-in features and returning the favor. He smelled the dozens of smokes and shots of whiskey on his breath.

"Yeah," said Rex, mustering the tone of voice that had gotten him past more immoveable guardians than this one. "My name is Rex Murphy, and I'm looking for Alice Dutton. I think she lives here. Or at least she used to."

"What do you want with my mother?" asked the man, and Rex was glad he'd at least come to the right place. He took the letter from his pocket and tapped it against his hand.

"I have something for her, a letter from an old friend."

The man's eyes narrowed. "You don't work for the Post Office," he said, sounding like he was accusing Rex of gross misrepresentation. Yeah, definitely a lawyer.

"You're right, I don't, I work for the *Arkham Advertiser*," said Rex, and the distaste that crossed the man's features told him all he needed to know of this guy's opinion on newshounds.

"Mother isn't receiving callers," said the man, holding out his hand. "If you give the letter to me, I'll see she gets it."

Rex flipped the letter up and shook his head. "Sorry, but I'd really like to give your mother this in person. It's sort of important."

"Really?" said the man, folding his arms in what Rex guessed was his big closing argument speech pose. "And why is that?"

"You'd never believe me if I told you," said Rex truthfully.

"Then I'm afraid I'll have to ask you to leave. Mother isn't well and doesn't need the likes of you disturbing her rest."

The man pushed the door closed, but Rex was expecting that. His foot was already over the threshold and the timber of the door thumped on his heavy brogues.

"Remove your foot this instant!" cried the man through the sliver of open doorway. "I'll have the police set on you."

"Just tell your mother the letter is from Luke Robinson."

The man's face changed instantly and the door was flung wide open. Rex found himself hauled inside by the lapels of his coat and Alice Dutton's angry son had him pinned against the wood paneling of a well-heeled entrance hall. Rex's arm and ribs were sending shooting bolts of agony into his eyes and he let out a groan of pain.

At least he was inside, though not quite in the manner he'd expected.

"What's your game, Murphy?" snapped the man, oblivious or uncaring of Rex's misery. "Have you come here to torment her? I ought to box your damn ears and have the police administer a beating you'd not soon forget."

Rex threw up a hand in surprise. "Woah, woah! I got some scars that ain't fully healed yet, fella. Why you getting all worked up? All I'm trying to do is deliver a letter."

"A letter from a dead man? I don't think so."

"Luke Robinson ain't dead," said Rex as the waves of pain began to diminish. "I spoke to him not long ago."

"You're a damn liar, Murphy," said the man. "Luke Robinson seduced my mother and ran off to Chicago. My father would have killed him, but I heard some thug in a speakeasy got there first and stuck a knife in his guts."

Rex tried to process what Alice Dutton's son was saying, but none of it made sense until he thought back to what the one who dwelled in the high house in the mist had said to Luke.

"Your mother was married," he said. "And she and Luke—"

The man's fist hit Rex squarely on the nose, hard enough to hurt, but not enough to do any real damage. Rex yelped and his hands flew to his face. Blood dripped onto his lip. The anger went out of the man and Rex rode the waves of fire that surged from his wounds. They'd be bleeding now, that was for sure.

"Clean yourself up and get out," said the man, handing him a handkerchief.

Rex took the silk cloth and blinked away tears of pain as he cleaned himself up. He looked at the man in a fresh light, now seeing the same robust physicality, the same dark hair, and the same classically proportioned features as the man who'd led them through the Dreamlands.

"You're just like him, you know," said Rex, rearranging his collar. "I can't believe I didn't see it the moment you opened the door."

"I look like him?" said the man. "How could you know that? He'd be in his nineties by now."

"He looks good for his age," said Rex, not yet wanting to get into the metaphysics of the Dreamlands or even sure he could begin to explain its languid flow of time.

"You say Robinson's alive? Where is he? In Boston?"

"No, he's not, and he won't be coming this way anytime soon," said Rex. "That's why he asked me to give Alice this letter."

"How do you even know him?"

"It's a long story and not one I'm inclined to tell you," said Rex. "Not because there's any scandal to it, well, not any more than you've just said, but I'm just not sure you'd believe me. Listen, I really need to give your mother this letter. I promised Luke I'd do that much."

"Why should I care what you promised that son of a bitch?"

Rex had no easy answer for him, but said, "Look, if it's any consolation, I'm pretty sure he didn't know about…you. He didn't know he had a son."

Before the man could answer, Luke heard shuffling footsteps on the landing above and looked up to see a dame who was old enough to have seen the signing of the Declaration of Independence. She might've been older than this building, but she had a steely core of determination in her, and Rex guessed she'd been a looker in her day.

"Lloyd," said the old lady. "Send Mr. Murphy up, please."

* * *

The upper parlor was tastefully appointed, a rich gal's place for sure, but not overtly so. Rex had been in some swanky places, and had always felt acutely uncomfortable, as though his skin had known he wasn't supposed to be there. A large fireplace burned low on one wall, needing fresh coal from the scuttle laid on it. A framed portrait of Alice Dutton and her son hung above it.

The rest of the room was filled with bric-a-brac from a lifetime spent traveling the globe: gilded trinket boxes from Arabia, Aboriginal carvings, Indian silks, jade figurines from the Orient, and a host of knickknacks from places he couldn't even guess. Rex took a moment to study the sepia toned images of Alice Dutton beside a biplane, atop a camel with the pyramids in the background, and on horseback in what looked like Monument Valley. His earlier suspicion was proved correct when he saw that Alice Dutton had indeed been a looker, with movie-star beauty and a dancer's figure. There were dozens more photographs, some from the wild places of the world, some at more formal occasions, but in each of them he saw the same thing.

Years of working with Minnie Klein had taught him how to look at a photograph, and the beaming smiles in every picture hid a secret sorrow.

"When my husband died, he left me a substantial bequest," said Alice, noting Rex's interest in the photographs. "From a guilty conscience or a misplaced sense of propriety, I expect."

"Looks like you made the most of it," said Rex. "Takes some serious scratch to get to some of these places."

"It was a *very* substantial bequest," said Alice, lowering herself into a chair by the fire with the aid of her son. Rex took a moment to study Lloyd Dutton. He had Luke's same fluid grace to his movement, and Rex wondered whether the dreamer would reconsider his decision never to return to the waking world if he knew he had a son.

Albeit a son now older than him, but still…

"Please, take a seat, Mr. Murphy," said Alice.

"Thanks, but call me Rex," he said, sitting opposite her. "I get antsy when folk call me Mr. Murphy, sounds like I'm in trouble or something."

"Are you in trouble?" asked Alice.

Rex shook his head. "No, at least not the sort I usually see."

"Then what sort of trouble *are* you in?" demanded Lloyd, and Rex saw it was taking every ounce of his willpower to keep his hurt anger in check. The worst of it was, Lloyd didn't know who he should be angry at: his mother for stepping out on her husband or Rex for bringing it up by coming here.

"It doesn't matter," said Rex. "All I'm here to do is give you this letter."

"And I suppose you want money for it?" said Lloyd.

"No," said Rex, holding out the letter. "I made a promise to give this to your mother, and that's all."

Lloyd took the letter and Rex saw his cheeks redden as years of hurt and shame surged to the fore. For a moment, Rex wondered if Lloyd was going to throw the letter in the fire, but the color drained from his face and he turned to hand it to his mother without a word.

Alice opened the envelope and unfolded a sheet of creamy paper. She slipped on a set of spectacles that hung around her neck and read the first lines.

Her eyes misted and her son was at her side in an instant.

"Mother?"

"I'm all right, dear," she said. "But I wonder if you wouldn't give Mr. Murphy and myself some time alone."

"Are you sure?" said Lloyd. "He's a reporter, you know. He could be here to blacken your name or rustle up a scandal. I won't let you be swindled by some two-bit huckster, Mother."

Rex didn't know whether to be more offended at being called a huckster or two-bit, but he let both insults pass unremarked. Alice shook her head and put a slender-fingered hand on her son's forearm.

"I don't think that's what Mr. Murphy is here for," she said, and Rex nodded with what he hoped was his most sincere smile. Lloyd protested some more, but that steely core of determination in his mother that Rex had seen earlier wasn't about to bend, and he withdrew from the room only with great reluctance.

When the door shut behind him, Alice returned to the letter's contents and read it twice before looking up. Rex saw a cocktail of emotions swimming in her eyes—hurt, regret, pride, and a bone-deep longing.

"You have done me a great service by coming here, Mr. Murphy," she said, her New England reserve almost cracking in the face of what she had just read. Rex knew better than to ask her what was in the letter, and was surprised to find he didn't want to know. Whatever it was, it was for Alice alone.

"He said he wished he'd given you it himself a long time ago," said Rex.

"But he never had the courage?"

"That's what he said, but I didn't peg him as a man without courage."

"You're right," said Alice with quiet dignity. "My husband was not a man afraid of violence, but Luke pursued me nonetheless."

"He helped me and my friends out of a real jam not so long ago," said Rex.

Alice smiled. "He never could resist a soul in need of rescue."

"You got that right," said Rex.

"Does he still go…*there*?" asked Alice.

Rex didn't have to ask where *there* was, but he was still surprised Alice knew of the Dreamlands as a place where a dreaming soul could live. He nodded slowly and ran a hand through his hair.

"Yeah, I think he's there for good now."

"So if I went there, could I see him again?"

"I reckon you could, Miss Dutton," said Rex. "I don't know for sure how it works, but I think so. If you really wanted to."

"But I would be so old," said Alice, her veneer of composure finally breaking down as tears spilled down her cheeks. "Luke wouldn't even recognize me."

Rex was on his feet and across the distance between them before he knew what he was doing. He took Alice's hand, feeling the dryness of her skin and the warmth that filled her.

"I've been there too, and I don't think it matters how old you are or how you look," said Rex, knowing even as he said the words that they were true. "It's all about how you dream yourself, and who cares about the years when you dream? I reckon if you went to Baharna you'd be the gal I see in all those photographs."

"You really think so?"

"I do," said Rex.

"You say you have traveled there?"

"Yeah."

"My son," said Alice. "It's been hard for him all these years, always knowing that something wasn't quite right, but never knowing why."

"Is that why he thinks Luke's dead?"

"I had to tell him something; it wasn't as though Luke was planning on ever coming back."

"I guess not," agreed Rex. "So what are we going to do?"

Alice smiled. "I'm going to sit by the fire, Rex, and I'd be obliged if you'd remain here until I fall asleep."

Rex smiled. "It would be my very real pleasure, Alice."

* * *

The strikers had started the day in an ugly mood and it had only gotten worse with every hour the owners of Blanchard's paint factory refused to meet their demands for better pay and working conditions. Gabriel Stone had spent three weeks working in the factory as an undercover Pinkerton agent and knew firsthand just how hard the management drove their workers.

The Thirteenth Amendment wasn't something Jack Blanchard had heard of, or if he had, he was paying it no damn mind at all. His factory was an ugly, redbrick building on the banks of the Hudson, a hop, skip, and a jump from Hell's Kitchen. Surrounded by high walls topped with broken glass set into beds of mortar, the factory's three tall stacks billowed toxic smoke, while its sluices dumped hundreds of gallons of caustic gunk into the water.

Gabriel had seen the oily froth on the water and smelled the acrid reek of chemical runoff. It was no wonder the workers were getting sick and burned. Gabriel was no chemist, but knew well enough that some substances ought to be kept away from untrained workers. After his time inside, learning all he could about the labor organizers and their plans of action against Jack Blanchard's tyranny, he'd developed the same hacking cough every worker seemed to have and his hands were red and blistered. After three weeks, he'd been ready to help the poor saps instead of sabotaging their efforts.

Hundreds of workers surrounded the gates of the factory, standing around drumfires and stamping their feet to keep the freezing cold at bay. A line of armed Pinkerton agents and hired goon squads kept them from entering the factory; two sullen lines of angry men separated by a hundred yards of snow-covered gravel. The mood was confrontational, but hadn't turned violent.

Yet.

Protest songs and rousing chants had started the day, followed by angry speeches given by drunks on stacked crates, but the hundreds-strong crowd was demanding something more immediate. A few of the more belligerent strikers had already gotten themselves brickbats and billy clubs. All it would take was one spark to turn the patch of ground between the strikers and Pinkertons into a battlefield.

Gabriel had shaved his beard and washed the dye out of his hair. He wore a long dark coat, a newsy cap pulled down, and a scarf around the lower half of his face, but it wouldn't be long until one of the angry workers recognized him as good old Mickey Clancy from Queens. He hadn't wanted this assignment, and had lobbied against the agency getting involved, but once Allan picked you for a job, you either put up or looked for alternative employment.

And Gabriel's unique set of skills weren't the kind most employers he'd want to work for particularly valued.

He had a trustworthy face and a way of carrying himself that told anyone he met that he was more than capable of handling himself in a tight spot. Just the kind of man the ringleaders of the strike needed. Their plan had been to storm the factory this morning and smash the latest delivery before it was shipped out to Pennsylvania, Virginia, and Maryland. Gabriel's tipoff had seen Jack Blanchard throw money at Allan Pinkerton and beg him to protect his wares and break the strikers.

Three of the four ringleaders had been dragged from their beds in the dead of night and given beatings they were lucky to live through. The fourth was in hiding and without their spokesmen, the mob had spent the day milling in confusion. And confusion was one of the most potent weapon in the strikebreaker's arsenal.

"Ach, these boys are all talk and no teeth," said Billy Sap, hefting his heavy nightstick. "We'll be standing here all day till they get too loaded to care and wander off."

Gabriel didn't know Billy's real surname, the folk at the agency just called him that because in Billy's world there wasn't a problem that wouldn't go away after a choice whack of his nightstick. Gabriel had held the nightstick once, and was surprised at its weight. Billy had laughed and told him he'd cored out the middle of his baton and replaced the hickory with a length of pig iron.

Anyone hit by that club was going down and wasn't getting back up in a hurry.

"I think you're wrong, Billy," said Gabriel, jerking a thumb over his shoulder where dozens of trucks were being loaded up in preparation for departure. The men doing the loading hid their faces with scarves, looking like outlaws from the dime-store novels about the Wild West. "When these gates open to let the trucks out, I reckon this could turn nasty."

"Suits me," laughed Billy, and he slapped his stick against his palm hard enough to leave a mark. "I been standing here in the freezing cold all day, so I ain't leaving without busting a few heads."

No one liked cracking heads more than Billy Sap, and Gabriel wished the fat thug had chosen somewhere else to stand. He heard a rumble of engines turning over and narrowed his eyes as he scanned the crowd of strikers, trying to spot who would be the one to start trouble.

That could be any one of the men shouting abuse at the Pinkertons and the men within the walls. The crowd was coming forward, the men in the front rows linking arms and singing.

"That's a nice touch," said Billy.

"What's that?"

"Singing hymns. Makes them look all peaceable-like."

Gabriel didn't answer. He heard the clatter of a heavy padlock being removed from the iron gates and the scrape of metal across the cobbles. The first of the trucks was coming out, its tires slipping on the frozen ground and cracking the ice in potholes. The shouting grew louder and Gabriel saw where the trouble would start an instant before it happened. A man in paint-spattered dungarees leaned back, his shoulder twisting as he swung a cobble he'd torn from the ground and lofted it into the air.

Like a stone launched from a medieval catapult, the cobble arced through the air and smashed through the lead truck's windshield. Glass shattered and Pinkerton men scattered as the truck veered to the left and wedged itself hard against the brick piers of the gates with a squeal of grinding metal. Gabriel saw blood on what glass was left in the windshield and knew this moment was the spark this powder keg had been waiting for.

"Hold the line!" shouted Gabriel as the striking workers surged forward, galvanized by the sight of their first success of the day.

"Come on, ye bastards!" shouted Billy Sap, racing out to meet the strikers. A handful of Pinkertons and the goon squads, as eager for a fight as the strikers, went with him. Gabriel turned and ran to the wedged truck. He hauled on the door and climbed inside as another brick bounced off the hood to strike the driver. He was still alive, but hurt bad, blood pouring from a deep gash in his forehead where the cobble had caught him. Glass peppered his cheeks and one razor shard was lodged in his throat.

"Hold tight, fella," said Gabriel, undoing his scarf to use as a makeshift bandage. "I'll get you out of here."

The driver tried to speak as Gabriel reached out to bind his neck. A jet of red squirted from the wound, drenching Gabriel in hot blood. The man's eyes rolled back and he slumped over the wheel. Gabriel had no choice but to haul him out of the way and take his place. Through a web of shattered glass, he saw strikers and Pinkertons engaged in a swirling free for all, batons and billy clubs rising and falling, cobbles and two-by-fours swinging like swords.

Miraculously, the truck's engine was still running, and Gabriel hauled the gearshift as he floored the gas pedal. He wrenched the wheel around. Sparks flared where the door of the cab ground against the brickwork. Smoke poured from the engine block. For a moment Gabriel thought he was stuck fast, but then the truck lurched forward like an unruly colt. He drove out of the gate and pulled off to the side of the road.

One look told Gabriel the driver was dead. It was so cold that steam rose from the gaping wound in his neck. There was nothing he could do for him and he swore that things had been allowed to get this far out of hand. Part of him knew he should keep driving and lead the remaining trucks away from this chaos, but Jack Blanchard wasn't paying his wages.

Gabriel was a Pinkerton man, and like it or not, he had to stand and fight.

He dropped from the truck's cab and pulled his own nightstick from the cloth loop he'd sewn in his long coat. It had a familiar heft and its leather-wrapped grip fit snugly in the callused palm of his right hand. He almost slipped on a patch of ice, but righted himself as the air misted with a fine snowfall.

Gabriel ran across the road between a gap in the rolling trucks and joined the Pinkerton men holding the line against the angry strikers. He saw Billy Sap put a man down with a savage blow to the side of the knee and then bludgeon him to the ground with a sharp crack to the back of the head. Blood sprayed and bone broke. The man collapsed, and Gabriel didn't know whether he'd ever get up again.

"Good to have you back, Gabe," said Charlie Kozinski, an iron-clad man from the Bronx. He'd worked as a night watchman at the East River docks until Allan Pinkerton's recruiters heard how he'd refused to take bribes from a bunch of bootleggers from Virginia and fought off six armed men when they came to make him change his mind.

"Gotta have someone here with a clear head," he replied, flexing his fingers on the grip of his stick.

Charlie nodded. "You see Billy?"

"Yeah," nodded Gabriel. "We live through this, I'm getting Allan to fire his ass."

"Right with you, Gabe," agreed Charlie.

The hurly burly of the melee abated for a moment as the strikers pulled back to lick their wounds. Most of the Pinkertons did likewise, but a few die-hards stood their ground like gladiatorial warriors, breathing hard and brandishing their nightsticks like broadswords. Some of the strikers crawled away, too battered and bloody to get to their feet. Billy Sap went in hard, administering solid slugs of his weighted stick and Gabriel's already fraying temper finally snapped.

"Wait here," he said, striding forward as Billy's club swung up once again.

Before it could descend in its crushing arc, Gabriel caught Billy's wrist and twisted it. Billy snarled and spun around, his other fist lashing out. Gabriel was expecting that and ducked, bringing his own nightstick into Billy's ample gut. The air whooshed from Billy and he doubled up, his eyes bulging in the sudden pain. He dropped his customized nightstick, and Gabriel kicked it into the ditch at the side of the road.

"I've had a bellyful of you, Billy Sap," he hissed as he dragged Billy back to the walls of the factory. "You're a damn maniac, and you're finished as a Pinkerton."

Billy Sap wasn't going without a fight. His feet scrabbled at the icy ground and he clawed at Gabriel like a wild animal. His blood was up, and he was fighting and roaring like Gabriel was trying to kill him. His hands tore at Gabriel's clothes, but all he managed was to pull Gabriel's newsy cap off.

A jab in the guts with the end of his stick calmed him down some, but by then the damage was done. Gabriel heard a shout go up from the strikers, a hurt, animal roar of betrayal and outrage. He couldn't hear the words, but knew he'd been recognized. He looked up and saw the faces of the men he'd been working and plotting alongside for the last few weeks. Each man wore an expression of disbelief and raw anger. They knew right away what he was and how their carefully laid plans had been pre-empted by the factory owners.

Gabriel saw their realization of his betrayal and though he'd always known what he was doing, it cut him deeper than any wound he'd been dealt in the war. The strikers surged forward again, and Gabriel knew they were going to tear him to pieces.

Could he say he didn't deserve it?

Before they could reach the waiting Pinkertons, a line of policemen in navy blue gabardine emerged from the side streets. Jack Blanchard's reach clearly extended to the politicians at Tammany Hall, and the bought and paid for policemen slammed into the strikers in a flurry of swinging truncheons and fists. Gabriel dropped Billy Sap and let out a shuddering breath that misted the air before him.

The last of the factory's trucks roared past and Gabriel watched as the gates were swung closed and swiftly locked once more. The masked workers within the walls gratefully retreated inside, and Gabriel didn't envy them their next backbreaking shift.

"Jesus, Gabe, and we're supposed to be the good guys," said Charlie, appearing at Gabriel's side as the police drove the strikers back to the alleyways and narrow streets leading back to the warrens of Hell's Kitchen.

Gabriel thought back to Arkham and said, "I don't even know if there's such a thing as good or bad anymore."

He felt Charlie look at him strangely and shrugged as if even he didn't know what he was saying anymore.

"You have that dream again?" asked Charlie.

Gabriel hesitated before answering. He'd told Charlie about his dream the other night in a Midtown juice-joint after one too many shots of rye. He'd had a nightmare where he'd watched his dead daughter drowning in a vast ocean of black water from the top of an impossibly tall cliff. Lydia had been screaming his name and begging for his help, but no matter how fast he ran, Gabriel couldn't reach the edge of the cliff to leap to her rescue.

"No," he said. "Just getting sick of working for guys I'd cross the street to avoid."

Gabriel had woken from his nightmare to find himself on the concourse of Penn Station with a ticket to Arkham in his hand he had no memory of buying. Charlie had looked at him warily and put it down to paint fumes and the trauma of his recent visit to the site of Lydia's murder. Gabriel hadn't been so sure, but had said nothing, knowing Charlie would never understand the horrifying truth of the things he'd learned in Arkham.

"I hear ya," said Charlie. "But you gotta do what you gotta do, Gabe. Jobs ain't exactly falling out the sky, so I'll work for whoever puts the sawbucks in my pocket. If it ain't me, it'll be more folk like Billy Sap here."

Gabriel didn't answer as he watched the last gasp of the brawl between the strikers and the police. The will to fight had been bled out of the strikers with the appearance of the lawmen, but that wasn't keeping the lawmen from extracting their pound of flesh. Gabriel watched snarling cops beat on one man he'd worked with on the mixing line, a decent enough fella from Pennsylvania by the name of Samuel Cooper who'd come to New York thinking its streets were paved with gold. The cops were working him over with thudding blows that would leave him black and blue for months.

Samuel Cooper was finding out the hard way that New York's streets were hard and cold, and most often paved with blood and shit.

Gabriel took a step forward, but Charlie put his hand on his arm and said, "Don't."

"Those guys are getting killed out there," said Gabriel. "They don't deserve this. All they want is to be able to work somewhere that isn't going to kill them with poison fumes. A decent day's wage for a decent day's work. That doesn't warrant this…bloodbath."

"You're right, it don't," said Charlie. A line of blood trickled from Charlie's temple and he had a lump the size of a duck egg there. "But it is what it is. Hell, at least it's those guys and not us on the receiving end."

"Not yet," agreed Gabriel, looking up at the darkening sky. "Not yet, but sooner or later we're all going to end up as *those guys*."

Chapter Three

Though the world was changing at an exponential rate, Oliver was pleased that some things appeared to be fixed in the fabric of the world. Aunt Lucy's diner was just such a place, and he had arranged to convene with Rex Murphy amid the breakfast crowd, the rattle of flatware, and the smell of cooking bacon and pancakes.

Rex was a changed man since their adventure in Kingsport. The hangdog weariness he'd worn like a second skin had been shed and a go-getting attitude was his new demeanor. He still looked like a hobo who'd found a nice suit and then slept under a bridge, but Oliver suspected that was some form of innate reporter's chic rather than a deliberate affectation.

"So I hope you had better luck in Boston," said Oliver as the waitress left after delivering their coffees and hash browns. "Dr. Hardstrom is proving to be most intransigent and the police aren't in a hurry to see Henry released. If we want him out of the asylum, it's going to take months of lawyers and judges and doctors arguing back and forth."

"And that's time we don't have, right, Professor?" said Rex, sipping his coffee awkwardly with his left hand. "Not if we want to get off to New York soon."

"Alexander will have drowned the world by then, yes."

Rex nodded and lifted his wounded arm. "And I'm not ready to get back in the water yet, but in answer to your question, yeah, I had some luck. I delivered Luke's letter and made an old gal very happy. Let's put it this way, if we ever see our dreaming friend again, I'm betting he's going to think we're the bee's knees."

Oliver smiled, pleased at this one piece of good news amid a slew of bad.

Despite repeated calls to his home in Providence, Oliver had heard nothing from George since he set off to retrieve his papers. He'd regretted leaving the old man to travel south alone, but George Gammell Angell was nothing if not capable. He would just have to trust that their venerable companion would find a way to make contact soon, or—failing that—they would pass into Providence on their way south to New York.

Nor was George's absence the only piece of bad news Oliver had for Rex.

Though Oliver had assured Henry they would have him out of Arkham Asylum before too long, the reality of the situation was proving to be quite different. The authorities of Arkham were still of the opinion that Henry Cartwright was a dangerous arsonist who'd burned down numerous buildings for reasons no one could adequately explain.

Dr. Hardstrom had lodged a vigorous campaign against Henry's release and Oliver could not refute that Henry had in fact caused those fires, even if it was completely out of his control. The truth was, of course, out of the question, but not even Rex could think of a convincing enough lie or misdirection to convince the good people of Arkham to release Henry Cartwright in a timely and legal fashion.

Which left Oliver and Rex only one option.

"We're going to have to bust Henry out, you realize that, don't you, Oliver?"

Oliver nodded, and was forced to admit to a certain frisson of excitement at the prospect of such an undertaking.

"This might be a foolish question, but have you ever done something like this before?" asked Oliver.

"Nope. You?"

"No, never," said Oliver.

They sat in silence for a moment, each man pondering on how they might remove an inmate from a facility designed to contain dangerous madmen. Oliver thought back to his Dr. Thorndyke novels and the tales of Jules Verne, trying to remember if any of them had involved such a caper.

"Have you any idea as to how we might go about this?" he asked.

Rex pulled a hip flask from the pocket of his coat.

"I surely do," said Rex. "Good old human weakness."

* * *

As far as hellish jail cells went, this Los Angeles sweatbox was right up there with Kilmainham Jail in Dublin. Finn Edwards had spent a year in that bleak place before the Lads in the Free State had shut it down. Frozen, beaten and starved, he'd done some hard time alongside some real hard men, but right now he'd give anything to have several thousand miles between him and the United States.

West coast light blazed in through the barred window, searing hot slats of baking sun like the heat rays of Wells's Martians. The stink of stale piss and puke, already pretty bad, was really starting to rise. Add that to his hangover, and Jaysus, there was a better than even chance of him complementing the smorgasbord of aromas with his own bile-flecked vomit.

How he'd gotten here was something of a mystery. Finn vaguely remembered a fist fight outside a speakeasy that claimed to sell genuine Irish malt, but which served caramel colored moonshine brewed in stills hidden in the San Bernardino Mountains. He seemed to remember calling the thick-necked barkeep a gobshite, but wasn't sure.

At first, it looked like all he'd be getting out of this night's descent into drunkenness was a thick ear and a black eye, but a few smashed bottles on the sidewalk had seen a fellow son of Erin come by. But where Finn was a roaring drunk ex-bootlegger, this one carried a bronze badge and a nightstick and had no pride when it came to mislabeled liquor.

Finn heard the man's County Mayo accent and roared with laughter, demanding to know what a bloody *culchie* was doing all this way out west. A sharp crack of wood to the jaw had put Finn on his back and loosened a few teeth into the bargain. He vaguely recalled being cuffed and thrown in the back of a truck, which gave him a stomach-lurching flashback to the one time he'd found himself in the back of a black and tan.

Then there were only spots of memory: a brightly lit building of squat brick, rattling iron doors, ratcheting locks and the moans of the damned as he'd been tossed into the drunk tank. Finn had tried to muster a last curse on his captors, but had passed out almost instantly.

He'd woken to find a rodent-faced man rummaging in his pockets for loose change.

Or at least he'd hoped that was what the man was doing.

"Away with ye," cried Finn, scrambling away and raising his fists like a boxer.

The man had retreated, leaving Finn stewing in what he fervently hoped was sweat. He blinked sleep away and took a deep breath.

Then wished he hadn't.

The stink of the drunk tank hit him like a blow, a physical presence in the cell that forced its way into him, past his clothes and pushing its way into his pores. It would take Finn a week to shed the reek of jail.

He shared the communal cell with ten other men—a slow night by LA's standards. Most were broken-down hobos who'd been swept up for trying to find a bed in the wrong park, but a few had the look of fellas who were new to the street and were still trying to find a way out of their predicament by looking in the bottom of a bottle.

A motley crew, to be sure, but spending each night in a jail cell with the dregs of the LA streets was the only way Finn had found to ensure he wouldn't end up on a train to Arkham.

The first time he'd found himself at La Grande station with a ticket in his hand, Finn had assumed he'd found it and wandered onto the concourse in a stupor. But when he headed for the exit, the guard told him he'd just bought the ticket a few minutes before.

Of all the places Finn could have bought a ticket for, Arkham was the *last* place he'd want to go. After that business with the flesh-eating cannibals, the alien monsters, and the trip into the underworld, he'd been bitten, bloodied and almost killed. Finn had recuperated in a soft bed at St. Mary's, but he'd checked himself out of the hospital as soon as he felt able and boarded a train to Los Angeles.

The blue skies and warm sunlight of California made it easier to keep everything that had happened in Arkham from his mind. The stories he'd learned on his mam's knee as a nipper had been grand, filled with faeries, great heroes, and devilish monsters from the sea, but the idea that things like that could ever be true was taking some getting used to.

No, Finn Edwards wouldn't willingly go back to cursed Arkham for a lifetime's supply of Guinness and fresh-baked farls.

He told himself that each morning, but three times he'd almost boarded an eastbound train without even knowing how he'd arrived at the station. The last time, Finn had woken to find himself seated in a pullman carriage with the wheels squealing on the track. He'd jumped from the train and run to the nearest liquor shack to drink himself insensible. He knew it was only a matter of time till he found himself stepping down onto a cold platform in Arkham's Northside, with no recollection of how he came to be there. Getting liquored up and spending the night in jail was the only way he knew to make sure that didn't happen.

Not a long-term plan, perhaps, but it was the only one he had.

Finn looked up as he heard the rattle of keys in a lock. The cell door was opened by a thickset cop who'd probably once walked a beat, but was now nothing more than a dead-eyed turnkey with a vicious temper.

"Right you disgusting lot, get the hell out of my jail," he said.

The drunks groaned at the prospect of facing a long day scraping enough coins together to get loaded, but hauled their ragged carcasses toward the door. Finn lingered by the wall until his jailer turned his soulless gaze on him.

"You too, Paddy."

"My name's not Paddy," said Finn.

"You talking back to me, son?" demanded the cop, hooking his thumbs into the strained leather of his belt. "In my own jail? Are all Micks as dumb as you?"

"Just saying," said Finn, pushing himself to his feet.

"Yeah, well keep your mouth shut or you'll spend another night here."

"Well, the bed's a bit lumpy, and the less said about the room service the better, but if you *could* fit me in, that'd be grand."

"A comedian, huh?" said the cop, grabbing Finn by the scruff of the neck in the manner common to lawmen from Dublin to New York, London to Glasgow. He hauled Finn out of the cell and marched him down a series of stone corridors to a heavy steel door. Early morning sunlight spilled through the door, and even though the calendars said it was winter, it felt like the West Coast hadn't heard.

The cop pushed Finn outside and he blinked in the harsh light of day, feeling the full weight of his hangover crash down on him. The alley behind the police station was dusty and dry, and the kicked out drunks milled around as though trying to decide where the best prospects of panhandling lay.

"Be seeing you," said the cop as the steel door slammed shut.

Finn had been in Los Angeles long enough to know where the Californian bootleggers plied their trade and turned west toward the ocean. He still had enough strength in his whiskey-sodden bones to unload barrels from boats, so there was always going to be some work for him if he looked hard enough.

So long as it paid enough to get him soused and thrown in a drunk tank.

So long as it kept him from getting on a train to Arkham.

* * *

His shift at Arkham Asylum had only just begun and already Monroe couldn't wait to get home. Ever since Henry Cartwright had arisen, Lazarus-like from his catatonia, Buck Monroe had been living in mortal fear that the man might remember the indignities heaped upon his unconscious frame. He'd barely been able to meet the man's eye, and those few times he had, Monroe had seen a weight of dreadful knowledge there.

If Cartwright remembered anything of how Monroe had treated him…might some of the others? If one man could miraculously rise from an apparently incurable stupor, could the others? And what stories might they tell?

This stretch of corridor smelled of fresh detergent, where an inmate had lost his lunch at the sight of an aspidistra plant recently installed in the courtyard garden. He'd been looking out the window at the far end of the corridor and had gone crazy at the sight of its leaves waving in the wind.

Monroe had watched him run halfway up the corridor before collapsing and puking all over the floor. It was hard to believe that one man could have that much in his gut, especially given the meager portions of slop the inmates were fed in here. No way was he picking a guy up from a pool of vomit, and had instead coordinated the clean up and removal of the screaming inmate.

He'd been shouting something about pre-human jungles and cities of gold under attack from polyps, but that was pretty tame for this place. At least he was using actual words and not some nonsensical gibberish.

Monroe swung his hickory club around on its leather loop, reassured by its presence, even though it was only supposed to be a deterrent, rather than anything intended for use. His hobnailed boots echoed from the stark walls, and he kept his eyes averted from the creepy paintings on the wall.

Dr. Hardstrom said they were therapeutic, that they helped the inmates express in images what they couldn't in words. Bullshit. You give a bunch of lunatics some paints and all you're going to get is their madnesses scrawled over the canvas. Monroe always felt the paintings were looking at him, even the ones without faces, as though they were windows into the bleeding soul of the asylum itself.

Monroe's halted in his walk.

Where had that thought come from?

His nerves were shot. He was thinking stuff as crazy as the inmates now.

Yeah, it was time to get the hell out of here and find a job that didn't involve sticking crazies with needles, washing your uniform of puke and shit every day, and having to fight off madmen who were convinced you were a monster.

He walked on through the moonlight slitting the floor in angular beams through the window bars, thinking of his future. Monroe had a buddy down in Boston who owned an auto-repair shop in Charlestown. He'd been handy with tools all his life, and he was sure he could get some work there. Yeah, that was the way to go. Get the hell out of Arkham and find an honest job that put his big hands and strong arms to proper use.

Monroe paused by the barred window, letting the night-time sounds of the asylum wash over him. The heavy building pressed in, solid and monolithic, and the sensation of being as much a prisoner as the inmates struck him like a blow. The plants in the garden outside waved in the winds caught in the courtyard, leafy bushes and drooping fronds that in a certain light *did* look kind of creepy.

Monroe flinched as he saw something move in the garden.

He squinted and pressed his face to the bars.

There was someone out there. A man, moving along the edge of the building.

Monroe thought about raising the alarm, but as the clouds parted and he saw the man's attire, he relaxed some. He jogged along the corridor to where the fire exit let out onto the courtyard. He unlocked the sheet metal door, then the heavy timber one to the outside before putting the ring of keys back on his belt. He looped the leather grip of his hickory club around his wrist and pushed the outer door open as quietly as he was able.

Monroe stepped down into the courtyard, keeping his eyes peeled on the spot he'd last seen the intruder. The clouds were covering the moon again, and a graveyard gloom hung over the vegetable garden. Again, that was something Hardstrom believed helped the inmates, but which Monroe thought was a waste of time.

A fitful spark flickered and died in the darkness and Monroe tightened his grip on the club. Someone trying to light a cigarette? Whoever the hell this was, they clearly didn't care about being seen.

"Hey, pal, you can't be out here," he called out, his voice echoing from the walls. "Come over here where I can see you."

A voice called out from farther down the path as a figure stepped into sight.

"Sure thing, pal," said Rex Murphy, holding out a packet of smokes. "You got a light?"

* * *

Oliver crouched in the dripping shadow of a highbush blueberry and watched as Rex and the thuggish bully, Monroe, shared a cigarette by the opened door to the asylum. He'd seen Monroe's aggressive body language as soon as the orderly had spotted Rex, but that had mellowed now he'd smoked one of the cigarettes Rex had obtained from Blind Rufus at the Commercial. To look at the pair of them, you could be forgiven for thinking they were two old friends of many years' acquaintance.

Rex produced a hip flask, filled with a honey-like amber liquid—also obtained from the blind man's speakeasy—and he and Monroe shared a belt of whatever liquor it contained. They spoke some more, and Oliver heard laughter, a sound as incongruous in this place of misery as jazz in a church.

The hip flask was passed back and forth, and Oliver felt his legs cramping up. The cold winds coming in from the Atlantic were particularly fierce around here. After numerous excursions around Arkham to prepare for tonight's escapade and their journey to Providence and thence to New York, Oliver was aching from top to tail. The last thing he needed was to be stuck out in the cold and the darkness.

A shadow moved over the window across the courtyard and Oliver looked up, keeping as still as was humanly possible. A figure moved past the window, a nurse in a starched uniform with a tightly wound bun of brown hair and ruby-red lips. She walked with slow deliberation, like a sleepwalker or someone in a mesmeric trance. One hand was pressed tightly to her side, the other held a raised hypodermic needle.

Though outwardly there should be nothing untoward in the sight of a nurse with a needle in an institution set up to care for the insane, the sight chilled Oliver to the bone. He looked back to where Rex and Monroe were talking enthusiastically, and decided he was going to have to move their timetable up a little.

He stepped from the shadow of the bush and strode across the courtyard. Monroe looked up at the sight of him, but instead of the expected hostility, Oliver saw only a glassy veneer of incomprehension. A blue haze surrounded the two men, and Oliver smelled fleeting exotic scents emanating from the cigarettes, not unlike those smoked by William Hillshore. His psychiatrist friend was fond of a strange Arabian leaf, but this smelled far more potent.

"Hey, Oliver," said Rex, as though they were all meeting in a friendly restaurant and not the courtyard of an insane asylum. "Buck here was just telling me how he's going into the auto-repair business, wasn't that right?"

Monroe nodded, and his smile was that of an innocent. Oliver had to remind himself that this man had been a constant thorn in his side for the last three years. Clearly the liquor and cigarettes obtained from Blind Rufus had demolished whatever antagonism Monroe carried with him.

"Really?" said Oliver. "That's very interesting, Rex, but don't you think we ought to be getting on?"

Oliver saw a hint of intoxication in the newshound's eyes. Where Monroe was utterly in thrall to the otherworldly tobacco and liquor, Rex had retained his sense of their purpose here and taken only tiny sips and inhalations. Monroe appeared not to notice that his newest drinking buddy was nowhere near as affected.

"You're right," said Rex, nodding sagely and turning to Monroe. "Listen, Buck, my good friend Oliver here, he needs to see his pal, Henry, you know? Henry Cartwright?"

"I know him," said Monroe. "He's the one that woke up."

"That's him," said Oliver. "Can you take us to him?"

"They never wake up," said Monroe.

"But Henry has," pressed Oliver, looking over his shoulder as he saw the needle-bearing nurse pass another window farther along the corridor. "And we do rather need to see him in a hurry."

"I didn't do nothing to him," said Monroe, his sudden lie childish in its directness. Oliver struggled to retain his equanimity in the face of this cowardly bully. He caught a slight shake of the head from Rex, and unclenched his fist. Whatever suggestive state the strange cigarettes and liquor had induced in Monroe would surely be undone by a fist to the face.

"Of course not, and I'm sure Henry will say the same when we speak to him."

"You think so?" begged Monroe, taking another hit from Rex's hip flask.

"I'm sure of it," said Oliver. "And if you take us to Henry's room, we'll make certain of that."

"Yeah," said Monroe, nodding. "Yeah, that's a good idea. We moved Cartwright to another room this morning, just along the east corridor."

Monroe pointed across the courtyard, and Oliver's heart sank as he saw the place the man indicated was where he had seen the nurse.

"Rex, we have to hurry," said Oliver.

The urgency in Oliver's voice was contagious and Rex nodded, subtly steering Monroe back to the door to the asylum while offering the man another cigarette. Oliver followed them in and turned to Monroe.

"Which room is Henry in? What number?"

Monroe stared blankly at him, as though struggling to remember why two strange men were standing in the corridors of Arkham Asylum with him.

"Quickly, man!" pressed Oliver, trying not to let his fear that something was terribly wrong overwhelm him. "The room, what number?"

"113," said Monroe. "Round the corner and to the left."

Oliver turned and sprinted away, leaving Rex to cajole the be-mused Monroe in his wake. He raced down the corridor, a nameless fear coalescing in the pit of his stomach at the thought of coming so close and failing at the final hurdle. He had no reason to assume the nurse he had seen should be of concern to him, but the strange sense of her being present at every turn unsettled him enough to fear the worst.

Oliver skidded around the corner in time to see a door slam shut halfway down the corridor.

He ran toward it, already knowing it would be room 113.

He heard footsteps behind him, but didn't dare wait for Rex's assistance.

Sure enough, the door was Henry's, and he barged in with a desperate shout on his lips.

"Henry! Wake up, for the love of God!"

The nurse with the blood-red lips stood above Henry Cartwright's sleeping form, the needle poised to pierce the exposed skin of his neck. Henry was stirring, but not quickly enough.

"Henry!" shouted Oliver, throwing himself at the nurse, any thoughts on the impropriety of striking a woman utterly forgotten. Oliver slammed into the nurse, intending to charge her back against the far wall.

And fell back with his shoulder screaming in pain at the impact.

If felt like he'd just run, full-tilt, into a steel girder.

The nurse looked at him with cold disdain, as though a man bursting in and attacking her was only something mildly unexpected. She hadn't moved an inch. Oliver was no linebacker, but he knew his wild charge should have moved her a little.

Henry pushed himself upright on his bed, his eyes widening in shock at the sight before him.

"Oliver?" said Henry. "What's going—"

Those words were all Henry managed before the nurse seized his neck in a powerful grip and slammed him back against the wall of his cell. Oliver picked himself up off the floor and grabbed the nurse's shoulders as she lowered the needle to Henry's neck once again. The cloth tore and a patch of skin was revealed, but just beyond the neckline of her uniform, the skin ended and was replaced by a plate of machined silver.

The skin blended seamlessly with the metal, and Oliver's grip loosened in horror. The nurse's head turned to face Oliver, rotating beyond the limit set by the arrangement of bones in the human body. While Henry fought to keep the needle from his neck, Oliver leapt for the hand bearing the needle.

"Henry, eyes right!" he shouted.

Having gained a measure of the nurse's strength, and knowing he could not overcome it, Oliver instead pushed her hand forwards. The needle passed a hair's breadth from Henry's turned neck and broke on the bare brick of the wall with a sharp metallic *tink*.

The nurse's head snapped around with an audible click and whine of pneumatics. An unintelligible screeching buzz, like a thousand angry wasps, erupted from her mouth, and a gaseous cloud exhaled between her red lips.

Oliver blinked as his vision blurred. His grip on the nurse's arm loosened as the soporific qualities of the cloud took effect. Oliver reached out to stop himself from falling and once again found the ragged edges of the nurse's uniform. The fabric tore away, revealing not a body of flesh and blood, but an anthropomorphic chassis of shimmering silver in the shape of a person.

At the center of this chassis, encased in a latticed cylinder of greenish glass, was a human brain. Filigreed with copper wires and electrodes, a jade-hued light limed the organ's ridged edges and meaty texture. Oliver recoiled from the horror of such a terrifying disembodiment. Even as he struggled to comprehend the nature of such nightmare surgery, he heard cries of astonishment from behind him.

This was no mortal being, but a horrid fusion of unnatural engineering and insanity, fashioned by minds beyond comprehension. Strange machinery, bronze and gold and crystalline, whirred around the brain and though it had no obvious sense-organs by which to see him, Oliver couldn't shake the notion that it was somehow *looking* directly at him.

The nurse, though deprived of her murderous needle, still held Henry tight in her mechanical grip and now began to tighten her hold on his neck. Henry struggled and kicked his legs like a gallows victim as the nurse began to choke the life from him.

"Gladys?" sobbed Monroe with the horror of a child. "What…?"

Rex and Monroe stood in the doorway to Henry's room, and

Oliver shook off the paralyzing shock holding him immobile. He surged to his feet and snatched the length of stout wood from Monroe's hand.

Henry's face was a livid shade of purple. His eyes were bulging and his tongue lolled from his mouth. Oliver swung the hickory club at the nurse's midriff with all his might. The wood struck the glass jar with a satisfying crack, and hairline fractures spread across its surface. Oliver swung again and this time was rewarded by a tiny jet of pinkish fluid squirting from a break in the glass.

The nurse swiped her free hand at Oliver and he was thrown across the room by the ferocious impact. He slammed into the wall with bone-jarring force and crashed down on the small cabinet allocated to the room. It smashed to splinters, and Oliver fell to the ground, the club slipping from his hand.

He rolled onto his side, bruised and breathless, in time to see Rex sweep up the club and take a swing that would have done an angry Ty Cobb proud. The sweet spot of the club struck just where Oliver had cracked the glass and the jar exploded in a shower of glittering fragments and stinking amniotic fluid. Rex staggered away from the nurse with a grunt of pain, dropping the club and clutching his side. A red stain soaked through Rex's shirt, but his Hail Mary had done its job.

The brain sliced itself on the broken shards of the jar and the lights on its attached electrodes flashed with terrified urgency. The astringent reek of embalming chemicals filled the room and the nurse jerked as though in the throes of electroconvulsive therapy.

She released Henry's throat and her body spasmed wildly, like a marionette operated by a demented puppeteer. Oliver scrambled from the nurse's path as she barged around the room with her hands flailing and a demented screeching blaring from her lips. The worse her convulsions became, the more the daggers of glass cut the exposed brain open.

With a last bray of anger, the nurse dropped to her knees and toppled to the floor. Oliver pushed himself to his feet, careful to avoid the growing pool of gelatinous pink liquid pouring from the smashed jar. Acrid smoke rose from the body, and Oliver was reminded of fat left too long on the griddle.

"Oliver?" gasped Henry, still fighting for breath. "Good God, what in heaven's name was that thing?"

Oliver shook his head, too shocked to answer.

"Whatever it was, it's dead now," said Rex, pressing his hand to his wounded side.

Monroe sank to the floor, holding onto the door for support. His eyes were wide and his jaw hung slack with incomprehension. Whispered prayers and childhood nonsense rhymes spilled from his lips, a last-ditch defense against the horror he had just witnessed.

Oliver wondered if it would be enough.

He wondered if *anything* would be enough.

The smoke rising from the nurse's body was growing thicker and more pungent, the apparently solid metal of her endoskeleton sagging like heated lengths of rubber. Molten droplets of metal fell to the floor, hissing like acid as they were reduced to their component atoms and dissipated in the atmosphere.

"My God!" cried Rex. "What's happening to…it?"

The very solidity of the nurse was being undone before their eyes, every passing moment reducing her bodily mass to a glutinous mass of inert fluid.

"I'm not sure," said Oliver, at last regaining his voice. "Perhaps the death of the brain is some kind of trigger for the self-immolation of the host body."

"Gladys?" said Monroe, reaching out to dip a finger in the expanding pool of steaming liquid. Tears streamed down the orderly's face and Oliver saw a faraway emptiness that had nothing to do with the narcotic cigarettes he had smoked. "She was so pretty. So pretty. She wasn't real? Gladys? My pretty one…she…"

Rex ducked his head out through the door as the sound of rattling keys and anxious voices echoed down the corridor.

"Time we skedaddled, fellas," said Rex. "We got Henry, an open door, and a car to take us to New York. It ain't gonna get any better than right now."

"Agreed," said Oliver, helping Henry across the almost entirely disintegrated body of the automaton nurse. Protoplasmic lumps of dissolving brain matter floated like gelid islands in the sopping mess, and Oliver wondered what manner of wretched soul would consent to being interred in such a ghastly fashion.

Or if such a condition had been imposed on it unwillingly.

He had little time for such concerns, as the sounds of voices and further doors being unbarred were getting closer by the second. Pausing only to help Henry gather up his clothes, they followed Rex out of the cell, leaving Monroe still slumped against the doorjamb, endlessly repeating his demented mantra to the lost Gladys.

"What should we do about Monroe?" asked Oliver.

"I guess we leave him," said Rex. "What else can we do?"

Though Oliver could not fault Rex's logic, it still sat ill to abandon a soul so obviously in need of assistance.

"We leave him," said Henry, his eyes cold and with a callous undertone to his words that brooked no disagreement. "Don't worry, Oliver, I'm sure Mr. Monroe will get the treatment he deserves here."

CHAPTER FOUR

The undoubtedly bizarre sight of what was left in Henry's room in the asylum kept the staff horrified long enough for Rex, Oliver, and Henry to reach the reporter's car. Though it had seen many better days, it was a reliable old gal, and its tires spat gravel as Oliver gunned the engine and sent them on their way through the less-traveled roads to the highway south.

Rex had planned to drive, but the pain of his reopened injury was too great, and Henry rebound his wound with the supplies Oliver and Rex had purchased earlier that day. This was Henry and Rex's first meeting in the flesh, and as introductions went, it had the virtue of dispensing with small talk, for nothing cuts to the heart of a man's character than how he deals with pain.

Rex bore his stoically, and between subdued grunts, he directed their passage along roads Oliver hadn't even known existed before now, keeping to the back ways and rutted paths barely wide enough for one of Mr. Ford's motorized contraptions.

"You do my job long enough, you get to see the secret places no one else cares to know about," explained Rex in answer to Oliver's query on how he had learned of such routes. "Especially in this town."

They drove for around twenty minutes before Rex was as

patched up as Henry's basic first aid could manage. Arkham was a sprinkling of occluded streetlights that were already fading as they followed a meandering route toward the city of Boston and routes southerly.

"Oliver," said Henry, leaning forward over the front seats. "I want to thank you for what you did tonight. Both of you. If you hadn't returned, that *thing* back there would have done for me. Killed me as I slept! I can never repay you for that."

"Don't be ridiculous, Henry," said Oliver. "There's no need. I told you I would get you out of that place, didn't I?"

Henry laughed, and it was a ray of sunshine on his soul to hear his old friend make so genuine a sound. "You did, it's true, but I never expected you to stage a good old-fashioned jailbreak."

"You know Oliver," said Rex. "Never likes to do anything by halves. After all, we traveled to another world to rescue you once already. Getting you out of Arkham Asylum was always going to be a cakewalk."

Henry sat back and ran his hands through his hair. "Well, you put it like that…"

The three of them laughed—nervous humor to pierce the strangeness of the night's events—and as it ebbed, silence overtook them as each man retreated into his own thoughts. Oliver kept one eye on the road, another on the rearview mirrors to watch for any signs of pursuit.

"Anything?" said Henry, twisting to look out the back window.

"No, at least nothing I can see," he replied.

"There won't be anyone after us," said Rex through gritted teeth. "At least nobody conventional. Not for a while."

"How can you be sure, Mr. Murphy?" asked Henry.

"Come on, surely you can call me Rex after what we just went through?"

"You're right, of course," agreed Henry. "But my question is still valid."

"Best case scenario: they'll think you're wandering the grounds of the asylum. Worst case scenario: they'll think you've gone running into the woods. They won't think you had help with a car standing by."

"What about Monroe?" asked Oliver. "He'll say we were there, won't he?"

"I doubt it," said Rex, managing to sound pleased and regretful at the same time. "You saw the state he was in. If he says anything about mechanical nurses with brain jars stuck in their chests, they'll have him fitted for a straightjacket by morning."

"If they haven't already," said Henry.

Oliver broke the silence that followed by saying, "Monroe wasn't an honorable man, nor even a particularly good one, but surely no one deserves to lose their mind so completely."

"Better him than you," said Henry, and there was no give in him.

"Trust me, Henry, I have seen horrors since last we spoke at length to make a brain in a jar seem quite prosaic."

"Perhaps," said Henry, doubtfully, "but one can never become inured to horror. I saw men in France wade knee-deep through blood at Belleau Wood without flinching, then watched as their sanity crumbled to ash at the sight of an injured dog. The human capacity for horror is a fickle thing, my friends, and hangs over an abyss by a frayed thread."

Oliver nodded, remembering how he had been shaped by his two great mentors. Henry's level-headed pragmatism and sober countenance had been the calming yin to the raging yang of Morley Dean's febrile excitements and sometimes overreaching passions. But like that Daoist concept, one could not exist without the other.

"So," continued Henry, "what is our plan of action?"

"First, we head past Boston to Providence to find out what's keeping George," said Oliver. "And then we head to New York to meet up with Morley Dean."

"Morley Dean? Your Alaskan explorer friend?"

"The very same," said Oliver. "He has a wealth of knowledge on the cult of the Old One. It was Morley that directed me to the cursed book in Miskatonic's library, you know? The one penned by the mad Arab?"

"I know of it," said Henry, "though I have not yet had the need to consult its pages."

"Count yourself as fortunate then, Henry," said Oliver, shivering as he recalled the sick sense of dread that filled him on reading of the doom of Atlantis and the terrible sacrifice its priests had made to defeat Cthulhu. "There was a passage of text in there I believe will help us prevent the rise of the sunken tomb, but we can't risk returning to Miskatonic. Alexander will be sure to have his agents watching for that, just as he sought to murder you, Henry."

"Does your friend have a copy of the book?" asked Rex.

Oliver shook his head. "No longer, regrettably. Thinking he was soon to perish, I'm afraid he donated it to an institution in San Francisco some years ago."

"San Francisco?" said Rex. "I know a few people out west."

"As do I," said Oliver, thinking of William Hillshore. "I believe we must draw in every ally we can in the coming days."

"Absolutely," agreed Henry. "Our enemies count monstrous creatures, diabolic automata, and psychotic murderers among their ranks. Though we risk our allies' sanity, we risk much more by not gathering them for this fight."

"The end of the world as we know it," said Oliver.

"Not if we can help it," said Rex.

* * *

The journey to Providence, a distance of around seventy miles or so, would normally have taken no more than a few hours, with a couple of stops to buy gas for the car, but with the obscure routes and tortuous diversions insisted upon by Rex—winding pathways through thickly forested byways and rutted tracks surely used only by bootleggers and gunrunners—it would be mid-morning before the car crossed the river at Pawtucket and entered the winding streets of Providence.

Henry and Oliver took shifts at driving, while Rex murmured directions from the backseat, always waking just long enough to steer them onto a fresh track at just the right moment. Traveling in the lonely glow of their headlights, Oliver felt like they might be the only men left alive on Earth, a foretaste of the desolation Alexander had planned for the world. Eventually, the darkness of night grudgingly gave way to daylight, and a chilly illumination that did little to dispel the isolation of their journey crept across the sparse woodlands and abandoned settlements through which they journeyed.

Only once or twice did they see fellow travelers, beaten up trucks laden with livestock or bales of hay, bolts of cloth or crudely labeled barrels they were careful not to look at too closely. The drivers and passengers on these rattling iron contraptions were rough country folk with leathered skin, black teeth, and hard eyes, bred tough by a lifetime spent eking a hardscrabble existence from a parsimonious landscape.

Oliver and Rex spoke to Henry of the last few years, world events, and local news, in an attempt to fill him in on the things he had missed during his spell at Arkham Asylum. It was a hopeless task, for so much had happened in the last three years as to render any such précis little more than a snapshot of the world's turning.

Between them, Rex and Oliver told Henry of the three-ring-circus of the Scopes trial, the shocking grotesquerie of the Leopold and Loeb murder, the death of the Bolshevik Lenin, Gertrude Ederle's swimming of the English Channel, and a score of other newsworthy events. But they would always return to the machinations of the Old One's devotees, as though caught in a conversational maelstrom that would always drag their thoughts back to this foolhardy quest to stop Alexander from seeing his mad plan to fruition.

The one topic Henry found hardest to leave alone was the matter of Charles Warren. Despite Oliver's best attempts to render the madman's final moments atop Kingsport Head, Henry maintained an irrational certainty that he had somehow survived his terrible fall. Rex contributed only minimally to these discussions until Henry happened to mention the oil interests Charles Warren had inherited from his father.

Rex sat up suddenly in the backseat, an action he clearly regretted as he pressed a hand to his injured side.

"Wait, wait…that lunatic on Kingsport Head was *that* Charles Warren? The mining magnate?"

"Alexander's partner in crime, yes," nodded Henry. "I know, it's hard to believe that such a man could contain his rages enough to run a multinational company. Then again, perhaps he was merely its figurehead, while a board of directors saw to its day to day running."

"Oh, this is bad," said Rex, sitting back and massaging his temple with his thumb and middle finger, as though trying to coax a reluctant fact to the fore. "The *Matilda*, that's where I remembered his name. I just didn't put the two together. Damn, Big Stan Goodman would've had my hide for missing that connection."

"What are you talking about, Rex?" said Oliver. "What connection?"

Rex paused a moment to gather his thoughts before answering.

"The Warren Mining Company, they launched a new ship a month or so back, the *Matilda*, some brand new, state of the art, deep-water construction vessel that was supposed to be able to extract oil from places no other ship could reach. For a while its press office was trumpeting its modern technology, stuff that was supposed to be out of this world in its sophistication, but no one ever saw any of it."

"I'm not seeing the connection," said Oliver.

"The *Matilda* set off for the South Pacific," said Rex. "And what do we think might lie somewhere below that particular stretch of ocean?"

"Good Lord," said Oliver. "With what Alexander learned from Amanda and the Eye of Infinite Stars…"

"And you know what's worse?" said Rex.

"There's something worse than our enemy having a ship en route to the approximate location of the Old One's sunken city with the means to affect the passage of the stars and raise the vile creature to the surface? This I *have* to hear," said Henry.

"Hey, don't shoot the messenger," said Rex.

"My apologies, Rex," said Henry. "It's just that with this revelation, our hopes of stopping Alexander seem ever more remote."

"Yeah, I get that," said Rex.

"So what is it that's worse?" asked Oliver, keeping his tired, sleep-limned eyes glued to the road as they approached a small township that a sign informed him was called North Attleborough.

"The *Matilda* set sail not long after Alexander's goons got that silver sphere of Finn's back," said Rex. "That can't be a coincidence. Oliver, you said that Kate Winthrop told you that the sphere is some kind of dimensional key, right?"

"Yes, she claimed it could open and close gateways between worlds," said Oliver. "I didn't believe her at first, but after we used it to escape the flying maggot creature into that dreadful underworld, I now know she was exactly right."

Rex nodded. "So all Alexander has to do is get that sphere somewhere near the sunken city and *voila*, the Old One's got a free ticket to anywhere in the world."

* * *

Oliver pulled the car to the curb by a gas station on the main street of North Attleborough, a quaint township that had clearly set its roots down early in colonial times. The buildings were picturesque and well-cared for, evidence of a through-line of trade and mercantile concerns that hadn't altogether dried up in the lean years since the war. Sunlight that had seemed so weak and listless on the road now shone with a golden charm that highlighted the Federal-style buildings and the glass and steel of the newer structures. The town had its feet firmly planted in the past, but its eyes were turned to the future.

November was well underway, but the cold and rain that plagued the eastern seaboard seemed not to reach this far inland, though Oliver knew they were only a little farther from the coast than they had been in Arkham. The hour was early, though not so early that the town's inhabitants weren't already up and about the business of the day. Providence was only a short drive away, but the car was driving on its last drops of gas, and all three men were in just as much need of refueling.

It had been decided that their purpose would be best served by arriving in New York without the need to immediately pause for breath. Oliver stepped out and took a breath, letting the clean air scour the uncirculated fumes of the car from his lungs. Henry shrugged on a coat, an ill-fitting garment that hung slack on his sparse frame where once it had clung like a second skin.

Rex unfolded his lanky frame from the back seat and took a moment to clean his glasses.

"I don't know about you fellas, but I could use some hot coffee and food," he said.

"Agreed," said Henry. "I recall you promised me a steak dinner, Oliver, but right now I'll settle for some eggs, bacon, and hash browns. Oh, and beans. They never gave us beans at the asylum, and God save me, but I missed them. Which is strange, because that's all they ever gave us in the Marines, and I hated them then."

"There's a diner across the road," said Rex, nodding toward a bustling place called the Red Stone Grill. "I'll go get some food ordered up and make sure to ask for extra beans, okay?"

Rex crossed the road while Oliver paid the attendant for enough gas to get them to New York, with a little extra in the tank in case of emergencies. Henry lit a cigarette that had languished in his coat pocket for years and cast nervous looks back up the road they had just traveled. Oliver knew it was unlikely the authorities would be looking for Henry here, but he understood his friend's anxiousness.

To have been locked away for so long must make this taste of freedom all the more precious. He felt desperately sorry for Henry, for the life he had known was gone, overturned in an instant by one man's evil. Three years gone in the blink of an eye. Oliver tried to imagine losing that much time, an eternity to a man of learning, and felt a yawning chasm open in his heart at the thought.

Oliver shied away from that line of reasoning and took a moment to rub his grainy eyes, letting the sight of small-town America reassure him with its intimate permanence. The people he saw on the sidewalks were the same as could be found in any town in America: good, honest, God-fearing people.

The trouble was they were afraid of the wrong god.

The gas station attendant took Oliver's money and handed back a handful of coins. Henry stubbed out his cigarette and the two of them crossed the road to the Red Stone Grill. Inside, the diner could have passed for Aunt Lucy's in a dim light, with the same manner of customers seated at wooden tables arranged around a curving service area. Rex sat reading a newspaper in a booth at the far end of the diner. His back was to the wall, with a good view of the door, and Oliver smiled to see he wasn't the only one who'd learned something from Gabriel Stone.

No sooner had they sat down than a waitress arrived with coffees and a tray bearing three plates laden with an indecent amount of bacon, sausages, scrambled eggs, and hash browns. Henry's plate was, as promised, heaped with beans, and the three men tucked in with the gusto of famine victims suddenly presented with an all-you-can-eat buffet.

They spoke little during this repast, each man taking a moment to enjoy the simple pleasure of a hot meal and the company of his fellows. Their cups were refilled and the plates cleared away, leaving them sated and energized for the final push to Providence and New York. Henry and Rex lit fresh cigarettes as they finished the last of their coffee and Oliver flicked through the pages of the paper. It was two days old, but much of the information it contained was still news to Oliver: an uprising in West Java, the beginnings of a restoration project in Williamsburg, and the disappearance of a Bostonian artist named Pickman.

Oliver skimmed the local news, and had turned the page when his brain caught up to a fleeting glimpse of a grainy daguerrotype. He turned the page back and a cold horror crept up his spine, coupled to a mounting sense of futility and sorrow.

"Oliver?" said Rex, seeing the color drain from his face. "What's the matter?"

No words would come, and Oliver placed the newspaper in the center of the table and pointed to the picture. Henry looked at the image without understanding until he read the name and dates written below it. Rex pushed his glasses up and pinched the bridge of his nose, letting the air escape his body like a deflating balloon. In deference to his companions' reactions, Henry picked up the newspaper and read the text aloud.

"It is with sadness that we report the passing of George Gammell Angell, Professor Emeritus of Semitic Languages at Brown University, Providence, Rhode Island. Professor Angell was widely known as an authority on ancient inscriptions, and his expertise had frequently been sought by the heads of many prominent museums throughout the country. Locally, interest has been intensified by the obscurity of the cause of death. The professor was said to have been stricken whilst returning from the Newport boat, falling suddenly, as witnesses said, after having been jostled by a nautical-type lately arrived in Providence on the same boat. Professor Angell had been following a short cut from the waterfront to his home on Williams Street, though physicians have been unable to attribute his collapse to any visible disorder. It has been concluded that some obscure lesion of the heart, induced by the brisk ascent of so steep a hill by so elderly a man, was responsible for his end. His passing at the age of ninety-two has deprived the world of Academia of a shining star in its firmament."

Henry put down the paper and Oliver felt his grief and guilt coalesce into a cold fury.

"I should never have let him go to Providence on his own," he said at last. "I knew it was a mistake, but I put him on that train and let him go. Damn it all, how could I have been so stupid? The man was ninety-two, for the love of God!"

Oliver's voice carried across the diner, and Rex put his hands on the table.

"This wasn't your fault, Oliver. George knew we were all at risk getting involved in this."

"I should have gone with him to Providence."

"Then you would be dead, too," said Henry. "Yes, our enemies have deprived us of a staunch ally, but had you been there, I do not doubt there would have been little you could have done. I know you know that, so you do your friend a disservice by letting his murder throw us from our course."

Oliver let out a pained breath. "George knew," he said.

"What?"

"I think he knew he wouldn't see this to the end. He dreamed of this in Kingsport."

"He dreamed of dying?" asked Henry.

"We *all* had strange dreams in Kingsport," said Rex. "It's that place, it gets inside your head."

"He knew he probably wouldn't live to rejoin us and he went anyway," said Oliver, his admiration for George growing ever more profound. Yet another strand supporting his fragile mental equilibrium began to unravel, and Oliver wondered how much more he could take. This entire enterprise was a Sword of Damocles whose hair-fine thread grew weaker with every fresh horror.

"And what about the papers he went to retrieve?" asked Rex. "Does Alexander have them now?"

Henry scanned the remainder of the obituary, and shook his head.

"Perhaps not," said Henry. "It says here that Professor Angell's papers and estate are to be executed by Francis Wayland Thurston of Boston, his great nephew. We should make contact with him."

"In time," said Oliver. "I promised George as much, but we would appear to be madmen were we to confront the fellow with tales of the Old One. Moreover, we don't have time to double back on ourselves and get to Boston. With the necessity of traveling to Providence removed, we should make all haste to New York."

Oliver pushed himself to his feet.

"George is dead," he sighed, "which tells us that Alexander knows everyone to whom we might turn for aid, and that their lives, too, are in danger."

"You think we might get to New York and find Morley Dean murdered?" asked Henry.

"From what I've heard of Morley Dean, I reckon he's able to keep himself safe," said Rex.

"For all our sakes, I hope so," said Oliver. "I sincerely hope so."

* * *

Leaving Paris was melancholy and thrilling at the same time. Minnie twisted in the front seat of the heavily built Crossley to lean out the passenger window and snap a picture of the skyline as they drove eastwards out of the city.

"Most people take picture of Paris as they arrive," said Tower from the driving seat.

"You've seen my pictures," said Minnie. "You know I'm not most people."

"True," said Tower with a solemn nod. "You take, how you say, *horrible* pictures."

"I prefer *grotesque*," said Minnie, seeing his sly grin, "but I'll take that as a compliment."

"I mean it as one," said Tower.

Minnie snapped a quick shot of Tower's profile with her new Zeiss before shutting the lens cover and squirming back into her seat. Purchased at a ruinous expense in New York prior to her departure for Le Havre, the Zeiss had been a godsend in terms of exposure speeds and portability. It was still heavy, but compared to the Brownie she'd used to capture pictures for the *Arkham Advertiser*, it was as light as a feather.

"You should not take my picture," said Tower. "I know much prettier things to put on film."

"Well you said I take horrible pictures," she said with mock seriousness.

"This is why we leave Paris, yes?" asked Tower. "To take horrible pictures."

"In a manner of speaking," said Minnie, snapping another quick shot of Paris.

Her guide and driver had come recommended by Christopher Fields—an English newspaper man Rex had told her to look up in Paris. Fields, who insisted she call him "Fieldsy," was a perfect gentleman and had shown her around the city for a few days before being called away by his editor to the deserts of Africa to report on some rum goings-on around the pyramids. In lieu of further guidance, Fieldsy had given her Tower's address in the Latin Quarter and a friendship had begun which Minnie knew would last to her dying day.

The last few weeks touring Paris had been the photographic equivalent of a pleasant landscape painting. Nice to look at for a while, but without any real vitality that kept her coming back for more.

She knew she was being ridiculous, of course. This was the Paris of Lautrec, of Gaugain, and the Moulin Rouge; a decadent city of light that was as far from Minnie's New England upbringing as could be imagined. She'd taken pictures of the boulevards, the Eiffel Tower, the Sacre Coeur, and every incredible sight that would thrill middletown America for years.

But it hadn't taken Minnie's practiced eye long to see that the best pictures were to be found in the faces of the Parisians themselves.

Their city had been at the forefront of the war effort and had only been saved from the Kaiser's soldiers after an allied victory at the Battle of the Marne. That brush with invasion had given its people a swagger and a sense of invulnerability that permeated every aspect of the city's daily life. In the wake of the war's horrors, Paris had embraced its newfound lease on life with gusto, becoming a lodestone for culture and decadence. Picasso and Dali painted here, and Hemingway—one of Rex's idols—lived and worked in one of its fashionable districts.

Yet it was in the ordinary men and women of the city that Minnie found true inspiration. The face of a man turned to his labors on an engine, a woman at a cooking pot, a child playing with a toy rifle. In their faces, Minnie saw the determination of a people who had stood on the edge of an abyss and stared back unflinching.

She had explored Paris thoroughly, seeking out the darkened alleyways of Poe's *Rue Morgue* and climbed the rickety wooden stairs to visit the lair of Hugo's hunchback. She had taken photographs that would fetch handsome prices in any of the rapidly proliferating gossip rags back home, but she wanted more. She wanted to see the scars of the war, the bruises left by the German war machine as it trampled the French landscape. She wanted to see the faces of the men and women who *hadn't* been spared the nightmare of occupation and devastation.

No magazine would buy such pictures, but that didn't matter. Minnie hadn't become a photographer to make money, but to see truth in the hidden faces of the world. She'd captured plenty of that in the grimy crevices of the States, but even the oldest places back there were shiny and new compared to Old Europe. This was a land whose history stretched back into the obscuring mists of antiquity, a country that couldn't be measured by a building raised in the last couple of centuries.

Minnie knew there was more than a hint of the perverse in her urge to see the raw wounds of war and the echoes of that in people's faces, but you couldn't find truth in comfort. Only in anguish did truth shine out, and Minnie was determined to capture that before she returned home to take pictures of county shows and small town nobodies for the *Arkham Advertiser*.

Which was why she and Tonton Tower were driving along the Rue d'Alembert and heading for the countryside. His name was, of course, not Tonton Tower, it was Matthieu Drouet, but every English-speaker in Paris knew him by that moniker. With the demeanor of a kindly uncle—Tonton—and his six foot nine frame—Tower—it was a name that felt like it had been given to him at birth by far-seeing parents.

Their route out of the city had been a circuitous one, weaving in and out of the busy streets to find a way east and north that wasn't blocked by swearing drovers, gridlocked cars (more than Minnie had seen, even on the streets of New York), or blocks of soldiers. Even now, finally clear of the city's leafy thoroughfares, they saw a great many soldiers marching about.

"Didn't anyone tell these guys the war ended eight years ago?" she said as Tower drove them past another group of uniformed men.

"Ah, but this is Paris," said Tower. "Every man who wishes to prosper must have served France against the Germans, no? Some of the young curse that they were too little to fight, and now take any chance to wave a gun around."

"I guess," said Minnie.

"They should get down on their knees in church and thank God they were too little."

Minnie gauged Tower's age as being somewhere around fifty, which meant he had almost certainly carried a gun during the war. He'd never mentioned anything about what he'd done during the war, and Minnie knew better than to ask.

But the confidence with which Tower did everything and the respect in which he was so obviously held, told her that he had been a man of some worth and courage in those days. Sometimes when he thought she wasn't looking, she'd see a faraway look in his eyes, as though he was seeing something everyone else was blind to, the cracks behind a freshly painted facade and the sorrow behind a painted smile. Minnie recognized a kindred spirit in Tower, and promised she'd buy Fieldsy a new bottle of Glenmorangie to replace the one they'd demolished that night on the Rue Stransky with an Irishman who'd claimed to be James Joyce.

Eventually they were clear of the battalions of soldiers and drove out into the countryside proper. She'd given Tower a particular destination, one she'd only recently become aware of, and had seen was only around sixty miles from Paris. Too close not to visit, though the thought of seeing where the nightmare of the cannibal ghouls had begun gave Minnie a vague sense of unease.

Château-Thierry.

The ruined castle where Alexander Templeton and Henry Cartwright had uncovered a long dead count's forgotten library of unholy knowledge. A place of infamy in local legend, a place she'd found precious few people willing to talk about and even less recorded in the otherwise comprehensive city archives. A battlefield where Henry Cartwright had called down the fire of an ancient god upon the heads of the German soldiers.

Surely such a benighted place of macabre history would yield incredible pictures, images that would hark back to the gothic horrors of the last century and which might provide Minnie with a glimpse into the mind of a madman. That some might consider such an aim morbid did not escape Minnie, but an almost physical imperative was tugging on her gut. The potential of capturing some aspect of Château-Thierry through her lens that everyone else had missed was too promising to resist.

Outside Paris, the quality of the roads quickly deteriorated, though Tower assured her that was only because he was following her instructions to take her off the beaten track, and they spent the morning driving through a countryside made flat by war.

Minnie saw no buildings beyond two stories high. Every church tower had been blown down by shellfire and even tall agricultural buildings had been wrecked and left to fall to ruin. Rebuilding work was underway wherever they went, but the bulk of that effort was in reconstructing the country's infrastructure and residencies. Minnie had caught the bug of *joie de vivre* in Paris, but that evaporated utterly as they drove past shattered farmsteads left to fall into disrepair and the detritus of a continental world war. Evidence of that war was scattered through fields that should have been rich with crops and deserted villages that ought to have been filled with life, but which were now little more than shell-gutted ruins.

"I didn't expect this," said Minnie, close to tears as they passed yet another empty collection of cottages and grave markers by the hundred. "It's been eight years since the Armistice."

"This is true," agreed Tower. "But there has never been a war like this one. People are still learning how to cope with the effects of such terrible carnage. But this is what you want, *non*, to take horrible pictures?"

"Yeah," said Minnie, "I guess it was."

Chapter Five

New York came upon them suddenly. Unlike the cities of the Midwest that gradually rose from the plains in ever-increasing steps, Manhattan appeared on the skyline like a punch to the gut. After a lengthy and largely silent drive along the coastline, stopping only briefly in New London, New Haven, and White Plain, Oliver brought them in through Mount Vernon, finally cresting a hill overlooking the sprawling tangle of the Bronx.

"The city that never sleeps," said Rex. "God, I've missed it."

Bright lights shone from thousands of buildings, towers, and tenements. Oliver had come to New York City a number of times, but never lost the thrill of seeing so monstrously vast an agglomeration of humanity. The vast towers of Manhattan Island reached up into the darkening sky, a number of winking lights from welding torches flickering along the vertiginous girders and scaffolds.

Long streets, arrow straight and arranged in a grid pattern of eminent sensibility, had been lifted wholesale from the architects of antiquity, and though its adoption had been vehemently opposed at the time, it had created a thoroughly modern-looking city. Henry took over driving duties, leaving Oliver and Rex to pore over a map, recently purchased in a book store in White Plain, and determine the best possible route to Morley Dean's apartment in Hell's Kitchen.

Getting to Midtown proved to be easy enough, but Oliver's belief that he would easily recall the layout of the streets and navigate them to 34th Street proved to be unfounded, and they circled city block after city block as they sought to make sense of the numbering system imposed on the burgeoning metropolis over a hundred years ago by well-meaning town planners.

"Damnation, Oliver," said Henry as they made what was clearly another wrong turn. "I thought you said you'd been here before."

"I have, but that was in the back of a taxi, and I was too busy looking at the towering structures around me to really take notice of my immediate surroundings."

"That's not what you said when we got to the edge of the city," pointed out Rex.

"I keep forgetting how big this city is," said Oliver.

"I think everyone does," said Henry.

The people of New York were, for the most part, a well-heeled crowd, dressed in the latest fashions and sporting dashing new haircuts. They laughed as they made their way down the streets, moving quickly from salon to salon, though the nature of the crowds changed the closer to Morley's address they drove. From the fashionable heights of Midtown to the immigrant tenements of Hell's Kitchen, the people became less carefree and more wary, as though they were resentful of outsiders coming into their domain.

"Is it just me, or does anyone else *really* hope we find Professor Dean's apartment soon?" said Rex, glancing over his shoulder through the narrow aperture in the rear canopy.

"It's not just you," echoed Henry and Oliver.

Eventually Oliver spotted a sign for 34th Street, and Henry pulled the car around. Narrower than the other streets they had repeatedly traversed, this road was darker than most, thanks to the numerous street lights that had been put out by rock-hurling street kids.

"This is the one," said Oliver, finally spotting a landmark he recognized, a grocery store where he had bought some apples the morning after he'd arrived at Morley's. "It's just a few dozen yards beyond. A green door with the number thirteen painted on the sidewalk."

"Thirteen?" said Henry. "Thank heavens I give no credence to superstition."

"After the last few days, you don't believe in bad luck numbers or stepping on a crack?" said Rex. "Sheesh, I'll be avoiding black cats or walking under ladders, and I'll be throwing salt over my shoulder the rest of my days, Professor."

"Why fear superstition when we know there are far worse things out there?"

"Good point," said Rex, as Henry brought the car to a halt at the curb.

Oliver all but bounded from the car, eager and terrified to discover the current health of his old mentor from Brown. Had he met the same fate as George or had the wily old professor's paranoia managed to keep the threat of Alexander's minions at bay? He crossed the sidewalk at a brisk clip, before a *sotto voce* shout from Rex pulled him up short.

"Oliver, wait! The door."

Oliver halted as though on the verge of stepping from a cliff and looked up at Morley Dean's building. The green door was just as he remembered it, sturdy and well-weathered, with what George had called elder signs etched into the woodwork of the jambs.

"What's the matter with it?" he asked.

"It's open," said Rex.

Now that Oliver looked closer, he saw that Rex was correct, but the significance of that eluded him. "So?"

"How many other front doors have you seen open in Hell's Kitchen?" said Rex. "You said this friend of yours was a nut for thinking bad things were out to get him. Does leaving a door open sound like something a man like that would do?"

"Oh, no," said Oliver, finally grasping Rex's meaning. He ran up the two steps to the door and barged it open, cold terror coalescing in his stomach at the thought that Morley might already be dead. Rex and Henry shouted his name, but Oliver didn't dare stop. The corridor within was gloomy, none of the wan illumination from the few streetlights beyond reaching within. A rank, chemical stink filled the air, like petroleum and ammonia blended together in some unholy cocktail.

Oliver blundered along the length of the corridor, knocking over a stacked pile of wooden crates and a collection of bottles that were invisible in the darkness. The glass broke with a sound like brittle thunder in the confines of the corridor, and Oliver's heart sank further as he saw a sliver of light at the edge of Morley's apartment door. Leaving the front door open might be a mistake made by another resident of the tenement, but Morley would never willingly have left the door to his apartment open.

The acrid reek was stronger here, and Oliver took hold of the door's chipped brass handle. Just as he was about to push the door open, he noticed a series of deep gouges torn through the woodwork of the frame. He'd seen marks similar to these before, when the ghoulish creatures had attacked him in his office. The claw marks appeared to end abruptly, as though some invisible barrier had prevented them from tearing fully through the wood.

Oliver bent to examine the claw marks, and the motion saved his life.

A booming, ear-shattering explosion ripped through the door at chest height, tearing a fist-sized hole in the thick wood of the door. Another closely followed, blowing the timber panels of the door to splinters. Shredded wood and glittering particulates filled the air, and Oliver rolled on the stone passageway with his hands locked over his ears.

A shape moved behind the remains of the door, a dark and shadowy outline carrying a sawn-off shotgun with two smoking barrels. The stock and barrel were canted at an angle as the gunman thumbed a pair of shells into the breech.

"You're not getting in, you hear me!" shouted the shape. "I've plenty more lunar caustic shells here! I'm not going anywhere, you interdimensional bastards!"

The shotgun snapped together and Oliver heard the click of the hammers being drawn back. He held out his hands in desperation, almost choking on the acrid fumes from the twin blasts.

"It's Oliver!" he shouted. "Oliver Grayson! Don't shoot! For the love of God, don't shoot!"

The shotgun didn't waver, but the shape resolved itself as a set of broad shoulders emerged from the smoke.

A bewildered and manic-looking face, one which had clearly stared too long at whatever was looking back from the abyss. For a sickening moment, Oliver wondered if he would pull the triggers and end his life right now.

"Oliver?" said Morley Dean. "What the devil are you doing here?"

* * *

It took a further fifteen minutes of haggling, cajoling, and questioning before Morley finally relented and opened the remains of his door to admit Oliver, Henry, and Rex. Morley quizzed Oliver relentlessly on the details of their Alaskan expedition and events of their last meeting to ensure he was exactly who he claimed to be. With this benchmark confirmed, Oliver was able to vouch for Henry and Rex, though he was acutely conscious of the fact that Morley did not unload or otherwise make the shotgun safe.

The inside of Morley's apartment was a snapshot of his current state of mind: chaotic and filled with all manner of esoterica and hideous renderings. The last time Oliver had visited his old mentor in New York, his apartment had been a more extreme version of his own home: an academic's collection of books, papers, and scholarly editions arranged without apparent thought for any system of organization.

Clearly something had happened in the meantime to drive Morley's haphazard way of life into overdrive. Torn books were strewn across the floor, and entire walls were pasted with the pages of a hundred or more broken-spined tomes. The window was entirely pasted over, with only a few spots of the night's deeper darkness visible through the scripted pages.

Every junction of wall and floor, every angle between the corners of the room, and every abutment of brickwork was smoothed to a soft curve with layered paper and pasted over with sheets of newsprint like papier-mâché. The overall effect was to render the interior of Morley's apartment like a scene from the inside of a Christmas snow globe, where a miniature landscape is covered in drifts of snow. Every square inch of wall was covered in arcane symbols and tightly wound handwriting—a mixture of Latin and Arabic, proto-Celtic, and what looked like ancient Egyptian hieroglyphs.

The symbols were a mix of elder signs and a grab bag of protective symbols from all walks of mythology and folklore. Clearly Morley was leaving no stone unturned when it came to his esoteric fortifications. The stink of chemical adhesives was almost overpowering, and pots of the stuff were stacked by the back door to Morley's apartment. A handful of books had escaped the purge, and lay stacked beneath a cloth that rounded their edges and reinforced the impression of undulant dunes of paper.

A glitter-sheen of strange iridescent dust coated the books and

Oliver saw a great deal of the stuff had been thrown onto the walls, where it had stuck on the wet paste.

"I love what you've done with the place," said Rex, stepping over a heap of discarded and ripped up books that would have made Armitage weep to see how they'd been mistreated.

"Morley, what in the name of God is going on here?" said Oliver.

"It's the angles, you see," said Morley, grabbing a wide sheet of paper formed from the stapled pages of Frazer's *The Golden Bough* and fixing it over the hole in his door with a pair of thumbtacks. "That's how they get in, angles in space-time, where the interstices of realities intermingle. It's quite obvious really, when you think about it. We look at one thing or the other, but we don't notice the spaces in between, do we? And that's how they get in!"

Oliver tried to hide his puzzlement and said, "That's how *who* get in?"

Morley stared at him with a look of disappointment, like a father let down by an underachieving son. "The hunting beasts. They've been loosed. I can hear them scratching at the walls, looking for a way in, but I'm too clever for them. I've smoothed the place out, kept the lattice from cohering and denied them a way in. They don't like that, oh no, it makes them so very angry, but better that than letting them in, eh?"

Though Oliver had introduced and vouched for the identities of his companions, Morley only now appeared to take proper note of them for the first time. He looked them up and down and said, "I'm assuming you're Rex Murphy."

"You assume right, Professor Dean," said Rex.

Morley laughed, a reedy cough of a sound. "Professor? It's been a long time since anyone's called me that. And you, Henry Cartwright, I heard you were catatonic in Arkham Asylum."

"Until very recently that was still the case," agreed Henry. "Not an experience I care to undergo again."

Morley nodded. "I spent some time in a sanitarium myself. Voluntarily, of course."

"You willingly subjected yourself to incarceration in an asylum?"

"Willingly is perhaps not the right word, but I knew that if I didn't seek help I would soon end up there unwillingly and with no means to extricate myself. Believe me, Mr. Cartwright, I understand the terror of mental breakdown."

"A little too well," whispered Rex to Oliver.

Morley stepped in close to the reporter, and the force of his gaze made Rex back up. His penetrating eyes were forceful and bored deep into Rex, taking his measure and judging his worth.

"Who else can face the madness that exists beyond the limited shores of our pitiful understanding but those who have tasted the bitter touch of insanity?" said Morley. "You've encountered the things we fight, I can see that, but what I can't comprehend is why you would be flippant about such things. Trust me, Mr. Murphy, you may have glimpsed a few squalid truths behind reality, but I have seen things that would drive stouter men than you screaming into the madhouse."

"I don't doubt it," said Rex, nodding to the smoothed outlines of the ceiling. "What is it you think is coming to get you?"

"I don't *think*, I *know*," said Morley. "It is a hunting beast that exists in the spaces between existence, at all possible points between all possible times and space. It is relentless, unflinching, unstoppable, and inhuman. No matter where its prey hides, through the endless cycles of time and space, it will draw ever closer to its quarry, never quitting its hunt until it has its victim's blood in its jaws."

"Some kind of hound?" asked Oliver.

"Nothing quite so prosaic," replied Morley, as a faint scratching seemed to emanate from a spot on the wall where a fireplace had once burned. "Though the analogy suits."

"And how do you know they're after you?" asked Rex, always keen to probe the logic of the impossible.

"You think I'm an idiot, Murphy?" snapped Morley, gripping the shotgun tightly. "I know they're after me because I know the truth of what happened to George Angell. I may not leave my apartment, but I am neither deaf nor blind to what goes on in the world beyond its walls. The secret whisperers gibber in the night of an approaching conjunction, an aberrant arrangement of stars and the rise of a great evil. Only a fool would fail to heed these signs and know that his card was marked. I am many things, Mr. Murphy, but a fool is not one of them."

"You know what happened to George?" said Oliver. "Then you know what happened at Kingsport? The *Persephone* and the Eye of Infinite Stars?"

"Yes, Oliver, I know," said Morley, and a hint of something paternal entered his voice, like the reassurance of a kindly grandfather. "And I know your friend betrayed you. Evil such as his can only be hidden for so long. He set his damned Polynesians on Angell and he has loosed his hounds to the hunt for me. But we should not speak of them. I am hidden from their sight for now, but even acknowledging their existence makes my spoor wax strong in their abhorrent senses."

Oliver knew better than to doubt Morley's certainty, and took a deep breath.

"Then you know why we are here?"

Morley nodded. "To enlist my help, though I fear I may be a poor ally trapped in a prison of my own making."

Henry weighed in to the discussion, though he was still wary of the shotgun Morley carried. "Listen, old man, Oliver believes the book you directed him to the last time you two spoke holds the key to the Old One's downfall, but we can't get to the copy Armitage keeps locked up at Miskatonic."

"You read it?" asked Morley, turning to Oliver.

"I did, though Armitage forbade me to take any notes."

"Wise of him," said Morley, pacing back and forth between the window and the cloth-covered books. "Always did have a sound head on his shoulders, that one. Should stand him in good stead when that Whateley fellow finally goes too far."

Oliver had no idea what that meant, but glossed over the cryptic remark, though he had heard numerous fanciful rumors concerning the Whateley family of Dunwich.

"We need to get hold of your copy of the *Necronomicon*," said Oliver, and instantly regretted it as the walls creaked with pressure, as though something enormous and bloated pressed against them from the other side.

"Hush, Oliver!" snapped Morley, bringing the shotgun up.

Creaks and groans and the moans of warping timber filled Morley's apartment, as though the building was being twisted by a playful giant. Frenzied scratching sounded from behind the walls, and paper ripped as the fabric of the room was pulled and stretched in impossible ways.

Morley dropped to his knees and placed one hand on the floor, fingers spread. He muttered unintelligible doggerel that blended approximate vowel sounds of ancient Assyrian and the sing-song cadences familiar to Oliver from the speech patterns of the Yopasi tribe of Pacific

Islanders. Loose pages fluttered from the ceiling and drifted like the feathers of dead birds before coming to rest on the floor.

"Too late," whispered Morley, shaking his head. "Damn it all, Oliver, have I taught you nothing? You know better than to utter the name of so damnable a tome at the best of times, but now you may have doomed us all! Stupid, stupid, stupid…"

Oliver's gaze was drawn to a flapping page near the top of the wall at the back of the apartment. It hung loose like a poorly applied strip of wallpaper, curling back on itself as it slowly detached itself from the wall. The wads of balled up paper behind it came loose and fell away from the wall, revealing the upper corner of the room, where two walls and the ceiling met in a confluence of three angles.

"Damn it," snarled Morley. "We may as well have just thrown open the door and rung the bloody dinner bell!"

"What's happening?" said Rex, backing away toward the window as yet another strip of torn pages sloughed from the walls like wet plaster. A vile stench of opened graves filled the room as a foul miasma poured from the upper corner of the room, like the vile extrusion of an overflowing sewer.

The suggestion of a fleshless crocodilian jaw pressed its way through the suddenly pliant matter of the world. Fangs like crooked needles of smoke and a questing blue tongue tasted the air. The four men clapped their hands to their ears as a skull-splitting howl of insatiable hunger erupted from the swirling miasma.

"Run," said Morley.

* * *

Morley's warning came not a moment too soon as the entire upper section of the apartment *folded* inwards, like a multitude of avalanches coming together. An explosion of paper erupted from the walls as something ghastly and vaporous pushed itself through, sloughing brick and plaster dust in its wake.

Loose pages glued themselves to its form, a nightmarish arrangement of clockwork limbs, membranous insectile anatomy, and a sinuous, feral quality common to the leaner wolfhounds. Oliver backed away in horror from the thing as it thrashed in the grip of the constricting apotropaic symbols Morley had etched there.

Its edges were defined by the paper, yet even they were inconstant and ever-shifting. The beast's jaws spread and black, vaporous breath issued forth like swamp gas. It was ancient, this thing, ancient and eternally hungry, an apex predator from the dawn of time against whom no distance or span of time was too great to cross in search of prey.

Oliver ran for the door as a whipping forelimb or flailing spine slashed out like a scything blade. He fell to the floor, knocking over a pile of brutalized books, and rolled onto his side in time to see Henry smashing the room's only window in search of an escape route. Cold air filled the apartment, and a gale-force wind screamed inside, pushing Henry back into the room. Rex threw himself at Henry as a vast paw with razored talons slashed toward the professor's back. The two men crashed to the ground, and the beast's claws gouged the brickwork, sending stone and timber flying and opening the apartment to the elements.

Cracks split the exposed walls, and the building visibly sagged as its load-bearing elements were subjected to forces their builders could never have conceived. The entire structure shrieked as walls collapsed and floors buckled with the arrival of the hunting creature.

The light fitting exploded, showering sparks of hot filament around the room, and numerous tiny flames eagerly fell on the library's worth of paper. A maelstrom of shredded pages swirled through Morley's room, trapped inside by the inexorable power of the beast. The room's ceiling stretched and cracked, as though a monstrous weight pressed down from above and Oliver scrambled away from the beast as the pages plastering its body began to disintegrate. He reached into his pocket for the elder sign-etched lump of soapstone given to him by the strange old man in Kingsport, taking comfort at its presence.

Morley stood defiant in the center of the room amid the growing conflagration of his burning books, with his sawn-off shotgun pulled tight to his shoulder. The creature saw him, though it possessed nothing Oliver could recognize as sensory apparatus, and its vile jaw cracked open with the sound of splitting bone.

His old mentor shouted something he couldn't hear and pulled the triggers of the shotgun.

The noise was deafening, but was swallowed by the crash of snapping girders and breaking stone. The creature bellowed in pain and every pane of glass within four blocks shattered into lethal splinters. Morley shouted something over the crash of the collapsing building, and this time Oliver recognized the words as being similar to those spoken by the man who'd lived at the top of Kingsport Head.

The iridescent dust that coated the walls and lay in drifts over the floor lifted into the air and began to burn like sprinkled gunpowder. The air erupted with sparks like miniature supernovas and the beast loosed another shriek of pain as the fires burned its amorphous and constantly shifting form.

"Go!" shouted Morley, thumbing fresh shells into the breech of his shotgun.

The beast convulsed and spasmed as the spots of flame swirled around it like a swarm of angry hornets.

"What is that?" shouted Oliver as Morley snapped the weapon shut.

"Lunar caustic," said Morley, walking backwards over the demolished facade of what had, until moments ago, been the front wall of his apartment. "Otherwise known as silver nitrate mixed with my own variant of one of Ibn Ghazi's lesser known concoctions. Painful to a human assailant, but quite agonizing to a creature not of this world."

The hunting beast thrashed like a fish on a hook, fighting to remain corporeal as the flaming dust attacked its unnatural substance. Cracks split the brickwork and Oliver heard the screams of the building's other occupants as floors buckled and tilted crazily.

"Good God," said Oliver. "All those people."

Morley hauled on Oliver's arm, pulling him away from the disintegrating building with Henry and Rex in tow. The crash of collapsing stone and snapping timbers continued even though it was clear that whatever power sustained the beast's existence had been nullified by Morley's words of power and the unique ammunition of his shotgun. The apartment was completely gone, and the beast's blasphemous form was surely crushed within the rubble.

"Hurry, Oliver," said Morley, moving down the street with an oddly crab-like gait. "We have to get away from here before the beast regains our scent."

"It's not dead?" said Rex.

Morley shook his head, resting the shotgun over his shoulder. "I've hurt it, but it will be back, you can be assured of that."

They stood at the corner of the block, and Morley looked along each avenue of escape.

"We have to get out of New York," said Morley. "Please tell me you came here with a plan to achieve that."

Oliver struggled to find his voice, too shocked at the sight of the monstrous beast's appearance and the terrible loss of life that had ensued. Even hundreds of yards away, it was possible to see that the entire building was gone, the dust-choked void like a recently excised tooth from a healthy gum. Rex's car was obscured by the billowing clouds of dust ejected by the building's demolition, but none of them would have ventured back down the street for all the tea in China.

"Well, we kinda thought we'd use my car to get to the train station, but…," said Rex, the words trailing off uselessly.

"Damnation," said Morley, pressing the shotgun to his side to better conceal it. "The police rarely venture into this neighborhood, but a disturbance of this magnitude will see them overcome that reticence soon enough."

"So where should we go?" asked Henry. "Do we know anyone in New York?"

"I know someone," said Oliver at last. "How far are we from West Bronx?"

* * *

The door was solid oak and secured by numerous heavy latches and bolts, but that didn't stop the man answering it with a thirty-eight special in his hand. Oliver breathed a sigh of relief as he recognized the face of the man holding the gun, but that relief swiftly evaporated when the barrel remained pointed unwaveringly at his heart.

"Tell your friend to lose the shotgun."

Morley knelt slowly and placed his weapon on the stoop with exaggerated care.

"Professor," said the man and, to Oliver's immense relief, eased the hammer down. "I thought I said I never wanted to hear from you again."

"Hello, Gabriel," said Oliver. "I'm afraid we need your help."

Oliver heard the sound of iron bars being withdrawn and chains being unlatched. The door eased open a fraction and Gabriel Stone said, "Get in, quickly. Before someone sees you."

Oliver and the others filed in, moving along a narrow hallway decorated with a woman's touch and hung with numerous photographs of a young girl who bore enough of a familial resemblance to Gabriel for him to recognize her as Stone's daughter. The parlor within was soberly appointed, with a few chairs and a wireless radio next to the fire. Like Oliver's home, albeit on a smaller scale, boxes of files and piles of documents lay strewn about as though Gabriel was hip deep in a case.

A bottle of liquor stood open, and five tumblers were set on the tray next to it.

"You expecting company?" said Rex, noting the same thing.

"Let's just say I've had a feeling I'd be having someone round my door sooner or later."

"Judging by the gun, you weren't expecting them to be all that pally."

Gabriel nodded at Rex's comment. "Let's just say being a Pinkerton's not all it used to be and leave it at that."

Oliver extended his hand, which Gabriel shook. It felt like a meeting of old comrades from a distant war. "It's good to see you, Gabriel," he said. "Even though it must be under such circumstances."

"What circumstances might those be?" said Gabriel, turning and pouring five hefty belts from the bottle and handing them around. "And who else you brought with you?"

"My name is Henry Cartwright," said Henry.

"And this is Morley Dean," said Oliver. "My old mentor from Brown."

Gabriel lifted his shot and the five of them touched their glasses together like generals on the morning of a decisive battle.

"Here's to your health; a long life and an easy death to you," said Gabriel, throwing back his shot. Despite the grimness of the toast, Oliver downed his drink, relishing the taste of what was clearly genuine rye, not something filtered through an automobile's radiator or cooked up in a bathtub with agricultural chemicals. The others did likewise, each man taking a moment to recover their wits after the burn of alcohol.

"Good stuff," said Rex.

"I don't drink anything that ain't the straight dope from Canada," said Gabriel, turning his penetrating gaze on Henry. "Cartwright? You're the guy in the asylum?"

"Manifestly not any more," said Henry.

"So you're not mad?"

"He never was," said Oliver, seeking to defuse the mounting tension between the two men. "Alexander arranged for him to read a page from an unholy manuscript that...*unhinged* Henry for a time, but we have overcome that to bring Henry back to us."

"Alexander?" said Gabriel. "Are you talking about Templeton?"

"Regrettably so," said Oliver. "Much has happened since last we spoke, and little of it good."

"Fill me in later," said Gabriel. "Just tell me what you want."

Chapter Six

The castle was everything Minnie had hoped for and more, a gothic arrangement of angular bastion towers, crumbling curtain walls, and saw-toothed ramparts. It emerged like a secret from the forest, as though the undergrowth sought to hide it from the eyes of passersby. They'd missed the turn at first, the approach road so overgrown and weed-choked that it seemed there was deliberate artifice in its obscuring.

"You are sure you want to go to this place?" Tower had asked as they cleared a path for the car. "We can find other castles to make photographs of, yes?"

"It's a bit late for second thoughts now," Minnie answered, and so they had driven down the narrow lanes toward the castle. The road was rutted and despite Tower's undoubted skill behind the wheel, the car managed to find every pothole along the way. For a road infrequently traveled, it felt like battalions of soldiers and their armored vehicles had deliberately broken the road up in their passing only the night before.

Eventually the trees and undergrowth thinned out, becoming shorn and blackened heat-fused stumps. The castle's immediate environs were utterly flat and devoid of life, a bleak battlefield that bore no relation to the natural healing of the landscape in the prefectures surrounding Château-Thierry.

Tower pulled the car to a halt in a patch of sunlight shining through a break in the outer wall of the castle, and Minnie knew she'd been right to insist they visit Château-Thierry. She hopped from the car like an eager child, removing her Zeiss from its case and checking her exposure settings before snapping a few establishing shots of the castle.

History was etched into its walls, the kind that stretched back to a time before European explorers had ever dared cross the western oceans. Men had first settled here over a thousand years ago, and you couldn't help but feel that. This incarnation of the castle wasn't nearly that old, but Minnie found that if she half-closed her eyes, she could picture armored warriors with polished iron helmets and spears patrolling the ramparts beneath banners emblazoned with lions rampant and fleur-de-lis.

A bridge with only one wall to keep you from falling into the drained moat led toward an open gateway between two tall towers, and Minnie knelt before the opening to take a shot of the murder holes. She shivered at the thought of how terrifying it must have been to attack a place like this, where you were so utterly vulnerable.

"It is not nice place this," said Tower, lingering by the car. "Many died here."

"Yeah," said Minnie. "I know. I met one of the guys that fought here during the war."

"I did not mean that," said Tower. "Even before the Germans, many met a bad end here."

Minnie nodded, passingly acquainted with the terrible experiments and nightmarish beliefs of the insane Comte D'Erlette. She knew nothing now remained of the library Alexander and Henry had found in the castle's catacombs, but she needed to see where this had all begun.

"I know that, Tower, but we do the memories of those people a disservice if we just ignore what happened to them."

The words felt shallow, even to her ears, but Tower just shrugged and gave a curt nod.

"You want to come in?" asked Minnie.

"No," said Tower, without his customary loquaciousness.

Minnie nodded and said, "I'll be back soon."

She turned and walked between the two towers, shivering in the shadows that lurked between them and finally emerging in a ruined courtyard, crisscrossed by stubs of walls that had once been structures. The romanesque keep was a shadow of its former height, its upper reaches jagged and broken where the stonework had fallen away. Minnie fancied she could still see the damage done by the peasantry as they stormed the vile Comte's stronghold and put an end to his unnatural practices.

She strolled the interior of the castle, taking a few shots of the internal ditches and those portions of the curtain wall that had survived with the least amount of damage. Given the tale Alexander had told them of the battle fought here, Minnie knew it was lucky to be standing at all. Portions of the castle had the consistency of Swiss cheese where machine gun fire had pock-marked the stone and artillery shells had razed entire walls.

Here and there, Minnie saw rusted bullet casings and telltale signs that the castle had once served as a billet for American soldiers. The remains of cigarette cartons and occasional pieces of kit that looked to be military were gathered in neat piles, putting Minnie in mind of votive offerings or a job of cleaning that had been left unfinished. She took pictures of each small pile, finding them immeasurably sad, but knowing that nothing she had photographed so far was *quite* what she was looking for.

Minnie made her way toward the keep, taking note of its rectangular solidity and the lack of weeds growing through the cracks in its mortared walls. Every other ruin they'd seen en route to the castle had been festooned with a drapery of vines and climbing weeds, but this squat, unlovely edifice was bereft of any such adornment.

"Odd," she said, hearing her voice echo though she had only whispered.

Slinging the Zeiss around her neck, Minnie peered through a doorway to the interior of the keep. The roof of the keep had long since been blown off or collapsed, yet the interior was gloomier than she would have expected.

"They made 'em small back then," she said, ducking below the lintel as she entered the keep. "Even by my standards."

Inside the keep was cold, a chill that seeped into the bones and lay there like an unsolicited guest overstaying their welcome. The sky was an oblong of pale white above her, and Minnie saw her breath feathering out before her. That didn't surprise her; it was, after all, getting deep into winter, but she hadn't noticed it until now. Was it *that* much colder in here?

She took out her camera once again, taking pictures of the interior, picking her way across the broken stones and rotted timber beams that had fallen from above. Outside, the stonework of the keep had been utterly bare of vegetation, but the opposite was true within. A tough gorse-like weed grew waist-high in the keep, its wiry thorns snagging her long dress and tearing the nylons that had cost her a pretty penny.

"Damn," said Minnie, inspecting the damage. "And Paris was just about getting me to like dressing all fashionable."

Minnie looked up as a pair of crows landed on corbels that had once supported the beams of an upper floor. The birds cawed, one after the other, looking down at her with their inscrutable eyes of black as though speaking directly to her.

"Yeah," she said, knowing she had a hell of a picture with the birds there. "That's just what I was thinking. Now just hold steady, huh?"

Minnie lifted her camera, slowly and carefully so as not to spook them, but before she could take the picture the undergrowth exploded at her feet. She let out a panicked yell and stumbled back as a swarming flock of crows erupted from the ground beside her. The birds flapped around Minnie in a black squall, at least two dozen squawking hellions that spiraled up and out of the roof of the keep like a pillar of tar-smoke. The Zeiss snapped picture after picture as her finger closed reflexively on the shutter release.

"Jesus jumping Christ," said Minnie when her heartbeat had returned to something like normality. "Where in God's name did they come from?"

The answer to her question was patently obvious, a hole in the ground she'd not noticed amid the tangled gorse. It was next to invisible, and but for the birds, she might have blundered over it and fallen who knew how far down.

Minnie knelt by the hole, now seeing a line of ancient bricks marking its outline. So it wasn't a sinkhole or anything natural, someone had cut this into the earth. Might this be the entrance to the catacombs beneath the castle? She peered into the hole, now seeing a set of weathered stone steps leading down into darkness. Every grain of common sense Minnie possessed—and she possessed plenty—told her to turn around and get out of this castle.

To go back to Tower and head back to Paris, to forget she'd ever come here.

"In for a penny…," said Minnie, and set off down the steps.

* * *

Roosevelt Field seemed like a poor place to begin a transatlantic journey, but it had the virtue of being so far off the beaten track on Long Island that Oliver was certain Alexander would not suspect they might come here. After making a telephone call, Gabriel drove them through the midnight streets of Manhattan, past the glittering lights and swaying revelers toward the 59th Street Bridge. The towering steel structure was a cantilevered wonder of technology, and as Gabriel drove them over the oil-dark waters of the East River, Oliver craned his neck to look at the deck above. Sparks from the elevated tracks rained down like molten shavings from a blacksmith's hammer strikes and the noise of the trains overhead was deafening.

They passed into Queens and drove through increasingly spread-out signs of habitation before eventually arriving at Garden City and an isolated collection of Quonset huts and sheet metal hangars surrounded by a chain-link fence. Most looked ready to blow away in the stiff winds coming off the Atlantic, their walls high and painted with letters and numbers that meant nothing to Oliver. The area had the air of an undefended military base.

Gabriel drove straight into the compound, past what looked like a security checkpoint with a man in a dark blue uniform sleeping with his feet up on a desk.

"Is this it?" asked Henry.

"What were you expecting?" asked Gabriel.

"Something a little busier, I suppose."

"Union Station it ain't, but you wanted to head west on the QT," said Gabriel, pointing to where half a dozen airplanes were tied down with cable stays. A pair of parallel runways, separated by a line of the long, curved-roof huts, ran the length of the compound—a distance that looked altogether too short for the launching of an aircraft.

"And you're sure this man can be trusted?" asked Morley.

"Chuck?" said Gabriel with a snort of laughter. "He's a bit of a daredevil, but, yeah, you can trust him. I knew him back when he trained with the Army Air Service. I never saw anyone fly a plane like him. Got a gift for it, he has."

"He'd better have, if he's going to get us airborne in this wretched weather," said Oliver.

"This? This is nothing," said Gabriel. "You should have seen it when he was barnstorming over Pensacola. Winds worse than an Oklahoma twister and rain that would have sent Noah himself running for hammer and nails."

Somewhat mollified, Oliver said nothing more as Gabriel pulled the Crossley to a halt in front of a Quonset hut emblazoned with a pair of wings and the letters RAC. Light spilled from its windows, together with the sound of good-natured banter. A head poked out the door, belonging to a slender-faced man wearing a flying cap, from which unruly strands of hair were poking. He smiled at the sight of Gabriel and all but bounded from the hut to grab his hand as the Pinkerton man stepped out of his car.

"What's cooking, Slim?" said Gabriel with a wide grin.

"Gabe!" cried the man. "Golly, gosh darn it, how the devil are you? I haven't seen you since you helped me get that bag of mail trucked from Wedron to Chicago."

"Trucked?" said Henry, stepping from the back of the Crossley with Oliver, Rex, and Morley. "I thought you flew the mail?"

The man, either Slim of Chuck, Oliver wasn't sure what to call him, nodded and gave an apologetic shrug that immediately endeared him to them.

"Yeah, normally that's what happens, but sometimes you and the plane have to part company. But, hey, the mail still got to Chicago. Thanks to good old, Pinkerton Gabe."

Chuck's manner was infectious, and Gabriel explained to the others, "I was heading to Chicago, tracking down a disgruntled heiress who'd just been told she'd been cut out of daddy's will and decided to go on the lam with the contents of his safe. I'd stopped in Wedron for the night when I hear this almighty ruckus in the field next to the bunkhouse I'd taken for the night. I look out the window and I see this pile of wreckage wrapped around a grain silo, then not five minutes later, Chuck here drops out of the sky on his parachute."

"Your plane crashed?" said Oliver, all his earlier fears returning tenfold.

"You try flying into Chicago at night and see how easy it is," said Chuck, though there was no malice to his words. "Gabe here helped me load the sacks into the back of this old tank of his and we drove straight through till morning to make sure the mail got delivered."

"Chuck takes his *Oath of Mail Messengers* seriously," said Gabriel.

"So these are the fellas you were telling me about?" said Chuck.

"Yeah, I'd be obliged if you could get us to San Francisco as soon as you can."

"Well, RAC's routes only go as far as Chicago, but now Crissy Field in 'Frisco has finally got some decent runways, I guess it's possible. I'll need to take the hundred galloner if we're to have a hope in hell of making it with extra bodies in the back. But I've always fancied trying to do a really long flight just to see how far I can push the old crate. If Maughan can do it, I'm sure I can, eh?"

"I never doubted it for a minute," said Gabe.

"You're coming with us?" said Oliver.

"You're damn right I am," said Gabriel. "Listen professors, if things are as bad as you say they are, then you're gonna need someone to watch your backs. And, no offense, Oliver, I saw you using a gun before and it wasn't pretty."

Oliver was overwhelmed by Gabriel's selfless decision, and simply nodded, knowing that any attempt to dissuade him would only offer offense.

"Thank you, Gabriel," he said. "Your aid is most welcome."

"Right," said Chuck, zipping up his thick, wool-lined flight coat. "Let's be getting you weighed and fitted with some good thermals. It gets damn cold at five hundred feet."

* * *

Bundled in the back of a heavily refitted military transport plane, Oliver began to seriously doubt the wisdom of this course of action. Stuffed in with the mail sacks, Oliver, Rex, Henry, Gabriel, and Morley were barely able to move, let alone get comfortable. Morley pored over the handful of papers he'd salvaged from his apartment, squinting in the dim light filtering back from the cockpit.

Burly ground crew tossed a seemingly endless succession of mail sacks into the plane until it was surely too heavy to ever get off the ground. Throughout the process Chuck checked every detail of the aircraft and double-checked his fuel to weight ratio charts. It was a journey of over seven hundred miles to Chicago, and with the extra weight the plane was carrying, the slightest miscalculation in the fuel load could see them drop into Lake Michigan instead of Bullard's Field.

"This marks a singular experience for all of us, I suppose," said Oliver, trying to make a pillow of a hessian mail sack. "The first time any of us have flown in an aircraft."

"Let's hope it's not the last time," groused Morley without looking up from his reading. "I hope this Chuck knows what he's doing."

"Of course he does," said Gabe, as the aircraft's engines roared to life with a throaty bellow. "They don't call him 'Lucky' for nothing."

* * *

The plane rolled slowly at first, gradually gaining speed as it careened down the runway to the edge of the airfield. Oliver didn't know whether to be grateful or terrified that he couldn't see where they were going. The interior of the plane was a bumping, juddering, throbbing bellow of noise and vibration. For the first time, he became grateful for the presence of the mail sacks and the padding they provided.

Oliver's stomach gave a sickening lurch as the plane hopped into the air, then let out a nervous cry as it bumped back down again. The engine noise sounded strained, like a truck laboring on a hill too steep for it to manage. Oliver closed his eyes, though it made no difference: the interior of the transport compartment was pitch dark anyway.

Once again, the plane bobbed into the air and Oliver braced himself for the thump of its undercarriage slamming back to earth. He felt the rubber of the tires kiss the tarmac, but then the plane lifted into the night sky with a triumphant roar. The propellor noise evened out and Oliver felt like he'd left his stomach back on the ground as he experienced a strange—and not entirely welcome—sense of emptiness beneath him.

Oliver wanted to ask how high up they were, but the noise in the plane was so great that even if he shouted he doubted anyone would hear him. He gripped onto the metal cords that threaded the interior as he felt the plane bank, and gritted his teeth as the plane lurched with the motion of the sacks.

He felt a hand in the darkness and grabbed hold of it. He didn't know whose it was, but held tight to it in fear as the aircraft turned west and continued to climb.

San Francisco here we come, thought Oliver.

* * *

Cobwebs hung around the walls of the stone passageway like Halloween decorations at a kid's party, and Minnie brushed them away as she descended the steps. She pressed herself to one wall for support, using the light from above to guide her footsteps. The light was reluctant to travel too far into the earth, and she couldn't say she blamed it. A wet, earthen smell wafted up from below and she wrinkled her nose at a faintly unpleasant aroma that lay beneath it.

She couldn't identify it precisely, but she recognized it from some of the squalid places she'd visited in pursuit of grotesque imagery. It was a smell of things not quite dead, of the imminence of death or the last breath of life before it was extinguished. The perfect smell for a catacomb.

Assuming that was what she was walking into and not just an open grave.

Minnie reached the bottom of the steps quicker than she thought she would, and extended her hand before here like a blind woman groping for something to hold onto. She felt the curve of an arched passage before her, this time tall enough for her to walk through without having to bend over. The stone beneath the earth was dry and brittle, fragments of rock flaking away under her fingertips. It felt like there was no moisture here, and never had been, just desiccated air and porous stone.

Minnie knew it would be foolish to move along this corridor. She had no idea what dangers might lurk ahead. A wild animal might be using this place as a lair or there could be sunken shafts or wells she might fall into. She wished she'd thought to bring a flashlight, but even as she formed that thought her eyes began to discern some of the details of her surroundings as the barest hint of light seeped into the tunnel.

It came from the far end of the tunnel, as though someone had lit a tiny candle that might be extinguished by the slightest breeze. The light was faint, but just enough to see by, and Minnie inched her way along the passageway with her Zeiss held before her like a protective talisman. It was too dark for a photograph, but Minnie kept her finger over the shutter release button anyway.

Perhaps the camera will see something I can't.

Minnie didn't know where that thought had come from, and was reminded of Rex and his random flashes of inspiration. She missed Rex and only recently had she come to realize how much they relied on one another. Individually they were good, but together they were something else.

But it was more than just a professional thing, and it had taken a journey of thousands of miles across the Atlantic to make her see her relationship with Rex for what it was.

She loved him, and though she knew he was oblivious to the fact, that didn't change how she felt.

Minnie stopped in her tracks, shaking her head at the ridiculousness of her train of thought.

"Mooning over a guy in the catacombs of a haunted castle," she said. "Way to go, Minnie."

Her voice echoed as she pressed on toward the fragile source of light.

Minnie carried on along the passageway, keeping her steps short and her mouth closed as the musty dry stench grew stronger. The passage turned and angled downwards again. The light was stronger now, and she could see more clearly where she was going. Motes of dust fell from the ceiling, and Minnie felt a moment's panic at the thought of being buried alive down here. She threw it off. After all, the passageway had stood this long and it would be the worst luck if it chose today to collapse.

Emboldened by that thought, Minnie followed the passageway down, emerging in a gloomy, barrel-vaulted chamber of black stone. Perhaps fifty foot square, splintered wood lay scattered throughout the space, as though a mob had rampaged through here and smashed all the furniture. A broken stone sculpture lay on its side against one wall, a representation of something she was glad she couldn't quite make out. Its broken plinth was decorated with murals, and drifts of plaster covered the floor where it had been hacked off the walls.

A tall, narrow desk sat in the middle of the chamber, the kind of thing she imagined a monk might sit at while spending thirty years or more illuminating some biblical manuscript. A guttering candle wavered on the desk, its flame dancing in a wind she couldn't feel.

And working at the desk with his back to her was a man in a long, black frock coat.

He turned at her arrival and she was struck by the cruel beauty of his features. Sharp, angular and patrician, almost reptilian. He smiled, and Minnie was simultaneously repulsed and intrigued by the captivating expression.

His smile lit up the room. Literally.

Light filled the space, and what was once a sepulchrally dark catacomb was transformed into the great hall of a castle lit by the warmth of a pair of banked fires. Bookshelves lined the walls and decadent paintings of forest bacchanals were hung in the spaces between them. Minnie's mouth fell open and she tasted a sour, bilious sensation in the back of her throat.

The man was now seated in a leather armchair before one of the fires, turning a bone-handled dagger over in his hands.

"Mademoiselle Klein," he said, beckoning Minnie to sit in the chair opposite. "Allow me to introduce myself. I am Francois-Honoré Balfour, the Comte D'Erlette."

* * *

On the sandy bluffs overlooking the ocean, Finn watched the waves crashing on the beach in angry swells. The Pacific, which Finn had heard was so blue it hurt the eyes to look at it, was as grey as slate and looked so cold it made him shiver through the woolen coat he'd stolen from the rack outside the thrift store. Even the half bottle of whiskey he'd drunk wasn't quite enough to keep the wind's icy fingers out.

The Santa Monica Pleasure Pier glittered in the darkness, the lights of its carousel and the distant sound of calliope music taking him back to his younger days. The beguiling light winking from the ballroom reminded Finn of the time his da had dragged him to Dublin in order to see the Irish International Exhibition in '07. Finn hadn't wanted to go, he'd just wanted to run with his mates, but he'd quickly shut his yapping mouth when he'd seen the vast array of automobiles, electric lights, and the great machines that billowed steam and lightning. There'd been a fair there too, but the young Finn hadn't been interested in that, too enraptured by the thousands of technological marvels on show. He'd seen great works of art, displays of life in foreign lands, and had spent a great deal of time at the Exhibition's recreation of a village in British Somaliland.

It had been a heady time, one that had opened the young Finn's eyes to the possibility of living a life beyond the cramped horizons of a British-ruled Ireland. Years later, after a spell of time fighting the Brits and ending up in Kilmainham for his trouble, Finn had had enough, and taken a steamer across the Atlantic to America.

Seeing Santa Monica made him wistful for the shores of his homeland, and Finn smiled at his drunken sentimentality.

"Ah, now, there's none as patriotic as an Irishman far from home," he said, taking another belt from the bottle. This was whiskey as the Americans made it, sweeter and less fiery than that of the Scots or Irish, but a pretty decent slug all the same. He'd put some time in with the hard lads of Los Angeles, working the secret piers and making sure he always spent every last dime of his cash on whiskey and women. His life had taken many a twist and turn, but at least he wasn't wasting money.

The wind coming in off the Pacific was biting and cold, and brought rogue strains of music with it. He couldn't tell what it was, but that there was still music in the world and people to dance was enough. It had been a long time since Finn had danced, but he still remembered all the moves to show a lass a good time on and off the dance floor.

Finn watched the swells as they spilled from the ballroom and promenaded the length of the pier, wrapped in furs and heavy coats. A lot of guys he'd met along the way resented folks with money, but Finn never had. He'd made his choices and they'd made theirs. You got what you worked for and you couldn't complain when a life of idleness didn't get you a room at the Savoy or a place at the top table.

"God love it, I'm practically an American," said Finn, draining the last of the bottle and lobbing it out over the sands. That was it. He'd nothing more to drink, but was many miles from the train station. Finn calculated the odds of him managing to get there in one piece with a bottle of whiskey coursing round his body were slim to none.

And that was just fine.

Finn put his hands in his pockets as a biting blast of wind swept the bluffs.

A couple of coins and a folded piece of paper. Finn threw the coins after the bottle and took out the paper. He unfolded the paper and groaned as he saw it was a transcontinental rail ticket to New York.

How the hell had he afforded this, and, more to the point, when had he bought it?

He'd spent his days working the docks, his nights in whatever drinking den would let an Irishman in. How could he *possibly* have gotten a ticket like this? Had he pick-pocketed some dandy on the sun-baked streets of Los Angeles?

Though he knew he was fighting a losing battle, Finn ripped up the ticket and threw it into the air. The Pacific wind blew it back in his face, and the torn shreds fluttered around him like confetti at a Dublin wedding.

Finn pushed himself to his feet and dusted his backside clear of sand.

"Well then," he said. "If there's one thing an Irishman loves, it's a lost cause."

Taking one last look at the Pacific and wishing it had been as blue as he'd been told, Finn turned south and began walking along the coast to Long Beach and La Grande railway station.

Part Two
Propagation, 1926

Working in the lab alone had become the norm for Kate Win-throp—ever since she'd blown up the electrical engineering laboratory of Miskatonic University's Tyner Annex a few months back. It wasn't that she was being shunned—was anyone *shunned* these days?—more that other people found excuses not to be in the labs whenever she was there. Kate was a diligent worker and did her part toward getting the university's proposed expedition to the Antarctic back on track after the setback of the lab's explosion. She worked methodically, and her work was scrupulously accurate. .

Even Dr. Dyer and Professor Pabodie seemed uneasy at her presence, even though, as men of science, they knew there was nothing "spooky" about her—like some of the undergraduates were saying. They just didn't like working with her.

Ordinarily, this would have upset her, but in point of fact, the isolation suited Kate just fine.

It gave her a chance to work on her flux stabilizer and study the extra-terrestrial rock she'd brought back from another world. She remembered the day Professor Grayson brought Finn Edwards to the electrical engineering laboratory with his mysterious silver sphere. It marked the day her life had taken yet another turn for the strange, and led to her escaping a monstrous beast—half-insect, half flying maggot—by jumping through an inter-dimensional gateway to a deathly world of even stranger monsters.

The grey rock on the workbench before Kate had come from that world, and every day she learned something more of its secrets. The university's equipment was only capable of detecting its more obvious properties, but even that was proving invaluable in her researches. With what she was learning, she had almost completed work on her flux stabilizer, a device that could manipulate disturbances in the localized space-time and prevent them from becoming dangerously unstable.

Previously she hadn't suspected what becoming unstable might mean, but firsthand experience had shown her *exactly* what it meant. And knowing that had allowed her to calibrate her machinery to locate such breaches in space-time and seal them shut.

The flux stabilizer sat next to the extraterrestrial rock ("the meteor," she called it if anyone asked), connected to a line of the new batteries developed by Dr. Hayes. The batteries hummed softly, while the flux stabilizer gave off a buzzing whine in tune with variations in the local magnetic field strength. Levels were rising, and the device had been picking up all sorts of strange jumps in field strength over the last few days.

What that meant or what it might signify Kate didn't know, but she dutifully recorded everything in her lab book. Column after column of numbers and diagrams filled its pages. She took the book everywhere and a folded map of Arkham glued into the back pages was marked with dozens of red Xs where Kate's best estimates of field disturbance had occurred.

Most were in the high ground to the north of Arkham, particularly around Meadow Hill, and Kate wondered if there might be a link between her readings and the local superstitions and legends that surrounded that bleak, rounded hilltop. Fires were said to burn on that hill, set by no man and which burned long into the night and by whose light demons capered.

Leaving the devices to purr on the workbench, Kate got up and stretched her back. She'd been sat hunched over for hours, noting readings on the vibrating needles, entering each fluctuation with dutiful care, and tracing the corresponding line on the accompanying graph. She looked up at the narrow horizontal slits of windows, surprised to see no light coming into the laboratory.

Had she been working *that* long?

Entirely possible, Kate thought, glancing back down at her notebook and seeing the long columns of numbers. Perhaps it was time to call it a night after all. Kate turned the dial on her measurement devices to zero and flicked the power switch to the off position. The humming noise of the batteries began to diminish and the flux stabilizer's whine bled off to a less irritating pitch before dying off altogether.

Kate walked over to the rack to pick up her long coat, and pushed her arms into the sleeves. She was buttoning up the front when she noticed something odd. The dials on the devices connected to the meteor were still bouncing high in the red and the batteries were still buzzing as though generating a charge. Wrapping her scarf around her neck, Kate returned to the workbench and bent low over the batteries.

She could still hear the faint buzz, but it wasn't coming from the batteries.

Kate looked up just as the windows exploded inwards. Glass fell in mirrored shards, and Kate scrambled away from the workbench as splintered daggers of wired glass fell around her. Kate blinked away shock as the terrible buzzing sound filled the laboratory. Two creatures, glistening and bloated, like leprous mosquitos, drifted just below the ceiling. A froth of smoky wings sprouted from their segmented backs and their thoraxes were a dreadful agglomeration of wet, clicking and undulant organs. A strange, forked metallic proboscis extruded from the wet meat head of one monster and Kate screamed in terror as she recognized them as vile kin to the creature that had attacked Ma's Boarding House.

A flash of blue light arced from the creature's forked device and the lights in the laboratory blew out in a cascade of molten filament. Sparking electrical current crackled between the creatures. Kate scrambled back toward the laboratory's entrance, craning her neck as she heard the door open and a rectangle of light was thrown out onto the painted floor.

"Don't come in!" she shouted. "For God's sake, run!"

Kate's back came up against another workbench and she used it to haul herself to her feet. The flying things dropped, but instead of coming after her, they landed on fresh-grown legs upon her workbench. Their heads flickered with strange colors and rapidly sprouting feelers brushed the surface of the flux stabilizer.

Kate's flesh crawled at the thought of those hideous appendages, and though she wasn't keen on the idea of abandoning her work, she liked the idea of hanging around even less. They didn't seem to care about her, so she eased herself along the bench as a man's shadow was thrown into the laboratory from the corridor beyond. She should shout another warning, but didn't want to startle the flying monsters and draw their attention. So far they were ignoring her, and that was just fine as far as Kate was concerned.

She reached the end of the bench and pulled up short as she saw the monstrous features of the man standing in the doorway. Like a child dressed in his father's suit, the man's clothes hung off his misshapen body like rags. A gagging reek of preservative chemicals and disinfectant washed off him. Kate screamed as she saw his mangled and bloody face was laid open to the bone. Skin peeled from his jawbone and his mouth moved in a horrid approximation of speech.

"Going somewhere, little girl?" gurgled Charles Warren.

* * *

Oliver woke, surprised to find he'd actually managed to sleep on so uncomfortable a bed. He blinked away a slight gumminess in his eyes and wondered how long he'd been asleep. He consulted his pocket watch, then realized he had no idea what time they'd taken off. It was close to six in the morning, which would normally mean complete darkness, but the rattling fuselage was bathed in a diffuse light. Dim, but enough to see by. Oliver tried to stretch, but found the motion next to impossible thanks to the cable stays holding the interior of the plane together. Morley was just as he had last seem him, poring over a sheaf of papers with a frown of consternation. Henry sat staring into space, picking nervously at the fabric of the mail sacks around him. Rex was fast asleep, his head canted awkwardly to the side and his glasses tipped back over his head.

"Feeling rested, Professor?" asked Gabriel, who sat like a guard dog with his thirty-eight special cradled in his lap.

"Not really, no," replied Oliver with his best *what are you going to do* shrug.

"Yeah, it's not the Astoria, but Chuck'll get us where we need to be."

"In one piece?"

Gabriel nodded. "He's a good kid, that one. Got dreams bigger than hauling banker's checks and money drafts. Mark my words, he'll do something that'll make him famous soon."

"I'm sure you're right," said Oliver, twisting his backside around to try and get comfortable. "Any idea where we are?"

Gabriel thought for a moment. "What time you got?"

Though he had just checked a moment ago, Oliver found he couldn't remember the time for the life of him, and pulled out his pocket watch again.

"Nearly six a.m."

"Then I'd guess we're somewhere over Indiana; Fort Wayne, maybe," said Gabriel. "Give or take another two hours and we'll be on the ground at Bullard's Field."

"Thank God," said Oliver.

They lapsed into silence for a few moments until Gabriel said, "I interviewed him once, you know, Charles Warren."

"You did?" asked Oliver. "When?"

"A year or two back," said Gabriel, turing the pistol over in his hands. "There'd been a bunch of bodies washing up along the Hudson and East Rivers, young girls, and the cops had them all down as working girls who'd run into a bad john, but one girl turned out to be Jessica Stanton, the daughter of Jeremiah Stanton."

"I don't know the name," said Oliver when Gabriel paused as though waiting for him to recognize it. "Should I?"

"I guess not," said Gabriel sadly. "We tend to forget the names and the faces of the dead, like we don't want a reminder. Jeremiah Stanton owns a medium-sized drilling outfit in the Midwest. A serious player, but not quite at Warren's level. Not yet. He figures he'll get his little girl a job in the typing pool at Warren's headquarters down at the docks, see if she can't get him a few juicy pointers to give him the inside track on Warren's operation, how he finds oil so accurately and how he gets to it so quickly."

"Warren's mining operation was that good?"

"I don't know the ins and outs of it, but, yeah, supposedly a lot of his richest finds were in places no one else had even thought about," said Gabriel. "And he was able to get it out of the ground in places his competitors said ought to be impossible to drill."

"I wonder if all of Alexander's cohorts from the war did as well," wondered Oliver.

"You know, I bet they did," agreed Gabriel. "But anyway, Old

Jeremiah thinks he's finally going to get one over on Warren, and he damn near throws a party when his little girl tells him she's been promoted to work as Warren's personal secretary. Jeremiah thinks he's hit pay dirt, but two days later the shore patrol on Governor's Island are pulling her corpse out of the water. At first they think she's fallen off one of the ferries, but then they turn her over, and it looks like she's been worked over by Jack Dempsey and Gene Tunney working in a tag team."

"Dear God," said Oliver. "You think Charles Warren killed her."

"Yeah, I do," said Gabriel. "Turns out so did her daddy, and when the cops wouldn't arrest Warren, he went down there like any father would to get his own justice. Tried to put six rounds into Charles, but he shot worse than you, Oliver. Put a lot of holes in Warren's office, but not a lot else."

"Did the police not intervene?" asked Henry. "About his daughter's murder, I mean?"

"They weren't even sure it was a murder," said Gabriel. "Medical examiner said she'd been in the water a few days, plenty of time to get smacked about by boats and rocks along the way. The water had washed off any real evidence, and she was written off as a 'tragic accident'."

"But her father wouldn't let it go," said Oliver.

"What father could?" said Gabriel, and Oliver was suddenly absurdly grateful he had no children of his own; he didn't think he could endure the terror of worrying about them. Oliver saw the grim set to Gabriel's jaw and saw an echo of what Jeremiah Stanton must have looked like with his daughter ripped from his life.

"Stanton called the Pinkertons and said he wanted no expense spared, that he wanted that son of a bitch Warren to pay for what he'd done. Me and a couple of other agents were assigned, and, sure, we found a bunch of girls who'd once worked for Warren, but none of them wanted to talk to us. I've seen plenty of scared people in my line of work, but I don't think I've seen anyone as frightened as those girls were when I mentioned Charles Warren. None of them said a word, clammed up like a nun's thighs when they knew why we were there. I could tell they'd been on the receiving end of a punch or three. A broken nose or cheek only heals so much, you know? But no matter what I said, none of 'em said so much as a single word."

Gabriel leaned back. "I figured since we weren't getting bupkis from the girls, it was time to go to the source. I arranged an interview with Warren down at the docks where they were building that big drilling rig ship of his, the *Matilda*, and I gotta say, right from the word go, I didn't like it."

"What would be to like?" said Henry. "The man was a beast. Even before we found that damn library, Warren was a killer. There was a rumor going around that he'd beaten an MP to death while he was drunk."

"Figures," said Gabriel. "So we meet in his office and I see plenty of young girls there, all looking like they got tacks on their seats or have just come out of some finishing school. It was weird, like walking into a room where everyone knows a secret you don't. Anyway, me and Charles have a sit down chat, and I ask him about Jessica Stanton. He makes all the right noises; sweet girl, a bit naïve and pretty. Terrible tragedy, blah, blah, blah. It's an act and I can see through it in a heartbeat. Trouble is, I can see Warren sees I see through it. And he doesn't care. We dance for a bit, before I decide I'm done playing with this asshole. So I lean forward and say, 'You know you're going to Hell for this one, right, Charles?'"

"What did he say to that?" asked Oliver.

Gabriel sighed and holstered his pistol. "Nothing that made sense at the time, but I kinda get now. He laughed and said, 'I've seen Hell, Mr. Stone, and it *welcomes* men like me.'"

* * *

Wakefulness came slowly, like a comfortable blanket slowly slipping from around her shoulders. Minnie resisted it as long as she could, still swaddled in the warmth of a comforting dream of candlelight and the crackling sound of logs on a fire. Her eyelids drifted upwards, languidly and without hurry. She saw the cloud-streaked sky lightening with the beginnings of dawn.

She was sitting down, in a chair, watching the sky move ahead of her. Through glass.

Minnie's head rolled to the side and she saw the bearded features of Tonton Tower driving the car. His expression was fixed, and his fingers held tight to the wheel in a white-knuckled grip. His cap was pushed back on his head, and she saw lines of worry etched around his eyes she'd not noticed before.

"Hey, you," she said.

Tower just about jumped out of his skin at the sound of her voice.

"*Merde!*" he shouted. He slammed on the brakes and the car screeched to a halt, skidding across the mud to end up straddling the verge at the side of the road.

"*Merde!*" shouted Tower again, slamming his palms down on the steering wheel.

Minnie took a moment to recover her equilibrium, her first instinct to check her Zeiss was still in once piece. It wasn't around her neck, and she didn't see it on the floor of the car at her feet.

"Where's my camera?" she said. "Tower, where's my camera?"

"Your camera? Mother of God, you worry about your camera?" snapped Tower, speaking ten to the dozen and windmilling his arms as he spoke. "You vanish for hours and you worry about your camera? You Americans are all crazy!"

"Woah, wait, what? Slow down, Tower. What are you talking about?"

"I be back soon, she says," growled Tower. "Just a few pictures, eh? You go into the castle, and an hour later, you still not come out. I wait another thirty minutes, but you still not come out. This is not, 'I be back soon,' so I get torch from car and go looking for you."

"I don't remember being gone that long," said Minnie, though she couldn't have said for certain how long she'd actually been away. "I think I found something…"

"You think so? Well, be nice of you to have told Tower that, Miss Minnie! I hunt the high and the low of that place, but you are nowhere to be found. I look for wells you might have fallen down, nothing. A ditch you might not have seen, nothing. And then I see you lying on your back in the middle of the keep, like you are lying down for a siesta like those lazy Spaniards."

"The keep," repeated Minnie. "I went in there, I think."

"You are playing games with Tonton Tower, I think."

"What do you mean?"

"I mean that I looked in the keep, many times, and then I look again, and there you are."

She saw real anger in his face, as though he truly thought she was playing some kind of trick on him or trying to make him look stupid. Minnie reached out and put a hand on his arm, feeling a quivering vibration of anger in his bones.

"Listen to me, Tower, and listen good," she said. "I'd never do anything like that. Not to you, not to anyone. I swear to you I don't know what happened. I...I remember exploring the castle, getting some good shots. There were some birds, I think. Ravens or crows, maybe. And I think there was a man, someone I thought I knew, but..."

Minnie's words trailed off as she realized how vague she was being. Had she fainted in the ruins or seen something so terrible she had fallen into some short-lived catatonic shock?

"A man?" said Tower, his anger instantly redirected. "Who?"

"I don't know," said Minnie, irritated at her own inability to remember. "I'm not even sure there *was* a man. I think there was, but I can't be sure. I'm sorry, I know this isn't helping, but I don't remember clearly what happened."

Tower nodded and let out a *laissez-faire* laugh.

"What else we expect, Miss Minnie?" he said. "We went exploring a haunted castle, after all."

Minnie smiled, letting out a breath that had held her chest tight for as long as she'd been awake.

"You put it like that and I'm amazed you found me at all."

"Don't joke, miss," said Tower, restarting the engine.

"Okay, I won't," said Minnie. "Now, about my camera, where is it?"

Tower pulled back onto the road, checking to make sure the road was clear—though who else would be on the road at this time in the morning was beyond Minnie, showing her ignorance of farming folk and their normal hours of work.

Tower jabbed a thumb over his shoulder to a blanket-wrapped bundle on the back seat. Minnie twisted and leaned over, grabbing the blanket and depositing it in her lap.

"Careful!" cried Tower, and Minnie jumped at the suddenness of it.

"Sheesh, okay, okay," she said. "It's just a camera, I'm not going to break it."

"Just a camera? No, is much more than camera. That lay beside you, and I thought someone tried to kill you, maybe."

Puzzled, Minnie unwrapped the blanket, finding her trusty Zeiss, its shot counter wound all the way to the end, and something wrapped in another layer. Putting her camera on the seat beside her, Minnie unfolded the last layer of blanket. Her eyes opened in shock, and she suddenly realized why Tower had been so worried.

A memory threatened to surface: a seated man amid debauched paintings who spoke of things beyond her understanding…

A silver-bladed dagger with a handle of polished bone lay on the blanket.

* * *

With a nerve-shredding landing at Chicago's Bullard's Field, the easy part of the journey was over, Chuck informed them. It was possible to make the eastern part of the journey in one go, but the journey onwards to San Francisco would require several stops along the way to refuel and, potentially, reorientate the aircraft.

Rex, Morley, Oliver, and Gabriel gratefully disembarked from the rear of the aircraft, which, they were gleefully informed by Chuck, was a prototype of Mr. Ford's, made from a brand new metal known as duralumin. Chuck called it the Tin Goose, and joked that he'd "taken it up for a spin" on a return flight from St. Louis, and no one had yet asked for it back.

After hurried visits to the toilet and a quick snack of cheese and stale bread from the flight hut, they clambered back aboard the Tin Goose. Chuck was already busy refueling the plane, keeping a close eye on the gauge and working out just how far he could fly before needing to fill up again. The good news was that, with no mail sacks to carry, the plane was substantially lighter and would fly higher and farther before having to refuel.

The notion that flying higher was a good thing took Oliver a moment to come to grips with. In the end he decided that Chuck knew more than him about such things, and that it was better not to think too hard about something so ridiculous as flying across the entirety of the United States.

This time, takeoff was a breeze. Despite its nickname, the airspace around Chicago was anything but windy, and the Tin Goose practically leapt into the sky, soaring up to the heavens before turning westwards for the endless cornfields of Iowa and the treeless prairies of Nebraska. Once over the prairie, they would land at Cheyenne to refuel before beginning the most dangerous leg of the journey, the crossing of the Rocky Mountains.

Assuming they survived that, it was a due west drop into Salt Lake City before a run over the corrugated desert of Nevada to Carson City for last-minute orientation and the final approach to San Francisco's Crissy Field.

It sounded simple when Chuck explained it, but when Oliver was shut in the sheet metal tail of the Tin Goose, it felt anything but. Without the padding of the mail sacks—which were now sorely missed—the four men had to sit on the freezing metal floor of the airplane's interior, turning what had already been a grueling endurance test into something even worse. In fits and starts they managed to sleep over the wide open spaces of the Midwest states, but no sooner had they recovered enough to stretch their legs in Cheyenne, than they were airborne again.

Oliver was exhausted, and saw that same exhaustion in the faces of his traveling companions. How Chuck was managing to cope with such an extended journey was beyond Oliver—though the young pilot seemed not to be affected by his length of time in the air. Instead, he seemed revitalized every time he approached the aircraft.

Oliver did not travel well at the best of times. The journey from Arkham to Baltimore to see his parents was enough to fill him with fear and loathing, though Oliver acknowledged it was the idea of setting out more than the journey itself that he detested.

No sooner were they in the air than this leg of the journey westwards promised to shake them out of any complacency they'd fallen into. The climb to crest the Rockies made the ascent from Roosevelt Field seem positively gentle in comparison. Rushing thermals and rogue squalls from hidden canyons made the air lousy with turbulence, and buffeted the plane like a leaf in a storm.

Chuck shouted back to them from the pilot's compartment, but the roar of the engines and the rushing of air past the fuselage made understanding his words and gestures a complex exercise in codebreaking. Now that the mail sacks were gone, it was possible to look out of the aircraft's windows, and even Morley was coaxed from his papers to stare with undisguised wonder at the incredible panorama before them.

The red stone of the mountains stretched up and around them as far as the eye could see, an unending vista of rock that barely a handful of men had seen from this vantage point. Oliver's fear vanished in an instant, replaced by a humbling sense of wonder at the sight of the earth so far below. Their shadow raced them on the ground, so far away it felt like it could not possibly belong to them.

Higher, the landscape was broken and snow-covered, and though the temperature in the plane plummeted, the rugged beauty of the view—like something from an earlier epoch of the world, where man had yet to make his mark—kept them glued to the glass. The winds here were fierce, slamming the plane from side to side, pushing it up into the air and dragging them down to earth the very next instant.

Oliver looked back down to earth, seeing their shadow undulate over the rocks, stretching and contracting as Chuck climbed and wove a path through the canyons. For a second it looked as though they had a twin shadow on the ground, but Oliver blinked and it seemed as though it split into a host of smaller shadows that scattered like startled ravens.

Suddenly it was gone, and Oliver looked back where he'd first noticed the shadow, but could see nothing and dismissed it as a visual phantom caused by tiredness and unfamiliar surroundings.

"Hey," said Rex warily. "Did anyone else just see that?"

"See what?" asked Henry, clambering over to the scuffed glass window.

"I'm not sure," said Rex. "Looked for a minute like we had two shadows."

"I saw that, too," said Oliver. "What do you think it means?"

"I got no idea," shrugged Rex. "Maybe we flew through a flock of birds or something?"

"Maybe that's normal when you fly this high," suggested Gabriel, though no one was convinced.

"It's not normal at all," said Morley, finally looking up from his notes. "It's hunting beasts set to destroy us."

"What?" said Rex. "How do you know that?"

Morley removed a small glass vial from his coat pocket. Stoppered with a copper banded lid, a black, crystalline rock—like a shard of napped obsidian—was suspended from a hair-fine strand of fibrous material, itself like an iridescent thread teased from a butterfly's wing.

"This was made for me in the Pillared City," said Morley. "One of the Devoured Sages stole the crystal from the black, lightless caverns of N'kai."

"What is it?" asked Henry.

"He told me it was the fossilized remains of one of the formless spawn creatures that dwell there in blind service to their slumbering master. The sage bound it within a Curwen flask with a membrane of hair said to have been plucked from Shathak's head."

Now that Oliver looked more closely, he saw the crystalline shard was vibrating at a subtle pitch, *clinking* against the glass with metronomic precision.

"Why is it doing that?" asked Oliver. "Tapping the glass like that?"

"The crystal is somehow…sentient," said Morley. "And it knows its own kind."

CHAPTER EIGHT

They watched the sky and ground beyond the aircraft for the next two hours, but Oliver began to suspect that Morley's alarmist proclamation had been nothing more than a hint of the paranoia that had driven him to barricade himself within his apartment. But then, hadn't his fears there been proven to be completely justified? Every time Oliver felt his eyelids closing or his attention wandering, he reminded himself of that fact.

Gabriel went up front to speak to Chuck and warn him that there might be others in the air with them. The pilot had looked puzzled, but agreed to keep an eye out for anything in their immediate airspace. Luckily the air at this height was crisp and clear, with good visibility all round. If there was anything flying nearby, Chuck assured Gabriel, they'd have plenty of warning. There was nothing to do but wait out the rest of the journey and keep a watchful eye at the windows. As Oliver wiped fatigue from his eyes, he felt Morley move closer to him.

"Nothing out there," said Oliver.

"Keep watching," said Morley, holding out the glass vial. "It's there all right."

The black shard vibrated against the glass, like a trapped insect trying to escape, and Oliver blinked as, just for a fraction of a second, it seemed the crystal looked back at him with a multitude of frozen eyes. He blinked away the image, once again seeing only the crystalline surface, pitted and napped by its forced removal from forgotten strata.

"If there is a beast out there hunting us, then why is it not attacking?" asked Oliver, not unreasonably, he thought.

"It's waiting and watching," said Morley.

"For what?"

Morley shrugged. "I don't know."

Oliver shook his head and was just about to return to the area of the fuselage he found the least uncomfortable when darkness dropped over every window as surely as if blackout curtains had been drawn across them. A powerful wind buffeted the airplane and Oliver was hurled to the floor as it was rammed downward by a powerful impact.

Morley cried out and Rex joined him as they tumbled over one another and the plane lurched sickeningly. Henry shouted something inaudible as the nose of the plane dipped alarmingly, and Gabriel clung to a stanchion with his pistol drawn—though how he planned to use it was a mystery. Oliver rolled across the floor of the plane, scrambling for a handhold, but finding nothing solid enough to arrest his wild spinning.

"What the hell?" shouted Chuck from the cockpit. "Hold on, everyone!"

The plane heeled over to the side and Oliver slid helplessly toward the fuselage. Something hard and metal slammed into his side, drawing a hissing grunt of pain from him. Light speared into the cabin where a long black spine pierced the thin metal skin of the airplane's roof and tore a gaping furrow. Cold air rammed into the compartment, together with the vile stench of something long dead.

Chuck threw the plane into a looping turn and the spine was withdrawn without a sound. Several more slamming blows dented the fuselage, all down the length of the plane, and a multitude of battering impacts screeched along its metal sides, like fingers down a blackboard. Oliver finally found a piece of internal structure solid enough to arrest his painful bouncing around the plane's interior and hauled himself up onto his haunches.

Chuck was throwing the plane through a host of insane maneuvers, as though revisiting his barnstorming days. It was making no difference to the assault, which continued unabated, and Oliver felt more and more of the impacts crater the plane's hull.

"What the hell's going on?" shouted Henry. "What's out there?"

No one had an answer for him, not even Morley, who was poring over his notes with feverish desperation. Oliver peered through the window nearest him, seeing patches of bright sky and utter darkness shimmering in a kaleidoscope of whirling change. The impression he had was of being surrounded by an infinitely vast flock of crows, swirling around the plane like the plague of locusts that had decimated ancient Egypt. He saw hints of lithe, whipping limbs, lashing tails, and flapping wings like those of loathsome, blood-drinking bats.

"Oh, Christ, this is it," said Rex, his voice almost lost in the roar of the engines and the wind howling through the rent in the upper fuselage. "Minnie, oh God, Minnie, why didn't I tell her I loved her…?"

Oliver tried not to give into such gloom, but for all he knew the ground was rushing up toward them right now. They could be seconds from death and not know it. Would it be painful, smashing into the ground in an out-of-control plane, or would it be so swift they wouldn't even know it had happened? Oliver hoped the latter, before shaking himself free of such morbidity.

"Morley!" he shouted. "Your notes, do they say anything of use? Can you stop this like you stopped the hound?"

Morley shook his head and Oliver tried vainly to think of some way of freeing them from this attack. A glass pane beside him smashed inward and a black, sinewy arm punched into the compartment. Glossy and utterly without features, like a shadow come to life, the arm ended in black-bladed fingertips that raked like a threshing machine. Henry cried out as the razored tips caressed his arm and parted the cloth of his thick coat like mist.

Oliver spun away as the clawed arm struck out blindly, horrified at the unnatural blankness of the limb. The oily semblance of a head pushed in through the window after the arm, a dreadful featureless facsimile of a face with a pair of inward-curling horns. Though frenzied in its attack, the creature made no sound, and its very silence was as terrifying as any ululating hunting cry.

Gabriel fired his thirty-eight special, and Oliver almost lost his grip as his hands flew to his ears at the deafening bangs. Gabriel's aim was true, but the creature gave no sign of any pain from the shots or any sign that it had felt them all. It was as if the bullets had passed straight through it, as though its outward form was no more substantial than smoke.

Another window smashed and a pair of whipping black arms forced themselves into the cabin, swiftly followed by another of the silent horned heads. The creature plucked Gabriel from his perch and its snapping claws began tearing at him with apparent fondness, like a parent tickling their child. Thudding booms ran the length of the plane as more and more of the black winged things slammed into the fuselage and began tearing its metallic hide.

"Hold on!" shouted Chuck, his voice almost swallowed by the violence of the attack.

The plane veered sharply downwards, and Oliver's stomach lurched violently as the world spun around and all sense of spatial awareness was thrown into disarray. Oliver flew up and slammed into the roof of the cabin before falling into its side. The breath was driven from him as his inner ear and eyes told him wildly differing tales of which way was up and which was down. He saw Rex and Morley fly back along the cabin to the tail section, as Gabriel was held fast by the monster ripping his thick clothes from his body. Henry was pressed flat against the fuselage, and Oliver had time to wonder how he had managed to hold himself fast when he saw a pair of black arms attempting to pull his friend from the aircraft.

Once again the plane spun out of control—or at least Oliver assumed it was out of control—and though he heard no sounds beyond the plane, he felt the frustration of the beasts as they lost their grip on its smooth outer surfaces. Henry fell to the floor and skidded down its length, clawing at the metal floor for purchase.

Oliver looked over Henry's flailing form, seeing into the cockpit and through the cracked glass. But what he saw only intensified his certainty that they were going to die. The red stone of the rockies spun crazily through the canopy. Just as Oliver was certain the plane was sure to smash itself to oblivion on the rocks, the ground looped away and the engines screamed in protest.

Chuck let out a rebel yell worthy of General Lee himself and the structure of the plane buckled and screeched as ground and sky switched places with shocking suddenness. The plane's belly skimmed the earth, and whipping branches of the tallest trees battered its underside.

Oliver gripped tight to a nearby stanchion, watching tall pillars of rock rear up before the plane and then suddenly veer away as Chuck threw the plane into a dizzying series of turns, climbs, and dives that threaded an acrobatic path through the narrow gullies and arroyos of the high peaks. Just as Oliver was certain the plane was going to crash into a sheer cliff of ocher stone, Chuck stood the plane on its wing and flew them through an eye-wateringly narrow canyon before throwing out the throttle and exploding into the air once again.

"We all okay back there?" shouted the young pilot.

No one had time to answer him as the black creatures threw themselves at the plane again, and Oliver wanted to scream in frustration. Was nothing going to shake these hunting beasts? A faceless head peered in through every window, and battering claws tore into the thin metal of the plane. Wind howled and Oliver fought to keep a grip of his precarious handhold.

Morley spilled into the companionway of the plane, his notes falling away and billowing like a flock of startled seagulls. Pages of arcane symbols and tightly wound text flew from the rents in the aircraft's fuselage, and Oliver saw the copper-stopped vial Morley had shown him just before the attack rolling down the floor of the plane.

The crystalline shard was rattling against the glass like an angry hornet, and once again Oliver saw the rippling suggestion of myriad eyes in its black depths. He remembered Morley saying it was a fragment of a creature that dwelled in the lightless depths of some unpronounceable cavern system. A mad idea occurred to Oliver and he dived down the length of the plane toward it.

The vial skittered away from him, but Oliver kept his gaze fixed upon it as Chuck threw the plane into a series of desperate maneuvers. A window nearby shattered and a damnably horned head pushed its way in, followed by a pair of loathsomely articulated arms that unfolded in its wake. Oliver fought past his revulsion and fear of the creature, crawling down the plane as his terror threatened to paralyze him.

His fingers closed on the vial as it rolled away again. Black claws like garden shears closed on Oliver's calf and he screamed as the razor sharp talons bit into the meat of his leg. He thrashed like a fish on a hook, but that only made the pain worse. He rolled onto his back, clutching the vial tightly. Oliver wasn't even sure his wild idea might have any basis in reality, but what else was left to try?

"Get the hell off our plane!" shouted Oliver and smashed the vial against the plane's metal ribs.

Even later, Oliver could never truly say for sure what happened next.

At the instant of the glass breaking, the interior of the plane was plunged into darkness. Not just the absence of light, but the total and utter negation of light's existence. It lasted only an instant, but in that instant, Oliver heard a terrible roaring, like an onrushing fleet of locomotives speeding over him. He caught a glimpse of something black and oily rushing through the air, a mobile slick of crude oil ramming out through the windows of the plane as a thousand bubbling eyes and mouths slithered across its geometrically expanding volume.

Then it was gone, and with it the attacking host of black-winged devils. Oliver scrambled to the nearest window as Chuck finally brought the plane level and began to gain altitude. Beneath and behind the plane was what looked like a swirling thundercloud, a titanic roiling mass of glistening blackness, flailing wings and sawing tails.

It sank to the ground as the battling mass grew too heavy to remain aloft.

Oliver saw it come into contact with the ground, but instead of drifting apart like a cloud, it exploded like a vast dirigible filled with viscous black tar. A few winged shapes tried to flee the blackness, but whipping tentacles of gelatinous mass dragged them back down, jealous of their ability to fly and know the light.

* * *

Several hours later, it became apparent that they had crested the highest peaks of the mountains and were descending. Thanks to the many tears in the plane's fabric, the noise from outside was considerable, and each man was wrapped in his coat and blankets to keep wind-chill at bay.

Little had been said in the wake of the attack, for no one had the words to express their terror at being so close to a fiery death in the sky. Oliver felt numb, his body still unable to process the sheer nightmarish quality of the devil beasts that had tried to bring them down. Every step of their journey was to be fraught with life-threatening nightmares, and he should have expected no less.

Alexander was not about to let them thwart his plans and would bend every effort into stopping them from interfering. What other powers or creatures could he call upon? Were these even the most terrible he could summon up from the blackest depths of the cosmos?

Oliver felt his grip on events beginning to slip and fought to hold onto their purpose.

Dimly he realized that someone was talking to him and he looked up through exhaustion-filled eyes. He blinked and shook his head.

"What?" he said.

"You did good back there," said Gabriel, one hand on Oliver's shoulder. "I don't know exactly what you did, but I'm pretty sure you saved our lives."

Oliver struggled to think of something to say. Speech had deserted him, and he didn't know how to react to what Gabriel was saying.

"Listen," said Gabriel, lowering his voice and leaning in so that no one else could hear him. "I know what it's like. To come that close to getting killed, I mean. You were in the frat house with me, and I heard what went down on that boat out in Kingsport Bay. You've looked death in the face, but there's only so long you can keep the fear and realization away. Eventually it gets you good, yeah? You get to realize just how close you're cutting it. Trust me, in the long run, that's a good thing. Means you really know what you're risking when you start something. I've seen beat cops with ten years on the street, guys who've faced down some of the scariest bad guys in New York, go to pieces when a seventy-pound housewife pulls a rolling pin after they've put the bracelets on their piece of shit husband. And you know what? It don't mean nothing. You lose it the first time or ten years after, it don't matter. We all got to face that moment sooner or later. What matters is what you do next, you get me, Oliver? You can go to pieces, that's fine. It's what you do afterward that matters, and we need you. Understand? We *need* you."

Oliver felt something inside him stand taller and he gave Gabriel a weak smile.

"So when did you face it?" he asked, then immediately regretted it when Gabriel's face hardened.

"You know when," was all he said.

"Of course," said Oliver. "I'm sorry, I didn't think."

Gabriel nodded, moving past Oliver's thoughtless remark and sitting back against the punctured fuselage to now include the others in their conversation. "So what *did* you do? How'd you get rid of those flying things."

"He released what was clearly more than a fossilized shard of the formless…*spawn* in the vial," said Morley.

"I'm no dinosaur expert, but my understanding of fossils is that they're dead," said Rex.

Morley shook his head, amused at Rex's naivety. "'That is not dead which can eternal lie,' Mr. Murphy. The Mad Arab's couplet refers to more than just the sleep of the Old Ones."

"You mean you *knew* that thing of yours was alive?" asked Henry.

"Only in the vaguest sense," admitted Morley. "I had assumed there was too little of its substance for any form of coherence or expansion. Clearly I was wrong. But what interests me more is how Oliver knew to smash the vial."

Oliver tried to articulate what he himself did not fully understand. He had not *known* that smashing the vial would achieve anything in particular, but some part of him had latched onto something Morley had said earlier.

"I thought it would hate them," he said at last, knowing that was a wholly inadequate answer.

"Hate them?" said Henry. "The flying creatures?"

"Yes. I suppose I thought that any creature whose entire existence had been somewhere black and lightless would hate anything that lived in the light and enjoyed the freedom of the skies. There wasn't any more to it than that, at least I don't think there was. It's hard to be sure."

"Well, whatever the heck it was, can't say I'm sorry you thought of it," said Rex. "You sure saved us back there."

"Absolutely," said Henry. "Now if Chuck can get us on the ground again before this plane falls apart, I'd be damnably grateful."

They laughed, but every one of them recognized the brittle nature of it. Not one a man amongst them had failed to feel the terror of imminent death in the air, and the brush with mortality had shaken them all.

Silence fell between them, and Oliver heard Chuck's good-natured curses from the front of the plane, as though he was having a running discourse with the weather. He hoped the young pilot wasn't tempting fate too much with his wild challenges and getting too cocky after the success of his wild flying.

They came upon the Salt Lake City beacons swiftly enough, then angled their course toward Carson City. The land beneath them was still wild and splendid, but after the majesty of the greatest mountain range in the United States and the attack of the flying beasts, it was hard to feel anything beyond relief at the sheer emptiness of this portion of the journey. For another three hours, Chuck flew a straight course over the gnarled rock and desert of Nevada, keeping their flight as level and smooth as was physically possible given the tattered state of his aircraft. He shouted back that everyone was to sit down and keep from moving around if they could possibly manage it.

At this stage of their journey, even the slightest element of fuel-saving could prove the difference between making it to Crissy Field or landing somewhere in Oakland.

Oliver hadn't realized how close to the wire this flight would run in terms of fuel, and fought to keep his limbs from shaking with cold as his stomach lurched with what he now knew was descent. He twisted his head to try and get a look at San Francisco from the air, but all he could see through the glass was a thick grey mist.

San Francisco, and particularly the sea within the enclosed bay, was notoriously foggy in the summer—and apparently the winter too—and Oliver could see nothing through the grey haze. He wondered what Chuck could see, and then remembered that they were flying into a military base.

Crissy Field was located at the northern tip of San Francisco in an area known as the Presidio, which had begun life as a Spanish garrison, then a Mexican fort, before finally being claimed by Americans in the middle of the nineteenth century. It had been a staging post, training ground, and an army hospital, remaining an important part of American military operations through the Civil War all the way to the Great War. Even now, the Presidio was evolving, with its focus now centered on Crissy Field and the growing importance of military aviation.

The plane banked sharply, and Oliver closed his eyes as the plane nosedived toward the ground at an angle surely too steep for landing. The fuselage at his back shuddered in protest, and the engine noise rose in pitch as the plane fought to make its meeting with the ground one that didn't involve wreckage and flames.

"After everything we've just been through, we're going to die coming into 'Frisco," said Rex, gripping the structural cabling tightly. "Aren't we?"

"Don't be an idiot," snapped Gabriel. "This is perfectly normal."

"You've done this before?"

"No, but I've seen Chuck land a plane before."

"Yeah, when he was a barnstormer and had a plane that wasn't full of holes! Last I checked, we weren't out to try and impress anyone with our landing."

"Rex is right. The plane's too badly damaged. We're about to crash!" cried Henry, his face drained utterly of color.

Oliver looked to Gabriel to shout at Henry to shut up and be sensible, but the Pinkerton man had nothing to say. Good God, was this the end of their journey? Were they about to crash somewhere in northern California within sight of their goal after surviving so dreadful a journey?

Then, with neck-wrenching suddenness, the plane's wild descent bottomed out and Oliver groaned as it felt like he'd left his stomach a hundred feet above him. Up and down were returned to their proper places in the world and the vertiginous descent was arrested in favor of a much more level flight path. Now Oliver could see a rocky headland rushing past the glass window beside him, steep cliffs and squat white buildings of adobe bricks.

Then the plane slammed down onto the runway, the undercarriage groaning with the force of impact. The Tin Goose bounced up into the air then came back down again with a much gentler touch. The tail dropped and the engines boomed as Chuck throttled them back. Oliver heard the whip-crack of cables on the torn fuselage as the flight control surfaces were employed to slow their headlong rush along the runway.

"Right!" shouted Chuck from the front of the plane. "Hold on to something, I'm going to use the Johnny Brake now!"

Oliver had no idea what that meant, but held tightly to the nearest cable stanchion as the aircraft ground a sudden, screeching, skidding halt. Rex slid forward and crashed into Henry, and Morley lost his grip as his surviving papers fell away from him. The sudden stop threw Oliver from his perch and he dropped onto his backside. Only Gabriel weathered the landing with his dignity intact.

The noise of the engines cut out and the sudden silence was a blessed relief after the incessant drone that had been their journey's constant accompaniment since leaving New York. Chuck emerged from the front part of the plane with a grin that belied how tired he must be.

"Fog made it a bit of a rough landing, fellas, couldn't quite see how close the ground was," he said with an unapologetic shrug that made Oliver want to strangle him. "But you know what they say: any landing you walk away from is a good one, right? Oh, by the way, welcome to San Francisco!"

Chapter Nine

San Francisco. The City by the Bay. Fog City…

This city owned all its names. The Presidio was wreathed in low-lying fog, almost completely obscuring the distant cliffs of Marin County across the water and the resurgent building that had sprung out of the 1906 earthquake. The road from the base wound through thick forests of redwood and eucalyptus, but once the military base was behind them, the full vista of San Francisco's rolling hills became apparent.

It had taken several hours to untangle the red tape generated by the unexpected arrival of Chuck's battered plane. A near-fatal collision with a migrating flock of birds was given as the reason for the emergency landing and the horrific state of the aircraft. Eyebrows were raised at the unlikeliness of such an event, but what other explanation could there be? Looking at the outside of the aircraft, Oliver felt a lead weight settle in his stomach. It looked like a voracious flock of metal-eating moths had turned the aircraft's structure into Swiss cheese, and his respect for Chuck's flying skills rose sharply.

Given that the Presidio was home to the 30th Infantry Regiment, the 19th Army Air Corps, and the California National Guard, their presence was deemed entirely undesirable. Only their pilot's easy charm (and the fact that he had just flown virtually non-stop from

Long Island) had convinced the angry officers that had originally come down to chew him out to quietly get rid of them. Only a few airmen in history had matched his flight, and none had matched him in time—though no one could say for sure how long their transcontinental flight had taken.

Once everyone's identity had been confirmed with a series of frantic phone calls to various universities, newspapers, and agencies, Oliver, Henry, Morley, Rex, and Gabriel were allowed to continue on their way. A granite-faced colonel advised them that Mr. Lindbergh would remain on base, and Oliver stared blankly at him until he realized the man meant Chuck. The pilot in question wished them a fond farewell, and they left him describing his incredible feat of aviation with copious hand gestures and referrals to tables and charts to eager air service flyers.

A military car took them to the gates of the Presidio, where they were unceremoniously dumped and told not to return. With the military unwilling to provide onward transport, a cab had been called—a terrestrial mode of travel with which Oliver was much relieved to reacquaint himself. The five men now journeyed into the heart of a city that had first been settled by Spanish colonists in 1776 while events of great magnitude were happening on the opposite coast.

Gold had made San Francisco; the California gold rush bringing thousands of workers westward and fleets of ships unmanned in the bay as their crews rushed to the prospecting fields. The city expanded exponentially, and areas like the Barbary coast quickly gained a reputation for lawlessness, drunkenness, and prostitution. But great wealth also brought great men, and many flourishing businesses had been founded on the back of Californian gold. Banks grew to invest the riches of the newly monied prospectors, and given such a mix of individuals, both rich and poor, San Francisco soon gained a reputation for its flamboyant stylings, stately hotels, and the ostentatious mansions on Nob Hill.

The railroad and port facilities helped turn the city into a thriving hub for trade, and with that much money flowing through the streets, a thriving art scene soon gained a reputation as daring and forward-thinking. By the turn of the century, San Francisco was one of the largest cities in America, a powerhouse of banking, a hub of industry, and with a free-thinking populace who valued their intellectual and progressive freedoms.

And it all nearly came to an end at 5:12 a.m. on April 18th, 1906.

An earthquake like no other struck San Francisco, demolishing almost three quarters of the city. Ruptured gas lines ignited and fires swept the ruins. Thousands died and thousands more fled the city, never to return. Much of the downtown area was destroyed and almost half the city's inhabitants were left homeless, camping in Golden Gate Park or the Presidio or along the coastline.

But the people of San Francisco were nothing if not resilient, and the rebuilding work was incredibly swift, with no half-measures allowed. Like the phoenix of legend, the city would rise from the ashes of its demise and be reborn. The mansions of Nob Hill became grand hotels, and civic buildings were reinvented in fresh, vibrant styles. The ashes of the past were swept away, and the city surged into the future.

All of this and more was explained at great length by their cab driver, a Fayette County man by the name of Floyd Butner, as he drove the short distance to the Jesuit College where William Hillshore awaited them. Floyd treated his cab like it was an unbroken colt being trained up for the Kentucky Derby, weaving between other cars and horse-drawn wagons as though racing to an unseen finish line.

Everything in San Francisco looked new, because everything in San Francisco *was* new. The same could be said for most of the buildings in America, but the spit-shined polish of this city was evident in the cleanliness and whiteness of everything they saw.

Morley sat hunched in the back, and Oliver was mystified at his agitated expression until he remembered his old mentor saying that the great earthquake had been no natural phenomenon—that it had been some great burrowing monster that had almost destroyed the city by the bay.

Oliver tried not to think too much on that.

Gabriel stared through the cab's windows like a child on the way to a fair, enthralled by the towering vistas around them. Where New York was so vast it prevented you from seeing much of its bulk except down its arrow-straight canyon streets, San Francisco was constructed on a much lower scale, with its many steeply rolling hills allowing a sightseer to view entire swathes of the city at a time.

The fog was lifting and Oliver saw the city spreading down the peninsula, the white and green and pinks of the hillside dwellings, the columned porticos of the sprawling hotels and the thriving density of the downtown business districts. A hundred or more ships clustered around the western quays and a number of ferries made the daily crossings to Oakland and Marin County.

"Quite a city you have here," said Rex, pressed in tightly with Oliver, Morley, and Henry in the back. In deference to Gabriel's height and muscular bulk, he'd called shotgun and occupied the seat next to Floyd.

"Yeah, it's a keeper, that's fer sure," drawled Floyd. "It ain't Louisville, but it ain't bad. I come here back in '94 and ain't found no reason to leave. Kinda like it here now, and the sea air keeps my busted lung filled up right and proper."

"You were here for the big quake?" asked Gabriel.

"I surely was," said Floyd. "Weren't much more'n a young buck, lookin' to strike it rich and get me one of them mansions up on Nob Hill. Had me an idea to breed horses, but the ranch got swallowed up by the earth and that was that."

"The ranch got swallowed up?" said Rex.

"Yup, quicker'n a man can blink," said Floyd. "Ain't had a quake like that since then, but I can feel there's a big one coming, that's fer sure."

"You think there's another quake coming?" said Gabriel. "How do you know that?"

Floyd waved a hand in a gesture that seemed to encompass the whole of the city. "We get tremors out here all the time, fellas. Just baby ones, mind, but most folks try and tell themselves it's just the old cable cars or them new-fangled electric streetcars. Not Floyd, no sir, his mama didn't raise no fools. I reckon it's only a matter of time till a real big one rips through this place and dumps us all in the ocean. Smart money says buy up land in Arizona and wait for it to become beachfront property. And you can write that down in you paper, Mr. Rex."

"How did you know I was a reporter?"

"You got the notepad, don't ya? Who else writes stuff down but a newsman? The rest of you all are surely professors or teachers, am I right or am I right? Well, except for you, Mr. Stone, your business is your business, I get that, I surely do."

"So what gave us away?" asked Oliver, finally summoning the will to speak.

"You got bundled out of the Presidio; no luggage and no place to stay. Only folks whose heads are too full of history and science be that dumb. Plus, and I mean you to take no offense at this, you don't none of you look like you done much in the way of hard laboring in your time. Soft pale skin looks like you spend most of your time indoors with your head in a book. I'm right, ain't I?"

"You're an astute observer, Mr. Butner," said Henry.

"Comes with the territory, Mr. Cartwright," laughed Floyd. "You spend a few years driving a cab, you get to see some things, you know what I mean? I seen some things turn you hair white and make you cross yourself and thank Lord God Almighty that you ain't done seen 'em since. I tell you this, I could write a damn book on the things I seen."

"Maybe you should," said Rex. "They say everyone has a book inside them."

"Kind of book *I'd* write, it best stay there, y'understand? I'd have me a lynch mob after me if I was to speak on the things I seen."

Oliver hid a welcome smirk as he took a last look at the Pacific, its surface a shimmering expanse of cerulean blue that was just as he'd always imagined it to be and which lifted his spirits immeasurably. Floyd kept up his running commentary on the districts they were passing through, together with slanderous insights into some of their inhabitants, but Oliver tuned them out, content to be thousands of miles away from the narrow streets of Arkham and back on *terra firma*. Until now, he hadn't realized just how oppressive the New England sky was, with its dark, Atlantic tones and the weight of bloody history pressing in from every nook and cranny.

Oliver had no doubt that California's history was no less bloody and had its own share of dark myths and legends, brought over by its original inhabitants and embellished by subsequent generations, but he doubted any possessed the same cosmic character as those slumbering beneath Arkham.

The buildings around their onrushing cab took on an altogether more familiar character, as did the young people moving between them. Oliver recognized the streets of a university campus and the hunched book-carrying gait of harried students moving between classes. A magnificent cathedral rose above the more utilitarian structures, and Oliver was reminded that this was a Catholic university. He was momentarily nostalgic for the simple pleasures of academic life; grading papers, peer-reviewing forthcoming articles intended for publication, staff-room gossip and indolent summer afternoons spent in a

Jules Verne novel. He glanced over at Henry and saw the same wistful expression he knew must be spread across his own features. The salve of the familiar was potent indeed, and Oliver felt the terror and numbness he had experienced on the plane recede to a shuttered space in the back of his mind.

"When this is all over, I hope I have classes to go back to," he said.

"My thoughts exactly," said Henry.

The cab pulled to a screeching halt at the curb of Fulton Street, in the shadow of the Jesuit College, a building constructed from quarried limestone. With the sun approaching its zenith, the brightness of the reflected light was dazzling, and Oliver shielded his eyes as he got out of the cab. Rex paid Floyd, who leaned out of the driver's side window with a lopsided grin.

He gave Rex a card and said, "You guys need to get around 'Frisco, you give my dispatcher a call and ask for Floyd, y'hear? I'll get you anywhere you need to be quicker'n anyone else, and you can take that to the bank."

"Thank you," said Oliver, as he spied a tall, broad-shouldered man smoking an elaborate pipe emerge from the gleaming white building. "We'll do that."

Floyd nodded and pulled into the flow of traffic amid a slew of blaring horns.

Oliver turned away as the man with the pipe approached with a broad grin.

"Oliver, dear boy," said William Hillshore. "'Friendship is a single soul dwelling in two bodies.'"

"Aristotle? You're making it too easy for me now, William," replied Oliver.

"True, but as a guest at my new posting, it seemed only fair to allow you a sense of superiority."

"'I would prefer even to fail with honor than win by cheating,'" returned Oliver.

"Sophocles, Oliver? How vulgar, give me Aeschylus any day," said Hillshore. "After all, who really desires to read about sons plotting their father's doom and bedding their mother?"

"Any time you two want to start talking in English would be nice," said Rex, interjecting his hand between Oliver and Hillshore. "Hello, I'm Rex Murphy, I work for the *Arkham Advertiser*."

"A pleasure, Mr. Murphy, but I assure you that Oliver and I were speaking nothing but the King's English, delving deep into the roots of what has made it such a rich and varied language in which to converse."

"Is that a fact?" said Rex with a playful grin. "You mean that wasn't some kind of one-upmanship game you two professors like to use to look smart in front of us mere mortals."

"Perhaps," allowed Hillshore, matching Rex's grin. "One must allow for an Englishman's vanity when in the United States. It behooves him to act superior to his colonial cousins once in a while to remind them of that which they turned their backs upon in revolution."

"All right, enough," said Gabriel. "I thought we were in a rush."

"Allow me to introduce Gabriel Stone," said Rex. "He's kind of impatient. This is Morley Dean, a clever fellow from Brown University. And last, but not least, someone I think you already met, Professor—"

"Henry Cartwright, as I live and breathe," said Hillshore, reaching forward to grasp Henry's hand and shake it profusely. "If I was not seeing it with my own eyes, I wouldn't believe it. You look a bloody sight better than the last time I saw you."

"That wouldn't be hard," said Henry. "I believe I should thank you for trying to help me when I was in Arkham Asylum. Oliver tells me you gave Dr. Hardstrom short shrift, and I should dearly have liked to see that."

Hillshore effected a posture of modesty, but Oliver could see his English friend was grateful for Henry's words.

"My pleasure entirely, dear boy," said Hillshore, turning to Oliver. "But I should like to know how you were able to release Henry from his mental bondage. Therein hangs a tale, I suspect?"

"And you would be right," said Oliver. "But remember how you said that some things are best spoken of in the light with strong tea to hand. Or failing that, good scotch?"

"I do indeed remember," said Hillshore.

"I think we're going to need the scotch," said Oliver.

* * *

Smell was the first sense to return to Kate, and with it came a bitingly cold, sterile aroma. It was, as close as she could envisage it, the smell of *absolutely nothing*. Her memory of that night in the laboratory was faultless, not for her the amnesia of wilting heroines in pulpy detective novels, and she tried to rationalize what she had seen with her empirical view of the world (a view that was getting shakier and shakier by the day). The flying beasts had attacked her laboratory, and the reason for that must surely have something to do with the silver sphere Finn Edwards had brought her and which had since been lost.

But what of the revolting corpse-man?

Where did he fit in?

Kate remembered an electrical crack and a virtually instantaneous sensation of being struck in the back by what felt like a hornet sting. Unconsciousness, followed by a span she had no way of measuring, then waking to the smell of nothing.

One by one, her other senses returned: a subtle humming vibration coming through the bench on which she was lying; a glare of white from the smoothly curved surfaces she could see above her. The air was clean and tasteless, as though rendered utterly sterile. Even cupping her hands over her mouth she couldn't discern the aftertaste of her breath. It was as if the atmosphere was being filtered and scrubbed even as she exhaled.

Kate sat up and took a proper inventory of her surroundings. She sat on a curved white bench extruded from one wall of a perfectly featureless room of white. No larger than her own bedroom, the walls were machine-smoothed and softly warm to the touch. She craned her neck and saw no obvious junction between the floor, walls or ceiling, as though the entire room had been pressed into existence as some kind of hollow modular block.

Even where the bench met the wall, she could neither see nor feel any seam where the two elements met. Kate had never heard of any such means of construction, its strangeness utterly alien to her engineer's nuts and bolts mentality. Kate put her palms flat on the wall and pressed an ear to its surface. It was very faintly warm, lending credence to her theory that this room had only recently been formed, like thermosetting Bakelite fresh from a mold. The surface was smoother than anything she had ever touched, even glass or polished stone.

Kate made a circuit of the room, keeping both her hands and her head pressed to the walls. She heard nothing more than the faint humming that permeated the room. A faint oscillation seemed to pass through the walls every now and then—some form of power transmission?—but beyond that she could shed no light on her surroundings.

Speaking of which, she could see no obvious light source. The stark illumination appeared to come from the walls themselves, though in such a diffuse manner that meant she cast no shadow. Then, with nothing left to keep her mind from settling on the terror of her abduction, the fear of what had happened to her clawed its way up from the pit of her stomach to her heart.

Kate had discovered a well of courage within herself she had hitherto never suspected, but frantic leaps into strange worlds, pursuits by terrifying monsters and capture by dead men was stretching her newfound bravery to the limit. Tears brimmed at the edges of her eyes, but she forced them down. She would not cry. She wouldn't give her captors the satisfaction.

She stood and made another circuit of the room, this time knocking at portions of the wall like a sleuth searching for a secret passageway in a gothic murder mystery. Each knock brought the same sound, an artificial thud that gave no clue as to what lay behind it. Only when she finished her circuit and sat down on the bench did a portion of the wall opposite her iris open like a machine valve to reveal another space beyond. Warily, Kate stepped through the opening, jumping back as it closed behind her in a reversal of how it had appeared.

The room beyond was identical in construction to the one in which she'd awoken, though it was larger and furnished with equipment like a laboratory. Curved white workbenches rose from the floor and upon them, Kate recognized elements that must surely have been taken from the Tyner Annex: her detection equipment, her flux stabilizer, and the rock she had brought back from the other world. Alongside that were tools and devices, the purposes of which she could not imagine. Some of the tools did not appear designed for human beings, requiring more limbs or fingers to operate, while the machinery was clearly intended to be employed by beings cut from a different anatomical cloth to Kate.

"Fascinating, aren't they?" said a cultured voice behind her, and Kate spun at the sound of it.

A tall man in an expensive-looking Brooks Brother's suit leaned on one of the tall white workbenches. His right hand was wrapped in bandages and his right arm was held at an awkward angle to his body, as though a badly broken bone had been poorly set. The man was examining a large machine that looked like the hybrid offspring of a giant monkey wrench and a jig-borer.

"I confess I don't know what half of them do," he said, "but then, I don't need to. After all, why have a dog and bark yourself?"

The man put the tool down and smiled at her, immediately putting her at ease. There was something familiar to his appearance, and it took her a moment to realize why. Her relief was immediate.

"Professor Templeton?" said Kate. "What are you doing here? Your arm…did they hurt you?"

He gave a wince of pain and said, "I'm afraid my injury was earned by my own eagerness. The defenses of the Atlantean exile had lasted the eons better than I had suspected."

Kate had no idea what that meant, but glossed over it for now. More important things occupied the forefront of her mind. "Did those flying things bring you here?"

"No, the Mi-Go work for me," said Professor Templeton. "They're the flying grub things, in case you were wondering. As does Charles Warren here."

The sense of smelling nothing at all was suddenly replaced by the smell of an open sewer and a barrel-load of caustic cleaning chemicals. Another door had slithered open and the bloated, dead man she'd seen at her laboratory limped inside. Without the insulation of adrenaline to cushion her, Kate screamed at the horror of what she was seeing. There was no way this man could possibly be alive. His body was broken in too many awful ways and the decay of the meat on his face was so pronounced that even his own mother wouldn't have recognized him. Black fluids leaked from tears in his skin and his bloated body was undulant with gaseous buildup.

She backed away, instinctively moving toward Professor Templeton.

"You'll forgive Charles's appearance, Kate—I can call you Kate, yes?—but he took a rather nasty spill from Kingsport Head," explained Alexander, gripping her arm tight enough to hurt. "His own fault, of course. Damn fool shouldn't have been up there in the first place, but even madmen must have their dreams."

"Please don't hurt me," said Kate, trying to pull free of his grip, but finding it impossible. "Please, Professor Templeton, what's going on here? I don't understand…"

"Of course you don't understand what's going on here, you are, after all, just another human ape. An upright hominid incapable of understanding just how insignificant and meaningless your very existence has become. No, that's wrong, you're worse than insignificant, you are actively part of the world's degeneration."

"What?" said Kate. "I haven't done anything."

Alexander pulled her around the workbench and Kate felt the dangerous madness within him, as though a mob of demons were at war behind his eyes. His posture and manner were outwardly relaxed, but she saw the tension in him, like a steel cable-stay stretched to the very limits of its tensile strength. At any moment he might snap.

"You're a clever girl, Kate," said Alexander. "A very clever girl, and that's why I had Charles bring you here. You see, I have a rather specific problem you can help me with."

"What kind of problem?" said Kate, searching the workbenches for one of the strange tools to perhaps use as a weapon.

"One you are uniquely qualified to confront," said Alexander as the rotten, stinking Charles Warren moved around the workbench toward them. "The Mi-Go are creative beings, no question of that; ask them to build you a habitat from intelligent materials crafted on the far side of the moon, no problem, but ask them to keep a gateway open for more than a few seconds and they just scratch their heads. Not that they *have* heads as you or I would understand it, but you get the idea."

"What in God's name are you talking about?"

Alexander stopped beside her flux stabilizer and rested his slender fingers on its complex arrangement of cogs, corkscrewing pipes, and crystals.

"This, my dear," said Alexander, "is a wonderful piece of work."

"Thank you," said Kate.

"Incredible, really. Unique. You have no idea of the manifold unintended consequences it took for you to come up with such a device. I mean, the odds against it are frankly astronomical."

Alexander dragged Kate to the far wall of the chamber and made a series of strange gestures with his free hand. A portion of its surface, roughly the size of a drawing room window, rippled like the surface of a glass of milk before clearing to become completely transparent. Kate stared through the newly revealed opening, suspecting that were she to extend her hand, she would meet resistance as solid as the walls.

"What is this place?" she asked. "What is it made of?"

"They tell me it's called tok'l metal, a ritual mineral found only on Yuggoth."

"Yuggoth?"

"Ah, yes, of course," said Alexander. "It's the world they come from, somewhere out near the very edges of the solar system, I believe."

By *they*, Kate took Alexander to mean the dozens of flying grub creatures buzzing through the air on wings that looked completely incapable of supporting their grotesque bodies. Kate had half-hoped that the creatures she had seen in Ma's Boarding House were some kind of mutant abnormality, a hideously deformed variant of an earthly creature, but Alexander naming them Mi-Go and the sight of so many similar beasts was surely proof positive that she was looking at a race of horrific aliens.

Her knees buckled at the thought of intelligent alien life actively working against humanity, feeling a giddy, light-headedness come over her. Alexander held her upright and pushed her hard against the transparent wall, which was, as she suspected, just as hard and unyielding as its opaque counterpart.

Kate took a steadying breath and forced herself to watch what the disgusting alien creatures were up to. They appeared to be building a towering machine that resembled the bizarre combinations of an orrery or a torquetum. It sat in the center of a secluded hollow atop a high hill crowned by a strange white stone. A dozen interlocking rings of copper-colored metal were arranged around a central platform reached by stairs that were subtly *wrong* in their arrangement of treads and risers. The widest ring was elliptical, perhaps thirty yards across from side to side, reaching perhaps forty yards at its highest point of rotation, and a complex series of cuneiform-like markings were etched into both its upper and lower facets.

Around the hollow's circumference, portions of the hillside had been planed flat, and jade-green statues placed upon ad-hoc plinths. They were vile, wet-looking carvings of something hunched and ape-like, winged with a nightmarish arrangement of eyes and squid-like tentacles for a face. Just looking at them gave Kate a bilious sensation of seasickness, and she returned her attention to the half-built mechanism the flying things Alexander had called Mi-Go were constructing.

Kate saw they were not constructing it alone. Where the Mi-Go were the architects, a host of degenerate beast creatures that clung to the shadows were clearly the laborers. They were filthy, dirt-encrusted things, vaguely canine, somewhat porcine, but Kate's revulsion reached new heights as she saw scraps of clothing: a straining belt, a ripped over-shirt, or the last remains of some colored long johns.

"Oh God…," said Kate, her hands reaching up to her face in horror.

"Ghoulish things, aren't they? Courtesy of the Comte D'Erlette's researches," said Alexander. "Poor specimens compared to what I was able to achieve with the athletic AQA boys, but you make do with what you have to hand."

"They were people," said Kate, her breath coming in short, panicked gasps.

"Barely," said Alexander. "They were nobodies, but now they get to be part of something magnificent, something epoch-changing. Just like you."

Groups of the wretched, hunched ghouls carried heavy spars of dense black metal, coils of iridescent cables and blocks of a green-veined stone that was clearly not native to these hills. Whatever purpose the device being built was to serve, it was some way yet from completion. The scientist in her wanted to know what it was, though she saw a terrible familiarity in some of the differing arrangements of components.

"What are they building?"

"I'm sure they have a name for it, but I don't think either of us would be able to pronounce it without extensive reconstructive surgeries to our vocal chords and some unpleasant-looking bio-mechanical augmentations," said Alexander as though they were speaking in the corridors of Miskatonic and she wasn't his prisoner. "Suffice to say that it will, essentially, be a larger version of your flux stabilizer, but with one important difference."

"Which is?"

"Don't rush me," snapped Alexander, and the mob of demons in his eyes flared in anger. "The Mi-Go are wondrous builders, but they have very literal sensibilities when it comes to extra-dimensional technologies, and they struggle to grasp the nuances of traveling between worlds in ways that don't involve wings. Which is a long-winded way of saying that instead of sealing a portal between worlds, the machine will hold one open. Or at least it will once you make the final modifications."

Kate struggled to comprehend why anyone would want to do such an insane thing, but before she could blurt out a stupid question to that effect, her mind was already forming scientific objections as to why it would be, at best, undesirable, and at worst, impossible.

"No, no, you can't do that…," she said. "The energy generation would be cumulative, you'd end up causing a cascade. More and more gateways would open and each one would have an exponential knock-on effect until…"

"Until the world would end?" finished Alexander.

"Yes. Until the world would end."

"Good, then you'd best get to work."

Kate looked at Alexander as though he were mad. "You don't really expect me to do this?"

Too late, Kate smelled the bloated-corpse stench of Charles as he came up behind her and clamped his hands on her shoulders in a crushing grip. The stench of an open grave wafted over her, a stench that no amount of chemicals could ever cover. Kate gagged as Charles leaned toward her, and she felt his desperate hunger for the warmth of her flesh.

"Of course I expect you to do this work," said Alexander.

"And if I say no?"

"Then I'll give you to Charles," said Alexander, and Kate flinched at the vehemence in his tone. "His lusts and appetites were obscene in life and I do not believe death has improved them. And trust me, Kate, you're just his type…"

Chapter Ten

Hillshore's offices in the Jesuit College were a carbon copy of those he had occupied at Cambridge University in England, and Oliver was immediately transported back through time at the familiar sights of the professor's books, wax cylinders, and esoterica. The faint, musty aroma of old paper gave Oliver a nostalgic remembrance of his time as an undergraduate, shuffling from library to lecture theater, from common rooms to course tutors' offices. Bright light shone through the high windows of the office, filtered through a yellowed patina of pipe smoke that gave everything a dusty, sunset hue.

"Some things never change, eh, William?" said Oliver.

"Some things never should, Oliver," returned Hillshore, clearing space on a number of stools and chairs for everyone to sit. "The curse of the modern world is that we all feel we have to keep moving or get left behind. Damnable times, if you ask me. What's wrong with enjoying what we have?"

"That's progress, Mr. Hillshore," said Rex. "Can't get in the way of it."

"Regrettably, I fear you are right, Mr. Murphy."

"Rex."

Hillshore nodded and placed the armful of collected papers on a table already sagging under the weight of students' work awaiting grades and reams of handwritten case notes. Eventually enough space was cleared for everyone to sit, while Hillshore perched on the edge of his desk, ignoring his own seat.

"So, Oliver, what brings you to San Francisco," asked Hillshore. "Your call from the Presidio was somewhat vague."

"Necessarily so, I'm afraid," said Oliver. "Gabriel here has instilled a maxim of trusting nobody into all of us, and I did not dare speak of our mission without having you standing before me."

Hillshore turned his gaze upon Gabriel, and his eyes narrowed as he took in the physical characteristics of the Pinkerton man and married them to the information Oliver had just given him.

"I suspect your trust is not lightly given, Mr. Stone, but once earned is near unbreakable," said Hillshore. "Your bearing is that of a military man, but not a serving one. Oliver's remark leads me to believe that you are in a form of law enforcement. Not the police, some private firm, perhaps the Pinkertons, yes?"

Despite himself, Gabriel was impressed and nodded slowly.

"Dead on, Mr. Hillshore, I do work for the Pinkertons, and let's just say that being careful is an occupational necessity in my line of work."

"Undeniably," agreed Hillshore, "but what line of work would a reporter, an anthropology professor, a scholar of ancient languages, a Brown man, and a Pinkerton be about that requires them to travel to San Francisco by plane and demands such a level of secrecy? I confess I am stumped and not a little intrigued."

Oliver hesitated before answering, knowing he would much rather spare his friend the true evil of the nightmare in which they were entangled. Given the cloak and dagger of their arrival, he would have to reveal something of the nature of their mission, but he hoped to spare Hillshore the true horror of all he had learned.

In the end Morley pre-empted Oliver and spoke first.

"A terrible threat to the world is arising, Professor Hillshore, the imminent awakening of an ancient god that threatens to destroy all life on Earth if we don't stop it. There is a book in the Markham-Hyde collection we must consult, a hideous tome I deposited there many years ago. As a fellow member of that library, we need you to vouchsafe us within its walls."

Oliver waited for Hillshore to openly mock Morley's outburst, but Hillshore's only reaction was to narrow his eyes and purse his lips, an expression he habitually fell into when applying his rigorous clinical abilities.

"I see," he said. "But to follow the logic of your statement, Mr. Dean, if you deposited a book with the custodians of the collection, you would also be a member of the library. Why do you not simply get the book yourself? Why do you need me?"

"Because I specifically instructed the custodians to never allow me within its walls again."

"Why would you insist on such a bizarre condition?"

"Because there is much in that book that should never be allowed in circulation."

"A heretic tome? I see. But if this book is so dangerous, why not just burn it?"

"I tried once," said Morley, and the memory caused his shoulders to slump as though a reservoir of air had been let out of his lungs. "I struck the match and held it next to the pages, but I couldn't do it. I couldn't burn it."

"Why not?" asked Hillshore, removing a curling wooden pipe from his coat pocket in what was surely a deliberate cue. "Surely so terrible a book would be better off burned?"

"Many have tried through the centuries to erase this book from history. None have succeeded."

"But you *could* have," said Hillshore, striking a match and letting the flame linger for a moment before touching it to the already-tamped down tobacco in the pipe's bowl. "I doubt the fact of previous individuals' failed attempts to destroy such a book would be enough to convince you that, match in hand, you too would fail."

Oliver watched Morley's face crumple in the face of Hillshore's dismissal, and felt a moment's wonder that he had not thought to ask why his friend had not simply destroyed the *Necronomicon* rather than hand it over to a select library. Henry, Rex, and Gabriel kept silent, understanding that this was a moment they dare not interrupt. The pungent aroma of Hillshore's pipe smoke filled the office, sweet and exotic with the scents of far-off places.

Morley shook his head, in regret and self-loathing. "Because I wanted to read it," he said, contempt for his weakness dripping from every word. "I stood with the flame burning closer to my fingertips and I knew I wanted to blow out the match and lose myself in the book's contents. I wanted to learn all I could, even though I knew it would drive me to madness."

"Madness? What kind of book can do such a thing?" asked Hillshore, and Oliver felt strangely relaxed as he breathed in more of the Englishman's pipe smoke.

"The kind no man should willingly choose to read," said Morley, his fingers knotted together like coiling snakes. "The kind a wretched few *must* read in order to safeguard the existence of the others. Its pages contain hints and legends of the most terrible things imaginable, but they also contain clues to their undoing. I decided that, rather than destroy it, I would place it with those who would see to its safe-keeping."

"And deny yourself the chance to access it again."

Morley nodded, his chest heaving with the effort of speaking. "Yes."

"I confess I know of no such books that could so damage a mind, but that you believe this to be the case and took steps to keep yourself from reading it tells me that you have a strong mind."

"Strong?" scoffed Morley. "No, I was weak. I should have burned it, but my all too human taste for the forbidden kept me from doing what I should have done."

"Nonsense," snapped Hillshore. "Whatever damage to the mind enabled you to believe this book was dangerous also allowed you to take steps to ensure it could not harm another living soul. Trust me, Mr. Dean, you are more resilient than you know."

Morley looked up, his eyes moist, but Oliver saw a poise in his spine that hadn't been there the last time he had traveled to New York. Morley Dean was no psychologist, but he recognized the value of a good insight.

"The first step to recovery, in psychoanalysis as in many things, is to recognize the wounding elements at hand and begin the process of divesting yourself of those things that enable the damage to be com-pounded."

"Then you'll help us?" asked Oliver.

Hillshore looked back at Morley and took a deep draw on his pipe.

"To be honest, I'm not sure I should."

"Why not?" asked Henry, rising to his feet with urgency. "Trust me, Professor Hillshore, this is a matter of grave importance. Morley may speak with a degree of melodrama, but that doesn't make him wrong. I have suffered at the hands of the men who will turn this book's contents to evil ends. You saw what had been done to me, how I had been abused, so when I say that we desperately need your help, you should know that I speak from a position of some authority."

Hillshore was unmoved by Henry's urgency, having faced far more serious outbursts from his shell-shocked patients at the Presidio Hospital.

"I have no doubt of your sincerity, Professor Cartwright, but I would be derelict in my duty as a psychiatrist were I to enable Morley to inflict further harm on his mental state by allowing him to consult a book that has clearly caused him no small amount of distress."

Rex rose from his chair and said, "Look, Professor Hillshore, I know this all sounds like hooey, but it's on the up and up, I swear. I remember when Oliver first told me about all this stuff I thought he was still drunk from the night before, but I swear to you that we wouldn't have busted Henry out of Arkham Asylum and flown across the country in the back of a barnstormer's plane if this wasn't serious."

Hillshore raised an eyebrow. "You broke Henry from Arkham Asylum?"

"In a manner of speaking," said Oliver. "A necessary evil, I assure you, for Dr. Hardstrom was unconvinced that Henry's mania was entirely passed."

"A not unreasonable position," said Hillshore, taking another puff on his pipe and retreating behind his desk to finally take a seat. "The mind seldom heals quickly or cleanly, but by degrees. Any such Lazarus-like elevation from diagnosed insanity must be viewed with some suspicion, but knowing something of Henry's condition, I can understand your frustration at his continued incarceration."

Hillshore looked over at Gabriel and said, "And where do you stand in all this, Mr. Stone? I sense you are a man of blunt reason, and I say that as no kind of insult. You are a man who deals in facts and cold, hard reality. What is your position on all this?"

Gabriel didn't answer for long seconds, staring at each of the men gathered in Hillshore's office before continuing.

"To be honest, I don't really understand much about cults and ancient gods or other crap like that," said Gabriel, and Oliver's heart sank. "But the man we're trying to stop had my little girl killed, and he's going to kill a lot more people before this is all done. And if that means we have to ask you to get a damn book out of a damn library to stop him, then I'm willing to do whatever it takes to make sure you help us."

Hillshore regarded Gabriel closely, his eyes darting around the

Pinkerton man's face as he matched words to expression, reading the intent behind his eyes.

"If I were being uncharitable, I could interpret that as a threat, Mr. Stone," said Hillshore.

"Interpret it how you like, it won't change anything."

Oliver stepped in and gave Gabriel a calming look. "William, no one's threatening you, but we desperately need your help. I wouldn't ask if it wasn't so hellishly important. In all the years we have known each other, have you ever known me to ask for something I could do myself?"

"No," admitted Hillshore, "but I fear you have made a wasted journey, Oliver. If you knew anything of the Markham-Hyde collection, then you would know that it is a reference library only, not a lending one. No one can take books from within its walls."

"Not even you?" said Oliver.

"Not even me," replied Hillshore. "I can sign you in, but the custodians evince the utmost rigor to ensure that none of their collection leaves its walls."

"Then we have to…borrow it," said Rex.

"I won't help you steal from the collection."

"We wouldn't be stealing it," said Oliver, leaning on Hillshore's desk and willing his friend to see that their need was genuine and pressing. "We borrow it for long enough to learn what we need and then we return it. You have my word on this."

Oliver could see Hillshore was far from convinced and said, "William, if our years of friendship have meant anything to you then you'll help us. Whatever assurances or guarantees you need to set your mind to rest as to the integrity of our purpose, I'll give you. Whatever questions you have when this matter is concluded I will answer. I promise you that. But, please, for the sake of everything we hold dear, please help us."

Hillshore said nothing, and the flame in his pipe had gone out by the time he answered.

"I don't like this one bit, Oliver, and your request is quite beyond the pale."

"I understand that," said Oliver. "And believe me, I would never dream of doing so were it not of the utmost importance. So you'll help us?"

"I keep the book with me at all times," said Hillshore, his face grim and his words freighted with deep sorrow. "It never leaves my sight and under no circumstances is Morley Dean to be allowed to consult its pages. My acquiescence is in no small measure due to the high regard in which I hold you, Oliver. But ask me something like this again and I will, regretfully, have to consider our friendship at an end."

* * *

Sneaking onto trains wasn't normally easy. The uniformed staff on the station platforms were always alert for freeloading bums trying to hitch a ride between cities. But the hustle and bustle in La Grande train station was so loud and chaotic that Finn could have marched a military band onto the empty boxcars and the bulls wouldn't have noticed.

It had been a few years since Finn had ridden the rails in an empty boxcar, but he'd long ago learned the trick to getting comfortable on the bare wooden floor and blocking out the noise of the engine, the smell of whatever had been transported previously, and the moving slats of light as the train turned. He'd snuck onto the train at noon, footsore and thirsty, with little but the clothes on his back and a canvas canteen of water to call his own. Not nearly enough to get him to New York and Arkham, but Finn had faith that the road would provide.

He wasn't alone in the boxcar, five wild-haired geezers that looked like Methuselah's uncles had climbed on just as the smoke-belching train had pulled out of the station heading east. And not long after the first big turn at Santa Fe Avenue, a family of four hauled themselves on: mama, papa, bambino, and bambina. Papa shouted in Italian, but no one made a move to help him. The man cursed at length as he lifted a battered steamer trunk that looked like it had been dragged behind a few trains already and had made the journey across the continent more than once. They found a corner and immediately set up shop with a cook stove and ragged bedding.

Finn put them from his mind, knowing they'd pass the rest of the journey in isolation unless more Italians joined somewhere along the line. Finn didn't care much for boxcar conversations anyway; they were invariably some hobo's tall tales or a desperate man's sob story. Neither interested Finn, though he'd listen to the King of England himself if he came aboard with some booze.

It was a long way to the East Coast, so Finn settled himself in as best he could as the wind whistled through the boxcar's warped slats. It never really got cold in Los Angeles, not like it did in Ireland, but even Finn had to concede that it was getting pretty sharp as the hours wore on. Though he tried to steer his thoughts away from Arkham and the nightmarish things he'd seen there, it was impossible to keep his thoughts from returning there.

Truth be told, he still wasn't sure why he was going back. He'd felt the urge in his bones, and resisted it for as long as he could, but the one thing he couldn't do was explain it. He was being called back to Arkham, that seemed certain, but by what and by who? Decades of Catholic upbringing told him it had to be God or one of His saints, but everything he'd learned from Oliver Grayson told him something quite different. There was no benevolent old guy on a cloud watching over the people of Earth, only a hideous collection of monstrous gods from beyond the stars who most certainly did not have the interests of mankind at heart.

And unlike any of the manmade pantheons of gods, these gods had no clear division of good and evil, no moral framework of any description at all. These monstrous beings were so utterly removed from humanity's understanding that such notions were irrelevant. There was no grand coalition of golden gods standing at the ready to save the day at the last moment, no divine savior waiting in the wings for when extinction loomed, and no holy book that told how it would all shake out in the end. Mankind was alone in the universe, and that cold, hostile fact terrified Finn more than any fanged monster or flesh-eating cannibal.

The day wore on and quickly got dark, the temperature dropping sharply and making Finn curse that he'd not helped the Italians as they produced an oil-burning stove and huddled around its small circle of warmth. A few of the old geezers tried to ingratiate themselves, but were given short shrift by Papa.

Sleep was impossible, and Finn resigned himself to a long night watching the stars wheel overhead. Once, their serene and watchful light had comforted Finn, but now he saw them for what they were: impossibly distant balls of light, between which the monsters who hid in the darkness watched and waited for their chance to strike.

They stopped at a few stations along the way, but the boxcar was far enough along the length of the train that it often didn't make it as far as the platform. The few times it did, he scrambled off and hid underneath the train or in the bushes off to the side until any railroad staff had retreated to the warmth of the station again. The cold worked to Finn's advantage, as none of the inspectors were getting paid enough to stay away from their stovepipe fires for long enough to be thorough.

Somewhere in Arizona—Phoenix perhaps—Finn was surprised when an angry-looking black mongrel appeared on the floor of the boxcar, thrown on and landing with an ease that suggested this wasn't the first train it had caught. A sprightly fella climbed in after the dog with a bindle tied to his back, and he took a moment to straighten his long hobo coat before taking in the measure of his fellow travelers.

Finn took a closer look at the man, thinking he saw something vaguely familiar in his profile. He couldn't place it and decided he was simply a hobo; behaving like a hobo and affecting all the usual hobo mannerisms.

"Top o' the morning to you fine fellas," said the man, taking off his torn flatcap and bowing to the Italian mama and bambina in the corner. "And a tip of the hat to you ladies. The name's Pete, though folks often just call me "Ashcan." This here's Duke, the finest traveling companion a man could wish for. Now we keep ourselves to ourselves, and we don't mean nobody no harm, so we'd appreciate the kindness of that attitude being returned."

The fella was loaded, swaying drunkenly from side to side. Or at least that's what Finn thought until he saw Pete was moving in perfect time with the rocking motion of the train and wasn't anywhere near as drunk as he was making out.

Pete found himself a place by the door not far from Finn, and the little dog hopped into the man's lap. Finn half-closed his eyes and watched the man: how his eyes roved the darkened landscape like the old men back in the Dublin pubs who knew there was a British informer somewhere in the crowd of drinkers. It was, Finn was shocked to realize, a look he recognized from the few times he'd caught sight of his own reflection: a look of regret and farewell, of taking one last look at everything before it was gone.

Despite himself, Finn pushed his hat back and said, "Where you headed, fella?"

Pete turned to look at him, as though surprised he'd been spoken to at all. Finn's suspicion that the man wasn't nearly as drunk as he was making out only grew stronger at scrutiny he saw in those gimlet eyes. The dog bared its teeth, but Pete stroked his mangy head and the animal lowered its head and appeared to go to sleep.

"A place you probably never heard of," said Pete.

"Try me," said Finn. "I've traveled from one end of this country to the other, and I heard of lots of different places."

"You Scottish?"

"Please," snorted Finn. "A proud son of Erin."

"Not proud enough to stay in Ireland, though."

Finn extended his arm, pointing through the open door of the boxcar. "The land of opportunity called to me. I heard the streets of New York were paved with gold, so I thought to myself, Finn lad, I'll have me some of that."

"You must have been disappointed," said Pete, his narrowed eyes never leaving Finn's.

"Away with ye," said Finn. "Sure, weren't they paved with gold right enough. Liquid gold. Whiskey and rye, fella. Man can make a living on that stuff, but it ain't without its…complications."

Pete laughed, but seemed no less wary. "What's your name, Irishman?"

"Finn Edwards, and I'm heading back east."

"Aren't we all?" said Pete. "We go where the boxcar takes us."

"I mean all the way east."

"Why you so keen to talk about where we're going?"

Finn shrugged, as though the matter were of no interest to him. "Just makin' conversation is all. You got a familiar look to you. Wondered if I'd maybe seen you out that way."

"Where you headed then?"

"Ah, now," said Finn. "I'll tell you mine if you tell me yours."

"Why do I get the feeling we already know the answer to each other's destination?" said Pete.

"Maybe because I finally recognized you, Pete."

"That a fact?"

"Aye," said Finn. "You used to come around O'Connell's, looking to spend some hours pushing brooms around."

"Buys a four bit room, eight by twelve," said Pete. "You're the Mick the Newburyport lads were looking to put a bullet in a few months back, ain't ya?"

"What can I say, I make friends easily, but enemies easier," said Finn. "It's the Irish way."

"Don't sound too different to the American way," said Pete.

"There's something to be said for that," agreed Finn, and the two men shared a smile.

"So what takes you back to Arkham?" asked Pete.

"You wouldn't believe me if I told you," said Finn.

Pete looked deep into Finn's eyes and gave a slow nod.

"I think I just might," he said.

* * *

Ever since she'd been a kid, Minnie had liked the sea. There was something deeply soothing in the warm, wet sound of it against a pier or on a beach. Calming and mediative, she'd sat for hours on the forest-bordered banks of the Miskatonic before it flowed into the city, throwing twigs into the water and imaging all the exotic places they might end up.

Le Havre possessed nothing of that calming influence. That it was an overcast morning, both cold and raining, hadn't helped her to form a positive impression of the city, but its bleak, twilight streets had been empty and silent as Tower drove her through the rains of the approaching storm to the port. They were pushed for time; the *Ile de France* was leaving inside of an hour, and she still didn't know if the ticket office had received her wire.

It seemed absurd to be leaving France so soon after arriving, but the imperative to leave and go back to the States had been building in her gut since her blackout in the castle keep. All she could think of was getting back to Arkham and seeing Rex, though she had no idea what had prompted such an undeniable urge. She knew—or at least she thought she knew—it had something do with what had happened below the castle, with the man who had spoken to her at length about…

Well, that was where things got fuzzy.

Minnie had no idea what the man had talked to her about or even if she'd actually met him. She sensed that what he had told her was something of great importance, but every time she tried to remember what it was, the memories of that meeting became even more unclear. She'd given up trying to think of who or what she'd encountered, hoping that, in time, the memories would return by themselves.

She'd sent a wire back to the States, addressed to Rex at the *Arkham Advertiser*, though she'd kept the strangeness of what had happened to a minimum, simply writing that she was returning on the *Ile de France* and that she carried something of great importance with her. Quite why she felt the urge to be so oblique, she didn't know, but sensed it was crucial she mention the silver-bladed dagger with the bone handle carefully.

It had taken much longer to get to Le Havre than they'd planned. A storm was ravaging France, and previously good roads were now minefields of sunken potholes and broken concrete, while the smaller roads Tower favored were swampy quagmires that were next to impossible to traverse. In the end, Tower's intimate knowledge of the countryside had brought them out on the coast road a few miles south of Le Havre. The shimmering glow of the port on the horizon was their guide, and Tower drove through its suburbs like a man possessed.

There could be no mistaking the road to the quayside, for hundreds of people were making their way toward the ship; many more than could possibly be traveling upon her, but the sailing of such a magnificent vessel was a sight to be savored. Tower threaded a path through the busy streets of the port with aplomb, using skill at the wheel and colorful language in equal measure.

Heavy trucks jammed the roads in addition to all the sightseers, but Tower zipped and darted into gaps Minnie swore weren't large enough for their car, but which miraculously opened up at their approach. The tall harbor buildings were beacons of light in the early morning mist, mysterious slabs of brick and stone that appeared menacing and banal at the same time.

Tower eased them past a stalled convoy of heavily laden trucks and their shouting drivers, pulling through a gap between the two closest vehicles. Two men yelled at them as they snuck past, but Minnie's attention was swallowed by the magnificent vessel moored at the water's edge.

The *Ile de France* wasn't the fastest ship on the high seas, nor was it the largest, but it was almost certainly the most beautiful. Constructed along the classical lines of an ocean-going liner, its three smokestacks were pitched at a rakish angle, and even from the quayside, Minnie could see the flourishes of its art deco stylings.

Wealthy passengers in the latest designs from Paris and Rome were making their way up a rococo-balustraded gangway, bedecked with fans, ivory-topped canes, and sporting all manner of fashionable accessories. Minnie suddenly felt woefully underdressed, and the thought of her suitcase filled with clothes that were at least five years old caused her cheeks to flush a deep red.

"Look at those fools," sneered Tower. "Like circus performers they are. Fashion has made them foolish and vain."

"Yeah, maybe," agreed Minnie. "But they look *good*."

"Good? A plucked hen for the oven looks good. These popinjays look just like the ones made a foot shorter by Madame Guillotine."

"Ha, you're just jealous," teased Minnie.

"Not one bit of it," said Tower archly. "I feel sorry for them that they need to dress like peacocks just to live their lives."

"I'd still like the chance to raid their wardrobe," said Minnie, staring at a handsome elderly woman in a form-fitting purple gown with asymmetrical panels that flattered her curvaceous maturity enormously and pulled in her waist to a literal hourglass figure. A brass cane topped with what looked like a hooded cobra rendered in gold and adorned with ruby eyes tapped at her side as she walked, and her lace-wrapped hat and veil made it look like her head was gauzed in smoke.

Minnie's eyes followed the woman until she embarked upon the ship and Tower pulled the car over to where the ticket office glowed with buzzing electric light. Tower got out and spoke to the two men behind the counter, gesturing animatedly as they shook their heads and tapped clipboards with elaborate fountain pens.

Minnie got out of the car in time to see Tower wrench the clipboard from one of the men and scan the list of names. He circled a name and thrust the clipboard back under their noses with a grunt that spoke volumes of his contempt for their intellectual capabilities. The second man rummaged through a stack of bills and eventually produced a ticket printed on heavy grain card.

Tower snatched the ticket from the man and handed it to Minnie.

The ticket was a thing of beauty, surely too lovely to be something so simple as a berth on an ocean liner. The cursive lettering was hand-written, the gold embossing like something you'd see on a royal proclamation. She understood enough of the language to get the gist of what was being said, and its overblown language was more like an invitation to a grand ball than a piece of card that told her which gangway to use and which cabin to sleep in.

"Fancy," she said.

"Like everything to do with this ship," said Tower, though she could tell even he was impressed by the flourish in the ticket's design.

Seeing her ticket, a pair of liveried porters approached their car and it took Tower an effort of will not to shoo them away and manhandle Minnie's luggage himself.

Arm in arm they strode toward the gangway, and Minnie felt a sudden stab of regret at the idea of leaving France. She hadn't been here long, but the deep sense of connection she felt to this place was something she hadn't expected to feel. She tightened her grip on Tower's arm as they approached the end of the gangway, feeling the amused stares of the fashionistas around her at her unforgivably prosaic attire.

Minnie felt a strange reluctance to approach the uniformed ship's officer at the foot of the gangway, knowing on the same instinctual level that served her so well as a photographer of the macabre that it would set her on a collision course with great pain.

"Mademoiselle?" said the officer.

Minnie held out her ticket and the man gave her a long look up and down before checking the name and number with those on his list. He checked again with a look of puzzlement before smiling in bewildered understanding.

"Ah, yes, of course," he said in perfect English. "Mademoiselle Klein, apologies for my confusion, but you have been allocated a new cabin."

"A new cabin?" said Minnie, trying to hide her disappointment. Clearly the officer had decided she wasn't top tier material and was unfit to mingle with the upper classes. She wondered how far down the boat she'd end up; right next to the engines or across from the bilge pumps?

"Yes, a suite in first class," said the officer, returning her ticket. "Welcome aboard the *Ile de France*."

Minnie took back her ticket as Tower turned her around with a fondly paternal smile.

"I think America wants you back," he said.

"Or France wants rid of me," returned Minnie.

Tower shook his head, his voice swelling with emotion. "*Non*, you are a daughter of France now, Minnie Klein. You will always have a place in her heart. You will always be welcome and when she calls to you, I think you will come back."

"Countries can call people back?"

"But of course!" exclaimed Tower. "Your homeland calls you back even now. And when France needs you, it will call to your heart and you must come."

Minnie wanted to laugh at Tower's words, to mock him in the teasing banter they'd shared since they'd met, but the words died in her mouth as she saw his sincerity. The idea was ridiculous, but she believed Tower, suddenly and with all her heart.

She nodded and said, "I will. I promise I will."

"I know this," said Tower, jerking his chin ahead. "Now get on board. Mingle with the beautiful people."

Minnie fought back a surge of tears, swallowing hard at the thought of leaving the country that had been so good to her, that had opened up and shown her its beauty and its wounds. The images she would take back on film were nothing to the feelings she'd take back in her heart. The idea that she would one day return gave her sudden hope that there was still something worth fighting for, that whatever darknesses might plague the world could be overcome.

A naïve hope, perhaps, but hope nonetheless.

CHAPTER ELEVEN

The ferry to Sausalito left from the busy Ferry Building on the northern tip of San Francisco, a crowded double-decked boat that plied the waters between the city and its neighboring counties every day. Oliver had taken some persuading that a boat was the best way to reach Marin County, for his memories of the *Persephone* were still recent and horrifying. To fly was impossible and held terrors just as potent as the water, but to drive around would take days they did not have. Oliver had, point-blank, refused to set foot from the shelter of the roomy passenger decks filled with hundreds of other commuters, claiming he was quite content to watch the approaching scarp of rock from within.

Knowing he was unlikely to be let within the library, even with Hillshore to vouch for him, Rex had remained in San Francisco, taking the time to write up his notes and perhaps file some copy with Harvey Gedney of the *Arkham Advertiser*.

"That's if I still have a job," the reporter had only half joked as he headed out into the city, leaving Morely behind in the apartment.

Gabriel and Hillshore rode up at the front of the ferry, taking in the glorious scenery to be had out on the water before the omnipresent fog of San Francisco made that impossible. Alcatraz island and Angel Island would pass to their right before they made their approach to

Sausalito. To their left the great gap of the Golden Gate was a portal to the achingly vast Pacific Ocean, a natural funnel of rock that even now the city fathers were looking to bridge. How such a vast span could be crossed at all was beyond Oliver, but he knew well that ingenuity and determination were two of his species most defining traits.

Banks of mist were already gathering at the edges of the cliffs, like an invading army just waiting for the defenders to relax their guard. Hillshore had told them that the mists would roll in at the slightest provocation, turning San Francisco into an island among the clouds, like the giant's kingdom raided by the intrepid Jack of the children's nursery rhyme.

To the right, Oakland and Richmond rose in stepped ridges, folding away into the middle distance as it eased into what was rapidly becoming known as wine country. Stuccoed villas of white and gold and pink nestled on the slopes, together with burgeoning communities of those who loved the Pacific climate, but didn't want to move back to a city that might be destroyed at any minute by the sudden upheaval of another earthquake.

Hillshore had described Sausalito as a sleepy, yachting community and Marin County as a sparsely populated region, home to a number of passable wineries and the summer abodes of the wealthy San Francisco set. Oliver was reminded of Long Island and the division of East Egg and West Egg of *The Great Gatsby*, wondering which of those places this latest destination would resemble.

"Do you really think we'll find something over in this library?" asked Henry, who had chosen to sit with Oliver inside.

Oliver sighed, resting his elbows on his knees and steepling his hands for his chin. Though he had pushed the fear that had settled in his gut after their plane ride, he could still feel that choking terror just waiting to rise up and suffocate him. Individually, each encounter with the forces at Alexander's disposal would have been enough to drive stouter men to insanity, but taken together it was almost too much. Oliver knew his grip on rationality was tenuous at best.

"I have to hope so, Henry," he said. "If it's not, then all we have done is carry ourselves farther away from our enemy. I consulted a copy of this book in the Miskatonic library, and I know the writings of the Atlantean priests hold the key to stopping Alexander. There are spells, incantations, and formulae there, terrible things that demand a terrible price, but I couldn't take them with me."

Henry nodded and put a comradely hand on Oliver's arm.

"This is difficult for you, I know," said Henry. "It's bad enough that we know what we know, but to have a trusted friend turn on you is the bitterest pill to swallow."

"Especially one who shows no compunction at utilizing every means at his disposal to kill us."

"Ah, yes, but for all that he has tried, he has not succeeded."

"Not yet."

"What was it you told me that the man on the White Ship said to you in Kingsport?"

"Basil Elton?"

"Yes, that's the fellow, the lighthouse keeper," said Henry. "Didn't he say that you had a hard road ahead, but that you had strong friends and more allies than you knew. I don't believe those were just empty words, Oliver. Look around at the people who aid you, look at the things you have done."

"Like what?" snapped Oliver. "We as good as gave the Eye of Infinite Stars to Alexander and we're no closer to stopping him. For all we know R'lyeh could rise tomorrow!"

The sea slapped harder against the boat at the mention of such a hideous place and the ferry lurched into a trough of water that sent a drenching spray over the bow before it righted itself.

"Listen to yourself, Oliver," snapped Henry. "You're not some raw recruit on the front lines, you're a seasoned veteran who knows more of the world's truths than most men ever will. You have fought the good fight longer than anyone could ask and you're still here. You could walk away any time you choose, yet you do not. I was trapped in a dimension beyond understanding, and you came to rescue me. You have survived things that would have killed a lesser man, or at least driven him to madness. You have saved a great deal of lives by your actions and, God willing, you will save many more. Now don't you dare think that we have achieved nothing or that we have no hope. We'll damn well fight Alexander until we can fight no more. Only when the last breath is driven from my lungs or the last drop of blood is spilled from my veins will I stop fighting. George Gammell Angell would never have given up, so neither will you."

Oliver let Henry's words flow through him, remembering that his friend had served in the US Marines for several years and hearing the echo of that old soldier in his voice. The despair he had hitherto not realized was infecting his soul was revealed like an approaching assassin, and in its unveiling were the seeds of its downfall.

But knowing Henry was right wasn't the same as accepting it.

Oliver said, "I know you're right, old friend, but it's hard to see how we few can make a difference."

"'All that is necessary for the triumph of evil is that good men do nothing,'" said Henry.

"And are we those good men, Henry?"

"If not us, then who?"

* * *

The ferry deposited them at the terminal, little more than a wobbling pier jutting from a concrete lot built on the rocky shore of Marin County. A pair of temporary-looking structures stood like grim sentinels by the water's edge, marked in the blue and red of the ferry company and staffed by bored men in wet-weather gear. A row of hardy evergreens screened the utilitarian ferry terminal from the more upmarket areas of the peninsula, and beyond the terminal, an electric railcar climbed to a plateau cut into the lower reaches of the headland.

Climbing aboard the busy railcar, Oliver, Henry, Gabriel, and Hillshore eventually emerged onto a parking lot, one filled with automobiles waiting to be engaged as taxicabs.

"Most of the places a person would want to visit are beyond walking distance," explained Hillshore archly. "Much like everywhere else in America. You are a nation that dislikes to perambulate, while an Englishman must exercise his right to walk where he pleases."

"So how far is the Markham-Hyde collection?" asked Gabriel.

"Perhaps twenty miles up the coast," said Hillshore. "It's a quite beautiful drive."

"Then let's get going," said Oliver, looking up at the slate-colored sky and the mist seeping through the Golden Gate. "That crossing was bad enough in daylight, and I don't think I fancy making it again in darkness, surrounded by mist."

The others concurred and a taxicab was swiftly procured at a rate just shy of ruinous.

"Where's Floyd when we need him?" asked Gabriel as he unfolded a sawbuck into the driver's palm and the others climbed in.

As Hillshore had promised, the drive was beautiful, swiftly traversing the steep and narrow roads of the town before moving inland toward the western coastline. Their route curled through acres of ordered farmland, gently sloping vineyards, and neat rows of Queen Anne and Federal style houses before finally cresting a gently sloping hill and winding down onto the coast road. The vastness of the Pacific stretched out to their left, an impossibly wide vista that made it possible to believe that the greater percentage of the Earth's surface was liquid. Oliver found it difficult to look westwards, for he knew what lurked beneath the seemingly placid waters.

The others knew too, but Oliver had read more and learned too much ever to feel anything other than cold dread at the sight of that unknowable expanse of ocean. The road hugged the cliffs, turning inland only infrequently to cross the bridge of a township whose name none of them caught before they were through.

Such communities were prosperous and clean, and the people inhabiting them well-dressed and well-fed. To see taxicabs driving north appeared to be a common occurrence, for their passage elicited no great notice from those they saw. Eventually, just before the road bent remorselessly eastward, the driver took an unmarked branch road that spurred back toward the coast in a series of ever-rising switchbacks. As the taxi rounded yet another hairpin bend, the road turned through a sudden ninety degree turn and the Markham-Hyde library was visible directly ahead of them.

Built right on the edge of the cliffs, the collection was housed in a sprawling, Colonial-style villa similar to the great mansions built by the plantation owners of New Orleans. Brilliantly white, with a facade of roof-height fluted columns and plum-colored shutters on each of its windows, Oliver wouldn't have been surprised to see a white-suited Southern gent emerge with muttonchop whiskers and his debutante daughter at his side as a troop of gallant Confederate horsemen rode by.

As a born and bred Yankee, Oliver had been brought up to pity the misguided fools that had followed Jefferson Davis and General Lee to war. And as heroic as the Union forces were in the Baltimore history books, they couldn't quite match the sheer roguish vibrancy of the southern forces in Oliver's teenage mind. Stories of JEB Stuart and Stonewall Jackson had given him what he now knew to be a romanticized version of the Confederacy, but one that still lingered in his adult mind.

"This is the place?" said Oliver.

"It is," confirmed Hillshore, his manner suddenly frosty now that the moment had come to make good on his promise to help them.

"Looks kinda deserted," observed Gabriel, as the taxi driver pulled around a long sweeping driveway of gravel. "I guess they don't get a lot of visitors out here."

"Any collection that houses the kinds of books we must consult is well left alone," said Henry, and Oliver was hard-pressed to disagree. As they drew closer to the building, Oliver saw the true scale of the Markham-Hyde collection as it stretched back from its ornate facade to the very edge of the cliff. At least twice as large as the library at Miskatonic University and at least the equal of Princeton's or Brown's.

As the taxi drew to a halt outside, a tall, whip-thin man in a sober black suit emerged onto the portico and stood with his hands laced behind his back. His features were gaunt to the point of being skeletal, and his thin eyes were hooded and dark. All that was missing was the tape measure for sizing up a client for a coffin.

"Who's he?" said Gabriel.

"He is the Custodian," said Hillshore.

"Does he have a name?" asked Oliver.

"Undoubtedly, but I have never learned it and he has never seen fit to divulge it."

Hillshore was first out of the car, with Oliver at his side. Henry and Gabriel came after them, and they climbed the steps to where the Custodian awaited them in the shadow of the columned entryway.

"Professor Hillshore," said the Custodian. "Your call was unexpected."

"My most sincere apologies, Custodian, but the need to consult your books was sudden and immediate."

"These are the gentlemen of whom you spoke?" said the thin man, casting appraising glances over the rest of them and taking their measure in a heartbeat.

"They are."

"And you vouch for their integrity?"

A beat. "Yes, I do."

Introductions were made, with Hillshore taking the time to establish each man's credentials, laud their academic achievements and extoll the virtues of their scholarly worth. With Gabriel, Hillshore presented his career as an honored serviceman and staunch upholder of the law. The Custodian listened to Hillshore's recitation without expression, giving no clue as to what effect, if any, the Englishman's words were having.

Eventually Hillshore stopped talking and the Custodian nodded. "Follow me."

The man spun on his heel and walked back into the building, his stride as purposeful as a drill sergeant's. Oliver and the others followed him within, entering an expansive circular vestibule of gleaming white. The walls were faced with ivory marble veined with gold, and the floor was a checkerboard pattern of black and white. A number of portraits of important-looking men and women hung between doors on the curved walls, each one glaring sternly down from their gilded frames. Stairs on both sides of the entrance curved up to a second level, and Oliver saw yet more painted patrician features staring down at him.

A small circular table sat in the center of the room, with a wide ledger upon it. The Custodian stood behind the table and indicated the archaic-looking fountain pen and ink pot beside the ledger.

"If you please," said the man.

Hillshore signed the book first, and passed the pen to Oliver. He drew some ink into the nib and signed his name beneath Hillshore's, feeling as though some irrevocable line had just been crossed by this act. Henry and Gabriel signed below his name, and he sensed they all felt that they were now bound together as conspirators. Whatever happened here, they were now all part of it.

The Custodian nodded, and Oliver was put in mind of Mephistopheles after Faustus accepts his deal with the Devil.

"Gentlemen," said the Custodian, looking directly at Oliver. "Do you know the name of the book or books you wish to consult?"

Oliver drew himself erect and said, "Yes. It is a book known as the *Necronomicon*."

The Custodian's unmoving facade slipped just for a fraction of a second, and Oliver saw a moment of hesitation and doubt in his eyes, as though he now regretted allowing them within his sanctum. It passed a heartbeat later, leaving Oliver to wonder if he'd seen it at all.

"Very well. Please follow me," said the Custodian. "And touch nothing."

* * *

Rex had already begun to like San Francisco on the drive from the Presidio to the Jesuit College, but walking the streets of the city with a crisp winter's wind in his face, he knew he was falling a little in love with the place. He rode the cable car up towards the heart of the city, feeling the layout of the place seep into him by some strange geographic osmosis.

Like any good newshound he could read the currents of a city that sluiced beneath the veneer of the obvious and the mundane. He recognized faces that were out of place, storefronts that weren't really storefronts, and the hangdog look of men and women staggering from nearby speakeasies. The cable car rode through a dolled-up part of town with closed curtains, fancy porches and cloth-hung stoop-lights that told him this was a street he could purchase the love of a good woman for two bucks an hour. It crested a hill and wound its way through a street of lawyers and accountants, and Rex liked that the two could sit happily cheek by jowl.

From up here, Rex could see out over the water. Alcatraz squatted on its rock like an encrusted barnacle, the military prisoners at least getting the benefit of the Pacific climate for most of the year. Rex had read a few pamphlets that had come out of Alcatraz during the war, and they were pretty powerful motivators not to get sent down. If conditions inside were even half as bad as he'd read, then it was no wonder that crime in San Francisco was damned low.

The cops here were tough as saddle leather, the ramrod straight sons of pioneers and grafters, but they knew enough of how the world really worked to bend when the occasion demanded. They were the kinds of guys you could reason with, maybe even offer a five-spot to get yourself out of a minor pickle, but who'd bust you on the head with a billy club if you stepped too far out of line.

Rex rode the cable cars and electric streetcars all morning, listening to the chatter of the locals, reading their papers and billboards, traversing the city backwards and forwards, left and right, feeling out the places he might later need to visit or avoid. He worked the town, talking to people he met along the way, hearing what was good in the theaters, where to eat and, more importantly, where to drink. He slummed it or put on airs and graces, as his listener demanded, and learned as much as he could of the city as he took the opportunity to flex the reporter's muscles that had lain dormant for far too long.

San Francisco still bore the scars of her brush with extinction, but her make up was good and she hid them well. And where the ruins of toppled structures did emerge from the intense rebuilding, they were like badges of honor or scars on the cheek of a prizefighter who came back from a twelve-round drubbing to deliver a knockout roundhouse.

Rex saw all this and more, gaining the insight of a local within three hours of setting out.

Yeah, there was a lot to like about San Francisco, but Rex had to remind himself that he wasn't here for the sights. And, truth be told, much as he was enjoying the refresher course in Journalist Instincts 101, he knew part of his morning's tour was just to put off the real reason he'd come out.

Calling the *Advertiser* was a job Rex would happily wander San Francisco all day to avoid.

Around noon, Rex had his first brush with what the folks round here had lived with every day since 1906, but willfully chose to ignore or had found a way to accept. Sitting on a bench in Russian Hill, eating a slice of oven-cooked dough topped with melted cheese, mushrooms, and olives he'd bought from an Italian guy wheeling around an oven on the back of a striped cart, Rex felt a subtle vibration beneath his feet.

It started as a gentle rumble that Rex first ascribed to a nearby cable car as it labored up the hill. Very quickly he realized there was more to it than that and sat bolt upright as the vibrations intensified and climbed up through the bench. Pebbles on the ground danced on the concrete around him and Rex felt a moment's panic as he saw nearby telegraph poles swaying and their wires cutting the air like whips.

The rumble built until it sounded like a New York subway train passing right underneath him, and Rex leapt to his feet, tossing his food away as he looked around for somewhere to hide.

Where the hell did you hide from an earthquake?

Then it was over, and Rex felt suddenly foolish as he stood unmoving in a crowd of people disembarking from the cable car. They walked past him with the faintly patronizing look of city folk seeing a hayseed coming down from the farm for the first time.

"Don't worry, pal," said a guy dressed in the pinstripe suit of a banker. "Mercalli wouldn't even rate that a three."

Rex just stared dumbly at him, not knowing who this Mercalli guy was or why he'd be rating earthquakes. Once Rex was certain the city wasn't about to fall into the sea like their cab driver had predicted, Rex decided he needed a drink.

He hopped onto the cable car before it set off again and got off at Chinatown, where a guy riding up to Nob Hill earlier in the day had told him was a swell place to get a decent rye. Calmer after the ride downhill, Rex took a moment to savor the sights of Chinatown, the red lanterns, the swarming mass of people of all ethnicities and from all walks of life, the bustling stalls like the souks of Cairo and the deafening shouts of the stall-holders. There was a good feeling here, a real melting pot of people from around the world that made Rex feel like the vaunted promise made on Lady Liberty's bronze plaque had been made good.

The stalls on either side of the street were laden with more produce, fancy goods, spices, and oriental knick-knacks than you could shake a stick at. Fireworks fizzed and spat sparks into the street and the smell of roasting meat on skewers made Rex's mouth water. Though he hadn't long eaten, he bought a platter of rice and meat swimming in aromatic sauces that smelled exotic and tasted even more so. He washed it down with a couple of cups of hot tea poured from a chained copper kettle suspended over an open fire that was probably illegal in such a built-up area, but which no one seemed to mind.

Fed and watered, Rex continued down the street with the confident poise of a local that meant the worst of the street hustlers and hawkers left him alone, looking for the blue door with an oriental symbol of two lightning bolts either side of a squared-off eight, sitting on top of what looked like a three-legged stool. He had no idea what that symbol meant, or even if he'd recognize it, but no sooner had he tried to visualize it than he saw a blue door with a faded symbol scratched into the woodwork. Rex squinted, cocking his head to the side, trying to match the description he'd been given with what he was seeing.

Deciding it was close enough, Rex walked up to the door and gave three knocks. The door opened and a heavyset Chinaman with a skullcap and long waistcoat ushered him in. A sweet-smelling cloud of vapor billowed from the door and made Rex's eyes water. Clearly alcohol wasn't the only intoxicating substance for sale within.

"You come in," said the man, beckoning urgently.

"Yeah, sure," said Rex, almost disappointed there hadn't been any of the password and secret handshake shenanigans that getting into an East Coast speakeasy usually required. He eased past the man, moving along a long corridor completely pasted in flyers he couldn't read or even tell whether they were the right way up. But as unfamiliar as the outside and language was, the interior spaces of the building were just like any other den of iniquity.

A long bar with a collection of genuine-looking liquors lined one wall, which told Rex this place almost never got raided by the cops. A bunch of tables were scattered around the room in front of a stage where an older woman in a sequined gown was singing a Broadway tune in Chinese like she was in front of the president himself.

"Gotta give her points for effort," said Rex under his breath.

A potent fog of smoke hung just below the low ceiling, and Rex was reminded of the tobacco smell in William Hillshore's office. It seemed the Englishman was no stranger to an illicit taste now and again, not that Rex particularly cared one way or another. Every man deserved to enjoy at least one vice without someone looking down their nose at him. After all, wasn't the punishment of a vice inherent in the very act of its indulgence? You drank, you got drunk and unhealthy, you overate, you got fat, you gambled, you lost your money. You chased the dragon, you lost days in a haze of fractured memories.

Rex knew that well enough to know that he dared not accept one of the long-stemmed pipes the Chinese grandfathers offered him as he approached the bar. He pulled up a seat and slapped a handful of coins on the polished wood. Its pitted surface was glossy with spilled hooch, the grain of the wood richly patinated with hard luck stories and tall tales.

He'd shut down most of his drinking in recent weeks, but the earthquake still had him spooked, and he figured he could use a shot or two to calm his jangling nerves.

"Gimme a rye, straight up, two fingers," said Rex to the barman, a Chinese kid who couldn't have been more than fifteen. *Hell*, thought Rex, *if you're gonna break the law running a speakeasy, might as well throw in a little child labor.* The kid brought him a chipped glass, and gave him a decent measure of what looked like the real McCoy.

"You got a phone in here, kid?" asked Rex.

All he got in reply was a blank look. Clearly language training here extended only to brands of whiskey and their cost. Rex asked again, louder this time, and mimed the act of speaking into a mouthpiece while cupping one hand over his ear.

"Phone?" he said again. "You got one?"

The kid nodded and held up three fingers. Rex understood and smiled. Some things you just didn't need to understand the other fella's lingo, you just had to know that all things had a price and that the world turned around that simple understanding.

"Sure, kid," said Rex, sliding three more coins across the bar. The money vanished into the kid's apron and he jerked a thumb to a bamboo screen covered in painted dragons and women in long dresses pouring tea for big guys dressed in armor and carrying long, subtly curved swords. Rex downed his drink, enjoying the taste, but knowing he shouldn't have too many more. Steadying his nerves and Dutch courage was one thing, but phoning his editor drunk was quite another.

Rex ducked behind the screen and sat on the high stool beside the phone. He picked up the earpiece and made the connection, giving the operator the numbers for the *Arkham Advertiser*'s offices. While he waited for his call to be connected, Rex listened to the distant buzz of voices in the earpiece, hearing a multitude of accents and voices just below the threshold of hearing. A thousand voices and a thousand messages passing back and forward across the country, a babble that was only ever going to get larger and more vocal. Who knew there were so many people with so much to say to one another?

The line buzzed and chirruped before a harsh click of connection told him the telephone had been lifted on the other end.

"Hey, who's this?" asked Rex, knowing that getting the first word in was always important.

"This is Darrell Simmons," said the voice on the other end of the line, clearly put on the back foot at Rex's quick-fire opening. "I mean, this is the *Arkham Advertiser*, Darrell Simmons speaking. How can I help you today, sir?"

"You can drop the 'sir' crap, Darrell, it's me, Rex."

"Rex?"

"Yeah, you know, Rex Murphy, superstar newshound for the august organ of Arkham reporting?"

"Rex, sheesh, where you been? Harvey's hopping mad here," said Darrell. "He's ready to string you up since you blew town. I can't use the words he used, but trust me, they'd have curled your toes, let me tell you."

"I'll bet he did," said Rex with a fond grin, thinking that to Darrell an exclamation like *sheesh* was tantamount to swearing like a drunken stevedore. The youngster was a photographer, a stringer who'd come on board the *Advertiser* to help carry the load since Minnie had waltzed off to France. A proud New Englander, he'd once tried to get Rex to come to a temperance meeting, little realizing that he was doomed to failure from the outset. A good kid with a good heart, Rex wondered how he'd survive in the offices of a newspaper. How long would it take him to become jaded like…

…*like me?*

Rex put that gloomy thought aside and said, "Listen, is the big man in? I need to talk to him."

"Harvey? Sure, Rex, he's here, but are you sure you want to talk to him right now?"

"That bad, huh?"

"Put it this way, Rex. If you don't have the story of the century to tell him, I think you're going to be looking for a new job soon."

"I kinda figured that," said Rex with a shrug. "Just go get him for me, will ya, Darrell?"

"Okay, Rex, but it's your funeral."

The line crackled and clunked as the receiver was put down and Rex heard the pleasing *clack, clack, clack* of busy typewriters. He could picture the unruly office of the *Advertiser*, the harried reporters with pens tucked behind their ears, reams of copy flying from their fingertips and Harvey Gedney looming over them all like the drum-pounding overseer in a slave galley.

"Murphy? You got a lot of nerve calling here like you still have a job," said Harvey Gedney as the receiver was picked up again. Rex could picture the florid, jowly face of the *Advertiser*'s editor as he spat down the line as though his errant reporter was right in front of him.

"Harvey, have I got a story or two for you," said Rex, as though his editor hadn't spoken.

"What makes you think I care, Rex? You vanish from the face of the Earth without a word, you don't file a story for a week and then I get a call from some military base in San Francisco asking if I know a Rex Murphy."

"What did you tell them?"

"I told them you were a good for nothing waste of space."

"Nice."

"I was being generous," said Harvey. "Are you really in San Francisco?"

"Yeah."

"And I'm supposed to keep your desk open while you're off gallivanting?"

"Damn straight," said Rex with a confidence he hoped would trigger Harvey's acquisitive nature.

"Give me one good reason not to fire you right now."

"Because you got no one in that office who gets you stories as good as I get."

"You haven't gotten me squat in months I couldn't get some second rate stringer to file."

"Okay, you got me on that one," admitted Rex, waving to the kid behind the bar to pour him another whiskey. "I've been running on fumes and goodwill for a while, but that's over now, and I've got some real good stuff for you."

"Yeah?" said Harvey, and Rex heard the sound of his redemption in the man's voice. "Okay, say I believe you, what kind of story you got that's going to get you of the hook?"

"I'm in San Francisco, right, and I flew with the air mail," said Rex, taking his drink and palming a few coins into the kid's hand. "All the way from Long Island."

"Right, sure you did, Rex," said Harvey. "And I swam all the way to Britain and back before breakfast."

"It's the straight dope, Harv," said Rex. "An RAC pilot called Chuck flew us out to Chicago, then over the Rockies and down through Nevada to California. Hell of a thing, Harvey. I can write it up so it's got action, exploration, and technology. Lenny Lunchpail will eat it up. You know I'm right, folks love stories like that. Come on, Harv, flying all the way across the country. How many folk can say they've done that?"

"I don't know, I'm not even sure I believe you did it."

"I swear to God, Harvey. I got Miskatonic professors with me who did it too, and we landed at the Presidio. Call 'em if you don't believe me."

"I will, you bet your bottom dollar I will," said Harvey. "And if I find out this is another of your big stories you won't share, then we're through. I'll fire you so fast you're head won't stop spinning, and there won't be a weekly rag from here to Timbuktu that'll hire your sorry ass."

"Understood, Harvey," said Rex, making a fist and punching out an imaginary opponent. "I'll get you something over by end of play today. How does that sound?"

"Sounds like another deadline you'll miss."

"No way, Harvey. This is a new day for us, just wait and see."

"It better be or you're history at the *Advertiser*," replied Harvey, and Rex had no doubt he meant every word of it.

"Okay, Harvey, gotta go," said Rex. "Pulitzer prize winning stories don't just write themselves."

A derisive snort was Harvey's only answer, and Rex took that as his cue to hang up, but before he replaced the receiver on its cradle, he heard Harvey say something else.

"Sorry, Harv, didn't catch that. What did you just say?"

"I said I've got a telegram for you, came all the way from France. From Minnie, I guess."

Rex felt his heart skip a beat at the thought of hearing from Minnie, and a surge of warmth spread through him at the sound of her name. Confused thoughts tumbled through Rex's head at the idea of Minnie getting back in touch. She'd been cagey about the idea of keeping up regular contact while she was abroad, and only once she'd walked out of his life had he understood why.

"You there, Rex?"

"Yeah," he managed. He could get Harvey to open the telegram and read it to him, but the thought of someone who knew Minnie seeing what she had to say before him sent a spasm of distaste through his body. And what if Minnie said something personal that ought to be kept between the two of them?

No, as much as it would mean a delay in finding out what she'd said, Rex knew he would rather never write again than have Harvey Gedney read the telegram down the telephone.

"Listen, I need a favor," began Rex, knowing he was stretching the bounds of Harvey's tolerance to breaking point. "I need you to forward that to me here in San Francisco."

"I'm not your damned errand boy, Rex," snapped Harvey.

"I know, I know. Trust me, I wouldn't ask if it wasn't important. Please, Harvey."

Whether some last kernel of goodwill or the imploring tone of Rex's voice was the kicker, Rex would never know, but he heard the editor's gruff acquiescence in the long sigh that followed.

"Okay, Rex, gimme an address and I'll get Western Union to telegraph it again later today. Good enough?"

Ignoring the sarcasm of Harvey's last words, Rex nodded.

"Yeah, Harvey," he said. "Good enough."

CHAPTER TWELVE

The opulence of the Markham-Hyde's exterior was reflected in the exquisite finishings of its interior. Oliver and the others followed the Custodian as he led them through octagonal rooms of opulence that would have shamed a Rockefeller or an Astor. From floor to ceiling the walls were faced with tall bookcases, handmade from gleaming crimson rosewood. The floors were polished terrazzo, and every room was hung with chandeliers that glittered like drooping ice shards.

"Impressive place you have here," said Gabriel. "Who pays for all this?"

"The collection has been patronized by many wealthy donors over the years since its inception," said the Custodian, without turning to face Gabriel.

The man's choice of words seemed odd, but Oliver couldn't quite put his finger on why.

"How long has the Markham-Hyde been in existence?" asked Henry. "I am familiar with most such collections, but I confess yours is one that has escaped my notice."

"The collection has always been there," said the Custodian. "It makes itself available to those that need it when they need it most."

Oliver shared a confused glance with Henry at the Custodian's answer, which seemed needlessly cryptic, but he was less concerned with the library's history than the provenance of the works contained within its walls.

The Custodian followed an unwaveringly straight course through the center of each room, too far from any of the shelves for Oliver to make out any of the titles, but as they passed through each door and the angle of the walls brought them closer, he saw the collection ranged from volumes of poetry, natural philosophy, eastern esoterica, to lurid fiction, celebrity autobiographies to dime-store erotica.

"You have a varied collection," said Oliver.

"Comprehensive is the word we prefer."

"It's certainly that," said Henry, pausing by a selection of anthropological tomes and pulling one from the shelf. "There's books and writers here I've never heard of. And you appear to have a book by Franz Boas: *Race, Language, and Culture*, with a publication date of 1940."

At last the Custodian halted his relentless march and spun on his heel.

"You were told not to touch anything, Professor Cartwright," he said, nodding at something behind them. Oliver turned and saw two men dressed in identical white suits that he hadn't been aware were shadowing them. The two men were broad-shouldered like Gabriel, and each had a face that was so bland and unremarkable that Oliver had trouble fixing their features into something he could actually assimilate as a human face.

They swept past him and as one man took the book from Henry's unresisting hands, the other steered him without apparent effort to the center of the room.

"I say!" remonstrated Henry. "Unhand me."

The man in the white suit complied with his demand, and Henry's ire seemed to vanish instantly as the touch was withdrawn, almost as though he had forgotten the insult done to him. The Custodian stepped to one side as the doorway he stood before swung open, revealing a room illuminated by the low light of the sun as it poured in through a far wall of glass.

Oliver moved past the Custodian, entering the room. It was a wide, semi-circular space with its flat wall immediately behind them and the crescent arc of its far wall completely formed of glass. Looking left and right, Oliver saw the entire room was cantilevered out over the cliffs, giving an unparalleled view over the Pacific Ocean. A series of tables were laid out in a staggered grid pattern, with discreet panels erected at each table edge to give readers a degree of privacy.

The room was empty at the moment, and the sense of space was quite dizzying.

"This is the Reading Room," said the Custodian. "The book you requested will be brought to you momentarily."

* * *

The Custodian and the two men in white suits withdrew as Gabriel moved to the window and Hillshore paced in circles, like an animal trapped in a snare. Henry took a seat at the nearest table, and Oliver, seeing no sense in wasting his energy and having no desire to approach the oceanic vista, sat next to him.

"Damn peculiar that book's publication date, eh, Henry?"

"What book?" said Henry.

Oliver looked askance at his friend. "The one apparently by Boas. The one you were just looking at."

Henry gave him a puzzled look. "I don't follow you, Oliver. I haven't looked at any of the books here. That queer fellow that brought us through the collection specifically told us not to, didn't he?"

"True," agreed Oliver, now less than certain he recalled the incident clearly. "I could have sworn you were looking at one of the collection's books."

"No, I'm sure I'd have remembered a book by Boas," said Henry.

"Yes, I'm sure you would," agreed Oliver, now sure that his own recall was at fault, though he found that he could not remember what had caused him to begin this line of questioning. He shook his head as the doors to the Reading Room opened and two more of the white suited men entered, one bearing a locked strongbox, the other a brass tray upon which rested a venomously green crystal supported in a small brass tripod, two ornate bells of Moorish appearance, and a clay jar like an ink pot that streamed aromatic smoke.

Gabriel turned from the view, his hand reflexively moving to his hip at the sight of the two men, though he evinced a strange look as his lawman's instincts tried and failed to memorize the salient details of their features. Hillshore studiously ignored the men, keeping his arms folded and his attention focused far out to sea.

The first man deposited the ink pot at the far end of the desk, before placing a bell to either side; one beside Oliver, the other beside Henry. The tripod bearing the green crystal he placed with exaggerated care in the center of the table. The second man placed the lockbox on the table and received a curiously notched key from the other. It fitted easily into the lock-plate and began turning of its own accord, making several ratcheting rotations before the box clicked open with a soft sigh that was like a breath of desert air.

The lid was opened, and a book produced. Its cover was red leather, pitted and worn with age and use. Oliver felt his skin crawl and the hairs on the back of his neck stand to attention at the sight of it. This was the *Necronomicon*, the dread book of the Mad Arab, the Al-Azif, the Book of the Dead—a tome for which hundreds had burned in the fires of the Inquisition and which had driven many more to madness over the centuries.

Once, this had belonged to Morley Dean, and the dread truths and cosmic horrors consigned to its pages had almost broken his mind into irreparable fragments. As it was, a great deal of Morley's psyche was still fractured, and Oliver hoped his own mental fortitude could withstand the strain of what he might find within. He had consulted the book once before, and knew well the toll it could take on a mind. Was he really prepared to delve into its blasphemous nightmares once again and risk his sanity by searching for what they needed? What unintentional damage might he wreak in his hunt for some clue that would aid them in their fight against Alexander? What racial memories of eons past might be unlocked by the damned formulae and occult keys contained within the *Necronomicon*?

Oliver reached for the book, but one of the men in white shook his head.

"Not yet," he said. "There are rules."

"Rules?" said Oliver.

"The smoke keeps burning throughout this consultation," said the man. "If, for any reason whatsoever, it stops burning, you close the book and each of you ring your bell immediately."

"Why do we need to ring the bell?" asked Oliver.

"It will summon us back to the Reading Room," said the man in white, tapping a manicured fingernail on the table beside the green crystal in the miniature tripod. "But if we cannot reach you in time, you must shatter the Serpent's Fang."

"The crystal?" asked Henry, clutching his own crystalline star. "Why, what is it?"

"Do you understand these rules?" said the man, ignoring the question.

"I do," confirmed Oliver, deciding he'd had enough mystery for one day. "But answer Henry please. What is that crystal?"

For a second Oliver thought the man was going to refuse to answer, but after some unheard communion he said, "A whisper of breath captured from the maw of Yig. The Father of Serpent's venom is not a painless death, but it will be better than what awaits those whom the book snares."

Gabriel approached the table and faced the two men with his hands on his hips. "Wait, are you telling me this is some kind of poison?"

"Yes," said the man, and both he and his identical companion withdrew to the library stacks beyond the Reading Room without another word. Oliver heard the snap of a lock being turned, though he couldn't see a keyhole in the timbers of the door. No sooner had the door closed than Hillshore stormed from the window and placed both hands on the table.

"Oliver, this has to stop," said Hillshore. "When you asked me to help, I had no idea you would drag me into…whatever this is. Smoke in jars, bells, poisonous crystals? What the devil is going on?"

"I'm not sure I can properly explain it, William," said Oliver. "All I can ask is that the trust you have shown me thus far extends just a little further. When Morley told you that this book was dangerous, he was not being melodramatic or indulging in some lunatic fantasy. This book *is* dangerous, and if its custodians require such precautions then so be it."

"I gotta say, Oliver, I kind of agree with William," said Gabriel. "Are you sure what's in there is so valuable that we gotta risk poison and the likes to get it?"

Oliver placed one hand on the textured leather binding of the hateful book, feeling the weight of blood and murder that had soaked the pages over the centuries. Oliver took a deep breath and addressed his next words to each of his companions.

"Whatever hideous dangers lurk within this book's pages, I cannot turn from facing them. There can be no price too high when the fate of the world is at stake. Ancient forces are moving to destroy the Earth and return it to its primordial state, a watery graveyard where a titanic god from beyond the stars would hold court over a drowned world of a billion corpses."

Oliver opened the cover of the *Necronomicon*, and it seemed he felt a sigh of release and a dark invitation that was seductive and repulsive at the same instant.

"What is one mind when set against such a terrible future?" said Oliver.

* * *

Except it wasn't just one mind. Henry Cartwright, brooking no argument, joined Oliver in his descent into the black gulfs of the *Necronomicon*. While Gabriel kept watch on the world through the glass wall overlooking the cliffs of Marin County, thinking of ways they could sneak the book past its custodians, Hillshore paced back and forth, gnawing on his fingertips at the thought of Oliver attempting to remove the *Necronomicon* from the Markham-Hyde collection.

Oliver had consulted its pages once before, but that occasion had—he now realized—been carefully orchestrated by Alexander, with precise page references and excerpts already established. This time there could be no such easy access to knowledge, and anything of value wrested from the book's pages would have to be unearthed with the painstaking rigor of the archaeologist.

Finding the pages he had read once before proved more difficult than Oliver had imagined. This was no mass-produced book run off Gutenberg's presses, but a hand-copied palimpsest scrawled by a host of deranged souls down the ages and correlated by a singularly lunatic compiler. Its contents bore a striking correlation to the tome kept under lock and key in Armitage's collection at Miskatonic, but its ordering was radically different.

Much that Oliver knew would haunt his nightmares until his dying day passed before his eyes; bestiaries of things that should not be, unholy descriptions of the rites by which they might be summoned and conversed, secret histories and doggerel prophecy. In some cases the nameless contributors attempted to reconcile what they had seen in twisted imagery; hellish renditions of creatures that no sane god would dare render in flesh. Nonsense syllables clashed together and many times Oliver felt his tongue attempting to shape the un-sounds they might make before reason intervened and he clamped his jaw shut.

Hours passed and yet they were no nearer to any solution or even a morsel of hope.

Henry paused in his inveterate note-taking to walk repeated circuits of the Reading Room, his skin pale and his eyes feverish. After so recently emerging from a catatonic state, Oliver could only admire the fortitude that had seen Henry come this far. As he walked, Henry turned a piece of azure crystal around in his hands. It was an artifact given to him by a merchant of the Dreamlands, a talisman to ward off the worst of the book's evil.

Oliver touched his own talisman, the soapstone glyph given to him in Kingsport. The never-ending succession of unknown histories that overturned everything he had been taught since childhood and the monstrosities that had once claimed this world as their own left him breathless and sweating. His heart beat on the inside of his chest as though he had matched the feats of Harold Abrahams and Eric Liddell. His finger traced a cursive pattern on the page before him, an undulating swirl of strange angles and beguiling whorls.

Something predatory loomed in his mind, and Oliver lifted his finger from the page as though burned. He flinched as the hideous touch of something utterly alien brushed his mind, an unheard howl of something impossibly distant as it was frustrated yet again. Oliver quickly turned the page, lest his digits be unwittingly used as a fleshy key to a lost prison hidden in space and time. His eyes alighted on the following page's text, and he sat bolt upright as he saw a reference to Nereus-Kai, the mad Atlantean priest who had brought salvation and doom to his island home.

"Henry!" exclaimed Oliver. "I've found it, by God, I think I've found it."

With obvious reluctance, Henry returned to the table. His skin was sheened in sweat, and his cheeks had a high, ruddy complexion that spoke of intense strain. Oliver hated that he had to impose such a burden on his friend, but without Henry's assistance, much of the text before him would be indecipherable.

Together they pieced together the narrative from the mishmash of Latin, Greek, and proto-Aramaic. Much of what they were reading was unfamiliar, this translation of the book carrying subtly different interpretations of the fall of Atlantis. The story was broadly similar: the attempt by the cultists of Cthulhu to destroy the only race of Men who could hope to stop the rise of their darkly dreaming deity.

Again, the war between the Atlanteans and the monstrous, aquatic beasts was described in gruesome detail, and this portion of the account held especial horror for Oliver, for he had encountered the hybrid descendants of these creatures in the dark waters of Kingsport. As the hours wore on and the translation of the *Necronomicon*'s tale of Atlantis became clearer, Hillshore and Gabriel were drawn in to hear its words. In a lowered voice, Oliver read out what he and Henry had gleaned from the pages, of how an exile of Atlantis had crafted a diabolical crystal with which to alter the configuration of the heavens like some demented clockmaker in order to bring the stars to a propitious alignment.

There then followed passages of verbose hyperbole of skies raining blood, continents hurled across oceans like skipping stones across a pond, and towering volcanoes being thrust from the seabed. Yet these titanic geological upheavals were nothing compared to the rise of Cthulhu's sunken city, the nightmarish sepulcher named R'lyeh. This cyclopean tomb-city broke the surface of the ocean and worldwide devastation followed in its wake.

But the Atlanteans were prepared for this, and Nereus-Kai unleashed the most powerful sorceries in order to defeat the hordes of Cthulhu besieging Atlantis and send R'lyeh back to the bottom of the ocean. In a shaking voice, Oliver spoke of how such power always came at a dreadful price.

Nereus-Kai had known that the aftermath of his great spell would be terrible. Just how terrible, he could not have suspected, or else he would never have dreamed of unleashing such potent magic. His spell had unmade the world, and such power was not meant to reside in the hands of mortals. Cthulhu and his minions were defeated, but the power of the spell doomed that which it had been wrought to save.

The heavens opened and the world split asunder. Atlantis broke apart and waves like mountains arose up to claim their prize. The pillared cities and gilded temples of Atlantis sank beneath the ocean, lost forever and wiped from the annals of history, save in the journals of madmen and the cartography of the insane.

Yet this rendition of the fall of Atlantis had a postscript lacking in the copy Oliver had previously consulted. In Armitage's version of the book, the spell of Nereus-Kai was rendered as polysyllabic gibberish that could not possibly be spoken accurately by a modern reader. Yet here the words were transliterated in what appeared to be a phonetic rendition, together with a scribbled note in the margins to the effect that this was but the first half of the great incantation.

The second half, it was claimed, had been sent to the Great Hall of Celaeno, a library of cosmic knowledge, though Oliver had no idea where such a place might be, having never encountered such a name in his years of scholarly pursuits.

"Read that last part back," instructed Hillshore.

"Which part?" asked Oliver, quite breathless from his retelling of the Atlantean war.

"Where the mad priest says he sent the second half of his spell."

Oliver traced his finger along the spidery script, finding the notation Hillshore had requested he read again.

"*And knowing the potency of what he had crafted, Nereus-Kai hid his spell from the sight of Men, locked in the red-litten vaults of Celaeno's Great Hall, where only those in the direst of need may seek it under the labyrinth.*"

Hillshore stood straight and rubbed his forehead, where a vein was pulsing with clockwork regularity. A layer of sweat beaded his forehead, and even Gabriel, pragmatic Gabriel Stone, looked worn thin by all they had heard.

"I thought so," said Hillshore. "Madness, all of it. Utter balderdash. And here you almost had me half convinced that there might be something to all this fantasy."

"Wait, what are you talking about, William?" said Oliver.

"Celaeno? That's where Nereus-Kai said he sent the second half of his spell?"

"Yes," said Oliver. "Do you know that name? What is it?"

"Celaeno is one of the seven stars in the constellation of Taurus," sighed Hillshore. "Part of the Pleiades cluster. In celestial terms, it is relatively close to Earth, around fourteen hundred light years from Earth, but is still inconceivably distant."

"How do you know this, William?" asked Gabriel, his shirt open at the neck and his tie askew.

"Amateur astronomy at Cambridge, dear boy," said Hillshore. "A bunch of us stargazers would gather on the Gog Magog hills and set up our telescopes to watch the heavens. Fascinating stuff, really, spent many a happy evening there taking notes and watching the silent stars go by. But my student days notwithstanding, I can say without fear of contradiction that this Atlantean priest, if he existed at all—which I'm now inclined to disbelieve—could not possibly have sent anything to Celaeno. It's ludicrous."

"Is it, William?" said Oliver. "In the face of everything we've learned, is it really so far-fetched that something could be projected out into the cosmos?"

Hillshore looked at Oliver in disbelief, as though unable to comprehend how an educated man could fail to see the lunacy inherent in what he was saying.

"Don't be ridiculous, Oliver," said Hillshore, backing away from the table and throwing his hands up in frustration. "You flew across one continent and it almost killed you. How is it possible that a man from an ancient culture traveled to a faraway star to deposit some piece of magical lore?"

"Does it matter how he got there?" said Henry. "Trust me, William, I have traveled to places I would never have believed possible, realms so far beyond anything I could have imagined that I would have laughed at you had you spoken to me of them. Distance is no barrier to travel when it is undertaken by the mind. You of all people should understand that. Has your profession not documented instances of astral projection, mental displacement, and the like?"

Hillshore snorted in derision. "It has, many times, but no such tale can be verified or corroborated and most are hoaxes engineered by charlatans. The rest are most likely the products of diseased minds, and are certainly nothing to be taken at face value. I have certainly never seen anything to convince me of the existence of such phenomena."

"Absence of evidence is not evidence of absence," said Oliver.

"A truism that is next to meaningless right now," snapped Hillshore. "Show me facts, Oliver."

Oliver gathered his thoughts to form a stinging rebuke when he noticed that the smoke curling from the ink pot on the desk had grown thin and almost transparent. It still filled the air with its exotic perfume, but what had begun as a thick plume of scented smoke was now little more than a slender tendril.

"Gentlemen," said Oliver, rising from the table. "I think we had best be going soon."

Henry, Gabriel, and Hillshore followed Oliver's gaze, but before any of them could say something, a grinding tremor shook the Reading Room. The chandelier overhead swayed as the building shook and the glass panels of the curved wall trembled in their frames. Oliver gripped the edge of the table for support as Gabriel and Hillshore staggered at the force of the sudden shock wave.

"Quick!" shouted Henry, still seated and with his hands spread on the table. "The bells!"

A deafening roar of splitting stone, like an onrushing avalanche came from deep beneath the earth as the smoke from the ink pot was finally exhausted.

"Oh, no…," said Oliver.

And the world turned upside down.

* * *

Hillshore's home in the Mission district was roomy and well-appointed, but it was woefully unsafe. Morley Dean had done his best to render its portals impassable to alien creatures and its fenestration unsuitable for ingress, but there was only so much he could do. The Englishman would no doubt complain about the gouges Morley's pocket-knife had torn in the window frames and cut into the architraves around his doors, but he'd thank Morley if only he knew what lurked out there in the shadows.

He dearly wished he still had his Sentinel Vial, but supposed it had served a useful purpose on the plane. The flying demons—a fatuous use of the word, but one Morley supposed fit well enough—had been utterly decimated by the creature within the vial. Morley tried not to think too hard about what might have happened had he dropped it accidentally in a crowded location during the years he had possessed it. If something attacked him while he paced from room to room in this dangerously unsafe environment, he would have no warning of its approach, save perhaps its stench or a feeling of intense cold.

Morley knew more than most men, even those privy to the ancient mysteries behind the fictive myths and legends built up by Humanity as a shield against the true horrors of the universe, yet even he knew too little. His time had not been wasted since the disastrous expedition to Alaska that had seen him cast from Brown as a scholarly pariah and numerous promising men and women lose their lives. Morley had traveled the globe extensively, always seeking out the marks and spoor of the unclean and the diabolical.

In Britain's deceptively green and pleasant lands, he had driven out a tribe of cannibalistic troglodyte folk dwelling in the dank caves beneath Nottingham Castle, while in London he had thwarted a plot to raise He Who Must Not Be Named. In the layered warrens beneath the streets of Edinburgh, Morley had shot the immortal revenant of Sawney Bean with a silver bullet recovered from the unmarked grave of a saint in Transylvania.

Amid the sands of the Egyptian desert, a reawakened Pharaoh and his army of monstrosities fashioned from the scraps of dead meat in his pyramid's Canopic jars had been returned to the afterlife, and in the veldt of the Transvaal, Morley and a nameless Sangoma ended the murderous rampage of a *naghtloeper* by thrusting a dagger of stone that had no earthly counterpart through its stolen heart.

Eastern Europe was a time he'd tried to wipe from his memory with alcohol and specially concocted narcotics, for the blackened ruins of a global war was fertile ground for the mad, the bloodthirsty, and the unnatural to hunt and plot and grow strong.

By Morley's reckoning, he had saved the world many times over, but no one would ever know.

Which was just fine as far as he was concerned. Anonymity was his best defense against the creatures of the elder dark and their mortal servants. To pass unseen or to be dismissed as a crank eccentric or a deranged lunatic was to hide in plain sight, and Morley cultivated the veneer of the deluded professor over a carefully analytical mind alloyed to a fearsome determination and zealous passion to thwart the enemies of Mankind wherever their tendrils arose.

It chafed at Morley to let others place themselves in harm's way while he waited for them to return. Yet after the last time he had come to San Francisco to undo the machinations of a cult whose claws had bitten deeply into the fabric of the world he had feared it would be the death of him. And rather than some innocent executor stumbling across his collection of unholy tomes and dread artifacts, Morley had bequeathed much of his library to the timeless custodians of Markham-Hyde.

In the end, his confrontation with the deathless avatar of that cult (upon the ghostly incarnation of a mighty bridge across the Golden Gate that was yet to be built) had seen him victorious, though gravely wounded in both body and mind. Morley had returned to New York, that teeming metropolis of lost and damaged souls, to find a place to hide amongst the millions that called that stone and steel hellhole home.

From there he had watched and waited, knowing that someday the cults of the Old Ones would attempt once more to bring their diabolical masters into the light once again. But as he waited, a faceless and nameless (but nameless no longer) enemy had moved against him, and worked his own arts to end Morley, dispatching a hunting beast that moved between the angles of space-time to track its prey.

With a synchronicity that hinted at design where Morley knew no design existed, Oliver and his companions had blundered into his life. Their mystery was one of which he had been only tangentially aware, yet there was a very real threat that Morley could not ignore. And though he had hoped never again to set foot in San Francisco, here he was on the West Coast, seeking a way to win a game where his opponent held all the advantage.

The sun was well past its zenith, and still he had no word from Oliver on the success or otherwise of their mission to the Markham-Hyde collection. Morley knew better than anyone how seriously the custodians took the security of the works stored upon their shelves, and just hoped that Oliver and the others were up to the task of removing that which they required.

Morley paused in his endless circuits of Hillshore's home to look out over the city. In the east, snow would be falling in New York, but here in California, the sky was still blue and the day was no chillier than a crisp autumnal afternoon. The window was now sealed shut, a series of nails hastily inscribed with elder signs hammered through the wood to the frames. He turned from the window and went back to the kitchen, filling a copper-bottomed kettle with water and placing it upon the stove.

He struck a match and turned the knob to begin the flow of gas. The flame lit and Morley put the kettle on the burner, letting the laws of physics do their work in the transmission of heat. He made another circuit of the house, stopping here and there to examine Hillshore's gilt diplomas and degrees, his certificates of commendation from the Presidio and photographs of more relaxed times.

Studying the framed photographs arranged on a dresser, Morley saw Hillshore in cricket whites, as a young graduate in the Great Court at Cambridge and, finally, standing with a group of friends wearing outlandish costumes and foppish grins around a bunting-wrapped pig wearing a top hat.

Morley grinned and put the picture down as the kettle began its whistling scream.

Before he could even turn around, a slamming impact struck the building and Morley put a hand out to steady himself as he heard a terrific rumble from somewhere far below. Like a subway train or a grinding Chicago L-train was tearing through the apartment, the noise was both distant and deafening. Hillshore's pictures and keepsakes tumbled to the floor and glass cracked beneath Morley's feet as he staggered back from the teetering dresser. Something heavy landed on the floor in the bedroom above.

He crawled on all fours to where the few papers he'd managed to salvage from his destroyed apartment in New York were gathered, knowing that they would be of no use, but wanting to keep them close anyway. Fragile things broke as the shock waves of the earthquake—for what else could this be?—continued, and cracks spread from the corners of the doors and windows.

The screaming of the kettle continued unabated, and Morley clung to the floor like a life raft as the rumbling, booming echoes of cracking rock and shifting earth moved on. Gradually the vibrations subsided and the structure of the building ceased its horrid motion.

Morley let out a sigh of relief, earthquakes being one of the many reasons he had chosen to stay away from San Francisco. Collective denial of the weird and the macabre was one thing, but believing that events which were geologically certain to occur would not happen again was lunacy. It was like living on the side of an active volcano and being surprised when a river of lava destroys your village.

Whistling, screaming, and howling, the kettle continued to boil away in the kitchen, and Morley pushed himself to his feet on unsteady legs, brushing dust that had fallen from the ceiling from his shoulders and trouser legs. He made his way to the kitchen, thinking that the Englishman's panacea of tea would be most welcome right about now.

Morley pulled up short as he saw the kettle lying on its side on the tiled floor, steaming water leaking from its curling spout.

The screaming wasn't coming from the kettle, but from the walls themselves.

And now Morley listened closer, he realized it wasn't screaming at all.

It was the howl of a hunting hound with the scent of its quarry.

CHAPTER THIRTEEN

Oliver's fingers brushed the surface of the Moorish bell, but before he could close his grip, the table tilted crazily as the floor heaved upwards like the back of a bucking bronco. The marble floor split apart and gouts of earth erupted from below. The bells spun away from the table, but the musical sound of their landing was swallowed in the cacophony of noise pounding the air.

The ground slammed into Oliver, though he swore he hadn't fallen, and the glass wall behind them shattered with a high-pitched crash. Thousands of glittering shards fell into the room, skittering daggers of diamond-sharp glass. A howling wind shrieked inside, incongruously accompanied by what Oliver swore sounded like some kind of distant Gregorian chant. Henry cried out as he was thrown sprawling, sliding down the tilting floor as a ragged slab of concrete erupted from below. Gabriel and Hillshore were nowhere to be seen behind the obscuring banks of dust thrown up by the room's collapse.

The heavy oaken table lay canted at an angle and Oliver saw that Morley's copy of the *Necronomicon* sat unmoving, as though glued to its surface. The green crystal had toppled from its wire-frame tripod and rolled in swirling arcs toward the edge. The floor heaved again and the crystal bounced closer to the table's edge. Oliver scrambled toward it over the cracked ruin of the floor, but already knew he would be too late.

The Serpent's Fang fell from the table, but before it landed on the marble, Gabriel Stone dove headlong out of the dust to catch it like a star pitcher in the World Series. Gabriel rolled, cupping the gemstone like an active grenade.

"I don't know what this thing does for sure, but I ain't in a hurry to find out," he said, slipping it into his coat pocket. Oliver nodded as the thunderous crashing sounds of a building collapsing sounded from all around them. Hillshore crawled from the settling dust, coughing and wiping blood from his forehead where a flying shard of glass had caught him.

"Good God, William, are you all right?" shouted Oliver, though he knew it was a foolish question.

"Just a graze, Oliver," said Hillshore with natural English under-statement. "I'll be fine."

The building groaned and a crack of splitting timber and steel re-minded Oliver that they were not out of the woods yet. Gabriel came to the same conclusion a moment later.

"Hell, this room's hung over a cliff," he said. "We gotta get out of here."

That was to prove easier said than done, for the spur of rock and the supports beneath them had subsided considerably. The broken floor was canted at an angle of around forty-five degrees, and it was only thanks to the numerous cracks in the marble that they were able to avoid slipping down to where the shattered glass wall opened out onto a hundreds of yards drop into the ocean.

"Come on!" shouted Oliver. "Everyone out. Hurry!"

Oliver moved up the buckled floor on all fours, feeling like a moun-taineer as he pulled himself along using cracks in the floor as hand-holds. Hillshore was already at the doors, and Gabriel soon joined him as they began tugging uselessly at the handles.

"It's no use," said Gabriel. "The doors are stuck. The quake's jammed them solid into the frames."

Oliver's heart sank, but he kept on going.

"Perhaps if all four of us help we can free the door from its frame," he shouted.

"It's worth a shot, Professor," replied Gabriel without halting his efforts to budge the door. "Climb up and we'll get to it."

Oliver looked back to where Henry followed him. His old friend had had the presence of mind to retrieve the *Necronomicon* from the table and held it clutched to his chest with one hand while attempting to pull himself up with his other hand. No easy task, but strangely it seemed as though every handhold and foothold was there within easy reach.

"Please hurry, Henry. I implore you!" shouted Oliver.

Henry looked up and there was a wild glint in his eye, as though in possessing the *Necronomicon* he was somehow beyond fear of death, like an obsessive who finally holds the precious object of their desire next to their heart. The look passed and Henry nodded, climbing higher toward Oliver.

"Take my hand!" cried Oliver as the floor crumpled and sagged, its angle relative to the cliffs becoming ever more acute. The reading table finally toppled, breaking apart as it was caught between two slabs of stone that crashed together like tectonic plates in a continental collision. Bracing his feet on a spur of split marble, Henry reached up with his hand outstretched. Oliver held his arm out, straining to make contact. The wind whipped by him from the shattered glass wall and again he heard the strange sound of distant chanting. He glanced up as his peripheral vision caught sight of movement over Henry's shoulder.

The line of the cliffs curved away to the north and south, and where it cleaved back out to sea, Oliver saw the ground was undulating with a grinding, splitting motion. His first instinct was to assume that this was some byproduct of the earthquake, but then he saw something vast and terrible break the surface of the grassy cliff top, a segmented ridge of armored plates and pulsating flesh that could not possibly belong to anything of this earth. No sooner had Oliver seen the bloated, yet sinuous monstrosity breach the earth's surface than it sank out of sight once more, tearing through the rock as easily as a fish moves through water.

Oliver's hand shook as though palsied at the sight of the thing beneath the earth. Its bulk had been impossible to guess, but as he saw the ruins of a farmhouse lying in the wake of the thing's passing, he suddenly understood its horrifying scale. Longer and wider than a freight train and just as fast, the vast worm-monster was a burrowing leviathan heading straight for them.

His mind refused to accept the existence of such a beast and Oliver felt his sanity fray yet further at this latest impossibility. The blood drained from his face and he closed his eyes, though he knew the horror of what he was seeing would never leave him. It was too much for one mind to take, too sustained an assault on reason to be endured. How sweet it would be to let go, to allow himself to surrender to hysteria and the inescapable abyss of madness. At least then he would not have to live with the sure and certain knowledge of Man's idiocy in believing himself preeminent among the universe's creations. Let the gods and monsters have this world, let them rule over an insignificant ball of rock populated by capering madmen!

Oliver felt himself succumbing to the lure of insanity when Henry's hand slapped hard into his own. Henry's fingers closed around Oliver's extended hand and something hard and warm pressed into the skin of his palm. Cold clarity surged through Oliver like the cool waters of a mountain spring, washing away the stringy, clogging detritus of his horror. Without being able to see it, he knew the elder sign Henry had brought back from the Dreamlands was held in their conjoined grip, and that its apotropaic properties were all that had pulled him back. That it was a temporary salve mattered not at all, it was enough for now.

"Pull me up, Oliver, there's a good fellow," said Henry with remarkable calm for a man hanging over a fatal drop into the ocean.

Oliver nodded and hauled with all his strength, pulling Henry up over the steepening angle of the floor. Stone shattered and steel buckled with grinding cracks and squeals as the last remaining fragments of glass fell from their frames. The roar of the approaching creature grew louder and Oliver saw entire swathes of the cliffs fall into the ocean like glaciers calving vast chunks of ice into the freezing ocean below.

"Gabriel, is that door open yet?" he shouted over his shoulder.

"Working on it," grunted Gabriel as he slammed his shoulder into the unmoving timbers. "Could use some help, though."

Henry nodded and scrambled up past Oliver, still holding the *Necronomicon* tightly. Oliver turned to follow him when he caught sight of something glittering in the ruin of the shattered reading table. At first he thought it was simply a piece of glass, but then he saw it was one of the Moorish bells the men in white had left them.

"No!" cried Henry as he realized what Oliver intended.

Oliver ignored him and slid down the disintegrating floor toward the table. Through cracks in the marble, he could see the waves crashing at the base of the cliff far, far below. If the remains of the Reading Room were to fall he would be killed instantly.

"Oliver, what in God's name are you doing? Get back here now, you dashed fool!" shouted Hillshore, lending his not inconsiderable strength to Gabriel's efforts to open the firmly wedged door. Oliver ignored them all and reached for the bell. It skittered way from his questing fingertips, but at last he was able to take hold of it and lift it toward him.

"Hurry up, man!" shouted Henry, reaching back to Oliver, much as he had done himself only moments ago. "Please, Oliver, take my hand!"

A booming explosion of stone below him caused Oliver to look down through the cracked floor, seeing a cascade of rubble falling to the ocean. The segmented bulk of the titanic rock-burrowing monster erupted from the cliff below him in an avalanche of liquefied earth and pulverized stone. Somewhat steeled to the likelihood of its grotesque appearance, Oliver watched with detached fascination as its body slithered out of the cliff.

A protean mass of abhorrent flesh, loathsomely worm-like yet elevated from such understandable vileness by its sheer unimaginable size, the creature's head was a mass of waving tentacles, each tens of yards long, and dripping in caustic slime. And at the heart of that writhing mass of rubbery, gelatinous appendages was a circular maw, ringed with chisel like nubs of what must be teeth, though each was the size of a tombstone.

The monster's vast form bent upwards, like a ridged length of intestinal tubing, and the waving, heaving mass of tentacles twitched as though sensing that the target of its destructive wrath was close. The sound of guttural, inhuman chanting gusted from its gnashing digestive tract, and Oliver smelled the disgusting reek of devoured earth and all the creatures therein that had been consumed.

More of the creature emerged from the cliff as it oozed up the cliff toward him.

Oliver lifted the Moorish bell, seeing the intricate swirls and latticework in its design; a design that was surely too ornate for so simple an object. Not knowing or understanding why he had risked his life for such a trivial, yet elaborate item, Oliver did the only thing he could think of to do with it.

He rang the bell.

* * *

The sound was magical, sweet like sugar and soft as church bells heard over a misty common on a lazy Sunday morning. Almost instantly, Oliver felt strong arms lift him from the disintegrating stone floor and haul him up toward the door. He could not see his rescuer, but saw the arms of a white suit as the Reading Room finally started to tumble into the sea. Like a waterfall of debris, the floor and walls of the room were dropping into the giant creature's gaping sphincter of a mouth, where it was ground to dust in a heartbeat.

"In future, please ring the bell *before* the shrouding smoke burns out," said one of the white-suited men as he pulled Oliver to safety.

Oliver twisted in the grip of his rescuer to see Henry, Gabriel, and Hillshore scrambling over the canted threshold of the Reading Room. The second of the men in white stood at the doorway, where only the twisted remains of the hinges and a few nubs of splintered wood remained to suggest there had been doors at all.

"What happened?" called Oliver.

Gabriel shook his head, looking as confused and bewildered as everyone else.

"Beats me," said the Pinkerton man. "One minute I'm beating my shoulder black and blue against the doors, the next they're flying halfway across the room in pieces and this guy's yanking me out of the room like I don't weigh more than a kid."

As if to emphasize the point, the man in white lifted Oliver through the doorway with childish ease into one of the many octagonal library rooms they had traversed en route to the Reading Room. Oliver had never been more grateful to have solid ground beneath his feet, but remembering the ease with which the devouring monster had smashed through the apparently solid bedrock of the peninsula, suddenly that didn't seem like such a safe place to be. In an awful series of cracking, tearing roars, the last of the Reading Room's structure finally gave in to gravity and ripped from the edge of the cliffs. The roar of falling masonry and grinding debris was deafening, and a billowing dust cloud forced them back from a doorway that now gaped into empty space.

"We need to keep moving," said Oliver with remarkable calm.

"You *think*?" said Gabriel, helping him to his feet as a hurricane of rotten air blasted into the library, followed by a hideous bellow of monstrous appetite and sing-song voices that chanted in guttural tongues not heard since a time before the coming of Mankind.

With the two men in white bringing up the rear, Oliver, Henry, Gabriel, and Hillshore turned and ran headlong through the library. This room too had suffered damage, though nothing as severe as the Reading Room. The shock waves of the earthquake had emptied the shelves and the floor was awash with books, all covered in a layer of dust spilling through cracks in the ceiling. A smashed chandelier lay in pieces in the center of the room, and gaping split lines ran in jagged traceries across the walls.

They had just reached the next set of doors when the rear of the library was demolished by a terrifyingly powerful collision. The booming impact threw them to the floor as the far wall was smashed inwards in a roaring tidal wave of destruction. Oliver saw a grinding darkness into which the tumbling debris was sucked and a flopping mass of glutinous, squid-like tentacles feeding shattered brickwork and beams smashed to matchwood into the devouring maw.

Oliver sprang to his feet as the cascade of rubble barreled toward them, bringing down yet more of the walls and ceiling. Bookcases exploded into splinters and irreplaceable books were pulped or shredded into millions of scraps of paper. Gabriel had his pistol drawn—though Oliver had not known he'd brought it with him—and fired shot after shot into the oncoming debris.

"You can't hurt it!" shouted Oliver. "It's too vast. Run!"

Like all good soldiers, Gabriel Stone knew when to fight and when to retreat, and this was very definitely a time for the latter. Henry and Hillshore followed the men in white through the doors, and Gabriel and Oliver were hot on their heels. The devouring monster smashed onwards in idiot pursuit, destroying the library as it went. Oliver and the others ran through library room after library room, each one subsequently leveled by the oncoming juggernaut in a cascading rain of destruction. The beast's speed was prodigious, but the very mass of the library was keeping it from overtaking them.

Oliver kept running, his lungs burning with the effort of escape. He could see no way to survive this attack, but kept going anyway. The sound of alien chanting was stronger now, overpowering even the crash and din of the collapsing library. He risked a glance over his shoulder in time to see a vast wave of rocky debris behind him and fronds of pulpy tentacles reaching blindly toward him.

A lashing pseudopod of vivid crimson whipped from the mouth of the pursuing monster and Oliver was hurled from his feet by the ferocity of the blow. He spun through the air and slammed with bone-cracking force through the double doors that led back to the checker-board vestibule. The portraits of the stern-faced patrons of the library looked down at him, and Oliver felt as though they glared their disapproval at what he had brought to their fine institution.

Looking back through the door, Oliver saw the gaping chasm-maw of the leviathan, its thrashing chisel teeth gnashing in hunger. Oliver tried to stand, but a restraining hand held him down.

He looked up to see the Custodian, gaunt and thin and shaking his head as though disappointed.

"Were our rules too difficult to follow?" he said.

Gabriel, Henry, and Hillshore were borne through the smashed remains of the double doors by the men in white, and no sooner were they over the threshold than the Custodian brought his hands together as though to applaud the thoroughness of the rock-devouring monstrosity.

If the beast's attack had been a rumbling buildup of noise and terror, the Custodian's response was one of singular sharpness. The sound of his hands connecting was like a peal of thunder or a lightning strike slamming down right next to Oliver's head. A booming crack of split stone echoed through the vestibule and a curtain of dust and iridescent smoke erupted from the ground.

And, just like that, the monster was gone.

And, just like that, so was the Markham-Hyde collection.

Oliver blinked away confused afterimages as a cold wind blew in his face.

In front of him he could see only blue sky, deepening to bruised purple. The entire rear wall of the vestibule had vanished save for a broken stub of concrete and timber hanging over empty space. The entire mass of the cliff upon which the deeper portions of the collection were built had simply sheared off, cut as cleanly as though a divine cleaver had slammed down.

Through the empty gap where the wall and library had been, Oliver saw the teeming city of San Francisco across the narrow waterway of the Golden Gate and the open expanse of the Pacific. Mist gathered over the water, and the lights of the distant city were already sparkling in the late afternoon sunshine.

"What the hell?" began Gabriel, though Oliver felt that didn't quite match the strangeness of what had just happened. Though every bone and muscle in his body protested in surging barbs of pain, Oliver climbed to his feet and looked over the edge of the building. A mountainous expanse of rock and wreckage tumbled downward, falling in a thunderous rain of debris into the ocean, where it landed in a series of titanic, never-ending booming splashes.

Amid the torrent of shattered rock and brickwork, Oliver saw the thrashing form of the bloated, worm-creature. Its slimy body fell with the remains of the library, but where the sea was no more inimical to the rocks that it would be to most living things, it was like an acid bath to the monster. It melted in the water, the liquid dissolving the alien matter of its body as easily as boiling water destroys ice. Grasping tentacles lashed like flailing whips, grasping outcroppings of rock in an attempt to save itself, but falling masonry pulped its groping feelers and it slumped back into the water with a hideous screeching quite unlike the chanting that had accompanied its assault.

Oliver watched the creature's dissolution impassively, shivering as its vast bulk was reduced to little more than an oily scum of jaundiced froth on the surface. He leaned out over the freshly shorn cliff face, swaying on the edge of a precipice, both mentally and physically. The surge of clarity and energy Henry's talisman had imparted drained from him and he felt the onset of pure, undiluted terror. His limbs began to shake and as he looked out over the bay, Oliver saw that it would be so terribly easy to end the brutalizing of his mind and soul.

All it would take was one step forward and all the pain and misery and horror would be over.

There was no promise of resurrection, no hope of a better life to come, and that was good.

Oliver felt his trembling limb begin to move, but a strong hand took hold of his arm.

"It's all right, Oliver, dear boy," said Hillshore. "I've got you."

* * *

The return to San Francisco over the water was one that neither Oliver nor any of the others relished, but the alternative, a round trip of many hundreds of miles north before curling in a clockwise hook to come into the city from the south was completely impractical. The Custodian had brooked no explanation of the awesome force with which he had sheared away the cliff upon which the collection had been built, and his bland-faced associates were politely forceful when they bundled the four of them into the back of a gleaming white Packard summoned from whereabouts unknown.

A driver who could have been brother to the men in white sat at the wheel, and his bearing suggested that no attempt ought to be made to leave the car once safely ensconced in the back. Not that Oliver had any intention of doing so. He wanted nothing more than to be away from this place, with its own secret mysteries and nightmarish associations. Though Henry had attempted to carry the *Necronomicon*—the only tome that appeared to have survived the complete and utter destruction of the library—into the Packard beneath his long coat, the Custodian had taken it from him with the ease of a seasoned pickpocket.

"I think this should remain with us," said the man.

Henry was about to protest, but Gabriel pushed him down into the car beside Oliver and said, "You'll get no argument from me, pal. This stuff's dangerous, right enough, and not just to a man's mind. I reckon we're all better off without it, don't you, Henry?"

"Not at all, I—," began Henry, but Hillshore cut him off.

"Professor Cartwright, I believe the Custodian speaks with our best interests at heart," said the psychiatrist, and Oliver had never loved his old friend more. Even after all the chaos and destruction around them, the Englishman still maintained his calming stiff upper lip. Under normal circumstances, Oliver would often tease William Hillshore for such starchy English reserve, but now he was pathetically grateful for it.

"You should listen to your friend," said the Custodian. "He has a rational mind, and that will serve him well in the days to come."

Henry gripped his carved elder sign close to his heart, and at length he nodded.

"Perhaps you are right," he said.

"You have your notes?" asked the Custodian.

Oliver was about to say that their notes were lost along with the library, but he felt in his pocket and found numerous pages of notations written in his own handwriting. He could not remember having folded them and placed them within his coat, but nothing of recent memory was clear or fixed with any certainty in his mind.

"Yes," he said. "I have them here."

"Good," said the Custodian. "And if I were you, I would burn them after your need for them has passed. Knowledge is power, and should be guarded well. At least until its purpose is served."

Gabriel looked back over the ruins of the collection. Only the facade of the building remained, hollow and bereft of any substance behind it, like the movie sets being built on the Hollywood backlots every day. The entire building and the ground upon which it had once stood were no more, swallowed by the ocean and lost forever.

"Everything's gone," said Gabriel, and the Custodian gave him a curious look. To Oliver's eyes it was part bemusement, part dawning understanding, and part indulgent.

"Markham-Hyde has always been here," said the Custodian, repeating his earlier words as they had traveled to the Reading Room. "It makes itself available to those that need it when they need it most. Its store of knowledge will come again somewhere else, under a different name in a different guise. But be assured, gentlemen, we will watch over it always."

Gabriel nodded stiffly, as though he'd seen a ghost, and quickly got into the capacious back seats with the rest of them. The door closed behind him and the Packard swung smoothly away from the crumbling facade. The automobile picked up speed as it drove away along the gravel drive, and Oliver could not resist a glance over his shoulder.

Portions of the upper facade were toppling into the ocean, and soon it would be as though the Markham-Hyde collection had never existed.

Oliver could see no sign of the Custodian or his associates.

* * *

The rest of the journey was made in silence, and even the prospect of another ferry ride, which had so unnerved Oliver on their first crossing, was insufficient to raise more then a grunt from any of the four men. The Packard dropped them at the parking lot above the ferry terminal, the mute chauffeur turning the car and driving back the way they had come.

Standing on the raised platform over the terminal, Oliver leaned his elbows on the iron railings and took a deep breath of sea air. Below them the electric railcar sounded its bell as it began another ascent.

The lights of a distant ferry swayed in the mist that lay thick and heavy over the bay as it labored toward the terminal. The ferry wasn't scheduled to arrive for another quarter of an hour, and none of them were ready to descend the steps to the quayside just yet. Henry lit a cigarette and Gabriel reloaded his pistol, both men reconciling the day's events in their own way.

Hillshore stood next to Oliver and quickly lit his pipe. The pungent aroma of his strange tobacco drifted on the air, and its very familiarity was a welcome anchor of solidity in Oliver's churning psyche as he stared down at the ferry terminal below.

"Do I have to pull you back from the edge again?" asked Hillshore, leaning over the railing.

"I guess that depends on what you mean, William."

Hillshore chuckled, a somber and inappropriate sound given the events of the day.

"Yes, I suppose it could be taken different ways," said Hillshore. "I was being flippant, but the deeper question still stands. If I had not taken hold of your arm, would you really have stepped from the cliff?"

Oliver considered the question. Once he would have laughed at so foolish a notion, but thinking back to the sense of release he'd felt when his leg had started to move toward the cliff, he didn't feel like laughing now.

"I don't know, maybe," he said, honest at last. "I might have. I think that, right then in that moment I might have, but you don't have to worry about me, William. It was a momentary insanity, nothing more, I'm quite all right now."

Hillshore stared at him, and Oliver recoiled from that look. He had seen that look on the face of clinicians throughout his life, most recently on the face of Dr. Hardstrom at Arkham Asylum. The analytical nature of his friend's perusal horrified Oliver with its implications, but Hillshore softened his gaze and turned his face to the ocean.

"I'm sorry, Oliver. Once a psychiatrist, always a psychiatrist."

"I told you, I'm all right now," repeated Oliver, angry now and needing to lash out. "I don't need your damned witch-doctor diagnosis."

Hillshore didn't react, his composure too studied to be ruffled by so obvious an outburst.

"I understand your anger, Oliver. It is a quite normal reaction to such a traumatic event. But to bottle up the emotions inside is a sure way to invite a psychotic breakdown," said Hillshore, leaning closer so that neither Henry nor Gabriel could hear what he said next. "I do not think the others saw what you considered at the edge of that cliff, but I have spent enough time with men who believe they wish to end their lives to recognize the look in the eyes they all have. And you had that selfsame look, Oliver. You have it now."

Oliver gripped the railing at the edge of the platform, wanting to argue with Hillshore's words, to spit them back in his face and tell him to leave him alone. But years of friendship could not be so easily undone and Oliver was pragmatic enough to recognize the worth of Hillshore's words and the nobility of his intent.

Instead of verbally abusing Hillshore, he shook his head, letting out a long, pent-up breath.

"I don't know how much more of this I can endure," he said at last. "It's too much for any one man to take. To know the things I know and to have seen what I've seen. It's too much. There's a limit to what any man's sanity can withstand, William, and I fear I'm operating way beyond my limits."

"You're right, of course," said Hillshore with a sagacious nod. "Every man has his limits, but that you fear you are beyond yours tells me the opposite is true. Only a fool would expect to go through a shocking event like that without some mental scarring. To acknowledge it is to accept that we are all mortal, all human and all capable of being broken by our experiences. But, and this is the part where I need you to listen closely to me, Oliver. Being broken does not mean it is impossible to be put back together again. I don't pretend to understand what happened up on that promontory, but I can see it is the tip of a much larger puzzle."

"You have no idea," agreed Oliver. "I tried to shield you from the worst of it."

"And the gesture is appreciated," said Hillshore with an involuntary shudder. "But if I am to help you through this and shore up your psyche, I must know everything."

Oliver did not reply, wishing he could spare his friend the full scale of the nightmarish things he had learned, but knowing he had little choice but to comply.

"You won't like it," he said. "Knowledge might very well be power, but once you have heard what I have to say, you will wish I had left you ignorant."

"I will be the judge of that, Oliver," said Hillshore as the ferry nosed through the mist and maneuvered itself toward the quayside. "After all, 'the only good is knowledge and the only evil is ignorance.'"

"Socrates," said Oliver with a forced smile.

"You see?" said Hillshore. "You're getting better already."

CHAPTER FOURTEEN

So far from land that it was possible to believe that no land existed, a lone ship charted a solitary course into latitudes shunned by most right-thinking seamen. From the upper decks of its bridge, it was just possible to see the curve of the earth on the horizon, though none who plied their maritime trades upon and below her decks cared enough to take notice.

Steel hulled and with a mass and structural solidity that far outweighed any cautious redundancy, the DCV *Matilda* was an ugly ship, a mongrel built from the carcasses of ships deemed unlucky by those who once sailed upon them or uninsurable by the great banking houses. Every portion of her construction was swathed in ill-omen and not a day had gone by without the blood of an innocent being spilled over her keel or poured by the gallon into her boilers.

To the outside world, the *Matilda* was a wonder of modern engineering, a triumph of Man's ingenuity and resourcefulness. Built, the outside world believed, to drill for oil in the world's most inaccessible spots, it could remain at sea far longer than any other vessel of its type and could range further in search of black gold than was believed possible or prudent.

Charles Warren had personally overseen the vessel's construction, firing every last one of the previous design team, from naval architects to engineers, and replacing them with hand-picked men of his own—who crafted an interior that would have confounded the senses of any shipwright unfortunate enough to venture below its decks.

At the behest of Alexander Templeton, the mining equipment was hurled overboard into the East River at the darkest moments of the night and replaced with bizarre items of alien technology brought in by hissing, buzzing creatures in the backs of sealed tankers. What was installed on the ship would have baffled the Earth's greatest scientists, for they had been crafted by engineers not of this world, creatures whose methodology and perceptions were not those of humans.

Nor did the oddity of the vessel stop at its internal structure or the technology it carried; its crew were a similarly mixed bunch. Composed primarily of men that could easily be mistaken for Polynesians or those whose evolutionary chain linking them to their piscine ancestors was far shorter than most, the *Matilda*'s crew had a piratical, ill-favored look to them.

There appeared to be no such thing as rank aboard the ship, save amongst those whose given tasks were to oversee the operation of the alien machinery or navigate the vessel on its long voyage from New York to the very heart of the Pacific Ocean. Its captain eschewed the quicker route through the recently opened Panama Canal or the more dangerous Straits of Magellan, knowing that no good could come of close inspection of its peculiar hull and even more peculiar contents.

Instead, the vessel traveled even farther south to the Drake Passage, a body of water first navigated by a Dutchman by the name of Willem Schouten in 1616, but which received its English language name from the explorer, Sir Francis Drake. This body of water lay between the farthest edge of Cape Horn and the South Shetland Islands of Antarctica. Connecting the western reaches of the Atlantic Ocean with the Pacific, it afforded the *Matilda* a perilous, but more or less empty sea route to its destination.

Few vessels bothered to travel this way, preferring the safer and quicker routes farther north, and the two Russian icebreakers wallowing in the glacial waters around the South Shetland Isles and the British scientific vessel returning to warmer climes were both given wide berths upon their sighting.

Drake Passage was an icy stretch of water, teeming with life, and had the crew cared to notice, they might have catalogued an abundance of whale species and bird life. But such natural wonders were of no interest to the crew, who spent their days maintaining the machinery of the vessel, keeping its decks free of ice and drinking a foul concoction brewed in its darkest bowels.

At length the *Matilda* crossed from the Atlantic to the Pacific and turned its prow west-northwest, a course that would eventually bring her to the coastline of New Zealand. The farther the ship sailed into the heart of the unknown, the deeper and stranger became the ocean. Majestic whales no longer attended the *Matilda*; rather shoals of malformed squid pulsed alongside her, battering themselves to death against her iron hull. Impossible blooms of noxious seaweed billowed up from unknown canyons of the ocean floor to foul the propellers, but their unique design cut through such entanglements with ease.

The seabirds that had once flown over the ship when it passed close to land had long since forsaken the *Matilda*, but evil-throated birds with leprous black plumage circled above her rusted gunwales until their strength gave out and they fell dead to the deck. A trail of oily matter, dead beasts and rotting oceanic vegetation followed in the wake of the *Matilda*, and by the time her captain called for dead stop, the ship had reached a point so close to the Pacific Pole of Inaccessibility at Southern Latitude 47º 9"S, Western Longitude 126º 43"W that it made a mockery of the notion of dry land.

There could no anchoring here, not when the ocean floor was so far below in eternal darkness, and it took the combined effort of the three specially crafted engines and propellers to keep the malicious currents and sourceless winds from sweeping the *Matilda* wildly off course.

In freezing conditions that were unknown in these waters and lashed by black rain, the swarthy crewmen began the true work of their journey. Vast silver-steel cargo containers were lifted from the cavernous holds and broken open to reveal struts of a white material brought to Earth by a race of winged engineer creatures from a world that would become known to earthly astronomers in years to come as Pluto.

Slowly and painstakingly, a latticed structure was built on the foredeck of the *Matilda*; a precisely engineered tower that rose to a height of a hundred yards. A complex arrangement of insulated copper wiring and high-energy batteries (that bore more than a striking resemblance to those being crafted by Dr. Dyer and Professor Pabodie of Miskatonic University) were installed upon a golden cupola at the summit.

The construction of the tower took several days, but with its completion, a figure clad in shimmering robes and bearing a wooden box on a canvas sling began the long climb to its top. The ascent was perilous, the alien metal slick with ice and rainwater, but at its end, the robed figure, a heavyset man with bronze skin and a face almost completely obscured by ritual tattoos, opened the wooden box.

Inside lay a shimmering crystal that shone with the light of captured stars, a cursed artifact wrought by an exile from a land long since consigned to the ocean floor. The Eye of Infinite Stars was set within the golden cupola and the high-energy cables affixed to its surface. The few black birds that still circled the *Matilda* attempted to dive onto the crystal, perhaps thinking to mar its smooth perfection with their beaks and claws and bodies. Marksmen stationed on the highest reaches of the ship picked them off one by one until the skies were clear for miles around.

And with the installation of the Eye, work on the second element of the *Matilda*'s unusual design was begun on her forked fantail. Tarpaulins were pulled from a monstrous assembly of chain winches and cable drums as yet another enormous container was brought up from the cavernous holds. A hundred or more crewmen worked to maneuver it from the crane's hook toward the rear of the vessel, whereupon an object of roughly spherical dimensions was carefully removed and assembled.

Adorned with gleaming metal protuberances and delicate wand-like spines, it resembled nothing so much as a mutant deep-sea urchin. One of the early builders of this ship had remarked that perhaps it might be some form of diving bell before being disabused of that notion by another, but the mistake in the device's purpose was understandable.

Connected to one end of a colossal cable as thick as a strongman's thigh, the device—with a silver sphere that had briefly been the property of Finn Edwards at its heart—was carefully eased from the back of the *Matilda* and lowered to the sea. The mutant squid creatures attempted to batter themselves against the device, but skilled harpooners and groups of mulatto crewmen armed with Browning machine guns kept them at bay while it sank beneath the waves on a slowly unravelling cable drum. It would take many days for the device to reach the prescribed depth, but such a span of time had been taken into account.

Night fell on the ocean and the stars burning in the deepest reaches of the galaxy seemed to turn in ways that would have horrified the great Ptolemy, who had penned the *Apotelesmatika*, which spoke of a hideous celestial arrangement known as the *Tempestus Mundus Incognitio*.

The storm that makes the world unknown.

Slowly the cable drum turned, and each rotation brought the end of the world that little bit closer.

* * *

Dresses had never been good to Minnie Klein, and that trend wasn't about to be reversed any time soon, she saw, looking into the full-length mirror on the back of her door. She'd acquired this dress under protest, a pale green formal number that made her look like a squashed lime, to serve as bridesmaid to a childhood friend. Her mother had forced her to keep it for dances and the like (though she'd never been to any) and she'd brought it to France on the off chance she had any need of something dressier than her normal skirt and jacket.

"Nope, Minnie, you ain't got the hips to carry this off, girl," she said, knowing she was being too hard on herself, but unable to shake the habit. Maybe if she wore a belt, or added a necklace or wore her hair up, or…

"Crap," said Minnie, after each attempt ended in failure.

Since when had going to dinner been such a pain in the back end? She'd eaten in the main dining room the first week, attracting stares from the other diners by virtue of her unfashionable attire until she'd given in and decided to make an effort. Except that effort wasn't yielding anything she'd be seen dead in outside of her mother's front room or a private cabin.

How it had come to pass that she'd been upgraded to a first-class cabin, Minnie didn't know, but it sure was a swell way to travel: a bed big enough for four people—though the thought of that made her blush—her own private bathing room, a walk-in wardrobe, and more space than an average family had to live in. Her shame at living so well lasted only as long as it took to unpack, but Minnie consoled herself by remembering that this wasn't her doing and she might as well enjoy it while it lasted.

She took another look at herself in the mirror and sighed, reaching around for the buttons. It wasn't easy, but she got the first one and was struggling to undo the second when there was a knock at her door. Minnie grimaced, her fingertips scrabbling at the button.

"Here, lassie, let me get that for you before you do yourself a mischief," said a woman's softly accented voice from the other side of the door.

Minnie opened the door with a sigh of relief then stopped dead as it occurred to her to wonder how the woman standing in her doorway had known she needed help. Without waiting for an invitation, the woman breezed into Minnie's cabin, taking a perfunctory look around before turning and beckoning her closer.

"Here, turn around, girl," she said in a voice that was used to being obeyed. "Let's get you presentable shall we?

"Wait, do I know you?" asked Minnie.

She didn't know the woman, but recognized her. This was the woman in the purple, form-fitting dress with the cobra-topped cane who'd boarded the *Ile de France* ahead of her.

"Not yet," said the woman, beckoning to people who'd been lurking out in the corridor. Four of the ship's stewards entered Minnie's cabin, each bearing an assortment of dresses, shoes, hat boxes, and mother-of-pearl jewelry cases. "But judging by that dress, it's high time you did."

"I'm sorry, who are you?"

The woman smiled and extended a silk-gloved hand. "Violet Tweedale, a pleasure to make your acquaintance. Now, quickly, lass, we haven't time to shilly shally. The captain's table meets for drinks in the Rococo Room in fifteen minutes, and we don't want to be late."

"The captain's table?" asked Minnie, feeling like she was drowning in a conversation that was spinning out of her control.

"Of course, my dear," said Violet, as though bemused by Minnie's confusion. "You've been at sea for seven days now and haven't said boo to a goose, it's most unseemly. It's time you were introduced. After all, everyone's dying of curiosity to know all about you."

"They are?"

"Of course they are," said Violet, selecting a dress and holding it up in front of Minnie with a pursed lip and furrowed brow. "No, that will never do. Mr. Thomson, hand me the scarlet number, no, not that one you silly boy, the Hartnell, yes that one, quickly now…"

Minnie knew better than to resist this tide and let it wash over her. With a dress and its accompaniments selected, the ship's stewards withdrew, leaving her alone with Violet who fussed and fretted like a mother hen until she was wrapped in silk and velvet, and clinched in a tight, yet bearable blouse that accentuated her figure. Throughout her sartorial transformation, Violet chatted amiably about the novel she was working on, a piece with the tentative title of *The Mammonist*, and the numerous society engagements she attended in London. Minnie barely got a word in edgeways, but being around Violet was like being at the eye of a benign storm, where wicked gossip, literary *bon mots*, and slanderous political opinion were bandied about willy nilly.

Eventually, Violet stood back and examined her handiwork critically, adding a choker with a ruby set in a golden iris and a flimsy silken scarf. Matching earrings and a tiara-like headpiece that made Minnie feel like a queen were added before Violet was satisfied.

"There, now you look presentable," she said. "Ah, wheesht, what am I saying? You look better than presentable, you look positively radiant, dear."

And for once Minnie had to agree. The part of her brain that was always finding fault with her clothes, her figure and her appearance in general was suddenly silenced, forced to concede that she was the bee's knees.

"Gosh…" was all she could think to say.

"You Americans," said Violet, shaking her head. "You're killing the King's English with your slang. Now, hurry now, they'll be popping the corks up there, and trust me, you don't want to be late when there's a bottle that's been open too long in the presence of old Wilberforce."

Violet took Minnie's hand and led her out into the teak-paneled corridor of the ship.

"Wait," said Minnie, digging in mental heels. "Thank you for… this, but how did you even know I needed some help? I mean, aside from seeing me over the last couple of days. How did you know I needed help now?"

Violet looked Minnie up and down with maternal fondness. "Och, didn't I tell you?"

"Tell me what?"

"I'm Violet Tweedale, and I'm a medium," said Violet, her earlier flightiness replaced with a cultivated brogue that had been formed in the well-to-do social circles of Edinburgh and honed in the salons of London. "A spiritualist and a psychic. I know when someone needs my help, and I'm not just talking about dresses."

* * *

Arm in arm, Violet and Minnie made their way along the ornate companionways of the ship toward the Rococo Room. The interior reminded Minnie of pictures she'd seen of Frank Lloyd Wright's proposed new works. This wasn't a ship, more a conceptual collision between an ocean-going palace and futurist manifesto. They passed through starkly furnished rooms of geometric precision, glass-walled capsules, and ornate public rooms with high ceilings, elaborate murals, exquisite furniture, and thick carpets that made walking in heels—something she found tricky at the best of times—even more of a challenge.

Women with beaded dresses and feathered fans and men in waistcoats and evening wear stared at them as they passed, each one accoutered in a wealth of oddly cut suits and bizarrely colored eyewear that ranged from simple monocles to what resembled goggles. They were a strange group of passengers, looking more like adventurers straight from the pages of Gernsback's *Amazing Stories* than European socialites.

Violet kept up a monologue on the ship's interior, and Minnie doubted even one of the crew could have given a more thorough or passionate description of its magnificence. Where other great ships of the line echoed the styles of the past or which could be found in the manors or châteaux of the land-dwelling elite, the *Ile de France* was something new entirely, a glittering rendition of the modern world, a celebration of the contemporary and the vibrantly new.

The Rococo Room was reached by means of a grand staircase that rose from the main deck to a playful interior that eschewed grandeur and symmetry, reveling in playful curves and a more florid approach to interior design. Where the main salons of first class were boldly colored, this room was a riot of pastels, asymmetrical designs, curves, and gold.

The entire room was designed as a work of art, filled with elegant furniture and coiling sculptures, its walls decorated with ornamental mirrors, tapestries, fashionable reliefs, and wall paintings. More of the exquisitely attired folk gathered here, drinking from tall-stemmed glasses with no bases, which were distributed by stewards in long greatcoats and ceramic harlequin masks.

Minnie didn't know where to look; every sight her eyes beheld was stranger than the last.

Here was a man with a bronze mouse in his breast pocket, a mouse that squeaked like a child's toy, and which appeared to move of its own accord. The woman he spoke to was tall and slender, wearing a mask fashioned from leather and bronze, but which appeared to move in harmony with the face below, as if somehow attached to the muscles beneath her skin.

Moving between the crowds, as though somehow *apart* from them all was a man who Minnie could only catch out of the corner of her eye, a man garbed in aristocratic clothes that looked enough like the people nearby not to stand out, but which were somehow more archaic, more *authentic*, than the riotous fashions on display around him. It seemed she felt his eyes upon her at all times, yet whenever she tried to look directly at him, he vanished behind a long fan or was obscured by the arrival of yet more curiously attired guests.

Eventually, Minnie gave up trying to get a proper look at this elusive man and watched as a woman in a long, floor-length gown of mirrors and mosaic chips circulated through the crowd. She moved as though floating above the ground, and Minnie almost giggled aloud at the thought of the woman being on wheels. Minnie wondered how she could have been so out of touch to have missed this new trend for the outlandish.

"I wish I'd brought the Zeiss," she said, and Violet laughed.

"Yes, they are a rather *unusual* set," she agreed. "Yet it is said there is no other culture that has produced a wittier, more elegant, and teasing dialogue full of elusive and camouflaging language and gestures, refined feelings, and subtle criticism."

"Said where?" said Minnie, smelling a quote.

"A book somewhere," said Violet, leading her toward the man with the golden mouse in his breast pocket and his willowy companion. "I don't remember exactly, but it sounds highfalutin', so it was probably written by a man. I much prefer simplicity in the narrative voice."

"Yeah," said Minnie, again feeling out of her depth and knowing she shouldn't. "Me too."

The man and woman turned at their approach, and the mouse squeaked happily. Minnie swore it winked at her too.

"Hellequine, Wilberforce; I'd like you to meet Miss Minnie Klein," said Violet.

The man was heavyset, but wore it well, and his costume (Minnie found it hard to think of his attire as simply *clothes*) was intricately assembled: a latticework of linen and lace, with slender copper wires trailing beneath his waistcoat. His trousers were ribbed with what looked like electrical cabling, and his hat was a stetson with a grinning snake skull worked into the hatband.

"A pleasure to make your acquaintance, Miss Klein," said the man in a refined English accent and taking her hand to deposit a soft kiss on the back of her hand. "Wilberforce Luis Torquemada at your service. And this little chap is Mordred."

In response to its name, the bronze mouse squeaked and ducked back inside the man's pocket.

"He's a little shy around new people," explained Wilberforce. "This is all a bit strange for him."

"I know how he feels," said Minnie, turning to the masked woman.

"And this is Hellequine d'Olt," said Violet. "A fellow devotee of the written word, a poet of some note in the Avignon region and a fellow practitioner of the Order. A sister of the Art, Hellequine has consented to return to London with me to further my education into the Mysteries."

"What mysteries?" asked Minnie.

"If she told you that, they would not be mysteries," said Hellequine.

"I guess not," said Minnie, studying the woman's face with a frank interest she hoped wasn't rude. The more she looked at the mask, the more she wondered if it was in fact a mask at all. It moved with the fluid suppleness of skin, yet was clearly artificial. Its manufacture was exquisite, a wondrous fusion of sculpture, embroidery, and metalworking. Its hinges and seams were all but invisible, and the green eyes that glittered behind the almond sockets were deep pools of secret knowledge.

"That's a hell of a mask you have," she said, deciding that directness was her best strategy, much as it had always been. "I've never seen anything like it."

"I would be surprised if you had," said Hellequine. "It is unique. Violet helped craft it after a particularly troublesome séance in Strasbourg a number of years ago. I think I would have gone mad without it."

Yeah, I think that ship might already have sailed, thought Minnie.

A steward handed her a drink, which Minnie was absurdly pleased to see was champagne. She sipped it carefully, enjoying the unique feel of the zesty bubbles on her tongue. She finished the drink far swifter than she intended and then wondered where to put the glass, since the stem ended in a crystalline point. A passing steward solved her dilemma by filling her glass, and Minnie took another mouthful.

"Minnie here is in need of our help," said Violet.

"Is she now?" said Hellequine, leaning in closer and Minnie saw the eager glint in her eyes through the mask.

"Am I now?" said Minnie.

"Ah, most interesting," observed Wilberforce. "You read her aura? It is troubled?"

"Very much so," said Violet. "I sensed it the moment she came aboard."

"My aura?" said Minnie. "What's wrong with my…aura?"

"Your memories, my dear girl," said Violet, reaching out to place her fingertips on Minnie's cheek.

"What about them?"

"Why, they've been tampered with. Didn't you know?"

Minnie hesitated. There *was* a gap in her memories, but how could Violet know that?

"Maybe," said Minnie, hedging her bets.

"Definitely. Someone has locked off a part of your mind with a psychic block, a mental dam if you will. It keeps you from understanding something important."

Despite herself, Minnie's interest was piqued. She had always turned her nose up at spiritualists and their mumbo-jumbo, but events of the last few months had turned her ideas of what was possible and what was ridiculous on their heads. She thought back to the episode back at Château-Thierry and her hazy recollection of what had happened beneath its crumbling keep.

"I'm right, aren't I?" said Violet.

"Yeah, I guess so," she said at last. "There is something, I think. Something I can't quite remember."

"I knew it!" said Violet with a delighted clap of her hands that took years off her.

"Do I smell a séance in our immediate future?" said Wilberforce with a gleeful smile.

"That you do, bonnie lad," said Violet as all three joined hands. "That you do."

* * *

Kate now knew she was somewhere in the hills to the north of Arkham, but that was about the only thing certain in her life right now. She'd long since lost track of time, as her prison in the alien metal habitat was always lit with the same stark illumination, and her work on the gigantic device was consuming all her attention.

Well, perhaps not all of it.

She saved some of it to maintain her near-constant sense of fear and horror at what she was being forced to do and the hideous things that surrounded her. The grave-creatures circled around her like carrion beasts waiting for a weary animal to give in to exhaustion, and the thought that they were just waiting to eat her brought Kate close to tears. Only once had a cadaverous beast tried to attack her, but no sooner had it leapt at her than one of the flying grub-creatures had eviscerated it with a blast of blue lightning from a trident-like weapon that unfolded from its rippling underside.

The charred corpse was dragged away by his fellows, and the next day Kate had seen a pile of broken, chewed bones atop a flat-topped rock that looked like an altar or a dinner table. None of the others dared attack Kate again, but she could tell they were just waiting for the moment their masters were done with her.

The flying creatures kept away from Kate, working in what appeared to be hermetically sealed bubble domes that sprouted like fungus on the upper slopes of the hill before a curious white monolith of unknown provenance. The creatures only emerged to attach some new device to the base of the silver tower or etch new symbols into the metal of the discs.

At the end of each day that saw a new alien addition to the device, Kate would find a sheaf of glossy, indestructible papers in her room. Filled with calculations that strained her tenuous grasp of inter-dimensional physics and extra-planar instability (terms she had coined just to articulate theoretical concepts she had no way of mathematically proving) the new data had to be incorporated into her own calculations and used to refine the orbits of the discs and their precise speeds of rotation.

Had the circumstances been different, Kate would have been thrilled to be working on such an incredible device. This was technology beyond anything even dreamed of at Miskatonic, or any other institution of higher learning for that matter. This was Nobel Prize winning engineering, the very pinnacle of her dreams of innovation.

Yet it was a poisoned chalice, a dream of achievement she dared not embrace. To succeed would be to usher in a cataclysmic armageddon of collapsing realities. The myriad planes she now knew existed beyond the world visible to human beings were kept apart by impermeable, invisible barriers for good reason. Kate had only the briefest glimpse into one of those worlds, and suspected it was one of the planes of lesser evil. On some gut level of instinct, Kate knew that realms of infinitely greater menace and horror existed, and that her device would break down the barriers keeping them separate from Earth.

At first she had tried to deliberately sabotage her work, but the alien creatures quickly detected her inserted errors. Alexander Templeton had come to her one day as she tried in vain to sleep in her shimmering, permanently lit cell.

"You shouldn't try to deceive them, you know," he said, appearing without warning at a newly irised doorway behind her.

Kate had leapt to her feet, exhausted but jolted instantly alert by the stench of Charles Warren as he entered through another hitherto unseen door.

"They might not have your innate grasp of this branch of science, but they know when someone is trying to subvert their work," said Alexander. He limped into the room, and Kate saw his arm had become even more twisted, as though whatever injury he had suffered to his hand was corrupting the rest of his body. Necrotic black tendrils emerged from his shirt collar like streaks of ink in the veins.

Kate shook her head. "No, I wasn't, I swear. But what you're asking…it's never been done before. Good God, it's never even been *thought* of before. I'm working in the dark here. This is science as no one's ever dreamed it. You have to give me some time to get my head around this, I can't just violate earthly laws at will you know!"

"It's perfectly natural what you are trying to do, Kate. I understand it, really I do, but it's quite useless," said Alexander. "They'll know when you are consciously working at cross purposes. And when they know, I'll know. And when I know, I'll have to let Charles loose on you."

"No, please, I swear…"

But Alexander was retreating from the room, leaving her alone with the debased, corpse-monster with a lopsided grin of animal hunger. His ruined eyes were bright with anticipation, and a blackened, swollen tongue slithered from between his lips.

"Do what you want with her, Charles, but make sure she can still work tomorrow."

Charles indicated his understanding with gurgling assent.

Kate screamed as the door shut behind Alexander.

CHAPTER FIFTEEN

The mood was somber as Hillshore poured each man a drink from his bottle of Talisker. Hillshore's hands were shaking as he poured the Skye malt, the delayed shock of what he had experienced at the Markham-Hyde collection now fully impacting on his system. Oliver raised the glass to his lips, letting the warm, peaty aroma of the drink take him back to the pubs of Cambridge, where he and Hillshore would solve the world's problems over the course of a night.

The memory was a good one and helped arrest his slide into the pit of deep depression which he had lately felt himself descending. He clung to it as a dying man clings to a spar of timber from his sunken ship, all the while knowing it will never be enough to bear him back to shore.

After stopping at the Jesuit College to see if Rex had returned from his wanderings (he had not), they left a message with the night porter as to where they could be found when he returned. Floyd Butner had conveyed them to Hillshore's residence, a two-story building with a grand mural depicting the rebuilding of the city on its ever-so-slightly leaning gable. It stood in the shadow of Recreation Park, though the baseball stadium was dark and abandoned in the off-season, and basked in a far milder climate than the rest of the city, with a pleasant view out over San Francisco Bay to the isolated landmass of Goat Island.

Morley had warily opened the door to them, and Hillshore had immediately remonstrated with him at the vandalism done to his architraves and window frames. Damage done to the house by the earthquake was only to be expected, raged Hillshore, but to have a guest abuse the hospitality of their host was the grossest breach of etiquette.

Further strife was avoided when Henry suggested they all share a drink, and Hillshore had fetched the Talisker with a stiff nod. Though the Englishman was furious at Morley's presumption, he had seen and learned enough from Oliver on the journey back from Marin County to understand that Morley's intentions had been honorable at least. Morley himself refused to sit, and paced the center of the room, continually sending panicked glances to the far corners of the room, as though expecting imminent attack.

Remembering what had happened in New York, Oliver was inclined to share his disquiet.

"Good Lord, Morley, sit down will you!" snapped Henry, standing at the fireplace with one elbow resting on the mantlepiece, where a carriage clock and keepsakes acquired over the years sat askew.

"Sit?" said Morley. "How can I sit at a time like this? Are you mad?"

Eventually Gabriel took hold of Morley and sat him down forcibly with a look that had quailed the hearts of New York's criminals for over a decade. Morley nodded and took a drink, which seemed to calm him.

A fire crackled in the hearth, though Oliver felt little warmth from the burning coals. The destruction of the Markham-Hyde collection had almost broken his tenuous grip on sanity, and he knew that, but for Hillshore's intervention, he would even now be lost in the delirium of lunacy. Oliver gripped the heavy glass tumbler of amber liquid, knowing that he was cursed to know too much, but blessed to have such strong friends around him.

Oliver raised his glass and said, "Gentlemen, a toast."

"A toast, Oliver?" said Hillshore. "Don't you think we have more pressing matters to discuss?"

"No," stated Oliver. "We don't. Raise your glasses."

One by one, Morley, Henry, Gabriel, and Hillshore did as Oliver commanded.

"My friends," began Oliver as a wave of emotion threatened to choke him. "Many times in the last few months the hopelessness of our plight has threatened to overwhelm me. The starkly terrifying vistas of which we have, of late, become aware are burdens no man should wish to bear, but bear them we must. No man can bear such burdens alone, and I could not have done so without you all by my side. I want to thank you all. To each of you, I owe a great debt I can never repay. Some of you I have known for many years, while others have come into my life only recently. Each of you has, in your own way, helped keep me from complete and utter collapse."

Oliver could see the effect his words were having, but plunged on, knowing that if he stopped now, he would never have the clarity to speak thusly again.

"You have kept me on the path," he said. "Gabriel, you forced me to confront my fear of death and understand the risks we take every moment of every day. William, but for you I would have gone mad, I think, and Henry, your determination to fight and inspirational words defeated my fear of failure. And Rex, were he here, I would thank for his ready wit and uncanny ability to cut through any gloom to deliver a ray of light to dispel any fear. And that is out greatest enemy: fear. Fear of the unknown, fear of death or fear of what Alexander might achieve if he succeeds in his hideous plan. So, for all that, and more besides, I thank each and every one of you. My friends and my comrades in arms."

Oliver drank, and the others did too, touched deeply by his words. Even the stoic features of Gabriel Stone softened at Oliver's toast. No one said anything for fear of spoiling the moment until a rattling trolley car went past bearing revelers heading to a late-night speakeasy.

Gabriel cleared his throat. "So, speaking of Rex, we've got no idea where he is. Should that worry us at all?"

"I suspect not," said Henry. "My acquaintanceship with Mr. Murphy is only recent, but I believe he is a born survivor and a man born under a lucky star. I heard what he did on *Persephone*, and if those beasts couldn't stop him, I doubt the seedier elements of San Francisco could do any worse."

"You're not wrong," said Oliver. "Any man who can leap from Kingsport Head into the unknown is a man who makes his own luck."

"So what do we think he's doing?" asked Gabriel.

"Knowing Rex, he's probably in some secret speakeasy getting a vital piece of the puzzle without which our endeavor will be a forlorn hope," said Oliver. "I'd bet the farm that the next we'll see of him is when he strolls in at the crack of dawn with the hangover from hell and a new clue."

Smiles were exchanged all around, and with the fate of Rex decided to be a benign one, the serious business of the evening began as Oliver brought out his notes he had taken from the cursed pages of the *Necronomicon*.

"So was today's excitement worth it?" asked Henry. "Are we any closer to stopping Alexander?"

"I believe so," said Oliver, running his finger along the transcribed phonetics he had copied. "This is the spell Nereus-Kai used to sink the star god's city, but it is incomplete."

"So what use is it?" asked Hillshore. "Is half a spell any good?"

"It is useless," said Morley. "In fact, it is worse than useless. To speak a partial spell is to invite disaster. It is to wield terrible powers and lack the means to control them. Yes, we are closer to stopping Alexander, but without the second part of the spell, we have nothing."

"And even if we had the other half," said Henry, "the book spoke of a terrible price to be paid for its efficacy. Nereus-Kai may have defeated the Old One with this spell, but Atlantis was sunk by its aftereffects. What might happen were we to cast it? We might lose the entire eastern seaboard!"

"If New York or Manhattan were lost beneath the waves, I should call that an improvement," said Morley, only half joking.

"Regardless of Morley's feelings toward New York, the matter is academic," said Oliver. "We only have half the spell. The other half is apparently beyond our reach."

An uneasy silence fell as each man recalled what the *Necronomicon* had to say on the location of the spell's missing components.

"Not necessarily," said Morley, and Hillshore rounded upon him.

"Great heavens, man, are we truly to believe that this Nereus-Kai fellow actually traveled to Celaeno?" asked Hillshore. "I don't wish to sound skeptical, Mr. Dean—God knows, I've had my eyes opened today—but how could such an impossible feat be achieved?"

Morley was quick with his answer. "The priest need not have traveled physically. There are ways and means of projecting a consciousness through the voids of space and time. Or perhaps he employed his magic to open a gateway through the aether to that distant star and did in fact walk on a distant world. Oliver and Rex traveled to a realm of dreams to rescue Henry, so such things should not strike us as being beyond the pale."

"You say that, Morley, but what can we do to achieve the same?" asked Henry. "Luke Robinson had an artifact that allowed Oliver to reach me across dimensions, but even if his device can reach across such vast gulfs of space, I doubt very much we could enlist Luke's help in this matter."

"There are several ways," said Morley. "Perilous ways, to be sure; mostly involving terrible bargains with interplanetary creatures, but I know of one avenue that may be within our grasp, though I hesitate to suggest even that…"

"I don't think we've got much choice," said Gabriel. "What do we need to do?"

Morley held up a cautionary hand. "Yes, I know a way we might follow in Nereus-Kai's mystical footsteps, but it will require some dangerously potent narcotics. A kind concocted by certain Oriental mystics, but the only place I knew of to obtain such drugs is back in New York."

Hillshore took out his pipe with exaggerated casualness and lit the bowl, filling the room with aromatic smoke as he took a draw on its stem.

"I think I might possibly know somewhere we could obtain narcotics," said the Englishman.

* * *

Dinner at the captain's table was a whirlwind of conversations that Minnie only dimly recalled through a haze of champagne and cigarette smoke. The captain, a dignified-looking man by the name of Joseph Blancart sat across from Minnie, and she idly wondered who was steering the boat just now, remembering a certain White Star liner that had sunk making a very similar journey after running into an inconvenient iceberg.

Violet was seated next to Minnie, and alternated between firing rapid bursts of conversation at her and Henri Villar, the ship's purser. A blonde woman with the sculpted, icy beauty of a movie star sat beside the captain, and Minnie knew she should recognize her, but her memory refused to dredge up the woman's name. Many of the large dining room's other occupants were staring in rapt fascination at her, and Minnie saw how skillfully she pretended not to notice, content to allow Wilberforce to monopolize her attention.

Though she scanned the hundred or so diners seated throughout the dining room, Minnie saw no sign of the strangely aristocratic man she'd half-glimpsed in the Rococo Room. She felt his eyes upon her even now, but knew there was no point in hunting him out. Whoever he was, he would make himself known to Minnie eventually, of that she was certain.

Hellequine sat beside a bearded man named Paul who spent most of the dinner sketching the other passengers on his napkin, while Minnie was seated next to a bullish man with dark hair and a thick mustache. He had been introduced to Minnie as Ernest, a writer working on revisions to his first novel. Minnie instantly realized that, like her, he had no real business being at this table. His tuxedo was clearly borrowed, and he was ill at ease with the refined airs and graces of his fellow diners. Minnie recognized a man that would most likely find a kindred spirit in Gabriel Stone, sensing that strange detachment of a former soldier in Ernest's brusque, spare replies to any question directed to him or his wife.

"Are there a lot of writers aboard this ship?" Minnie asked Violet between mouthfuls of champagne. "Everyone here seems to be a writer or an artist."

Violet laughed. "We are itinerant souls who claim to be artists and writers because we simply can't think of anything else to do. He's on his way back to America from Pamplona where he's going to sign a book deal that I think will do very well for him."

Minnie nodded, and the rest of the dinner passed in a pleasant blur. Wine was served, a fabulously expensive vintage that Minnie didn't doubt had a price tag that would make her head spin, along with food that was refined and served on china plates. Much of the conversation revolved around the inability of the current generation to find their place in the world in the wake of the Great War.

Ernest had much to say on this and his words were delivered like gut punches. He and Paul engaged in a spirited debate on the modern era's pursuit of vapid gratification, and Minnie watched as their debate transformed into an argument the more the alcohol flowed. After more courses than Minnie could ever remember having in one meal, the dinner table broke up when the captain graciously excused himself. The movie star woman also departed, to Wilberforce's chagrin, though not before attracting the eye of a handsome rake in a shimmering tuxedo at a nearby table, who swiftly followed her from the dining room with a spring in his step.

With these departures, Violet now turned to Minnie and said, "Thank goodness that's over. Right, dearie, I think it's time we found out what's been monkeying with your memories, don't you?"

* * *

They retired to Violet's suite, which though ostensibly the same as Minnie's had an altogether grander aspect to it. Books belonging to Violet were stacked on a bookshelf that looked out of place against one wall, and a large, circular table was set in the middle of the room. Along with Wilberforce and Hellequine, Ernest and his wife, Hadley, had accompanied them back to Violet's suite, together with the artist, Paul.

"Right, shall we begin?" said Violet.

"Oughtn't we have a drink first?" asked Ernest, already helping himself to a large measure of brandy from a crystal decanter.

"If you must," said Violet, fetching some black candles from a dresser and arranging them around the table so that one sat before each of the seven seats. Hellequine doused the electric lights while Wilberforce lit the candles with a gold lighter embossed with the image of two intersected triangles forming a six-pointed star.

Minnie felt a flush of excitement, tinged with a not unwelcome frisson of trepidation. Stable, solid Minnie had never done anything like this in her life, and the thought of venturing into this decadent world of spiritualism make her cheeks ruddy and her breathing shallow. Ernest handed Minnie a drink with a curt nod and Hadley gave her a soft smile that made her seem acutely vulnerable.

"Right, you sit here, Minnie," commanded Violet as the others took their seats around the table. Violet sat opposite her, with Hellequine and Wilberforce to either side. Paul and Ernest were wisely separated, with Paul taking Minnie's left hand, and Ernest taking her right. Hadley sat between Ernest and Hellequine, her eyes darting nervously around the table. The candle light carved canyons of shadow into everyone's features, and their faces seemed to float out of the gloom— though that was probably thanks to the fact that pretty much everyone was wearing black. A shiver traveled the length of Minnie's spine, like someone walking across her grave. Given what they were about to attempt, she tried to shake that image from her mind.

"So how do we do this?" asked Minnie, taking a deep breath. "What do I need to do?"

"You don't need to do anything, dear," explained Violet, closing her eyes as her exhalations became shallow and breathy. "Just let us do the hard work. The spirits don't know you yet, and they're skittish little buggers at the best of times, let me tell you!"

"Then perhaps you'd best not insult them, Violet," said Hellequine.

"Aye, I suppose you're right," said Violet brightly. "Right, come on everyone, join hands and close your eyes."

"I say, is this really kosher?" asked Hadley, taking Violet's and her husband's hand. "I mean, you hear stories and this all sounds a bit devilish, you know? Like those fellow in the Hellfire clubs."

"Hadley's right," snapped Ernest. "I remember reading about that Houdini fellow going around exposing charlatans. I won't be made to look like a fool, I'll tell you that for nothing. If this isn't on the up and up, someone's in for a damn thrashing."

Ernest's grip on Minnie's hand tightened as he spoke, and she felt the full force of his masculinity in its strength. Her eyes flickered open, seeing the strong line of his jaw and the pugnacious slope of his forehead. This was a man whose force of personality was almost physical, and for Violet's sake, she hoped this wasn't a fool's errand they were on.

"You'll see soon enough whether this is real or not," said Hellequine, her voice rendered macabre through her mask and her eyes blazing in the flickering light of the black candles. "We should begin, the spirits are restive tonight. They are transient at best, but water discomfits them greatly."

Was it just Minnie's imagination or did she hear a suggestion of a mocking laugh?

She closed her eyes again, feeling the same chill that had made her shiver earlier.

Against her expectations, it was Wilberforce who began proceedings.

"Spirits of air and land, we beseech thee to make yourselves known to us. Breach the walls separating the worlds of the living and the dead so that we may partake of your wisdom. No earthly constraints bind you, no mortal cares concern you. You, who are beings of light and aether, whose ascent of the Tree of Life nears completion, pray speak with us this night."

"Speak to us," said Hellequine and Violet in unison.

"Those who are dead and yet live on, whose dreams reach out to the living, wield these vessels we present you and grant us a measure of your light."

Minnie felt Ernest's hand tighten on hers, letting her eyes open a crack. Everyone still sat where they were, though the candles had burned down farther than she would have expected in so short a time. She was startled to see her breath feather the air in front of her and she blinked as it seemed the cabin was suddenly filled with a yellowish green mist.

Its source was Hellequine, whose head was tipped back and her artificially wrought mouth pulled open in a silent scream. The coiling mist issued from between her ceramic lips and Minnie saw her eyes were wide with fear.

"Spirits, are you here?" asked Wilberforce. "Give us a sign that you hear us?"

Minnie wanted to scream that the spirits were here all right, but her mouth was as locked closed as Hellequine's was open. She tried to disengage her hand from Ernest's and Paul's, but her fingers were fixed in place. No one else seemed to be aware of any change in their environment, and she could do nothing to warn them.

Hellequine jerked, as though some invisible assailant had taken her by the scruff of the neck in a rough grip. Her mouth snapped shut and her head suddenly slammed forward onto the table. The handmade mask cracked and Minnie jumped in shock as the wood of the table splintered under the force of the impact. A candle skittered across the table, leaving a trail of hot wax in its wake. Minnie drew in a cold intake of air as she saw the wax formed what looked like a dagger aimed at her heart.

Hadley screamed and Paul cried out in terror. Violet jerked in her chair as though being strangled and Wilberforce had turned a horrid shade of purple as his tongue protruded from his mouth. Spittle flew from his lips and even Ernest was shocked rigid.

Hellequine's head rose from the table, moving jerkily like a poorly operated marionette.

"Good God," hissed Ernest. "What the devil is going on here?"

Hellequine's face tilted to the side and Minnie gasped as she saw the damage done to the mask.

"No god and no devil," she said, though the voice was not Hellequine's. "Man has quite enough evil in him without need of deities."

Shattered clumps of fabric and porcelain hung loose from the once-beautiful mask, and beneath them, Minnie saw a portion of Hellequine's ruined flesh. Stripped of skin and bare to red muscle and bone, her cheek and jaw were like tenderized meat hung in a butcher's window.

Her eyes sat, lidless and unnaturally wide in sockets pared back to the skull.

Just looking at her made Minnie's flesh crawl and it didn't bear thinking about how painful it must be to live like that. The exposed eye rotated to fix on her and Hellequine's jaw worked up and down, testing its limitations and working itself from side to side as though she was learning how to speak with a different mouth.

"Ah, Minnie," said Hellequine. "I wondered how long it would be until you attempted to remember our time together. It almost pains me that it took you so long."

"Who are you?" said Minnie, angered by the supercilious tone of condescension. The voice, which she already knew was not Hellequine's was, she now realized, that of a man.

"So fragile, the human form," said Hellequine, ignoring her question and rotating her head. "It takes almost no force at all to ruin it. I was continually amazed that our insect species was able to conquer the globe when all others had failed. Aside from the insects, of course. The more we adorn our tender forms with the trappings of civilization, the more we forget our animal past, the bestial roots that made us superior in the first place."

"I asked you a question."

"All in good time," said Hellequine, reaching up to pluck broken pieces of the mask from her face. She turned each piece around, studying it intently before dropping it to the floor beside her. No one moved, and Minnie doubted any of the participants in this séance *could* move.

"You're the man I saw beneath the castle, aren't you?"

"Very perceptive of you," said Hellequine. "Did you receive my gift?"

"The dagger?"

"Yes."

Minnie nodded, though even that took considerable effort. Even speaking required her to force the word up her throat and past her teeth.

"Most excellent, my dear. I would hate for you to have forgotten it. It will be *so* important if you are to punish the thief."

Minnie tried to follow his words, slowly beginning to understand their import. Portions of her time beneath the castle returned to her; the handsome aristocratic man with the refined, yet vaguely disturbing air of over-familiarity to him. She remembered his soothing tones, laced with a very fine anger and outrage. The fury of a master whose work has been perverted by a rank amateur.

"You're the Comte D'Erlette," said Minnie, a choking fear threatening to suck the air from her lungs at the thought of being in the presence of so legendary a debaucher.

"Francois-Honoré Balfour at your service, my lady," said Hellequine with an exaggerated tip of the head. Minnie felt acrid bile at the back of her throat, but forced it down as she looked at the terrified, pain-contorted faces of her fellow guests at the séance. Violet and Wilberforce gagged and spluttered, while the rest of the table were pinned in their seats by some unknown force.

"Let them go," said Minnie. "Whatever it is you want, it's with me, isn't it? Let the others go."

Hellequine—or, rather, the Comte D'Erlette—shook her head. "No, for I do so enjoy watching people in pain."

"Why?" said Minnie, unable to comprehend such a thing.

"Suffering is power," said the comte. "If you know anything of me, then you should appreciate that. My library was filled with ancient books that spoke of ways to grow in power by such means, blood rituals and the most sublime tortures that lesser men would baulk at inflicting, but in which I reveled. I learned everything of human nature by such means, for no man or woman is as naked as when they are pleading for their life. Princes or peasants, it is irrelevant; everyone weeps and begs when their veins are open and their bones are broken. But when I learned that by such arts we could return to our bestial heritage and unlock the power of our ancient, primal selves…ah, my lady, *that* was when I understood my destiny."

"What destiny?" asked Minnie. The thought of learning more of the comte's deviltry repulsed her, but she knew she could learn much more were she to let him speak. The Comte D'Erlette was clearly a man in love with the sound of his own voice, and she guessed it had been a long time since he had been in a position to hear it.

"To show Humanity the error of their ways, to show Men how to reclaim their lost heritage."

Minnie almost laughed in his face at so egotistical a motive, so nonsensical a desire, but the sight of Hellequine's bloody face and the fear and pain around the table kept her silent.

Hellequine leaned forward. "You are special, did you know that, my dear? Do you know what it takes for me to take notice of those who trespass in the ruins of my home? In the years since the Sun King's peasant rabble stormed my castle, many have trod freely where would once have been a death sentence. Soldiers, farmers and even grazing animals."

Minnie heard outrage in the comte's voice, his fury that what had once been his seat of power had been violated by mere mortals and beasts.

"I gauged them all, judged their merit or, rather, their lack thereof, and do you know how many were worthy of notice? Just one, my lady, just one. You."

"Me?"

Hellequine nodded. "Yes, for you are just like me."

"I'm *nothing* like you," spat Minnie.

"Oh, but you are, my dear," purred Hellequine. "You have an eye for the macabre, you see the truth of the world behind its facile veneer of civilization. You seek out the dark places where that truth dares to show its naked flesh. It is a harsh life to see what others do not, but it is a necessary one. You alone of all your companions know that."

"No," repeated Minnie. "I'm not like you. I could *never* be like you."

"Foolish girl, don't you see? Everyone has the potential to be just like me, all it takes is the right push," said Hellequine, wagging an admonishing finger. "But no one is *exactly* like me, no matter how many of my stolen books they read or how much of my lore they think they possess."

"What the hell are you talking about?" said Minnie, tiring of the comte's theatrics and feeling a measure of her volition returning to her limbs.

"The thief who took my library for himself, who stood upon the shoulders of a giant and turned my work to serve his own squalid grief," spat Hellequine. "He turns the means to reclaim humanity's birthright to the crafting of dirt-grubbing perversions of my great work."

Hellequine leaned forward, fixing Minnie with a maddened stare. "And I would not see my work so debased."

* * *

The first Finn knew of the railroad bulls was when one kicked him square in the crotch and hauled him by the scruff of the neck across the boxcar. It was dark and he'd been asleep. He hadn't felt the train stopping. That was stupid. Pain filled his body, tears and snot mingling on his face as the bulls rousted the boxcar's inhabitants with billy clubs, hickory switches, and hobnailed boots.

Men and women were screaming and shouting, but Finn couldn't many sense of it.

They'd stopped and he hadn't kept a look out for bulls just waiting to roust them.

Finn tried to fight the man off, but meaty fingers dug into his neck with unbreakable force. The throbbing ache in his groin was spreading up into his belly, and Finn leaned over as a spasm of bilious nausea surged up his throat. He leaned over and puked out the meager contents of his guts, making sure to get as much as possible on the guy holding him. Acrid vomit splashed the bull's boots and the grip on his neck loosened.

"Ah, Christ on the Cross, you stinking hobo bastard!" shouted the bull, and Finn slithered from his grip as the man recoiled from the stink. Finn tried to get to his feet, but his legs were like rubber and went out from under him. He rolled, scrabbling for the edge of the boxcar. He had no idea where the train was, but jumping ship and trying to grab another was a damn sight more appealing than taking a beating from a posse of angry railroad thugs.

A few of the other hobos had already jumped from the boxcar. Finn saw Pete was already outside, with Duke jumping up and down and yapping for all he was worth. The old Arkham hobo frantically waved at him to get out of the boxcar.

"Jump!" shouted Pete. "Ain't worth a beating to stay on board this one."

Finn nodded, hearing angry shouting in Italian, and turned as he heard Mama screaming at their attackers. Papa was standing with his fists raised like he was the Marquis of Queensbury and had already put one of the bulls on his ass, but the others weren't playing by the same rules. Mama was on her knees with blood pouring down her face as she kept her bambinos out of harm's way.

The railroad guy who'd had hold of Finn was coming at him. Finn knew he ought to get the hell off this train, but felt a surge of righteous anger toward these bullies. The puked-upon guy swung his billy club, but Finn ducked and returned the favor by punching his fist straight into the man's groin. He doubled up and his chin met Finn's knee on the way up.

Papa went down, and three bulls laid into him with clubs. Finn shoulder charged them like a Dublin hurling player in sight of the crossbars. One went flying out of the boxcar, dropping his hickory club as he went. Finn swept it up and brandished it like Nuada of the Silver Hand himself.

"This, lads, is like a hurley," said Finn, "used in the Irish game of hurling, a cross between hockey and murder."

Finn swung the club and a second bull went down, knocked senseless by the blow and Finn roared with the release of fury. The last thug turned tail and leapt from the boxcar like beelzebub himself was on his tail, and Finn threw the club after him.

"This is my train, now, ye gobshites!" he yelled into the darkness.

Finn held himself upright using the edge of the door and sucked in heaving breaths as the adrenaline drained out of him like water through a collapsing dam. Papa hauled himself upright and started gibbering at him in a mixture of Italian and broken English.

"You save us," he said, blood streaming from his busted forehead. "*Grazie tanto! Grazie tanto!*"

Finn nodded and backed away from the man. His head was cracked open like the side of a boiled egg, but he was still standing, which said a lot for what a tough son of a bitch he was. Mama shooed her little ones off the train and helped her husband as he swayed with concussion.

"Here," said Mama, looking deep into his eyes. "You take. Hyacinth keep you safe when dark waters rise."

She pressed something into his hand before he could protest, and Finn looked down to see a silver medallion on a thin chain coiled in the palm of his hand. Upon both faces was a saintly looking figure of a monk or friar holding the Holy Sacrament and what looked like a statue of the virgin Mary.

He shook his head and said, "No, you don't need—"

But it was too late, Mama was already helping Papa out of the boxcar. Finn was about to go after her and ask her who Hyacinth was, but the breath heaved in his lungs and the pain in his groin returned with a vengeance. Finn sank to his knees, watching as Mama, Papa, and the kids vanished into the darkness and a fresh falling of snow.

"Jesus Christ and all his wee saints, that hurts," he groaned.

Finn's eyes watered and he cupped his bruised nethers as he heard the yapping of a barking dog behind him. Pete knocked on the box-car's door and said, "If you're finished playing the big damn hero, it's time we got the hell away from here."

Finn sagged against the door and nodded. "Yeah, I think you might be onto something there, Pete. Any idea where we are?"

"Judging by how damn cold and windy it is," said Pete, "I'd say Chicago."

"Chicago?" said Finn, climbing down from the boxcar with a wince of pain. "Shite and bugger, we're still hundreds of miles away."

Pete helped Finn down, and the cold clawed up into his bones through the threadbare soles of his boots. Snow was falling in earnest now, and an evil wind found every tear in his coat and every exposed slice of skin. He was instantly shivering.

"Christ," he swore. "Now how we going to get to Arkham?"

"The road provides," said Pete with cryptic hobo wisdom. "The road will provide."

Part Three
Inundation, 1926

Chapter Sixteen

The sun was just beginning to lighten the eastern sky by the time Hillshore returned home, haggard and strung out from the previous day's exertions and a night of hunting down opiates of a singular nature. Gabriel Stone opened the door to him, with one hand on the butt of his thirty-eight special, and a pungent reek of tobacco and other, less identifiable aromas, came in with the Englishman.

"You don't mind me saying, Doc, but you look like hell," said Gabriel, scanning the sidewalk outside the house for any sign of observers.

"It's professor, actually," said Hillshore, hanging up his coat and hat.

Hillshore stumbled into the front room of his house and rubbed his unshaven chin. Oliver roused himself from the couch at the sound of Hillshore's voice and blinked away sleep residue in his eyes. He sat up and stifled a yawn, seeing Henry fast asleep at the far end of the couch. Someone—Gabriel most likely—had thrown a blanket over him and he snored softly and peacefully.

Oliver envied him. His sleep had been filled with nightmares of gaping maws and black chasms opening beneath his feet to drag him down into an abyss from which there could be no escape. He didn't need Hillshore's insight to guess what that might signify, and tried to push the worst remnants of the dreams to the back of his mind.

"Still no sign of Rex?" asked Oliver.

"Not yet, but there's plenty of drinking dens that'll still be jumping," said Gabriel, holstering his pistol and heading to the kitchen. "I'll get some tea on in case he comes in anytime soon."

Hillshore nodded in thanks and slumped in an easy chair beside the fire. Oliver didn't think he'd ever seen his fellow professor look so tired. Even the long nights of rag week, where the students ran riot through the quiet streets of Cambridge and kept all and sundry awake with their charitable revels, had not seen him look so ground down and exhausted. The fingers of one hand beat a nervous tattoo on the chair's armrest, while the other picked at a frayed thread on his shirt collar.

"Did you get it?" asked Morley, leaning forward from the opposite chair in which he'd spent the night writing out notes, diagrams and precise instructions on page after page of a yellow legal pad.

Hillshore took a moment to gather his thoughts, and Oliver saw it was taking all his old friend's concentration to summon a cogent answer. God only knew how he had managed to drive across town and back again. It he hadn't hit a pedestrian somewhere along the way it would be a miracle.

"Yes, Morley, I obtained some, but it cost me dearly," said Hillshore.

Henry roused himself from his end of the couch and sat up with a start.

"Hillshore, you're back," he said, yawning as he did so. "You met with success?"

"He did," said Morley, rising from his seat and attempting to order his notes in a manner that might be understood by someone other than himself. "So we have no time to waste."

Morley left the room, clutching his notes and muttering to himself.

Oliver knew Morley was right, but dearly wished they could take some time to recuperate and recharge their flagging batteries. A man could only fight for so long before he could take no more, and each of them had pushed against those limits for longer than any of them could have foreseen. It was madness to press on at such speed, but what choice did they have?

Gabriel returned from the kitchen bearing a silver tray, upon which were five cups, a milk jug, and a pot of restorative tea. He set the tray down and reached for the pot, but Hillshore stopped him.

"You have only just poured in the boiling water?" he asked.

"Yeah," said Gabriel. "Should be nice and hot, just like we need."

"You Americans," said Hillshore, with a remonstrative shake of the head. "How little you know. Pouring all those crates into Boston harbor has given you a barbarian's approach to tea-making."

"What's to know? Boil the water, pour it in, then pour it out."

"Heathen," said Hillshore with the indulgent tone of a connoisseur instructing a layman.

"First of all, the teapot must be warmed," explained Hillshore. "And, pray tell, how many spoonfuls of tea did you put in the pot."

"Five, one for each of us."

"Ah, then you forgot the golden rule. One per person and one for the pot," said Hillshore. "And one cannot simply pour the tea straight away, it must be left to infuse for five minutes or else you will lose the essential flavors of the brew."

"Jeez, Professor, it's just a cup of tea."

"There is no such thing as *just* a cup of tea, Mr. Stone. I would be obliged if you would fetch another spoonful of tea for the pot, please. And a strainer, we don't want to be picking tea leaves from between our teeth for the next few days, do we?"

"William," said Oliver. "Perhaps this isn't the best time to—"

"No, Oliver," snapped Hillshore, slamming his fist down on the armrest. "It is *exactly* the right time. A global empire was founded on the back of properly brewed tea, won by men who knew the value of things done the right way. This tea will be too weak, and all true tea lovers not only like their tea strong, but like it a little stronger with each year that passes."

Gabriel returned with a loaded spoonful of tea and added it to the pot. Satisfied, Hillshore stirred the liquid and arranged their cups before him as his calm demeanor reasserted itself.

"And now the thorny issue of milk," he said. "Opinion is divided as to the correct order for its addition. Some maintain it should be added before the tea is poured, to prevent the milk from scalding. Others believe it should be added afterwards, to better regulate the amount."

Oliver said nothing, letting Hillshore expound on the proper etiquette of tea-making, knowing from bitter experience that focusing on apparently inconsequential details was a means of coping with great mental stress.

"I maintain that adding the milk afterwards is correct, as it allows the individual to arrive at their preferred balance of sweetness and bitterness. And now to the pouring."

Hillshore poured five cups through the strainer, and Oliver noticed how his hands—which had previously been agitated and restless—were now as steady as a surgeon's. Hillshore took the liberty of adding milk to each man's cup and sat back with the contented sigh of a man who has maintained standards while the world around him crumbled.

"Now, under normal circumstances, I would say we ought to allow the tea to cool to its optimum temperature, but in this instance, I think we can forego that last prescription."

Oliver took a drink of his tea and smiled.

"I think that's the best cup of tea I've ever had," he said.

"Standards, dear boy," said Hillshore. "Even in trying times they must be maintained. *Especially* in trying times. This world would be a far better place were its people mindful of that. Now, remember, gentlemen, this is not a highball glass, it is a teacup and it has a handle."

In deference to Hillshore, they sipped their tea as though in the presence of royalty until Morley returned with an armful of carefully annotated notes. He had removed his jacket and loosened his tie, a febrile excitement causing the muscles of his face to twitch and dance. His enthusiasm was infectious and Oliver felt his trepidation at this course of action diluted by the possibility of success.

"You look excited to be courting such danger," said Henry.

"Wouldn't you be? If we do this correctly, our consciousnesses will speed across the cosmos to another world. Only a privileged few are ever afforded such an opportunity."

"And if it goes wrong?"

Morley waved his hand to dismiss Henry's concern. "True, our minds may become forever detached from our bodies, but against the world's destruction, is that not a risk we ought to be willing to take?"

"Wait, what does *that* mean?" asked Gabriel. "You mean you might not come back?"

"A very real possibility," acknowledged Morley, arranging his notes on the table by the bay window. "But not one you will need to entertain, Mr. Stone. Only Henry, Oliver, and I will be traveling."

"Why only you three?"

"Someone has to stay here and keep our bodies safe," said Morley. He finished laying out his notes and turned to face Gabriel. "I have only known you a short time, Mr. Stone, but I already feel you are a man who prefers to meet his enemies face to face, man to man with a gun in your hand. Where we are going there will be no enemies that can be faced by such means, but if Alexander suspects what we plan, he may well send his human agents or creatures of the darkness to kill us. Of all of us, I believe you will have the best chance of stopping them and ensuring we have bodies to which our spirits may return. There is none among our company I would rather have standing guard over me."

"You put it like that…," said Gabriel, finishing his tea and drawing his pistol.

"And you, Professor Hillshore," continued Morley. "You understand Latin, I presume?"

"*Alenda lux ubi orta libertas*," said Hillshore.

"Cherished indeed," agreed Morley, indicating that Hillshore should approach. Morley indicated the reams of notes he had made.

"You will be our anchor to this world, Professor. These are memory hooks, if you will. Spoken aloud, they will act as beacons to our spirits when we are ready to come back. They will be, in effect, breadcrumbs we can follow home. We need someone who knows us well, to speak of us, to remind us of who we are and where we belong. Mr. Stone will keep us safe while we travel, but we need you to bring us back."

Hillshore scanned the notes, nodding as he saw how thorough Morley had been in his preparations. He quickly grasped what Morley's notes would achieve and sat at the table, scanning them with greater thoroughness.

"How will we know when you are ready to come back?" asked Hillshore without looking up from his studies.

"You will hear us," Morley assured him. "Have no fear of that. And now, the drug. I presume you have more pipes, Hillshore?"

"In the top drawer of the bureau."

Morley retrieved the pipes, each one a thing of beauty in itself: one carved in the shape of a rearing dragon, another like a carnyx horn, and the last a simple bamboo pipe with a gentle curve that reminded Oliver of those employed by the Yopasi. Hillshore handed Morley a square of cartridge paper folded over and sealed with a blob of blue wax stamped with a Chinese character.

"I hope that will be enough for our purposes, Morley," said Hillshore. "The look old Lang Fu gave me when I passed him your requirements was quite beyond the pale. I think he was ready to refuse, but when I impressed upon him the urgency of our need, he finally relented."

Morley broke the seal and carefully unfolded the square of paper. As each triangular section was lifted, the potent fumes of the drug filled the air. Stronger than any incense, its smell was exotic and strange, triggering sensory reactions to which Oliver could put no name.

"Yes, this should suffice," said Morley, placing the paper in the center of the table next to the teapot. He began filling each pipe with a yellowish, granular powder that looked like coarse sand mixed with crushed leaves, tamping down the mixture with the aid of a clean spoon. The carnyx horn pipe he passed to Henry, the Yopasi pipe to Oliver, and kept the dragon pipe for himself.

"Are we ready?" asked Morley as each man held up his pipe. Gabriel sat with his thirty-eight special cradled in his lap, facing the door and with an unobstructed view of the windows. Hillshore had arranged Morley's notes around him in the manner of a detective on the verge of a breakthrough. Henry, Oliver, and Morley remained seated by the fire.

"As I will ever be," said Oliver.

"Ready," agreed Henry. "I have traveled to the Dreamlands, but I suspect this will be my strangest journey of all."

"I believe I have the measure of what is required," said Hillshore.

"And there ain't nobody getting in here without taking a bullet to the head," said Gabriel.

"Just be careful you don't shoot Rex if he returns," pointed out Oliver.

Gabriel gave him a withering glance and Oliver shrugged.

"Right," said Morley, retrieving a taper from the fire and lighting his pipe. The smell of the opiate cocktail Hillshore had procured waxed strongly as Morley lit Henry's pipe, and finally Oliver's.

"Breathe deeply, but naturally," advised Morley. "This concoction can be quite strong."

* * *

Oliver inhaled a draught of the heady smoke, feeling it circulate with jagged ferocity in his lungs. He wanted to cough, to expel the fire he felt building in his chest, but Morley shook his head and he managed to suppress his natural reflex. He let out a breath, already feeling a warm numbness spread through him like syrup. He blinked as he saw the suggestion of colored smoke lifting off everything around him.

He took another draw on the pipe, now enjoying the drowsy heat that enveloped him like a comfortable blanket. His fingertips were tingling now, leaving bright streamers in the air as he moved the pipe back and forth from his mouth. He looked over to Henry, to see how his old friend was coping, and blinked away a shimmering afterimage.

"I say, Henry," said Oliver. "Did you know that there's two of you sitting in that chair?"

Henry turned to face him with a dreamy look on his face, and Oliver tried to reconcile what he was seeing with what he knew of the natural order of things. It seemed he was seeing *two* Henry's, like a pair of photographic negatives showing the same image placed one on top of the other, but slightly off center. One Henry had turned toward him, while the other remained utterly static, like a waxwork in a museum.

"Good grief, Oliver," replied Henry, lifting one hand to stare at it as though he had never before noticed its presence. "So there is. And are you aware you're floating above your chair?"

Oliver looked down to see that Henry was correct. A version of himself still sat in Hillshore's armchair, a smoking pipe still clenched between his teeth, while another, insubstantial, version of himself had drifted ever so slightly higher like an untethered hot air balloon.

"I am, aren't I? How curious," he said. "Morley, is that normal?"

Morley Dean was likewise a shimmering image of himself, disembodied from his recumbent form on the chair. He too had the vaguely confused look of a man who has woken to find he cannot recall how he came to be in this place, but it vanished swiftly as Morley's will reasserted itself.

"The smoke has done its work, gentlemen," said Morley, looking up to the ceiling.

Except there *was* no ceiling.

The upper reaches of Hillshore's house had vanished, replaced with the glittering arch of heaven. Stars in their billions wheeled above them, a universe of impossible vastness and complexity. The walls of the house were diminishing, blowing away like morning mist in a stiff breeze until there was nothing left of the structure whatsoever. Only the floor remained, and even that was shrinking like a melting ice floe.

Oliver felt panic welling up in his chest as what he knew as reality faded from sight to be replaced by the stellar vista of unimaginable gulfs of space. This was the universe revealed, the howling cosmic wilderness in which his species lived their insignificant lives in the blink of an eye. Galaxies spun lazily in the distance, each turn of a spiral arm taking millions of years to complete. Each spray of light in the dark was a realm where stars lived and died and entire civilizations might have risen and become extinct without anyone on Earth having been aware of them.

The sheer scale of what spread out before them was impossible to grasp, and Oliver felt his mind buckle at the incomprehensible distances and spans of time. He wanted to drop to his knees, but the floor had vanished beneath him, leaving his shimmering body of light floating in the emptiness of space, cold and alone.

"Hold to my voice," said Morley, and the ethereal form of his old mentor hove into view, drifting like a gentle comet. "Yes, we are motes of dust in the universe, but we are here together and we have purpose that unites us. Keep to that at all times and you will not lose your way."

Henry appeared at his side and the presence of his fellow travelers brought a reassurance of scale with which Oliver's mind could cope. Silver threads trailed behind Henry and Morley like glittering fishing lines that vanished into the darkness beneath them—though he was coming to realize that such spatial terms were meaningless here. Oliver too had a silver thread, and though he had no idea what it represented, he knew it was vital that it not be broken.

"My God," said Oliver. "It's full of stars…"

Morley pointed to where a group of seven suns spun like tiny fireflies in the distance.

"The Pleiades cluster," he said. "The fourth star is our destination, between the stars Alcyone and Electra on one side, and Maia and Taygeta on the other. *Unaussprechlichen Kulten* speaks of a Great

Hall being found upon the red-litten wastes of Celaeno. That matches Nereus-Kai's description of the library."

"How do we get there?" asked Henry. "It's so very far away."

Morley grinned. "Where we are, Henry, *nothing* is far away."

And Oliver cried aloud as the stars and galaxies flashed past him at the speed of thought.

* * *

Over the years, Gabriel had developed many tricks of the trade to keep from sleep on a job after long hours awake. Rocking back and forth from his heels to the balls of his feet, stamping (which had the added benefit of keeping your feet warm in the cold), and singing to himself. Whistling worked too, as did reciting lists of presidents, old girlfriends, or places he'd still like to visit one day.

"Do you have to keep up that infernal whistling?" said Hillshore. "And, for God's sake, please sit down instead of stomping around the house."

All of his tried and tested methods were, unfortunately, no use when he was forced to share a room with a nervy Englishman who was studying the notes and instructions of a highly strung professor.

"Sorry, Professor Hillshore," said Gabriel. "Just trying to stay alert."

"I understand that, but is there any way you could do it quietly? After all, we are adrift in uncharted territory here."

"Tell me about it."

Hillshore's scolding manner softened. "Yes, I imagine this must be quite a change from your usual line of work, Mr. Stone."

"Gabriel."

"If I am to call you Gabriel, then I will forego insisting upon my honorific."

"Your what?"

"You don't need to call me professor," said Hillshore. "William will be just fine."

"Thanks, and, yeah, you're right," said Gabriel, rubbing his face and flexing his fingers on the walnut grip of his pistol. "Being around those guys ain't exactly strikebreaking or hunting down missing persons or bank robbers. Ever since I met them, I keep pinching myself to make sure I'm not dreaming or going nuts."

"And have you come to a conclusion?"

"About what?"

"Whether you are going nuts?"

"I'll get back to you on that one, Prof—, I mean, William."

"As I shall to you," agreed Hillshore. "In the space of a day I have had my entire worldview turned upside down. Even after what we saw at the Markham-Hyde collection, I can still scarcely credit its truth. My mind baulks at accepting such hideous notions, but the psychologist in me knows how easily the mind can turn from hard truths and fashion fantasies to avoid their bitter realities."

Gabriel moved around the room as Hillshore spoke, glancing out each window for any sign of trouble. This time of day, the streets weren't empty, but neither were they particularly busy. A few moms walked past with young kids in prams, a beat cop smoked on a corner, and some Portuguese types lounged on a stoop eating chicken legs. Gabriel dismissed them all, his instincts telling him that, for once, they didn't have to worry about something breaking down the door and attacking them. He caught himself in the act of complacency, knowing that was right about the time you'd get blindsided by a brickbat to the head.

"Reality ain't all it's cracked up to be," he said, returning to his seat by the door. "Or so I'm told."

"It never was," said Hillshore, lighting a cigarette and rising from his table to check on the three travelers. The smell of the smoke was still strong, though the narcotic pipes had long since burned down. Oliver, Henry, and Morley stared vacantly into space with their eyes wide open, as unmoving as store mannequins.

To say it was unsettling was an understatement.

"You sure they're all right?"

Hillshore sighed. "I have medical training, but this…this is somewhat beyond my remit, Gabriel," he said, placing two fingertips on Oliver's neck and holding the tip of his cigarette before his mouth.

The plume of smoke twitched, but only barely.

"He has a pulse, and breath," said Hillshore. "Aside from that I have no idea where they are or what they might be experiencing. The mind has incredible powers of self-deception, and whatever tales they return with may be just that: tales conjured in the depths of an opium delusion. Trust me, I know whereof I speak."

"Yeah, but what if they all come back with the same story?"

"Then we shall have a very different conundrum on our hands," said Hillshore, moving to check on Henry and Morley. "How to document this incident in a manner that will not see me laughed out of the Psychiatry Association."

Gabriel chuckled. "Yeah, good luck with that."

"Yes, perhaps you are right," agreed Hillshore. "Methinks this is an incident best left unreported."

"So, there's just one thing I don't understand, William."

"Just one?"

"Well, one in particular," said Gabriel, checking a weapon he already knew was as ready to fire as it would ever be. "When Morley gave you all those notes about how to bring them back…"

"Yes?" said Hillshore when Gabriel didn't continue.

"He said that you'd be their anchor to the world, that you'd speak about them and remind them of who they were. He said that would somehow act as a signal flare or something to them. You'd be the lighthouse that brings them home."

"Breadcrumbs, Morley called them," said Hillshore.

"Sure, sure," said Gabriel. "But like I said there's a big problem with that."

"And what would that be?"

"It sounds okay as far as Oliver's concerned," said Gabriel. "But you don't know Morley and Henry at all. And neither do I."

* * *

It could have been instantaneous or an infinitely vast span of time. Oliver would never know how long passed, but no sooner had he blinked than the stars were gone. A sudden, overwhelming sense of dislocation swept through him at so instantaneous a journey and change of surroundings. He dropped to his knees, his senses reeling, dizzy and so churned as to make him feel violently sick.

"Don't worry," said a voice beside him he knew he ought to recognize. "The sickness will pass. It's not real sickness anyway, just what your mind believes you *should* feel."

The idea of a believed sickness seemed so absurd that the moment he thought of it as such, the sensation vanished. Oliver's memory of who had spoken returned to him, and he looked up to see Morley Dean standing at the foot of a smooth outcrop of red-veined stone. All traces of nausea and the brain-fogging narcotic had vanished from

Oliver's mind, and in their place was a sense of bodily freedom and clarity of thought.

Oliver rose to his feet, finding himself on the edge of a vast plain of black rock, over which moaning winds blew squalling tides of ocher mist that rose and fell like theater curtains. He was cold, and the ground beneath him was hard and glassy, volcanic, but somehow inert. Oliver shielded his eyes and mouth from drifting dust, like coarse sand on a Maryland shoreline. The air tasted bitter and metallic, as though he were breathing air of unknown chemical composition.

"Henry?" said Oliver, turning a full circle, his voice sounding strangely distant.

"I'm here," said Henry, and Oliver saw his friend emerge from the mist with his neck craned to the sky. Oliver followed his gaze, and saw the stars had vanished. The unending panorama of the universe was now a heavy crimson sky, thick with particulate matter and violent with atmospheric storms.

"We're here," said Morley, somewhat unnecessarily.

Oliver turned a full circuit, scanning the thunderheads in the far distance and the vast, empty expanse of wasteland surrounding them. If there was a bleaker place to be found in the universe, he was hard pressed to imagine it. As far as the eye could see was emptiness— broken plains of crazed stone like the parched floor of Death Valley. Here and there, he could see a suggestion of a structure raised by alien hands, but no sooner did he notice any such hints of habitation than they were obscured by wind-blown mist.

It felt like the world was being worn away by the winds, an entire civilization and all its works eroded over the course of millions of years. What folly were the works of sentient beings in the face of such deep universal time…

"There's nothing here," he said with hollow finality.

"It has to be," said Morley. "Such libraries do not easily end their days."

"Like Markham-Hyde?" suggested Henry. "That ended. Not easily, but it ended."

"Whatever was once here, it's gone now," said Oliver, bending to cup a handful of the grey dust in the palm of his hand before letting it trickle between his fingers. "It's dust now, nothing but dust."

"So have we come all this way for nothing?" asked Henry.

"No," insisted Morley. "The Great Hall is here, I know it."

"Then where is it?" demanded Oliver. "Look around you, man. This is a dead rock. There is nothing left alive, and even the bones of whatever race once dwelled here are nothing more than dust and ash."

Morley refused to be browbeaten and said, "This world is dead, yes, but entertain for a moment the possibility that its very desolation might be exactly why it was chosen to house a repository of forbidden knowledge. Would you build a library of horrors where just anyone might walk in and steal the secrets of the universe?"

That paused Oliver in his recriminations, and he took a deep breath.

"You're right, Morley, I apologize," he said. "I was just expecting something…"

"Easier," said Henry, completing Oliver's thought.

"Yes, I suppose so, though I shouldn't have," said Oliver. "What of my experience over the last few months has been easy? Very well, if this is indeed where we are meant to be, how do we proceed?"

The question was a good one, and the three of them climbed to the top of the nearby outcrop of rock. It rose hundreds of yards like a vast runway and afforded them an unrivaled view of their surroundings, though there was, at first, not much more to see than there had been on the ground.

Scoured rock tundra extended to the horizon in all directions, where the toothed summits of mountains were just visible through the clouds of abrasive dust.

"If this Great Hall *is* here, then we have a long walk to reach it," said Henry. "Or do distances not matter at all while we travel thusly?"

"We are beings of light and thought, Henry," said Morley. "Though in such a place, we are bound by the conceits and limitations our minds impose upon us to a certain extent. Our forms are limited by those physical constrains we imagine would act upon our physical bodies. Given time, we might attempt to unlearn such limitations, but whether we have such time is debatable."

While Henry and Morley talked of relative distance and thought-imagined travel, Oliver continued to search the landscape for any hints that they might not have come to this place in vain or that the object of their search might be closer than they imagined. He saw nothing that gave him any hope of that, simply more unending vistas of dead rock, emptied river beds, and thrusting peaks of black rock crowning the horizon.

The swirling clouds of dust made a mockery of any serious attempt to discern their surroundings, and Oliver had to continually shield his eyes and wipe gritty debris from his face. It seemed the storms that kept the dust moving around Celaeno conspired to keep its secrets.

Once he would have dismissed such an idea as ludicrous, but Morley's notion that perhaps this library had been placed on such a doomed world deliberately made him wonder if there were not some specific artifice on the occluding nature of the winds. Determined that no mere dust was going to keep them from their goal, Oliver returned his gaze to the desolate landscape.

Once again he saw hints of this world's previous existence: stubs of petrified forests and the dust-filled canyons of mighty riverbeds. The peaks of the mountains were rounded and smooth where the endless winds had eroded their jagged summits, and Oliver was reminded of the hills around Arkham, where dark rituals were said to have been enacted in ages past and strange stones still stood proud on their gorse-napped slopes.

He saw nothing of any note until he observed that the mountain-tops in one particular direction were not rounded like the others, but stepped and regular. The billowing clouds of dust jealously obscured the geometric peaks, but Oliver knew that what he had seen was im-portant. He was put in mind of the ancient pyramids of Chichen Itza or the stepped ruins of Machu Picchu.

Surely against so abrasive a wind, no such regularity could exist naturally.

Which led Oliver to one inescapable conclusion.

"That isn't a natural formation," he said.

"Oliver?" asked Morley. "What is it?"

Oliver thought of what Morley had said of them *un*learning how their mortal bodies behaved in this incorporeal existence. He could scarcely credit that this was not his physical body here on this far dis-tant world; it felt real, it felt heavy and solid and made of meat and bone. And yet it could not possible be here. It *had* to be a body of light and thought, of spirit and aether.

And such a body needed no physical constraints to hold it bound to physical norms.

Oliver closed his eyes and held the image of the stepped peaks in his mind, picturing himself and the others standing before them, like Carter before the most intact pharaonic tomb in the Valley of the Kings.

Sudden vertigo seized him and a lurching sensation of weight-lessness. The same dislocation Oliver had felt when Morley had brought them through the stars made his head spin, and a terrible, aching cold suffused his limbs. He felt…*thin*, as though somehow less defined or able to maintain his faculties. Once, when Oliver was a child, he had been at the bottom of a pile of children playing in the park. The weight on his chest had been crushing, squeezing the air from his lungs and leaving him wheezing for breath like a landed fish. By the time the laughing children had eventually moved on to play somewhere else, Oliver had almost blacked out and his panic had left him with a lingering claustrophobia for many years after.

That feeling of constriction and confinement returned with a vengeance, and Oliver fought for air he knew he wasn't really breathing and tried to push back walls he knew were not closing in on him.

"Good God above!" cried Henry from afar. "Oliver, what did you do?"

Oliver released a shuddering breath, seeing that he was on his hands and knees, though he had no recollection of falling. The ground was no longer rocky and veined with quartz-like deposits, but soft black sand into which his fingers were sunk. He heard the sound of water, though that was surely ridiculous; hadn't they seen the evidence of numerous cracked riverbeds that had baked dry eons ago?

Morley appeared at his side and helped him to his feet. He brushed coarse black sand from Oliver's knees and shook his head in wonderment.

"By Jove, Oliver, you're a natural at mastering out-of-body traveling!"

"I certainly don't feel like a master of anything right now," answered Oliver, looking up to see a bleak shoreline stretching for miles in all directions.

The three of them stood on the very edges of a steel grey lake or river of colossal proportions, as uninviting a body of water as Oliver had ever seen. Not so much as a single ripple marred its mirror-smooth surface, yet its depths remained unknown for its deeps were utterly dark.

"Understandable," said Morley, examining him critically, as though for signs of injury. "Our spirit forms have a limited amount of energy, so we will only be able to sustain our presence here for a finite amount of time. Believe you me, our bodies will be quite enervated by the time Hillshore brings us back to Earth."

Oliver held onto Morley as another enfeebling wave of nausea swept through him.

"What's wrong with me?" he said.

"It's quite normal," said Morley. "Well, as normal as an endeavor such as this can ever be. As I said, to indulge in activities beyond what your mind tells you is physically possible requires a great deal of the body's energy. When that energy is depleted, well, I shouldn't like to find out what might happen."

"You mean you don't know?" asked Henry.

"Not as such," admitted Morley. "I have never sought to exceed my limitations."

"So can we die here? Is it as Luke described the Dreamlands, where if a man should die, he would instantly be transported back to the waking world?"

Morley shook his head. "I am afraid I can offer no such guarantees, Henry. Should you die while traveling in this manner, your body will die, for no mortal shell can exist without its spirit. Even injury here will leave its mark, repercussions I call them. A cut to the hand on your spirit form would appear on your flesh back on Earth."

Henry's cheeks flushed an angry red and his fists balled at his sides.

"And you didn't think to mention this before we smoked that damnable tobacco?"

Morley shrugged. "It would have made no difference. We still had to make the journey."

"Morley is right," said Oliver, staring across the enormous lake to where the towering scarps of the mountains reared up like a wall at the end of the universe. "In any case, we're here."

Without the cloying mists of the dead plateau, the details of what had drawn Oliver's attention was plain to the others. Henry gasped in awed astonishment, and even Morley was rendered speechless by the unimaginable scale of what lay on the other side of the lake.

The upper reaches of the mountains were not naturally formed peaks, but the titanic spires of a vast black edifice raised by the hands of some long-vanished alien race. Carved from the face of the mountain like Jordan's Petra, the entire cliff was the facade of the most monstrous building imaginable. Vast columns of basalt, shadowed gateways and obscene statuary of glistening obsidian adorned its frontage, alongside weirdly angled architectural embellishments that defied easy understanding and confounded every notion of perspective.

Everything was orders of magnitude grander in scale than anything that could be constructed on Earth, rendering the magnificent achievements of human builders meaningless—statues like buildings and columns hundreds of feet high. Flitting things of shadow roosted in its crumbling eaves, made tiny by scale, and Oliver tried not to imagine what manner of creature might call such a place home.

"The Great Hall of Celaeno, I presume," said Oliver.

CHAPTER SEVENTEEN

The afternoon wore on, with no movement from the three travelers and no sign that anything was happening behind their dead-eyed stares. Gabriel's eyes were heavy, but he kept on the move to stave off the sleep that threatened to take him every time he blinked. Hillshore supported his head in his hands, poring over the notes Morley had left him.

Over the last hour, he and Hillshore had pooled their combined knowledge of Henry Cartwright and Morley Dean, but the results of that brainstorming barely filled a single sheet of the legal pad. Hillshore knew more of Henry from having read his case notes prior to his recent consultation at Arkham Asylum, but of Morley, they knew little.

"Had you ever heard of Morley before we got to San Francisco?" asked Gabriel.

"I had heard of him, yes, but I knew little of real substance about the man," said Hillshore, with a weary shake of the head. "Only what little Oliver had told me from his time at Brown. I seem to recall something of his latter disgrace and removal from the university, but of his subsequent dealings I'm afraid I know nothing. What about you? Did Morley speak to you en route to San Francisco of anything we might use?"

"He wasn't the talkative type," said Gabriel. "At least not with any-thing that told me who he was or what kind of a man he is. I'm pretty good at picking up on that kind of thing—you have to be as a Pinker-ton—but Morley kept his cards so close to his chest, I doubt even he could read 'em."

Hillshore tapped his pencil against the notes Morley had left him.

"Then we shall have to hope that these phrases and memory hooks are enough to bring him back along with the others. Perhaps in their shared experience, it might be enough to bring Oliver back with mem-ories and self-knowledge."

"What do you mean?"

"Bring one back, and we bring them all back," said Hillshore. "I am afraid it is all we have."

Gabriel yawned and rubbed the heels of his palms against his eyes. Blinking away afterimages, he frowned as he looked over at Oliver. Nothing had obviously changed, at least nothing his trained eye could yet perceive, but there was something definitely different about Oliver.

"What the hell…?" said Gabriel, rising from his seat by the stairs and crossing Hillshore's front room in three quick strides.

"Gabriel?" said Hillshore, looking up from his notes. "Is something the matter?"

"I don't know, maybe. Something's different."

"Different? What?"

Gabriel tried to figure that out. Outwardly, Oliver seemed just as he had the last time Gabriel had checked on him, but then he saw what he'd missed the first time, something so obvious that he couldn't believe he hadn't seen it.

Oliver's eyes were closed and his left hand was clenching the edge of the armchair in a white-knuckle grip.

"Good God," said Hillshore. "Look!"

A line of blood ran from Oliver's nose, and his flesh paled visibly before their eyes. Oliver's mouth eased open a fraction and an icy breath sighed from the depths of his lungs. Gabriel coughed at the stale smell: partly tobacco smoke, partly metallic, and partly that of something spoiled.

"What the hell's wrong with him?" demanded Gabriel, watching Oliver's eyes darting furiously behind his closed lids. "Is he having a fit or something?"

Hillshore bent to take Oliver's pulse, and Gabriel knew something was *really* wrong at the look of surprise on the Englishman's face.

"His heart rate is elevated," said Hillshore. "Considerably."

"How considerably?"

"Dangerously so, I'd say."

"So what do we do? Wake him up?"

"Dear Lord, no!" cried Hillshore. "It's dangerous enough to wake a sleepwalker or one hypnotized, I dread to think what me might risk by awakening one whose mind is traveling across the galaxy."

"So we sit with our thumbs up our asses and do nothing?"

Oliver's back arched and both Gabriel and Hillshore jumped back in surprise. Gabriel automatically reached for his gun, though there was no obvious target. Oliver slumped back in his chair, and the Yo-pasi pipe he had smoked fell to the floor in a scatter of ashes. Gabriel and Hillshore returned to his side, and the difference in Oliver was shocking.

His face had aged ten years in an instant. Streaks of white now threaded his hair, the lines around his eyes and mouth were more pronounced, and his jowls sat looser on his jawline. Oliver's chest rose and fell in fitful inhalations and labored exhalations, like an emphysemic old man after decades of smoking.

"Holy Christ," said Gabriel. "What's happened to him? Jesus, we've got to wake him up!"

"No!" said Hillshore, reaching out to grab Gabriel's hand. "Morley's notes spoke of this."

Hillshore ran back to the table as Gabriel knelt helplessly by Oliver's chair. He wanted to shake the man by his shoulders, to shout in his face and tell him to wake the hell up, but Gabriel Stone wasn't a man of reckless impulses. If Hillshore said it was dangerous to wake Oliver prematurely, he'd take that to the bank.

"Hurry, Professor, I think it's getting worse."

Hillshore rummaged through the notes Morley had left him, skimming his spidery writing as fast as was humanly possible.

"Damn you, Morley, your penmanship is atrocious," snapped Hillshore.

Oliver's chest hiked, and another breath of impossible, non-terrestrial air escaped his lips.

"Aha!" cried Hillshore, holding a page triumphantly aloft. "Here."

"What does it say?" said Gabriel, trying not to reach out to Oliver, even just to hold his hand to let him know there was a friend nearby. "Can we stop this?"

Hillshore knelt beside Gabriel and shook his head. "No, if what Morley has written here is correct, an astral traveler has only a limited reserve of energy with which to remain separate from his physical body. I suspect that such *repercussions*, as Morley calls them, on the physical body are a sign of some injury Oliver's subtle body has suffered."

"You mean he's being attacked?"

Hillshore looked up from the page. "A distinct possibility. Or perhaps some other trauma or unexpected expenditure of effort has depleted his energies."

"Right," said Gabriel. "I've heard enough. We're waking him up."

"No," said Hillshore. "We must stay the course, my friend. Morley's notes warn that we might see some ghastly effects of so arduous a journey. He demands that we hold true to our purpose and not flinch from letting them complete their task, no matter what we might see."

"You mean he knew this would happen?" demanded Gabriel.

"I believe he suspected such an outcome was possible, yes," said Hillshore.

Gabriel stood and began pacing the room, his hand on his hips as he tried to think of what to do. To be helpless when his friends were in danger was anathema to him. Gabriel prided himself on always being there for the man next to him, to fight as hard for him as he would for himself, because that was what men of action and honor did.

"There's nothing we can do but wait and pray they are near their goal," said Hillshore. "And, when the time comes, we will wake them, I assure you."

"And when will that be?"

"I suspect we will know when it is time," said Hillshore. "Now sit down, and I will prepare us some fresh tea. God knows, we could both use some Earl Grey."

Gabriel nodded slowly and said, "I don't do well on the bench, William."

"Nor I," said Hillshore at the kitchen door. "Woe betide the schoolmaster who didn't put *me* in the starting eleven of the Eton cricket team."

* * *

The great river vanished to the horizon in both directions, but further along the shoreline the three travelers found an ancient jetty of cerulean stone that jutted out into the water. It appeared to have been built directly upon the lake, and the impenetrable nature of the water made it impossible to tell how its solid mass was supported. Oliver saw a long, flat-bottomed boat moored to a bollard fashioned from the same queer, greenish soapstone as the elder sign inscribed talisman the old man of Kingsport had given him.

Like the ferryboat of Charon, the boat's prow and stern were raised, though there was no skeletal steersman to guide them.

"Now that's damn peculiar," said Henry as they advanced cautiously along the jetty's length.

"What?"

"This boat, it was made for passengers of human scale," said Henry. "Everything else here is so vast. Why is there a boat we might make use of?"

"Probably because we are not the first men to make use of this library," said Morley, stepping off the stone jetty and onto the boat. His weight barely unsettled the boat, and the ripples of its movement reached scarcely a foot before being swallowed by the water.

"We're not?"

"Do you think no others would have made this trip? We found it with relative ease did we not?"

"Ease?" exclaimed Henry. "If that's what you call ease, then God help us all when you think a task might present a challenge!"

"There's a boat," said Oliver, ending their bickering by climbing down next to Morley. "So let us be thankful for small mercies, yes?"

Henry bit back a retort and nodded, also climbing aboard.

No sooner were all three aboard than the boat slipped its moorings and turned its bow toward the far shore, just as Oliver had hoped it might. With no visible current or flow, its course was arrow-straight, knifing through water that parted before its bladed prow with the viscosity of oil.

Henry stared straight ahead, as did Morley, but Oliver sat in the center of the boat, weary beyond words. He had brought them to the library with unexpected swiftness, but at a greater cost to his well-being than he had allowed the others to know. His body felt light, insubstantial, and he knew that if he closed his eyes and drifted off to sleep, his friends would turn around and find him gone.

But that was the easy path, to fade away and let others shoulder a burden he had taken upon himself. He blinked away treacherous sleep and stared up at the gargantuan structure of the black library, marveling that such a thing could every be constructed by beings of flesh and blood. Then again, perhaps it had been raised by other, older beings—ancient gods with the means to craft anything their unknowable minds could conceive.

Just looking at its titanic immensity seemed to press down on Oliver, crushing him into his seat with the stark fact of his insignificance. Despite Morley's belief that other men had come here before, Oliver knew that such mortal trespasses would not lightly be tolerated. Whatever secrets lay within this mighty hall would be jealously guarded. Armitage and the mysterious custodians of the Markham-Hyde collection were formidable enough, but what guardians of knowledge might this alien library boast?

Oliver looked out over the water, its glacial stillness barely troubled by their passage. He could see nothing of its hidden depths, yet had the troubling sensation of vast leviathans plying the icy submarine world below them. Indeed, he had a potent sense of something so close that were he to reach his hand into the water, he might brush some noxious hide, a mass of scales or the leathery texture of something reptilian.

And just for a second, it seemed as though Oliver looked into the black reaches below them to see such a beast, a many-eyed, tentacled behemoth left over from an earlier epoch of the universe and which extinction would not claim. He recoiled from the sight of the beast, breathless and horrified, wanting nothing more than to be off this boat before its monstrous bulk broke the surface.

"Oliver?" called Morley from the bow. "Are you all right?"

"I'm fine," he called back as the opacity of the water was restored. "Are we almost at the shore?"

"There's another jetty," said Henry, pointing out over the water.

Oliver followed Henry's outstretched arm and saw there was indeed a jetty, identical to the one from which they had begun this crossing. The last hundred yards to that jetty were the longest in Oliver's life, as he became convinced the underwater horror would rise up and devour them before they had a chance to disembark.

The boat moored itself at the jetty, and Morley was the first off. He helped Henry out and reached down to assist Oliver. He smiled weakly as Morley pulled him up.

"Thank you," he said. "I think bringing us to this place took more out of me than I thought."

Morley looked him square in the eye and said, "I know *exactly* how much it took out of you, my friend. Just remember what I said about us having finite reserves of spiritual energy. We must be done with this place before we exhaust ourselves and cannot return."

"I will remember that, Morley," said Oliver. "You have my word, no more stupidity."

Morley gave one of his short, bitter laughs. "It was stupidity that brought us here in the first place. A little more will probably see us home."

Oliver, Henry, and Morley set off along the jetty, feeling even more dwarfed by the soaring structure now that they approached it. An immense portico of black stone was the obvious way in, but its carven steps were scaled to the strides of giants and impassable.

"So how do we get in?" wondered Henry.

Morley had no immediate answer, but the closer they drew to its outer edges, the more Oliver saw the library had not escaped the ravages of time unscathed. Portions of its structure had collapsed, while others were incomplete, as though some great catastrophe had eradicated its builders before they could complete their great work.

"There must be some way in," said Morley. "Those who came before us must have found a way to gain entrance. A postern or some secret means we have yet to discover."

"Or a great big avalanche," said Oliver, pointing to where one of the colossal statues from the portico's cracked pediment had fallen and carved a path through the corner of the stairs, like a breach in a medieval castle walls. Rubble filled the breach, but such was the destructive mass of the fallen statue, that it had been crushed to a scale just manageable for humans.

"You think we can climb that?" asked Henry doubtfully.

"I climbed Kingsport Head in the dark," said Oliver. "I think we can manage this."

It took them another half hour to reach the bottom of the rubble slope, by which time Oliver was breathing heavily. He knew now it was not the physical exertion, but the demands on his very soul that just being here was exacting. Were Henry and Morley feeling the same? Could any man ever return whole after such an ordeal?

Each block was as huge as those used to construct the pyramids, and the statue that had crushed them was thankfully lying on its side with its face turned from them. Oliver had little doubt that its unsettling geometries and alien anatomy would be abhorrent to his sight, and had no wish to know what abomination had been carved there. With little choice but to attempt the climb, the three men clambered up onto the debris, grunting and groaning with effort as they climbed higher and higher toward the inner sanctums of the Great Hall.

Only after several hours' effort did they finally reach the end of their climb, hauling their exhausted bodies into the shadow of the great pediment. The far wall was fashioned from enormous blocks of polished black stone, with a towering set of bronze gates at its center. Each gate was decorated with more sigils and terrible imagery, but Oliver paid it no attention, his mind too brutalized to register fresh horrors of alien artifice. For a moment, he feared their climb had been for nothing, then saw a sliver of light that was probably tens of yards wide between the two great gates.

The floor beneath them was polished jet, glossy, and reflective. Seeing what was reflected, Oliver looked up at the underside of the portico. Thousands upon thousands of nesting, winged things, like a host of bats hung in repose, just waiting for darkness so that they might hunt again. He saw the others notice them, and they hurried their steps toward the sliver of light between the bronze gates.

The crossed the distance as quickly and quietly as possible, not knowing what manner of creature roosted above them, and keen to remain ignorant of their undoubtedly hostile nature. The vast gates soared above them as they approached, far larger than even the giants for whom the stairs had been carved could possibly have required.

Even from without, it was possible to feel the weight of terrible knowledge within.

The stench of ancient pages, rotting paper, and stagnant air wafted through the gap in the doors, which—as Oliver had suspected—was at least two dozen yards wide. A haze of dust obscured the deeper reaches of the Great Hall, but Oliver had the impression of towering shelves, vast balconies, and endless archives where the greatest secrets of the universe could be hidden from sight. A soft whisper drifted through the gates, like distant voices in earnest discourse somewhere in a forgotten portion of the library.

"You said we might not be the first to consult the library," said Oliver.

"Yes, that's correct," answered Morley. "What of it?"

Oliver tilted his head to the side, straining to catch the faint sounds from within, once again hearing the soft, wet sound of what might have been words.

Tekeli-li, Tekeli-li, Tekeli-li…

"Maybe we're not alone here," said Oliver.

* * *

Though the outside of the library had suffered damage, it was still spectacular in its cyclopean scale, and while the interior was constructed on no less a grand scale, it had not weathered the millennia nearly. so well. Passing through the great doors, Oliver, Henry, and Morley found themselves in a cavernous hall, a vast open space with tier after tier of black stone balconies rising to the ceiling. Noxious red light poured in through enormous holes in the roof, and the floor was thick with encrusted white residue.

The collapsed sections of the roof lay in piles of shattered stonework, gold and green veined marble blocks as big as trucks lying scattered about like unfinished sculptures. Dust lay heavily, and the air of neglect and abandonment within the library was palpable.

Vast spiral staircases, of the same proportions as the steps of the portico, connected the great tiers, and each level was filled with stone shelves that groaned under the weight of heavy books, racks of scrolls and clay tablets. Oliver saw tiered repositories of forbidden tomes stretching away into the distance, and galleries branched off from this main nave with no less a quantity of knowledge.

All the libraries of Earth could combine their works and still they would not equal a fraction of these treasures.

"I hope you know where we need to look," said Henry. "We could spend a lifetime on one tier alone."

"A hundred lifetimes," said Morley, "but Henry is right. Did the Mad Arab's book give any clue as to where we might find the second half of the Atlantean's spell?"

Oliver thought back to the words he had read in the *Necronomicon*, before realizing he had no need of recall. The last words of Nereus-Kai were written on the sheaf of notes the Custodian of Markham-Hyde had given him as they left the wreckage of the collection; notes in his own hand, but which he had no memory of writing. Oliver unfolded the pages and traced his finger down the lines of text until he found what he was looking for.

"And knowing the potency of what he had crafted, Nereus-Kai hid his spell from the sight of Men, locked in the red-litten vaults of Celaeno's Great Hall, where only those in the direst of need may seek it under the labyrinth."

"Well, I think we qualify as being in the direst need," said Morley. "Though as guides go, it lacks something in specifics."

"No, it's quite specific," said Henry, kneeling to obtain a fragment of stone with a sharp edge.

"It is?" asked Oliver.

"Yes," said Henry, looking up at him as though it must surely be obvious. "The labyrinth? Come on, Oliver. Even Prothero Fitzgibbons knew that was the symbol of Atlantis. Plato's description of the layout of Atlantis speaks of its inner sanctum being formed around a series of concentrically shaped canals."

Henry used the sharp-edged stone to draw out what he was describing, a layout that was unmistakably that of a labyrinth.

"The spiral labyrinth has long been seen as the symbol of life, from the Hopi Indians to the Aztecs, to the natives of the Nazca plains. Across the world to almost every culture, including Minoan Crete, we see the unmistakable evidence of the labyrinth as a universal symbol. The stone circles of Britain and France, through to Sicily and Malta, and beyond it to the African continent also show a reverence for this symbol."

"That doesn't necessarily link it to Atlantis," pointed out Morley.

"No," agreed Henry, holding up a finger to stall further objections. "But bear with me, my friends, for I have seen this symbol many times in my researches."

Henry stood and began pacing, using his hands as much as his words to communicate his passion and reasoning. He grinned infectiously, and Oliver only ever recalled seeing Henry this animated when on the verge of an insightful breakthrough.

"Now, the widespread use of the labyrinth icon has often been seen as the inspiration for an ancient symbol to represent the physical outline of our galaxy. That may well be the case, but as with so many things in the ancient world, it is also capable of double or even triple significance. I believe it is conceivable that perhaps the spread of this symbol had just one intention: to preserve the memory of Poseidon's island. If we accept Nereus-Kai's story at face value, Atlantis had been sunk beneath the waves, and the rest of the world cast into turmoil. To secure its memory, a lasting emblem survived, the labyrinth emblem of Atlantis. We find and follow the labyrinth symbol and it will lead us to what we came for."

"A symbol like that?" said Morley with a grin to match Henry's.

Oliver looked at a great block of basalt Morley was pointing to: a shaped rock that had fallen from the library's roof. Carved into its upper surfaces was a perfectly circular spiral pattern.

"Yes," said Henry. "Exactly like that."

* * *

They followed the labyrinth symbol down the main nave of the library, scanning left and right for any further instances of its appearance. The echoing abandonment of the library pressed in around them, though every now and then, Oliver would hear the distant susurration of distant voices, whispering that existed just below the threshold of hearing. He told himself it was the rustle of wings from the bat-like creatures above, but could never quite convince himself of that.

The deeper into the Great Hall they penetrated, the stranger it became.

A gallery to their left had partially subsided into the rock upon which the library had been built, and a cove of black water lapped at the base of the stone shelves. Hundreds of books and scrolls floated in the water, their contents lost forever. In contrast to the still waters outside, this body of water bubbled and frothed, lapping hungrily at the shelves as through seeking to drag more books to a watery grave.

Strange lights that cast no shadows illuminated areas of the shelves that ought to be shrouded in darkness, and every now and again Oliver heard a persistent scratching that seemed to come from the air itself, like a dog left out in the rain. Each time he sought the source of the sound, he could find nothing untoward, but the feeling persisted. His eyes scanned the far corners of the library, but whatever was producing the sound remained invisible.

A vague sense of unease possessed Oliver, a nagging primal urge telling him that they should not be here. He told himself that was an entirely reasonable feeling, but the sense that it came from an outside agency would not leave him. A distorted wail echoed from deep inside the library, somewhere between a wolf howl and the screech of an owl. Oliver flinched and looked up, but none of the bat creatures had moved more than the occasional rustle of wings.

"What was *that*?" asked Henry.

"Something best avoided I suspect," said Morley.

No more was said, and the sound did not come again, so they pressed on, following the fleeting sightings of the Atlantean labyrinth symbol toward their goal. Oozing pools of black liquid, like noxious tar pits bubbled and popped where fallen masonry had smashed through the floor slabs. A foul stench, like a hundred cesspools combined, wafted from the pits with each protoplasmic bubble that burst, and tendrils of tar-like ooze burped and slithered across the floor before being dragged back.

Oliver was reminded of the thing in the vial that had fought the winged creatures on Chuck's plane, but if there was anything sentient within the tar, it paid them no mind. Again and again they saw the labyrinth symbol, and it did indeed seem to be leading them on through the library, inscribed on particular galleries, pathways and clear routes through the debris and bubbling pools.

On a tier hundreds of feet above them, Oliver fancied he saw a man dressed in the sober suit of a New Englander. He appeared to be writing in a leather-bound journal, but no sooner had Oliver caught sight of him than he vanished into stacks as though fearful at being discovered.

At length the labyrinth symbols led them to a ruined gallery hundreds of feet wide and virtually inaccessible thanks to more of the bubbling pits of tar. The stench here was abominable, and Oliver covered his mouth and nose with a handkerchief. A great rent in the ceiling let in a ruddy light, and motes of glittering volcanic dust spun in gusts of wind blown in through a wide crack in the far wall that ran from floor to ceiling. Rubble covered the ground and innumerable pages torn from the thousands of books on the cracked and broken shelves fluttered in the air like a flock of white-winged gulls.

"This must be the place," said Henry.

"How do you know?" asked Morley.

"There's nowhere else to go. This is a closed gallery."

"Apart from the great crack in the wall," pointed out Oliver.

"True, but I suspect we can discount it as a means of progress."

Oliver walked a slow circuit of the gallery's center, trying to guess how many books filled its shelves. The sheer impossibility of finding one book amongst so many was disheartening. This gallery alone was home to thousands of books, tens of thousands. The task was impossible, but wasn't everything they had achieved thus far been impossible?

"There's so many books," said Morley. "Where to begin?"

"Just as before," said Henry. "Look for the labyrinth. On a shelf, a piece of debris, drawn on the floor. It could be anywhere, so spread out."

The three men separated, each taking a different path through the rubble and scanning everything around them for the labyrinth symbol that had brought them this far. Oliver hoped that whenever Nereus-Kai had hidden the second half of his spell, it had been after whatever cataclysm had destroyed the stone staircases, for there was no way to access the higher tiers of shelves. Perhaps some rudimentary form of platform could be built from the rubble, enabling them to reach the second or third tier, but the dozens above that would forever remain beyond their reach.

While Morley searched the region around the crack in the wall and Henry the shelves and debris near where they had entered the gallery, Oliver walked a slowly widening circle at its center. He kept his eyes roving from side to side, letting his focus relax as he tried to avoid fixating on any one detail. Instead, he kept the image of the Atlantean labyrinth at the forefront of his mind and let his eyes drift as they sought a match.

Oliver's pocket watch had long since ceased keeping time, but surely hours had passed with no sign of the labyrinth symbol. He began to despair of ever finding it before their time on this world was done. He had no idea how Morley or Henry were feeling, but knew he was very nearly at the end of his endurance. If there was something here to be found, they would need to find it soon.

So exhausted was Oliver, and so subtly was the labyrinth worked into the play of rocks that he almost missed it. He stopped in his tracks and carefully retraced his steps, careful to ensure he disturbed nothing that wasn't already out of place.

Oliver moved slowly, trying to move in exactly the same way he had before. Each time he saw a hint of the symbol, it was maddeningly incomplete, but as he shifted, tilted and eventually managed to recreate his exact posture and bodily inclination, he finally saw the complete symbol.

It was a conjunction of numerous pieces of rubble, each carved with a portion of the symbol. Meaningless on their own, but viewed from a precise place and at a precise angle, they reformed in a marvel-ous piece of optical trickery to recreate the entire symbol.

"Where only those in the direst of need may seek it…," said Oliver with a wry smile.

Without moving his head, he lifted his voice so the others could hear.

"I've found it! The labyrinth, it's here."

Morley and Henry hurried over, and after a moment's explanation, Oliver moved aside to allow the others to see what he had seen. Con-fusion swiftly became understanding as each man finally formed the symbol contained in the many rocks.

"Clever," said Henry.

"We can admire the old priest's cunning later," said Morley, already setting off in the direction indicated by the Atlantean spiral, a book-shelf thick with heavy volumes of forgotten lore. He circled around one of the bubbling tar pits, grimacing distastefully as it burped a stream of polluted matter onto the ground before him. Oliver watched as Morley began running his hands along the shelves, hunting for something perhaps only detectable by touch now that they knew the labyrinth symbols would not always be so simple to find.

"Shall we?" said Henry. "The sooner we find this damn book the better. As exciting as this was to begin with, I have a bad feeling about this place. It's like…it's like it doesn't want us here. The library, I mean. Preposterous, I know; that a building could want us gone, but there you have it."

Henry shrugged, to show how ridiculous he knew he was being, but not quite convincing Oliver of his certainty. He put a hand on Henry's shoulder and shook his head.

"You're not being ridiculous, old friend," he said. "There's more than just rock in the bones of this building, but I'm not sure I want to find out what that might be."

"Never a truer word spoken," agreed Henry as they set off after Morley.

The stench of the tar pit assailed them as they approached and again it bubbled with activity, as though something beneath the sur-face sensed their approach. A series of stinking vapor pockets swelled and burst on the rippling surface of the black ooze, spattering a slick of black ichor onto the ground before Oliver. He glanced down and saw the surface was once again as smooth as glass, and reflected in its black opacity was a spiral symbol he had come to know well over the last few hours.

"Henry, wait," said Oliver.

"What?"

Oliver didn't answer, and knelt beside the tar pool. Its surface churned once again, obliterating the fleeting image of the labyrinth. The odor rising from the pool was freighted with decaying matter, protoplasmic chemical tangs and undigested matter. It was the stomach contents of a whale washed up on a beach in summer. He turned his head to the side, again hearing the faint whisper he had heard as they stood outside the library.

Tekeli-li, Tekeli-li…

Before, he had no specific idea where the sound originated. Now he knew.

It was coming from the black ooze.

"Oliver, shouldn't we be helping Morley?" asked Henry, looking in disgust at the black pool of glutinous liquid, but sensing Oliver's sudden pique of interest. "Wait, did you see something?"

"I'm not certain," replied Oliver.

Except he was certain. He'd seen the Atlantean symbol in the ooze, and there could only be one location such a placement could indicate. Oliver removed his coat and handed it to Henry, who took it with a bemused look on his face.

"Oliver, what are you doing?" asked Henry as he rolled up his sleeve.

"It's here," said Oliver, leaning down. "This is the last symbol."

"Good Lord, you cannot be contemplating what I think you are contemplating."

"Not contemplating, Henry," said Oliver, plunging his arm into the black sludge. "Doing."

Chapter Eighteen

The feeling was like immersing his arm in hot jelly filled with wriggling movement, as though an entire colony of worms surrounded his limb in curiosity. The black ooze moved in a way that no normal fluid, however viscous, should behave. No law of fluid dynamics could have explained the sucking, hungry movement of the black slurry around Oliver's arm, and there was only one inescapable conclusion.

The black fluid was aware of him on some level.

Nothing that could be called true cognition, but perhaps an animalistic understanding that something new had entered its habitat. Oliver felt its sucking, questing exploration of his flesh and tried to hold back the leprous horror its touch engendered. Instead, he opened his fingers and moved his arm back and forth through the sludgy depths.

"Oliver, for the love of God, please take your arm out of there," begged Henry.

"No, what we are looking for, it's here, I know it," said Oliver, as the suction on his arm increased. He felt himself being pulled down into the pool, and reached back with his other arm. "Hold my arm, make sure I don't get pulled in. Morley, some help would be appreciated."

Morley turned at the sound of his name and his jaw dropped open as he saw what Oliver was doing. He shook his head in disbelief, but turned from the bookshelves and ran over to help. Both Henry and Morley took hold of Oliver's shoulders. His immediate descent was halted, but he felt the pressure within the pit increase, as though whatever primal intelligence lay beneath grew angry at being denied its sport.

Oliver reached as deep as he could, forcing his hand back and forth as he searched for something to tell him he wasn't completely mad for doing this. Worm-like caresses slithered around his questing fingers, but he felt nothing else, no sign of a submerged book or any other treasure.

"It's getting stronger, Oliver," said Henry.

Oliver already knew that. The bubbling surface of the pool was getting closer to his face with every passing second, and he could sense its bristling appetite. The grip on his arm was increasingly painful, a crushing strength that was only growing more intense the longer his arm remained submerged. His face was an inch from the pool when a froth of bubbles rose to the surface, but instead of bursting to vent toxic fumes, they rolled over and Oliver found himself staring into a slick of unblinking eyes.

Milky with cataracts and red-rimmed pupils, the eyes were hideously part-evolved, but Oliver knew with sickening certainty that they saw him clearly enough. He retched in revulsion, feeling his gorge rise at the sight of hundreds of floating, disembodied eyes.

"My God," he heard Morley say. Oliver didn't dare open his mouth for fear that some of the ooze might find its way down his throat. The black liquid spilled over the edges of the pit, and Oliver heard a sickening sloshing from every corner of the gallery as the other pits of dark matter reacted to some unheard communication passing between the fluid creatures.

Then, so fleetingly he could have believed he had imagined it, Oliver's fingers brushed something solid within the protoplasmic entity. He reached for it again, feeling its sharply defined edges and scrabbling in the muck to grasp it. His fingers slipped and slithered over it, but at last he pulled it into his palm and closed a fist around it.

The effect was instantaneous and shocking in its intensity.

The pressure on Oliver's arm vanished instantly, and he found himself looking into a deep fissure in the rock, a bottomless, empty abyss that disappeared into the bowels of the planet. Dizzying vertigo seized

Oliver, and the three of them fell back from the edge of the pit with the sudden release. They sprawled, breathless, until Oliver disengaged himself from Henry and Morley. He sat back on his haunches, holding out what he had removed from the pit.

A black gem that beat like a human heart, a multi-faceted gem of darkness that was the midnight twin of the Eye of Infinite Stars.

"What is it?" asked Morley.

"I don't know," said Oliver. "But it's what we came for, I know it. This is what Nereus-Kai hid."

At the mention of the dead Atlantean priest's name, the black gem writhed in Oliver's grip and he was forced to release it. Contrary to all laws of physics and sense, the gem didn't drop, and remained suspended in the air. It spun on its central axis, and it appeared to be growing larger with every revolution. The three travelers stood and backed away as the gem began to unfold, its every facet flipping over to reveal yet more darkly reflective matter within.

"What is it doing?" said Oliver, though the question was purely rhetorical. No one could possibly have an answer. As the gem continued to expand and unfold, an anthropomorphic shape became apparent. A vastly tall, broadly built figure was forming out of the blackness, as though the combined matter of the oozing fluid within the pit had been appropriated and pressed into service giving it a form.

The blackness continued to expand until it was a titanic figure of a man, a full head and shoulders taller than Oliver, who stood just over six foot. Like a three dimensional shadow peeled from a wall and given its freedom, the shape had no features beyond its outline, though hints of crashing waves and myriad looping spiral patterns churned invisibly in its substance.

Oliver knew he should be afraid of this dark apparition, but felt nothing beyond an infinite sadness at its presence. Gossamer-fine mist spun around the form, like oily smoke curling from a gasoline fire, giving the form the suggestion of billowing robes or vestments.

"Nereus-Kai," he whispered, and the shadow man seemed to shudder at the sound.

"Good God, Oliver, do you believe this is he?" asked Henry.

"I know it is," he replied, tears welling in his eyes as the most awful sense of loss and pain filled him. "Or at least a remnant of what he once was."

"The priest didn't just hide his spell on Celaeno, he hid himself…," breathed Morley in awe.

"Oliver, Morley, look…," whispered Henry, pointing to the other pits and cracks in the ground where the tarry liquids bubbled and seethed. Vast black shapes were hauling their gelatinous bulk from the tar, hideous and formless beasts without shape or anatomy, merely shifting amoeba-like congeries of half-formed, fluid-like tentacles, and horridly malformed proto-limbs. A morbid greenish illumination flickered across their inconstant bulk as hundreds of rheumy eyes and gnashing mouths oozed into existence. Each organ existed only momentarily before being subsumed in the gelatinous mass once again, only to be replaced by hundreds more a second later.

"The guardians of the library," said Morley, eyes wide in astonishment. "The texts spoke of the shoggoths being long dead."

"Clearly the texts were wrong," said Henry, as the beasts blocked the entrance to the gallery with their shifting, undulant bodies. "Are they dangerous?"

"Oh, absurdly so," said Morley. "If we try to take so much as a page beyond the library's walls they will destroy us in an instant."

"Now you tell us," hissed Oliver as the towering figure of Nereus-Kai extended one of its ebon limbs, fingers outstretched, and Oliver felt his own arm rising to meet it. The sadness he felt at the sight of this pathetic, wretched shard of a man who had once overturned the world was almost too much to bear. Emotions surged through Oliver, a complex morass of guilt, colossal pride, loneliness, regret, and hatred—all distilled into a cosmically potent wellspring of energy.

Energy that Nereus-Kai was offering to pass on.

"Oliver, are you sure about this?" said Henry, keeping one eye on the creatures Morley had named the shoggoths. The beasts neither advanced nor retreated, but stood sentinel upon intruders who had accessed something of the library's contents.

"No," said Oliver as memories that were not his flashed through his mind: painful, horrific recollections of a war against monsters and a desperate fight for survival, when the world was brought to the edge of ruin. That war had been fought with weapons too terrible to imagine and had brought the human race to extinction's precipice. Tears flowed down Oliver's face, and he knew Nereus-Kai, or whatever remaining aspect of that mighty priest this shade represented, was not showing him these images to hurt him.

He was showing him them as a warning.

To show him of the consequences of failure.

And to remind him of the price of success.

"I understand," said Oliver, and their fingertips touched.

* * *

A cold wind whipped through Rex the moment he stepped down onto the platform, cutting through his thick winter coat like it wasn't even there. He'd heard the stories about this city, how cold it was and how the wind sliced between its soaring skyscrapers like a thousand icy knives. He knew men who'd skied the glaciers on Mount Nygaard in Norway and said it wasn't as cold as this place. Right now, Rex could well believe it.

The station was a busy one, as he'd expected, and he hefted the kit bag he'd purchased at the Army surplus store on his way to the Oakland Terminal (a station that, for some reason, the locals called the Mole), where he'd bought the fastest ticket back east. Of course, fastest wasn't quite as fast as Chuck had crossed the country, and the train had steamed its way through Santa Barbara, Los Angeles, Tucson, El Paso, San Antonio, Houston, New Orleans, Jackson, Memphis, and St. Louis before finally reaching its destination. Every stop along the way was a nightmare of waiting and worrying, and each hour that passed in travel was a lifetime.

Rex walked up to the nearest guy in the uniform of the Southern Pacific and tipped his hat.

"Hey, buddy, where can a guy get the next train to New York?"

"Just over there, sir," said the man, pointing to a ticket booth thronged with passengers eager to be on their way.

"Thanks," said Rex pushing through crowds on the platform to join the line.

Everyone ahead of him looked too well-fed, but Rex knew they weren't fat, just well wrapped up. He wished he'd thought to bring more warm clothes, but he hadn't really expected this place to be as cold as he'd been led to believe. He'd left San Francisco in a mad scramble, too fast to even leave a message for Oliver and the others, but once he made contact again he was sure they'd understand his reasons for leaving in such a hurry.

Depending on when the next train east departed, he'd see about placing a call to the Jesuit College and leaving a message for Hillshore. Or if he could charm the operator enough, maybe he'd be able to get Hillshore's home number—if he even had a telephone. Judging by the wax cylinders in his office, it seemed the Englishman liked to keep things old-fashioned.

Rex stamped his feet to keep them warm as he joined the queue, a trick Gabriel had taught him while they'd been waiting for Chuck's plane to be prepped for the second leg of their journey west. Thinking back to that moment told him he really should have known this place was going to be cold. Rex shrugged, thinking that soon it wouldn't matter. He'd be slumped in a Pullman car with his pencil burning up the pages of the legal pad he'd bought from the train's purser.

Every stop along the way, he'd filed copy with Harvey, nothing as good as his telling of the transcontinental trip by air, but good enough to at least keep his editor from firing him. Rex didn't think he'd worked this hard since Egypt, when he and Fieldsy had run a bet to see how many stories they could file with Reuters before the end of a booze-fueled week of unrest and revolution.

He didn't really want to write, but it kept his mind from dwelling on the telegram Minnie had sent him and the fear that clawed his heart every time he thought of it.

Minnie was returning from France, which was amazing news, but for one problem.

She was heading to Arkham and she didn't know that Alexander was now their enemy.

Minnie would walk right into harm's way, and Rex had no way to contact her.

He'd left messages with Harvey at the *Advertiser* to tell her to stay away from Alexander if she made contact with the office, and had left identical messages with Minnie's folks. They didn't care for him much, but he'd made them promise to pass on his warning as soon as she made contact. He hoped that would be enough to keep her from Alexander, but he couldn't be sure.

So here he was, eastbound to New York, dashing to rescue the woman he loved from a black-hearted villain.

Rex almost laughed aloud at the absurd sentimentalism of the gesture, its gothic melodrama like something from a dime-store novel or a Douglas Fairbanks movie.

But the danger was very real, and the thought of Minnie walking unwittingly into the lair of the monster that had started this madness was too terrible to contemplate.

A hand tugged his elbow as he neared the front of the queue and Rex smelled the hobo before he saw him. He pulled his elbow away as the bum shook a tin cup beside him.

"Ah, God love ye, sir, you wouldn't be depriving a man of a chance to get himself a wee bite, now would ye?" said the hobo.

"A bite?" said Rex, without turning around. "I give you any change and you're just going to spend it on booze."

"Ah, now, and isn't it every Irishman's right to get himself a drink, eh?" said the hobo. "Don't you agree, Mr. Murphy?"

Rex turned at the sound of his name, and stared in astonishment at a man he had last seen cut to ribbons after a nasty encounter with the same flesh-eating ghouls that had been praying on the young women of Arkham.

"Mr. Edwards?" said Rex.

"Sure now, aren't we pals enough you can call me Finn?"

Rex nodded, still too amazed that he was talking to Finn Edwards to think straight.

"Yeah, I know, I don't look my best these days, Mr. Murphy," continued Finn, "but that's what happens when you don't travel first class like the swells."

"What are you doing in Chicago?" said Rex as a murmur of disapproval built behind him in the queue. Rex ignored it. "Last time I saw you was in a hospital bed at St. Mary's."

"Aye, and wasn't it grand being tended to by all the pretty nurses, but I took to me heels as soon as they said I was fit and well."

"You never made contact with us again."

"No, and for that I am truly sorry, Mr. Murphy," said Finn with a genuine sigh of regret. "But I had me some…difficulties with a bunch of lads up Newburyport way, and let's just say they're not good Catholic boys with a handy line in forgiveness."

"I see," said Rex, knowing full well how dangerous and bloody the liquor wars could be. "Then Chicago sure seems like a risky place to come if you're having bootlegger problems."

"Aye, you'd have the truth of it, Mr. Murphy, that you would, but see I'm only making what I'd call a temporary stop here. I'm actually trying to get back to Arkham."

"You are?"

"Aye, though if you were to ask me why, I'd be hard pressed to give you a reason that wouldn't sound like I was stark, raving mad."

Rex could relate to that.

"Funnily enough, I'm heading there myself," said Rex. "To rescue a fair maiden, so to speak."

"Grand," said Finn. "Jaysus, aren't we a pair of soft-headed eejits, Mr. Murphy?"

The queue moved forward and Rex found himself at the ticket booth, a hatched-faced man with a bushy white beard enquiring where he wanted to go. Rex looked from the ticket-master to Finn and pulled his billfold from his coat pocket.

"Arkham, Massachusetts," said Rex. "Two tickets, please."

* * *

The moment of connection was wondrous and agonizing at the same time, a pulsing moment of fiery rebirth. And what birth was not painful? The dark man before Oliver seemed to swell until it seemed the great vault of the library could no longer contain his immensity. Though he had no mouth with which to speak, a string of burning letters that had no business ever being spoken in this particular order seared themselves onto Oliver's mind.

This was the second half of the spell, the means they sought to thwart Alexander's plans to unmake the world. The words he had copied from the ancient pages of the *Necronomicon* chained themselves to these new incantations, formulae, and damned consonants. A woven symphony of unwords that violated the human capacity for speech with their blasphemous sounds.

The power of the Atlantean priest, even in this much-reduced form was immense, the touch on Oliver's mind indiscriminate and ungentle. Unvisited caverns of his memories were filled with illumination and a host of memories long thought forgotten were ushered out into the light.

In one sublime instant, Oliver lived his entire life over again, every organic memory stored by the inadequate fleshy organ within his skull flashing through his consciousness with a speed beyond understanding, yet within his grasp to experience. He lived his happy boyhood years in Baltimore, the love of his household, the years at Brown, and everything in between.

The words of Basil Elton, the lighthouse keeper of Kingsport returned to him.

You have strong friends and more allies than you know…

Never more was a truer word spoken, saw Oliver as he comprehended the array of men and women who had supported him, befriended him, loved him, and been part of the warp and weft of the grand tapestry of his life. His had been a life lived well, a journey favored by kind stars and blessed with fine companions.

And with that valedictory thought uppermost in his head, the connection to Nereus-Kai was broken and Oliver sagged into Henry and Morley's arms. They caught him and lowered him to the ground as he let out a great, heaving exhalation.

"Good God, Oliver, are you all right?" cried Henry.

Oliver nodded, watching as the silhouette form of the long-dead priest began to fade, becoming fainter with every heartbeat. Its task fulfilled, it had no ties to bind it to this place and its matter was falling to dissolution. Behind the priest's decaying outline, Oliver saw the seething mass of shoggoths, their protean forms growing ever more restive. By means of senses Oliver could not begin to guess at, they knew he now carried knowledge not meant to leave the library.

"I'm completely fine," said Oliver, taking a deep breath and feeling more energized than he had in months. "Really, I feel quite exhilarated. Stronger than ever, in fact."

Oliver climbed to his feet, the earlier enervation and slump of spirit now quite forgotten. His body was stronger than ever, reinvigorated by contact with Nereus-Kai, as though the Atlantean had bridged a gap in human existence spanning tens of thousands of years to impart a measure of his own strength to his successor…

"That's what I am," said Oliver.

"What?" asked Morley.

"I'm his successor," said Oliver. "I'm to finish what he began."

"A dangerous mantle to inherit," said Morley.

"If I ever get the chance," said Oliver, backing away from the roiling shoggoths as they advanced like a dark tide into the gallery. They moved like a black lava flow, unhurried, but devastating nonetheless. Where they touched the rock it was pulverized beneath their bulk or pushed aside by quasi-formed limbs extruded for that purpose and then withdrawn back into their plasmic bodies.

Blind, idiot eyes burst and formed on the liquid surfaces of their bodies, and that damnable recitation was gibbered from every mouth like a mantra whose meaning they had long forgotten.

Tekeli-li, Tekeli-li, Tekeli-li…

"These things are not going to let us leave, are they?" said Oliver.

"Did those texts that erroneously supposed them extinct give any clue as to how they might be fought or evaded?" asked Henry.

"That detail was, sad to say, absent," said Morley. "Though I welcome any suggestions."

Oliver was about to answer when he heard the faint scratching sound come again. He looked around for its source, but was again frustrated. The sound was familiar, and it took a moment for him to recall where he had heard it before.

In Morley's apartment, right before the reptilian hound had torn the place apart.

"Morley?" he said.

"I hear it," said Morley, his eyes alight with comprehension. "That's it, that's how he knew…"

"How *who* knew?" said Oliver. "Knew what?"

"Alexander," said Morley with sudden fury. "It's how he knew how to find us all this time. How else could he have known to dispatch those flying creatures to attack our plane or bind the burrower beneath to demolish the Markham-Hyde collection?"

"How?" demanded Henry, as the scratching sound grew more distinct.

"The creature he loosed when he knew you had consulted me, the hunting beast that stalks the angles between time and space! It had my spoor all along and to a sorcerer of Alexander's skill, it would be a simple matter to set other, less-spatially dependent creatures to destroy us using that self-same scent. Damn it all, how could I have been so naïve to allow myself to believe it had forsaken the hunt?"

"It's here? Now?" said Oliver.

"Soon," said Morley, turning in circles as he scanned the corners and angles of the gallery, from its vaulted ceiling to its junctions of wall and tiers of shelves. "Can't you hear it tearing at the interstices? Soon it will have ripped itself a crack through which its ghastly body can manifest."

"I don't suppose you have any more of that lunar caustic about your person?" asked Oliver. "Or your shotgun?"

"No, regrettably not," said Morley, looking up in horror as the confluence of roof slabs directly above them began to warp, their solidity being undone by a creature to whom stellar distances and geological epochs of time were no barrier in its pursuit of quarry. Rock and dust fell from the roof as a deafening howl filled the gallery. Billowing, lightning-shot smoke spilled outward, like blood red paint poured into a jar of water. It swam in the air against all natural laws, swelling like a monstrous animal fetus growing too fast and too unnaturally. Limbs extruded from the smoky mass, spindly and lathered with immaterial flesh that stretched and glistened like insectile chitin. Long jaws and compound eyes were agonizingly birthed, followed by a fleshy tongue that was more tentacle than taste organ.

"What do we do, Morley?" asked Henry, retrieving a hefty weight of stone from the floor to use as a weapon.

"That will be no defense against such a creature," said Morley.

"Once a soldier, always a soldier," said Henry.

The howling beast's body forced itself from the unnatural geometries the roof, though Oliver could yet make out no real solidity of form, merely a smoky outline of threshing blade limbs and the predator's maw. In seconds the entirety of the creature would have forced the alien matter of its body into the gallery.

And then they would all die.

That it was their astral forms that would be torn to shreds made no difference. Morley had made it clear what would happen to their Earthly bodies were these imagined physiologies to be killed.

Oliver followed Henry's example and found himself a stout club of rock.

"Were you not listening, Oliver?" said Morley. "You cannot fight such a beast with a rock. Nor can it be defeated by the jawbone of an ass, sharp sticks, foul language, or even a gatling gun."

"Perhaps not, but better to attempt some resistance than to meekly accept our fate."

"Of course you're right, Oliver," said Morley with a serene calm that Oliver liked not at all.

"Then pick up a damn rock and let's go down fighting."

Morley smiled at Oliver and shook his head. "No, my old friend. I have never shirked from the clamor of battle, but I think knowledge shall be our best weapon in this case. Well, that and a tide of angry shoggoths."

"What are you talking about?"

"Gentlemen, it has been my honor and privilege to have fought the good fight with you," said Morley turning and running toward the nearest shelf of books. Before Oliver could shout a warning, the screaming hunting beast completed its violent birth into the world and its spiked, many-angled, howling form fell through the distorted air.

It landed on bent and twisted limbs that sparked with rasping claws and spines. Its form spun and warped within its own orbit, a spiraling tumult of forms too alien to name. It defied any easy classification of form, but Oliver's terrified mind imprinted a vaguely canine form to its myriad guises, grafting form and shape and function to its predatory angles.

Morley had a book in his arms, a heavy tome with mahogany binding and faded lettering, and he was running. He ran with all the speed of an Olympian athlete, one arm pistoning as he bolted for the vast crack in the rear wall of the gallery that led out onto the desolate plains beyond.

No sooner had he set off than the shoggoths barreled forward in a roaring tsunami of oily black matter, their nonsensical chanting rising to a deafening crescendo. The hunting beast pounced, lithe as a cat, whipping blade limbs and snapping jaw aiming to tear Morley apart.

Oliver and Henry had no choice but to bolt for the other side of the gallery or else be crushed by the thunderous mass of the shoggoths. Oliver leapt for a boulder the size of a Model T and dragged himself onto its upper surfaces as the protoplasmic beast caromed against it. Weighing tens of tons, the boulder spun around like a pebble, nearly throwing Oliver down into the morass of glutinous black matter. Henry had scaled one of the lower shelves, hauling his legs up beneath him as the library's amorphous guardians pursued Morley.

"No!" cried Oliver as he saw the hunting hound smash Morley from his feet with a swipe of a vast, taloned paw of stringy meat and iron-hard bone. "Oh, God! Morley, no!"

The hound reared up on multiple hind legs, howling its triumph.

"Morley!" screamed Oliver as the hound descended upon his friend.

And then the tide of shoggoths smashed into the hunting beast like an awful collision of freight trains.

Their bodies slammed it against the wall of shelves, sending an avalanche of books raining down. Bodies that appeared to be liquid and compliant now turned solid and murderous. Whipping tentacles of unimaginable density pummeled the hound as a thousand broken-toothed mouths formed to bite savage chunks from its body.

The hound fought back, its own body easily capable of reforming in response to attack. Cleaving limbs, tearing claws, and its trap-like jaws tore into the mass of the shoggoths, ripping vast clods of matter loose from the writhing mass of tentacles and lashing pseudopods.

It became impossible to separate the swirling combatants, their inconstant anatomies flowing and running into one another as they fought. Morley was lost from sight as the floor cracked and the walls broke apart with the violence of the creatures' struggle. The gallery's structure groaned under stresses it was never intended to endure as vast slabs of rock fell from the roof. Oliver shielded his eyes from the billowing clouds of dust and wreckage.

"Henry!" shouted Oliver, seeing only a dim outline of his friend, still clinging to the shelves.

"Oliver!" returned Henry. "You are still alive! I feared the worst."

Oliver leapt onto the wall, gripping the edge of the shelves tightly, and began shimmying toward Henry. Hand over hand he made his way along the shelf, holding tight as the monsters continued to fight and reduce this repository of ancient knowledge to rubble. At last he reached Henry, and the two men shared a look of profound relief.

"Come on," he shouted over the crashing din of battle.

"Where?"

"Outside," said Oliver.

"But the guardians!" protested Henry.

"Are otherwise occupied," said Oliver. "Now come on!"

And so saying, Oliver dropped from the shelf. The floor was buckled and smashed, like the aftermath of a powerful earthquake. Slabs of rock jutted upwards at strange angles and plumes of dust and stinking vapor billowed from the crypts below. Oliver landed badly and fell to one knee.

Henry dropped next to him and hauled him to his feet.

"Up!" shouted Henry. "If we're going to make a run for it, then let's damn well do it!"

Oliver nodded, and together they ran for the crack in the wall from which Morley had sought to escape. Except Oliver knew he had no expectation of escape, only the hope that the library's guardians would be distraction enough to keep the hound at bay and allow Oliver to make a break for freedom.

Oliver fought his way over a nightmare landscape of broken boulders, rubble, and debris. His hands were torn bloody, but he kept going. Morley had bought them time with his incredible sacrifice, time Oliver was not about to waste. Henry forged his own path, keeping pace with Oliver with the steely determination of an ex-soldier. Together, they reached the vast rip in the building's structure and though neither had expected to live to reach it, neither could bring himself to leave a friend behind without a last look over their shoulder.

But there was nothing to see.

The hound had been swallowed by the thrashing mass of black tentacles and sopping, tarry flesh, its angular body incapable of harming a host of beasts whose bodies were utterly without form and whose very existence was defined by that formlessness.

Oliver saw no sign of Morley and emotion threatened to choke him.

Myriad eyes turned to face them, but there was nothing these guardian creatures could do to stop them from bearing their precious knowledge from the confines of the library. Oliver silently bade Morley farewell, knowing he would grieve his old mentor later, and swearing that Alexander would pay for all the lives he had ruined. He and Henry stepped from the library as the boiling mass of dark, oily flesh lapped against the jagged tear. Unable to stop the two men, they battered themselves impotently against the walls, but neither Henry nor Oliver looked back.

Such was the scale of the library that it took them several hours to circle around to its imposing facade, time in which neither man said so much as a single word to the other. When at last they reached the glacially still lake, Henry started to make his way along the jetty toward the boat that sat unmoving on the water.

Oliver took his arm and shook his head.

"No, Henry," said Oliver, staring at the sinister darkness of the glacially cold lake. "I suspect the shoggoths are not the only things preventing trespassers from leaving here with stolen knowledge."

Henry looked out over the water, now made even more unwelcome by the thought of a submarine behemoth just waiting to attack.

"Then how are we to return?"

Oliver looked up to the red sky as hot winds brought more squalls of mist and dust down from the mountains. Morley would know how. Morley always had an answer, a riddle from a cryptic book that allowed them to proceed.

But Morley wasn't here, and Oliver could think of only one route home.

"We call to Hillshore and Gabriel," said Oliver. "And we hope they hear us."

The stink of of smelling salts filled the front room, together with other, less recognizable aromas as Hillshore brewed up various concoctions from Morley's tersely inscribed notes. Gabriel sat on a stool beside Oliver's chair, aghast at the change that had come over the man. He wore the face of an old man, aged before his time and that change was only getting worse. His skin had gone from pale to ashen, like a corpse dragged out of the Hudson on a winter's morning.

Henry was marginally better, though he too looked drawn and gaunt. But Morley, Jesus…

Morley had collapsed into himself, his body looking like it had had all the air sucked out of it and the flesh dissolved from the bones. Morley Dean was visibly wasting away before them.

"William!" shouted Gabriel into the kitchen. "How's it going with Morley's brew?"

"I'm getting there," answered Hillshore, "but Morley's handwriting is not the easiest in the world to decipher."

"Well, hurry it up, I don't think these guys have got much longer."

As if to confirm that point, Oliver's chest heaved, as though fighting to draw a breath, and Gabriel squeezed his hand tightly.

"Come on, Oliver," he said. "Hold on. Come back to us, y'hear?"

Gabriel looked over at Henry, seeing the old man slumped in his chair like a drunk. The left side of his face was locked rigid, like a stroke victim, and red-tinged foam gathered at the corner of his mouth.

"That goes double for you too, Henry."

Hillshore arrived bearing a platter of cups and a pot that steamed with a noxious reek of elements that seemed more likely to finish them off than bring them back. The Englishman placed the tray in the center of his table, and placed three cups in a row on the tray.

"I think, given the circumstances, we can forego the usual etiquette," he said.

"Yeah, I think so," snapped Gabriel. "Just pour the damn drink."

"Times of stress are no excuse for poor manners," said Hillshore, pouring three cups of a yellowish liquid that looked like something siphoned from a septic tank. Gabriel's nose wrinkled and he felt tears prick the corners of his eyes at some acidic property of the steam.

"Christ, what the hell's in that?"

Hillshore shrugged as he filled the last cup. "Some ordinary household items, together with some powder Morley left for this express purpose. Heaven only knows what it is, but his instructions were most precise, if somewhat cryptically rendered on the page."

"Here, pass me a cup," said Gabriel, snapping his fingers. "I'll give this one to Oliver, you give one to Morley."

"And Henry?"

"We'll get to him afterwards. You've heard of triage, right? Well, Morley's the one that needs help the most, so hop to it, Professor."

Hillshore nodded and Gabriel took the proffered cup. Oliver was in no state to drink on his own, so Gabriel tilted his head back and gently pried open his mouth. Such was the rigid paralysis induced by Hillshore's drug, that once he'd moved Oliver into position, he didn't need to hold him there. It was like moving a shop's dummy.

The vile brew in the cup smoked and bubbled with heat and God knew what else. He wouldn't willingly pour this down someone's throat, but what choice did he have?

"This is gonna hurt like a son of a bitch, Oliver," said Gabriel. "And you'll have one hell of a sore throat when you wake up, but I you can yell at me later, okay? Just so long as you wake up."

Mouthing a prayer to a god he no longer believed in, Gabriel tipped the contents of the cup down Oliver's throat. He could see the angry red weals rise up on the inside of Oliver's mouth, but beyond the physiological response, Gabriel might as well have been pouring warm honey down Oliver's throat for all the reaction he got.

"It's not working," he said, hearing the gurgle of liquid pouring down Henry's throat.

"This is not all Morley's notes tell us to do, remember?"

"Yeah, yeah," said Gabriel, dropping the cup on the carpet. He saw Hillshore's irritated glance, and shook his head. He'd deal with the Englishman's ire on his treatment of the teacup later. "You're right, we've got to bring them back, yeah?"

"We are their guides," said Hillshore, carefully placing his cup back on its saucer. "We bring them home with our voices, our memories, and our shared experiences, yes? Speak to Oliver, speak to him of the things you have done together."

"Shouldn't you do that? I mean, you know him better than I do."

"But how well do you know Morley? Or Henry?" pointed out Hillshore. "I at least am acquainted with Henry via his case notes and my previous examination."

"And Morley?"

Hillshore didn't answer at first and Gabriel shot him a glance.

"You spoke of triage?" said Hillshore imperiously. "This is no different. Speak to Oliver, I will speak to Henry. And if we can, we will both speak to Morley. Understood?"

Gabriel nodded, now seeing the solid bedrock within Hillshore that many failed to see.

"Okay," he said, getting a grip on himself. He turned to look at Oliver, horrified at the transformation this journey had inflicted upon him.

"Right, Oliver," he began. "It's been a while, but here goes. We haven't known each other that long, but I stood beside you when the bullets were flying and there were monsters all around us. You remember that? I don't think you'd ever held a gun before then, but you shot like you meant it. Couldn't hit anything worth a damn, but you went in with me and you didn't look back. There's not many men I can say that about, and I've stood shoulder to shoulder with some of the best."

Was it just his imagination, or did one of Oliver's eyelids flicker?

"Right, and then when you turned up on my doorstep. Christ, I don't want to think how close you came to getting a bullet through your head. And right away, I knew it was trouble, but God damn it, I couldn't walk away from it. You're a good man, Oliver, and this ain't ending here, you get me? We don't travel the whole way across the country just for you to check out seated in a damn armchair, you hear me? The man that brought Amanda out of that burning basement doesn't get to go that way. No way, not on my watch…"

Gabriel's words trailed off, and his head sank to his chest. Dimly, he heard Hillshore speaking in low tones to Henry, but the words were too soft to hear. He caught references to Henry's military service and to what the Englishman knew of Oliver and Henry's shared friendship. Hillshore barely knew Henry, but he was still talking, still finding ways to bring him back. Gabriel knew he could do nothing less, and he searched for a common memory that wasn't simply a recounting of the last few days.

"Damn it," he said. "I got nothing, Professor. I'm all out."

He gripped Oliver's hand tightly, feeling the thinness of the bones beneath. It felt like he was holding the hand of a wizened grandfather, wheezing out his last breaths on a hospital bed.

"Oliver, you're coming back and you're going to damn well finish this thing, and once we put Alexander six feet under, we're going to go for a steak dinner at Aunt Lucy's. I'm going to bring a bottle of twenty-year-old malt, and we're going to drink that bastard dry. And if any flatfoot tries to stop us, I'll tell him to go to hell, because we just saved the world. You hear me?"

And it seemed Oliver did, for Gabriel felt the pressure of his grip returned.

Gabriel looked up and he felt like laughing as he saw the vacant, empty look fade from Oliver's eyes. The color surged back into his face as his back arched and Oliver drew in a great, sucking breath, like a drowning man brought miraculously to the surface.

"I got him, William, I got him!"

Oliver's hands clenched into fists and Gabriel flinched as he let out a piercing scream.

Behind him, Henry coughed and spluttered as his spirit was dragged back to his body, the look of a corpse fading from his flesh as the spark of animation and vitality was breathed back into him. Henry doubled up, retching and dry heaving, but clearly back in the seat of his consciousness. Gabriel stood and took hold of Oliver's shoulders, pressing him back into his chair.

"Oliver!" he cried. "Oliver. It's me, Gabriel. You're back. You're back in San Francisco. In William's house. You're back, it's over!"

Oliver fought him, but after such an ordeal, he was no match for Gabriel's strength.

"Oliver!" shouted Gabriel, in a voice used to cutting across the lines of strikebreakers.

Gradually Oliver's struggles subsided and he looked up at Gabriel with recognition and relief.

"Gabriel? Good God, man, I thought we'd never see you again."

"You're back," said Gabriel. "And Henry, too."

"Morley!" cried Oliver, attempting to rise, but finding that the effort was quite beyond him.

Gabriel turned and found Hillshore kneeling beside Morley Dean, reading from notes prepared by the very man he was trying to save.

"Help me up, Gabriel," commanded Oliver, and Gabriel nodded.

Hooking an arm under Oliver's shoulders, Gabriel lifted Oliver from the chair and brought him closer to Morley. He kicked over a stool from beside the fireplace and deposited Oliver next to his old mentor, but kept a firm grip on his shoulders.

"Morley," said Oliver, taking his old friend's hand. "It's Oliver, we made it back. You did it."

Hillshore helped Henry over, and both he and Oliver spoke to Morley, telling him of their safe return. Only after a few minutes, did Gabriel realize they were not speaking to Morley with the intention of bringing him back.

They were saying goodbye.

"God damn it all to hell," swore Gabriel, slamming a fist into his palm. "We didn't know enough about Morley and we left it too late. This is our fault."

Hillshore stood beside him and shook his head. "No, I fear that no amount of ministrations on our part could have brought Morley Dean back to us."

Gabriel looked up as tears filled his eyes.

"No," he said, moving past Oliver and Henry to place two fingers on Morley's neck. "He's still alive, so he's still out there. We can bring him back. Oliver, you know Morley best, speak to him for God's sake. Speak to him about Brown University or something! Your Alaskan expedition! Something, come on, before it's too late."

"I'm afraid it's already too late for Morley," said Oliver.

"Why?" demanded Gabriel. "What happened while you were gone? Why didn't Morley come back with you both?"

"The hunting beast," said Oliver. "The one that destroyed his apartment in New York? It finally caught up to him."

"You mean he's dead?" asked Gabriel, shaking his head. "No, that can't be. Look, he's still alive, he has a pulse. How can he be dead?"

Oliver let out a shuddering breath, and Gabriel forced himself to do likewise. His simmering grief was making him angry, and no one made good decisions or spoke with a sensible tongue while in the grip of anger.

"We found the second part of Nereus-Kai's spell," said Oliver, "but the library's guardians were not about to let us take it from there. Morley bought us time to escape."

"How?"

"Morley was caught in the midst of a battle between the hunting beast and the library's guardians," said Oliver, and Gabriel saw he was fighting to contain his emotions. "He did not make it out."

"So that's it? Is he…gone…for good?"

Oliver shared a look with Henry and said, "I don't know, Gabriel. I wish I did."

Henry said, "I don't know if there is any correlation to what I experienced in the Dreamlands, but I remember Morley saying that if the spirit died, the body would die too."

"So how does that help us?" asked Gabriel.

"Morley's body is patently still alive," said Henry. "It is entirely possible that his mind is still out there, looking for a way back."

"You're right," said Hillshore. "Then we will not give up on Morley."

"We won't," said Oliver. "Just like I never gave up on Henry."

"So how do we get him back?" said Gabriel, but only silence answered his question.

Eventually Oliver pulled himself to his feet and said, "I think the one person best qualified to answer that is the one whose spirit is lost to us. And we do not have time to bring him back now."

"You're just going to leave him?"

Oliver nodded, and Gabriel saw something die in him, a decision made that he hated but which had to be made.

"For now, yes," said Oliver. "If Morley is still out there, we'll find him, but we don't have time to do it now. William, you have already done so much, more than we could ever have asked of you, but I must ask one more boon."

"You do not need to ask, Oliver," said Hillshore. "Morley's care will be my number one priority, my friend. I will have him taken to the Presidio's medical facility, and if there is a way to bring him back, rest assured I shall do my utmost to find it."

Oliver shook Hillshore's hand. "Thank you, William. When this business is concluded, I will return to San Francisco to help you."

"As will I," said Henry. "I owe Morley Dean my life."

"And I'm in, too," said Gabriel. "If there's anything I can actually do."

Oliver placed a hand on Gabriel's shoulder. "By God, man. You brought me back, I should be surprised if there is anything a man like you can't do."

"I don't know about that, but thanks anyway," said Gabriel, though Oliver's words had touched him deeply. He took a deep breath and said, "So we're a man down, what do we do now?"

All four men shared a solemn look. With Morley left to Hillshore's care and Rex's whereabouts unknown, it was left to Oliver, Gabriel, and Henry to stand against Alexander.

And that left only one possible destination.

"We leave for Arkham," said Oliver. "Tonight."

* * *

The machine stood starkly silver against the night sky, a gleaming affront to all laws of physics and reality. Kate Winthrop's theories underpinned its construction and her calculations had helped refine its axis of spin, speed variables, and a hundred other aspects of its design.

Knowing that, Kate knew that no other person on Earth could hate themselves more right now.

She watched the ghoulish creatures attaching yet more lengths of cable to what she had come to understand were alien generator mechanisms. Kate had studied the waveforms of that energy on glass-fronted display panels, and knew that whatever motive force empowered the device did so by means no human technology was capable of replicating.

Kate slumped against her workbench, exhausted beyond any level of tiredness she had ever known. Even in her undergraduate days she had never felt this tired. But then her undergraduate days hadn't been filled with terror and pain (at least until Professor Young's terrible accident in the laboratory). Her notes were strewn around the bench, marked with technical notations that, on any other day, would have earned her the highest accolades from the greatest universities of the world.

But if Kate had her way she would burn everything.

She had tried to do just that with the heated tip of a soldering iron, but the paper had proved to be utterly indestructible. Neither fire nor water could damage it, and she could not tear it however much she tried. She could write upon it as normal, but once written upon, no mark she made could be unmade.

Kate sat in what was now her laboratory, the same sterile workplace she had first encountered Alexander Templeton. She knew better than to assume she was truly alone. Once, she had tried to steal a pair of bladed clippers to use as a weapon, but no sooner had she secreted it about her person than the shambling corpse-man, Charles, had come in and removed it.

The memory brought a shudder to her limbs and a moan of distaste to her lips.

Following her attempt to sabotage the device, Professor Templeton had allowed Charles to beat her and, but for some deep-rooted instinct to obey, Kate felt sure he would have killed her. As it was, her struggles had earned her a mass of purple bruises down her arms, a swollen jaw, and a pair of black eyes. Nothing that had prevented her from being forced to work after a few hours rest, just enough to remind her that no delays or interference would be tolerated.

Afterwards she had tried to kill herself.

Using the soldering iron to shatter one of the glass readout screens, Kate had wrenched out a long, dagger-like shard and brought it up to her neck, fully intending to cut her throat. The edge had barely pierced the skin at her jugular when a screeching sonic wave filled the laboratory and the glass turned to powder in her hands.

The broken machine had been repaired during her following sleep cycle and from that day onwards, Charles Warren watched her every move like a Komodo dragon just waiting for its prey to succumb to the bacteria and venom of its bite. The stench of his rotting body filled the laboratory, and the loathsome touch of his hungry eyes upon her flesh sickened Kate to her stomach.

She had seen Alexander Templeton only once since their first meeting, standing at the edge of the hillside and looking down on the twinkling lights of Arkham through a sheeting torrent of rain. Kate was soaked through, but welcomed the discomfort. Professor Templeton had appeared at her side and she had been shocked at the transformations wracking his body. His arm hung at his side, appearing to be completely paralyzed, and the necrotic black lines rising up over his collar had spread across his neck and face in an oily spiderweb.

Droplets of water followed the curve of the lines, as though they were grooves in his skin.

"Soon this will be gone," Alexander had said. "Washed away by the dark waters of a reborn god."

"Someone will stop you," Kate had said, more out of a need for defiance than any real expectation she would be proved right.

Alexander shook his head, though the gesture was clearly difficult. "No one can stop me. No one knows there is anything *to* stop. At least no one left alive."

"Someone will have noticed that I'm gone," said Kate. "Professor Pabodie or Dr. Dyer will see I'm not in the laboratory and make enquiries."

Alexander laughed and said, "If you are missed at all, the people who take pains to keep out of your way will be glad of your absence. In the end it won't matter, the device is almost complete."

That was true, the device's calibrations were all but finished, and though she had tried to stretch the task for as long as possible in the hope that someone might stop this insanity, Kate knew in her heart that no one was coming.

"And then the rest of the world will go away too…," she said.

"And who will be left to miss that?" said Alexander.

* * *

Until she set foot on the dock of the Port of New York, Minnie hadn't realized just how much she'd missed the States. The air scooched into her lungs like an old friend, wet and cold and filled with a heady mix of saltwater, oil and gumption. Rain barraged the docks, but that didn't keep them from being awash with people: stevedores already unloading the baggage from the cavernous holds, porters waiting to take the bags and trunks of the rich folk, friends and family of those who were returning home.

And, of course, the unscrupulous just waiting to take advantage of those who were new to these shores. She saw a few unsavory types lock their eyes on her as she descended the gangway, but gave them all withering looks that told them she could manage her one bag perfectly well, thank you very much.

The day was already on the way out, the sun folding itself over the horizon, and the shadows of New York were thrown out over the docks like giant black fingers. The wooden gangway was slippery with rain, so Minnie held tight to the gilded handrail as she made her way down to the quayside. As much as she had convinced herself that she'd miss Paris, she couldn't deny the thrill of getting back to her own country, brash and new and vulgar though it might be.

It had been a hell of a journey getting here, though.

In the aftermath of the disastrous séance in Violet's cabin, Minnie had become a virtual *persona non grata* aboard the *Ile de France*. The comte's spirit had departed after delivering his chilling warning, leaving Hellequine to faint dead away from the pain of her exposed flesh. Wilberforce, himself florid-faced and breathless from the encounter, ushered Paul, Minnie, Ernest, and Hadley from the room, while Violet tended to Hellequine with matronly tenderness.

The last Minnie saw of Hellequine was her being lifted bodily to the bedroom in Violet's arms.

No further invitations to the captain's table had been forthcoming, and Minnie had returned to the isolation in which she had spent her first few days aboard the ship. Only once had she seen Wilberforce on one of the promenade decks, but he had assiduously ignored her and changed his course to avoid her.

She wanted to be upset at this, but, in truth, the isolation suited her. It gave her time to think on all that the comte had said. Clearly there was more to the theft of his books than she knew, which, Minnie admitted, wasn't much to begin with. All she knew was what Alexander and the others had told her of the Comte D'Erlette's castle.

Minnie didn't like to think too much on what the comte had told her. Hell, she didn't even like to think that it had been him at all. She kept trying to think of ways Violet, Hellequine, and the others might have been hoodwinked into thinking that a long-dead aristocrat had told her anything, but every time she went over the events of that night she came to the inescapable conclusion that it had been all too real.

The comte had known too much of her life, too many things that none of the gathered spiritualists could possibly have known or even suspected from their brief encounter that night. And as much as his revelations had hit close to uncomfortable truths, Minnie was no stranger to such things. Hadn't her parents sent her to the head shrinkers at the asylum for just that reason.

Perhaps she *did* have a taste for the macabre, but someone had to…

She caught herself slipping into a daydream and carried on down the gangway, feeling the rain plastering her skin through the turned up collar of her thick coat. Minnie shook off thoughts of the comte's words, knowing his anger had not been directed at her, but at those who had stolen his library from beneath Château-Thierry.

One of those men was, as far as she knew, still catatonic in Arkham Asylum, and she had no idea where Alexander was. Presumably hitting the books with Oliver in search of some way to stop the Star God's cultists from bringing the sunken city to the surface. What part Minnie had yet to play in whatever dramas were unfolding, she didn't know, but her gut was telling her it involved the muslin-wrapped dagger stowed in her bag.

Minnie didn't like the idea that some old dead guy wanted her to stick his blade in a living, breathing human being. She knew she'd brought the dagger halfway across the world for a purpose (and surely there could be only one purpose for such a weapon) but didn't like to think that purpose might be her murdering someone.

Minnie stepped off the gangway onto the quayside, taking the hand of the French Line officer stationed at the bottom to wish departing passengers a safe onward journey. The man bent to kiss her hand and gave her a smile that almost made her believe that he wasn't being paid to do it.

"Au revoir, mademoiselle Klein," he said. "I hope we will see you again on the *Ile de France*."

"I doubt my budget will stretch that far, but I sure do hope so," replied Minnie. "Say, do you mind?"

"Mademoiselle?" asked the officer.

Minnie pulled her Zeiss from her bag and flipped off the lens cover. The man visibly preened, and Minnie snapped a few shots of him with the boat in the background.

"What's your name?" asked Minnie. "So I know what to write on the back of the picture."

"It is Fabien," said the young officer. "With an *e*, Mademoiselle Klein."

"Thanks, Fabien," said Minnie, moving away from the ship. "Happy sailing."

Now she needed to find a taxi before all this rain washed her back out to sea.

A voice calling her name stopped her just as she reached the Custom's Building and was fumbling for her red-covered passport. Minnie turned and felt a jolt of surprise and unease as she saw Violet Tweedale bustling toward here, wrapped in a thick wax-jacket and with a deerstalker hat pressed down on her head.

"Minnie!" she cried. "I'm so glad I caught you, lassie!"

The Scottish medium was red-cheeked and breathless by the time she stood before Minnie, and took a moment to catch her breath before speaking.

"Oh, dearie, I'm all at sixes and sevens," she said. "Give me a wee moment to get my puff back."

"What do you want, Violet?" asked Minnie, in no mood to humor the woman's theatrics.

"No need for that snippy tone, dear," said Violet.

"Oh, isn't there?"

"Not a bit of it. And here's me just come to give you a last wee bit of advice."

"What advice?" demanded Minnie. "I got the feeling you and your bunch of spiritualists didn't want anything to do with me."

"Whatever gave you that impression?"

Minnie tried to muster an appropriate response, but words failed her.

"Och, here, come in away out of the rain," said Violet, taking hold of Minnie's arm and steering her into the Customs Building, where the hundreds of people disembarking from the vessels thronging the port would be processed before being allowed into the country.

A babble of languages filled the columned building, the voices of Europe and beyond clamoring at the borders and looking to be granted access to the promised land. Families from far distant countries who carried everything they owned pressed at the high desks at the far end of the hall, while armed men in dark uniforms kept the peace as best they could. Minnie and the other passengers of the *Ile de France* wouldn't have to queue with them, but had a separate aisle down which they could enter the country.

"Walk with me, Minnie," said Violet, taking her arm and leaving her no room to argue as they walked slowly toward the uniformed staff at the United States border. Ahead, Minnie saw Ernest and Hadley go through without so much as a glance from the desk sergeant. Neither of them looked back.

"What do you want, Violet?" repeated Minnie.

"I just wanted to say how sorry I was about what happened that night," said Violet. "It took all of us by surprise, and no mistake. We're dabblers, really, though Hellequine's had a few notable successes in her time. A few…unfortunate instances too, but more positive than bad."

"I think what happened aboard ship definitely qualifies as bad."

"No doubt about that," agreed Violet. "But that's by the by. What's of much more interest to me is that dagger you're carrying in your bag."

"How do you know about that?"

"*Please*," said Violet, pulling a face. "Medium, dear. Spiritualist. I know things. And I saw the way that wax spilled from the candle. Too regular and symmetrical by half. I know a sign when I see one, my dear. Now, I don't know where you're going with that weapon, but I'll tell you one thing, it's not for you."

"What do you mean?" said Minnie. "It was given to me, who else would it be for?"

"Trust me, dear, it's not for you," said Violet. "You are many things, Minnie Klein, but a murderer isn't one of them. Whoever that comte fellow was who poked his head out from the spirit world, he's not half as clever as he thinks he is. And he doesn't know you at all if he thinks you'll stab someone."

"You don't know me either," said Minnie.

"I know people," countered Violet with an indulgent smile. "I know a good person when I see one and you're one of the best I've met."

"If I'm so nice how come you and your friends left me out in the cold for the rest of the trip?"

"My dear, what could we possibly have said to you? No, you needed that time to yourself."

Much as she wanted to argue with Violet, Minnie knew the woman was right. She had missed the *idea* of company more than the company itself.

"Okay, say I believe you," asked Minnie. "Who's this old pig-sticker for?"

"Ah, now there I cannot help you, dearie, but if I were you, I'd look for someone who'd be only too glad to stick that in the guts of a man just like the comte."

They had arrived at the desk that marked the beginning of the United States proper, and Minnie felt like she was a child at school as she looked up at the uniformed man on his raised podium. The moment passed as he took their names and stamped their passports without pause.

Violet and Minnie passed out of the Customs Building into the darkness of a New York evening.

Minnie wrinkled her nose at the heavy rain.

"Here," said Violet, lifting the umbrella from the crook of her elbow. "Take this. I have another."

"Thank you," said Minnie, as Violet made her way to where a gleaming Cadillac with a bright blue paint job awas parked. A liveried footman awaited her with a fresh umbrella. Violet climbed into the car and leaned out of the window.

"Now don't forget what I said, dearie. It's not for you."

Minnie waved, surprisingly sad to see the gregarious Violet go on her way. It'd be pretty nice to have a fancy car like that waiting to collect her from the docks, but Minnie guessed she'd have to marry a king or get real rich real quick before that was likely to happen.

As it turned out she didn't have to do either of those things.

A battered red Ford pulled up into the spot vacated by Violet's Cadillac, and a familiar face emerged from the driver's side window with a goofy, boyish grin plastered across his face.

"Hey, pretty lady…need a ride?" said Rex Murphy.

Chapter Twenty

Traveling cross country by train felt unbearably slow compared to how Oliver and the others had traversed it before. The mood in the Pullman carriage they had booked for themselves was somber, for they were two men down on the return leg to Arkham.

Leaving Morley Dean behind had been difficult, but what other choice was there? As catatonic has Henry had been before him, it was just as likely that Morley might remain so for as long if not longer. None of them wanted to contemplate the idea that Morley might never wake up.

Hillshore had not accompanied them to the station, but had wished them well and again offered his oath that he would give Morley his personal attention at the Presidio. Normally reserved for military patients, Hillshore promised he would see that Morley was allocated a bed where he would be as safe as it was possible to be.

Floyd Butner had driven them through the rain to the Hyde Street Pier in North Beach in record time, and though it meant yet another trip on a ferry, they had caught the last train to New York and saved the necessity of waiting until morning for another. Henry, Oliver, and Gabriel were exhausted after the ordeal of the trip west and events subsequent to their landing, and had purchased the use of a Pullman sleeping car for their exclusive use on the route east to New York.

"Hell, if we're going to save the world from Alexander, we're gonna need some rest," Gabriel had said, when both Oliver and Henry had balked at the cost of such a berth. But Gabriel's logic was sound, and thus a great deal of money had changed hands to secure themselves a well-appointed suite for the journey.

Two days had passed since their departure from San Francisco, two days in which the deluge of rain had yet to cease and was grim portent for the coming confrontation. Oliver and Henry had slept a great deal of that time, missing the sodden sight of Salt Lake City and a water-logged Denver as they crossed the vast expanse of America en route to Chicago. Gabriel kept watch over them, though he too rested when one or other of the professors awoke.

Conversation was minimal, and restricted to their basic require-ments as they ate, slept, and refreshed themselves. Already Oliver and Henry were looking better after long bouts of dreamless sleep and numerous hearty meals emboldened by surreptitious shots of genuine Canadian rye from the dining car's accommodating steward.

A rain and windswept Chicago came and went, and after wait-ing several hours wending their way through the waterlogged farm-land of eastern Pennsylvania they were finally hitched to a South-ern Pacific engine at Manhattan's Grand Central for the final push to Massachusetts.

Less than three hours separated them from Arkham, and each man had two fingers of scotch in front of him. The genuine article from the Highlands, courtesy of the amenable steward. If this was to be their last drink, then it was damn well going to be a good one.

Rain battered the roof of the Pullman and its rhythmic tattoo was a constant accompaniment on their journey north. Morley's notes, together with every scrap of knowledge they had amassed, was spread on the table before them: a few books, a legal pad of hastily scribbled notes, and the folded piece of paper the Custodian of Markham-Hyde had given Oliver.

"This is a poor trove of knowledge when measured in relation to all it has cost us to amass," said Oliver, leafing through the pages of Morley's cramped script.

"Yet we know more than we did when we set out," pointed out Henry. "We have the second part of the spell Nereus-Kai used to de-feat Cthulhu. And our resolve is stronger than ever. Alexander may have bloodied us, but we remain unbowed."

"Yeah," agreed Gabriel. "He keeps taking swings at us, but he ain't put us down yet."

"I'll try not to dwell on that 'yet,' Gabriel," said Oliver, forcing a weak smile. "But you are right. For all that we have lost, we are still here, still alive. That is something."

"It's more than something, Professor," said Gabriel, sipping his whiskey at a connoisseur's measured pace. "Think of everything we've survived, all that we've done. Yeah, it's not been easy, and we've lost good people along the way, but one way or another this is ending soon."

"Either we stop Alexander or he kills us and the world ends," said Oliver.

"We're not going to *stop* Alexander, we're going to kill him," said Gabriel, placing his whiskey on the table and looking Oliver in the eye. "This ends with the world still turning, and it's gonna end with that bastard dead. For my Lydia and for everyone else he's murdered along the way. You'll do what you have to do, Oliver, but I'm putting a bullet in Alexander Templeton."

"You'll get no argument from me on that score," said Henry. "That swine cost me three years of my life and left me for dead in an insane asylum. Give me a gun and I'll put bullets in him myself."

Oliver sighed and rubbed a hand over his face, a face he could feel was already old before its time, weathered and worn by the vicissitudes of unlooked-for knowledge and adventure. He looked out the carriage window, seeing only the solemn greyness of impending darkness. Heavy rain streaked the glass, as it had all the way east, and Oliver feared they might already be too late. Rivers were bursting their banks all along their route, radio bulletins spoke of storm winds lashing the coastlines, and the black clouds overhead were swollen with yet more biblical quantities of rain.

"Ordinarily, I would try and dissuade anyone from taking a human life," he said at last, tearing his gaze away from the downpour beyond the glass, "but in this case I can think of no one who deserves death more than Alexander."

"At least we're agreed on that," said Gabriel. "But we gotta figure he's not going to be alone."

"You think he'll have, what, cultists?" asked Henry.

"Yeah, maybe, or maybe he'll have some of his old army buddies from back when he was burning Germans in Belleau Wood," said Gabriel. "Or more of those monsters. How do we know they all got burned up in the AQA frat house? And what about those flying buzzard, insect things that chased you into that other world with Finn

Edwards and Kate Winthrop? I think we're looking at Alexander having some serious muscle with him, human or otherwise."

"We three alone can't hope to take on such an army," said Henry. "It's been a while since my days in the Marine Corps, but even I know such odds are tantamount to suicide."

"Yeah, I was part of a few attacks like that during the war," said Gabriel. "And let me tell you, it wasn't pretty."

"So what do you suggest?" asked Oliver.

"Well, first thing we gotta do is figure out where the hell he is."

"Alexander will be in Arkham," said Oliver flatly. "It's the one thing I know for sure."

"How? How do you know that, Oliver?" asked Henry.

"It's something you yourself told me, old friend," answered Oliver. "You told me that there was cosmological significance to Arkham, that it sits at a confluence of alignments and draws the mystical, the unholy, and the macabre. Alexander knew that too; he was drawn to Arkham like a moth to a flame because he knew it was a center of activity for the Old Ones. Arkham is a place where metaphysical energies and cosmic forces converge. If there is anywhere in this world we will find Alexander, it is in Arkham."

Gabriel sat back and said, "Okay then, so he's in Arkham, but even for a small New England town, it's still pretty big. A lot of places to hide."

"Alexander will not be hiding," said Henry emphatically. "Wherever he is, and however he plans to bring his schemes to fruition, it will not be in the shadows. He wants us to see our doom coming."

"So what do we look for?" asked Gabriel.

"I don't know," confessed Oliver, draining his whiskey. "But we will know it when it begins."

"I can probably rustle up a few Pinkertons to help us out," said Gabriel. "Not many, but maybe enough to make a difference. There's a few guys left that'll come if I ask."

"What will you tell them?"

Gabriel grinned. "I'll tell 'em there's a bunch of Bolsheviks hiding out in the town," he said. "And I'll tell 'em there's a bottle of good scotch in it for them. That ought to bring enough big guys with billy clubs and thirty-eight specials."

* * *

By the time the train pulled into Arkham, night had well and truly fallen. Rain battered the gothic vault of Northside Station as the train heaved its glistening bulk into its shelter. Water gushed from its tenders and fell in a steady rain from the steps and couplings. Uniformed staff moved to secure the locomotive and direct passengers from Boston onwards to connecting trains to Newburyport and Portland.

Gabriel disembarked first, scanning the scattered faces gathered on the platform, though there were few enough of them. The howling winds, icy cold, and torrential rainstorm had kept the people of Arkham indoors far more efficiently than any curfew.

Oliver and Henry followed Gabriel onto the platform, each man looking around nervously for any sign that Alexander had anticipated their arrival and prepared accordingly.

But as they moved off down the platform toward the waiting ranks of taxicabs, it wasn't an emissary of Alexander's that accosted them, but a young girl with dark eyes.

Dressed in short pants and a flatcap that was much too big for her, the girl's hair was coal dark and spilled over her shoulders in wet streaks. With skin that was pale to the point of translucence, and features startlingly serious in one so young, she stood unmoving in front of them with her hand outstretched. Gabriel reached for his wallet, but the girl shook her head.

"I ain't looking for change," she said. "But if you've got any, I won't say no."

"So what are you looking for?" asked Gabriel.

"Him," said the girl, and Oliver's eyes widened in surprise when he realized he recognized the girl.

"I know you," he said, struggling to remember where he had seen her.

"Yeah, you gave me a dollar."

"That's right," said Oliver as the memory resurfaced. "New York, Penn Station. It's Wendy, isn't it?"

"Yeah, and you're Oliver, right?"

"That's right," said Oliver. "How did you know that?"

"From the same guy who told me to give you this," said Wendy, handing Oliver a sealed envelope.

Oliver took the envelope and ripped it open. "What was this man's name?"

Wendy shrugged. "He didn't tell me and I didn't ask, but he had a trustworthy face."

Gabriel pressed a folded ten dollar bill into Wendy's hand as Oliver removed a calling card from the envelope, worn around the edges and decorated on one side with the gothic letterhead of the *Arkham Advertiser*.

"Thanks, mister," said Wendy, pocketing the cash before turning and skipping away.

"Wait," called Oliver after her retreating back. "Did you ever find your father?"

Wendy looked back over her shoulder, and her serious face broke into a grin that made her a child again. "Yeah, I did," she said. "And now I've got to go help him get my mom."

Oliver smiled and a warmth filled him that he had not felt in a long time. Even in the midst of impending armageddon, spots of light could still be seen against the darkness.

"What does it say?" asked Henry, nodding at the calling card.

Oliver turned it over and read the words inked on the back.

"It says, 'Meet us at the Blind Man's joint.'"

* * *

The cab from the station dropped them on an anonymous street that Oliver must have walked down a dozen times in his years in Arkham and never once noticed anything untoward. Water bounced from the gleaming, rain-slick sidewalk, and as Oliver fumbled with an umbrella he'd purchased at the station, Gabriel ran across the road. The Pinkerton man stopped at a door that looked just like any other on the street until Oliver noticed the deadbolts at top and bottom, and the letterbox at eye level.

Henry paid the cab driver, who drove off in a spray of water, though by now both men were soaked through from the rain. By the time they'd crossed the street, Gabriel already had the door open and a hunched doorman in a dirty shirt and stinking canvas trousers was gesturing down a flight of stairs.

"Like Cerberus at the gates of the underworld," said Henry as he and Oliver followed Gabriel downstairs, past a man with skin so dark it made his eyes gleam like chips of ivory and into a scene like something from a Dionysian bacchanal.

Not even a flood to rival that of Noah's could keep the dancers and drinkers away.

The Commercial was packed to the rafters with women who were beautiful and painted, and men who were dashing and handsome. A band of jazzmen played a fast, syncopated beat on stage, and women in knee-length skirts danced the Charleston shoulder to shoulder with handsome beaus in baggy pants and tight waistcoats. A bar ran the length of one wall, where a pair of theatrical bartenders created neon-bright cocktails and poured arcing streams of liquor into shot glasses with wild flourishes to thrilled applause.

"Good Lord," said Henry. "How are all these people not deafened?"

Oliver had taken a drink in his home and elsewhere, of course, but he had never yet set foot in a speakeasy. The Commercial's tables were surrounded by people who laughed a little too loud and whose smiles were just a little too fixed to be convincing.

"It's somehow desperate," said Oliver, hating that his sentiment was so similar to something Alexander had once said. "It feels like some elaborate charade everyone one knows about, but no one dares shatter the illusion."

"I wonder if other cities around the world are similarly boisterous," said Henry. "Perhaps they sense the coming change in the world."

"Who cares why they're here?" said Gabriel, though his face was hard and flinty. It took Oliver a moment to recognize why. His daughter had been abducted from the Commercial, taken back to the AQA frat house and murdered. To walk into this place must have brought a surge of terrible memories for Gabriel, but little trace of that was evident on his face. Oliver was again filled with admiration for Gabriel's courage.

"Of course," said Oliver, scanning the crowd for a familiar face. None of the drinkers or dancers were known to him, but the more he absorbed the myriad sensations of the speakeasy, the less he could begrudge these people their passions. For all its inherent falseness, the pulsating, throughly modern vibe touched him too; the noise, the thrill, the sheer abandon with which these partygoers shed their inhibitions like a layer of skin. The illicit fug of smoke and cheap perfume filled the air with a willfully decadent atmosphere, and he could already feel his toes tapping to the infectious rhythm of the music.

"Kinda gets into your blood, don't it?" said a broad-shouldered man with pockmarked black skin appearing at Oliver's side. "Even a buttoned-up college professor like you can feel it. Oh, there's hope for the white man yet."

The man wore a heavy velvet topcoat and thick glasses that were so dark as to surely be opaque. A foul-smelling cigarette that put Oliver in mind of Hillshore's Arabian leaf glowed in one meaty hand and he drank from a highball glass.

"We were given a card…," said Oliver, trailing off as he saw the creased lines of scar tissue around the edges of the man's eyes. "Are you Rufus?"

"Ain't no other," agreed the man. "And this here's my joint. Everybody comes to Rufus sooner or later, and sooner or later, everybody come back. Now, you all need a drink."

"No, thank you," said Oliver. "As I said, we received a card."

"You need a drink," repeated Rufus. "And that wasn't no question. Come on now and follow me, I got some people who be real keen to make your acquaintance again."

And without waiting for an answer, Rufus turned and plunged headlong into the dancers, leaving curiously aromatic cigarette smoke in his wake. For all the heaving back and forth going on all across the dance floor, not a single person collided with him, Rufus leaned, swayed and twisted in time with their movements.

"I thought he was supposed to be blind," said Henry.

"I think he is," replied Oliver, following Rufus into the crowd.

But where Rufus moved with effortless ease, Oliver, Henry, and Gabriel were elbowed, kneed and trod upon as they tried to keep in sight of the blind man. Eventually they emerged on the far side of the dance floor, where a table was set up in the shadows around the corner and where the volume of the music was almost completely attenuated.

Seated at the table were three people Oliver had given up any expectation of ever seeing again.

Rex Murphy, Minnie Klein, and Finn Edwards.

All three looked up and their smiles of welcome were heartwarming. Rex stubbed out the cigarette he was smoking and bounded to his feet. He closed the distance between him and Oliver in two strides and took his hand in a crushing grip.

"Christ on a crutch, fellas, it's good to see you again!" he said.

* * *

Extra chairs were dragged over, and the weary travelers sat at the table, with swift introductions made for the benefit of Henry and those who had not yet made his acquaintance. Rufus stood at the end of their table long enough for drinks to be brought, his knowing grin never once faltering.

"Right, now that you good folks is sorted for tasty beverages, I think I'll leave you to it."

With the departure of the speakeasy's owner, Minnie stood and leaned over the table to give Oliver and Gabriel bear hugs that belied her short stature with their force.

"You're both soaked," said Minnie, releasing Oliver with a grimace. "But it's good to see you again."

"It's raining outside," said Oliver with a stupid grin on his face. "We thought you were in France, Minnie. I mean, I'm overjoyed to see you, but what brought you back so soon?"

"A couple of things," said Minnie coyly, sitting back down as Finn Edwards raised his glass from the table in a toast.

"How are ye, Professor?" said Finn. "Thought I'd seen the last of this place, that's fer sure."

"I didn't expect to see you back in Arkham, Mr. Edwards," said Oliver.

"And I'll tell you this for nothing, Professor, I didn't expect to be back myself," agreed Finn. "But it's funny how things work out, isn't it? The farther I tried to get away from here, the more it kept pulling me back. I met an old hobo feller on the boxcars by the name of Pete who felt the same way. Every time he tried to leave Arkham, sooner or later he'd find the road would bring him back. I guess it brought you back too, eh?"

"I suppose it did," said Oliver as Gabriel shook Rex's hand, half angry, half relived.

"Rex Murphy, God damn you," said Gabriel. "Where the hell did you get to? We didn't know what happened to your sorry hide. Sure, we thought you might be drunk in a gutter somewhere, but you left for Arkham? Why? And didn't you damn well think to let us know?"

Rex shrugged and said, "Yeah, I know I left in kind of a hurry, and I'm sorry for the vanishing act. I left messages at Hillshore's office, but his prissy secretary wouldn't give me his home telephone. I know I left you guys in the lurch, but my editor forwarded a telegram from Minnie saying she was on her way back to Arkham. She didn't know that Alexander was the bad guy, so I had to come and warn her."

"My knight in shining armor," said Minnie, weaving her fingers around Rex's.

"I got her just off the boat and we've been, uh, laying low for a few days," said Rex, striking a match. "You know, catching up. She's up to speed about our trip out west, or at least as much of it as I know. Hey, speaking of which, where's Morley?"

A look of shared sorrow passed between Oliver, Henry, and Gabriel, one Rex wasn't slow to pick up on. The match hovered in the air before the end of Rex's cigarette, the dancing light reflected in the round lenses of his glasses.

"Something bad happened, didn't it?"

And so Oliver explained all that had happened in San Francisco: the destruction of the Markham-Hyde collection, and their astral journey to Celaeno. He told the others of how Morley had sacrificed himself in order to allow Henry and Oliver to escape the library with the knowledge they needed to defeat Alexander. Despite the continued music from the band, Oliver felt the weight of silence around the table. Finn and Minnie had never met Morley Dean, but even without the benefit of his friendship, they understood the keenness of his loss.

"But his body…?" said Finn. "It's still alive, yeah? So there's a chance he could still come back?"

"An outside chance," said Oliver. "He would have known more than I, but I fear the chances of Morley Dean returning to us are lamentably slight."

"Ah, now don't write your friend off that easily," said Finn, nodding in Henry's direction. "Sure, didn't you get your old pal back when no one said he'd ever recover his marbles?"

"That I did," said Oliver, grateful for Finn's optimism. "And Morley is in good hands, so I'll keep on believing that I'll speak to him again someday."

With everyone up to speed on current events, Minnie brought out a cloth-wrapped bundle and laid it in the center of the table.

"Remember I said that a couple of things brought me back to Arkham?" she said, with an unconscious glance in Rex's direction. "Well, this is the other one."

"What is it?" asked Oliver.

Minnie unwrapped the bundle, and a silver dagger was revealed. It glittered in the half-light of the speakeasy, and Oliver felt an unaccountable loathing for this weapon of murder.

"What is it?" he asked. "I mean, I know *what* it is, but why did it bring you back to Arkham?"

"I was given this at Château-Thierry," said Minnie, and Henry let out a gasp of surprise.

"Given it? By whom?" said Henry.

"By the Comte D'Erlette," answered Minnie.

Henry all but pushed himself away from the table, his face twisted in horror as he relived the time he had spent at that nightmare castle. He stared at the bladed weapon in disgust, and Oliver saw the temptation in his eyes to sweep up the blade and snap it on the cement floor of the speakeasy.

"You should not have brought that back," said Henry. "No good can come of anything from that abode of the damned. It's a cursed weapon, and the only reason you have been given it is to do harm."

"I thought so at first, but now I'm not so sure," said Minnie, going on to tell them of the disastrous séance aboard the *Ile de France* and the discourse she had shared with the long-dead Frenchman. "I got the impression he was more mad that someone had taken his work and messed it up than the fact of them being stolen."

"Like a virtuoso whose works are butchered by a rank amateur," said Oliver.

"Yeah," said Minnie. "I guess. The comte had some crazy idea that he could return humanity to its primal, true nature, but was hopping mad that whoever had taken his books was using them for his own ends instead of some messed up vision of savage nobility."

"You think the comte gave you this dagger to kill Alexander?"

"No, not me," said Minnie. "I'm pretty sure it's not meant for me."

"Then who?" asked Gabriel.

Before anyone could answer, Blind Rufus appeared at the end of their table with a tray of glasses.

"You folks are looking a mite parched," he said, circling the table and laying down a drink before each of them. "These are on the house, in case you wondering who got to pay."

He circled the table, placing a drink precisely before each member of their group. Oliver tried to catch an angle whereby he might see behind the inscrutable man's glasses, but all he saw were the edges of puckered scar tissue. Rufus turned toward Oliver, as though sensing his scrutiny.

"Trust me, professor man, you don't wanna know what's behind these eyes," said Rufus. "Turn your hair white as summer moonlight."

A glass of pure Tennessee bourbon sat before Oliver, and he saw that everyone else around the table had a drink that, from the look in their eyes, was the perfect choice for their tastes.

Then Oliver noticed something odd.

"Hey, Rufus," said Rex, noticing the same thing. "There's two drinks too many."

Rufus laughed and the noise rolled over the table, seeming to come from somewhere impossibly deep within the man.

"No, sir, when it comes to drinks, I don't make no mistakes," said Rufus. "There's just the right number of drinks here for everyone, or I'll be a monkey's uncle."

Two dancers detached from the crowd on the floor and approached the table. Both were dressed in spruced-up hand-me-downs from a thrift store, but in the Commercial it didn't seem to matter what you wore as long as you wore it well.

"Professor Grayson?" said the younger of the girls, a light sheen of sweat on her brow and a faint redness to her pale cheeks. "What are you doing here?"

"Amanda?" said Oliver. "Rita?"

The last Miskatonic students to have been abducted by Alexander's cannibal ghoul cult squeezed into the bench seat next to Rex and Minnie. Both had weathered their horrible experience well, the robustly immortal blush of youth giving them the mental fortitude to put it far behind them.

Amanda took a drink from the glass before her.

"That's a real ritzy knife," she said.

"Yeah," said Minnie, sliding it across the table with a grin of understanding. "It's for you."

CHAPTER TWENTY-ONE

As soon as Amanda and Rita had sat down, Oliver felt a sense of completeness, of all the pieces in a jigsaw finally being arranged in a manner that allowed them to fit. He remembered feeling something similar when he'd sat in Aunt Lucy's after meeting Rex, Minnie, and Gabriel. More than just a shared sense of purpose, but a feeling that some ineffable part of their composition was no longer missing. Amanda and Rita's disappearance had been the driver that brought them all together, and Oliver realized now that it there could be no finishing this without them.

"I hope you ain't about to tell me that some of those AQA frat boys is still on the loose," said Rita, sipping her drink and scanning the faces around the table. "Because that would really ruin my night."

"You said you got them all, Professor Grayson," said Amanda, still looking at the dagger as though she didn't quite know what to do with it.

"We did," said Oliver. "At least we're pretty darn sure we did."

Rita looked over at Gabriel. "That right? You killed them all."

With the exception of Henry, Rita had met every one of them in the hospital after her escape from the frat house. She and Amanda both knew that the men and women gathered round this table in this club, could only augur more trouble.

"We killed them all," said Gabriel. "And the ones we didn't shoot got burned in the fire. Yeah, they're all dead. You have my word."

That seemed to satisfy Rita, and she said, "So why you all here? And don't tell me it's cause you love jazz and fruity cocktails. It's the guy in the red robe, ain't it? He's back."

Oliver felt the others around the table look to him for how to proceed. That Rita and Amanda were now part of their band seemed a given, and Oliver suspected that were he to try and protect them by sending them away, they would simply refuse.

"Yes," said Oliver. "He's back. And we know who he is now, though it might be difficult for you to believe at first. It's Alexander Templeton."

"Professor Templeton?" said Amanda, and Oliver could well understand her shock at such a revelation. Oliver had seen Alexander's treachery unmasked face-to-face, and *he* still had trouble reconciling the idea of him being the villain of this drama.

"I'm afraid so. He deceived us all, and now he plans to plunge the world into destruction. All the questions he was asking about your dreams, Amanda? That was all so he can raise the sunken city of a long dead god that has lain beneath the ocean since before the rise of life on Earth as we know it. I know that's a lot to take in, but we would not be here if it were not the truth."

"The city I saw…in my dreams…?" said Amanda. "It's real?"

"It is," said Oliver. "And if we do not stop Alexander, it will soon be rising."

Amanda lifted the dagger from the table, and though she was a slight college student, the weapon looked entirely suitable for her to bear. Like Arthur and Excalibur, Jim Bowie and his knife, or Davey Crocket and his Beautiful Betsy, the silver dagger from the depths of a debauched French aristocrat's Château was unquestionably Amanda's.

"And Professor Templeton was the one who…hurt me and Rita?"

"Yeah, him and his twisted frat boys," said Gabriel. "We killed all the ones that took you, but he might have made more and he might have worse than that to back him up now. You sure you're ready for this?"

"Wait," said Henry. "Are you sure, Gabriel?"

"Yeah, I'm sure, Henry," said Gabriel, rapping his knuckles on the table. "Rita escaped from these bastards and put one of them down with nothing more than a splintered bone. These gals are tougher than you think."

"You got that right," said Rita. "Us Crescent City girls are meaner than a gator in heat when you get us riled up. And Amanda? Don't think that cause she wearing a dress up to her knees that she's a soft city girl. She shot one of them monsters and blew his head clean off."

Oliver remembered that moment vividly; the leaping ghoul with its jaws spread wide and its claws ready to tear out his entrails. But for Amanda's dead eye shot, it would have done just that.

"I mean no offense," said Henry, furiously backpedaling, "for you are clearly feisty young ladies, but there is every chance we may not return from this encounter."

Amanda and Rita looked at one another, and Oliver was struck by the strength and determination he saw in their faces. He already knew they were much stronger than anyone might credit, and to have survived in that cannibal hellhole was nothing short of miraculous.

"If there is anyone who deserves to be here for the end of this affair, it is you girls," said Oliver.

"Damn right," said Rita. "So where do we find that son of a bitch, Templeton?"

"Mind if I join you folks?" said Rufus, pulling up a chair and lighting a long cheroot.

* * *

The owner of the speakeasy reclined on his chair, a crooked smile splitting his face as one of the bartenders brought him a triple shot of Kentucky bourbon. He took a long slug of his drink and a heavy draw on his malodorous smoke. A billowing cloud plumed above him as he exhaled and he tapped a flurry of ash from the lighted tip.

"Hell of a thing, this rain, ain't it?" he said at last.

"The rain?" said Gabriel.

"Yeah, you know, the wet stuff that falls from the sky," said Rufus. "We been getting a lot of it these days, yeah? So much rain...I ain't seen rain like this since the Vagabond Hurricane back in '03, back when I was tending bar on the boardwalk in Atlantic City. Chased those rich swells back inside, lickety-split, let me tell you. Not that the casinos minded."

"Yes, the rain is terrible," agreed Oliver, sensing Rufus had more on his mind than the weather.

"What are you, English?" said Rita. "Who cares about the damn weather? Ain't we got better things to talk about, like where we find that bastard Templeton."

"Man, she a firecracker, ain't she?" laughed Rufus.

"That she is," said Gabriel. "But she has a point."

Rufus leaned forward and jabbed his stinking cheroot in Gabriel's direction with a short shake of the head. "And so do I, Pinkerton man. Rufus don't say nothing that don't have meaning to those that gots the smarts to hear it. You listen up, you might just learn something of interest."

Satisfied his point had been made, Rufus puffed contentedly and took another shot of bourbon.

"You were saying about the rain?" said Oliver, knowing he'd need to indulge the old man's theatrics if he wanted him to open up.

"Sure, yeah, the rain," mused Rufus, as though Oliver had only just now brought it up. "Big storm coming, that's for sure, one a fearful man might think was set to wash away the world. Yeah, a man might think that, but this ain't gonna be no storm, not like we ever seen. This is gonna be the world toppled up over on its ass again…"

"Again?" said Henry. "You're saying this has happened before?"

"Hell, I'm just an old blind man in a jazz club, what do I know?" said Rufus. "But if I was a gambling man, I'd say that when the big old hoodoo you aiming to stop seeing the light first came here, it weren't no picnic for the things that lived on this here rock. Up went down and down went up. Now, like I say, I just a poor dumb blind boy from West Chicago, but I don't reckon I want to see that happen again."

"None of us do," said Oliver, wishing he could hurry Rufus along. But as frustrating as it was, Rufus was not a man to be bullied into haste.

"Then I'd be looking up to the hills around this old town," said Rufus. "Some real bad storms up in them deep gullies near the top of Meadow Hill. Not rain so much, but bad lightning, the kind I seen shoot *up* into the sky, you know?"

"I don't think I've ever seen lightning shoot *into* the sky," said Oliver.

"Nor I," said Henry, also understanding that he had to dance to Rufus's tune. "That would be exceptionally unusual."

"Unusual?" said Rufus. "Yeah, that be one word for it, Mr. Cartwright. Peculiar, that be another. Downright unnatural be better. Lightning that go up into the sky, fire dancing in the clouds…yeah, I reckon if you was to climb the highest of them hills in the north, you'd see some sights make you wish you was as blind as me."

"I understand," said Oliver. "And thank you."

"Thank me?" said Rufus before finishing his drink and rising from his seat. "Fo' what? I just here having a civil talk about all this rain we been having. Now, you folks take care now, y'hear. I don't reckon this storm's gonna break tonight, so you all go off and do whatever it is makes you happiest in the world. Like my mama always told me, even if I knew that tomorrow the world would go to pieces, I'd still plant me an apple tree."

And with that cryptic piece of advice, Rufus departed, leaving only the whiff of his cheroot in his wake. The music, which had until now been background noise swelled to a level that was—to Oliver's ears— deafening.

"So what do we do now?" said Minnie.

"You heard what Rufus said," replied Oliver. "Go and spend to-night doing whatever it is makes you happiest in the world."

"And what about tomorrow?" asked Henry.

"We'll meet in Independence Square," said Oliver. "At dawn. Then we climb Meadow Hill and we end this once and for all."

Gabriel pushed back his chair and shook Oliver's hand. "Till to-morrow, then."

"Tomorrow," said Oliver.

Gabriel turned and made his way through the crowds of dancers as Minnie and Rex came from behind the table. Rex put his arms around Oliver and said, "We'll see you tomorrow, Oliver, and I'll sort out some transport to get us up into the hills. But right now, Minnie and me, well we got a lot of catching up to do. Plenty of things to say that ought to have been said a long time ago."

"I understand, Rex," said Oliver with a smile as Minnie leaned up to give him a kiss on the cheek.

Finn finished his drink with a flourish and stretched his arms out in front of him. He cracked his knuckles and rotated his shoulders like a challenger about to go ten rounds with a heavyweight prizefighter.

"Grand," said Finn. "I'll be off too, Professor. There's a few lads I want to see over at O'Connell's and have a wee word with."

"I'll not ask," said Oliver.

"Probably best not to, aye," agreed Finn with a beaming grin.

Henry stood and gave Oliver a salute.

"Henry, don't be ridiculous," said Oliver, offering his hand. "I was never a soldier, and you're not in the Marine Corp anymore."

"Oliver, it has been an honor to be at your side through all this madness," said Henry, shaking his hand with the formality of a general inspecting his troops. "You might not have served in the military, but you have displayed bravery that would have done the Corp proud."

"Where will you go?" asked Oliver as Henry buttoned up his coat.

Henry relaxed and smiled. "I believe I'll just walk," he said. "It's been so long since I have seen Arkham that I think I'll just remind myself what it is we're trying to save."

"What about the rain?" said Oliver. "You'll be soaked."

"If you want to see a rainbow," said Henry. "You have to put up with a little rain."

Oliver watched Henry go and turned to the latest additions to their group. Amanda and Rita were straightening their dresses and fixing their hair. Amanda tapped her feet and Rita was already shaking her shoulders in time to the beat.

"Ladies, do you need a cab called?" he asked.

Rita laughed and said, "Nope, we're gonna stay here."

"You're staying?"

"Yes," said Amanda. "If the world's ending tomorrow, what else are we going to do but dance?"

* * *

The Asbury Church was a solid, brick-built structure just around the corner from Independence Square, and was as good as any a place to spend the night. Gabriel didn't feel much like sleeping, and he sure as hell didn't want to spend it in the jazz club where his baby girl had been snatched.

Rainwater dripped from the ends of his fingertips as he held a lighted taper over the candle, but the wick caught first time, swelling from a tiny glow to a healthy flame. Soon it would be extinguished, but while it burned, Gabriel would enjoy its fleeting radiance.

With two candles lit, he blew the taper out and looked up at the marble white image of Christ at the far end of the nave, trying to fathom any meaning in the man's suffering.

"They say you died for our sins," said Gabriel. "Then how come this world's still such a mess?"

The carving's serene face provided no answer, not that he'd expected one.

The candles he'd lit were not alone. Three others burned on the offering plate, lit by people who'd since left. Gabriel instinctively crossed himself and retreated to the nearest pew.

The wood was old, golden Massachusetts pine, worn smooth by decades of pious backsides. It creaked pleasantly as Gabriel sat and laced his hands together on his lap. Knowing what he knew now, he wondered if there was any point in prayer. If even half of what he'd learned in recent months was true, then he was most likely wasting his time here.

Except, Gabriel knew he wasn't.

He wasn't here for God or any thoughts of piety.

He was here for his wife and daughter.

Masie Lafayette had made Gabriel Stone the happiest man alive, a New Orleans singer who'd made a decent, if unspectacular living, singing in the chorus lines of the theater shows that were springing up all down Broadway. They'd married in 1905 and two years later were blessed with a daughter, Lydia Lafayette Stone. The next ten years had been tough, with Masie finding it harder and harder to get work in the shows with each passing year. To make ends meet, Gabriel had taken Pinkerton work that took him farther and farther afield from New York and his family.

Time and distance drove a wedge between him and his Masie, and when the Spanish Flu took her in 1920, it was all Gabriel could do to keep from eating the barrel of his thirty-eight special. All that stopped him was the thought of leaving his thirteen-year-old daughter alone in New York.

Five years after Masie's death, Gabriel lost his daughter too.

Murdered by the man he was going to kill tomorrow.

Gabriel took out a pewter pocket watch from inside his coat and flipped it open. He'd removed the clockwork mechanisms and replaced them with two photographs, one of a beautiful bayou girl in her wedding dress, the other of a young girl who possessed the same sculpted cheekbones, wide brown eyes, and coquettish smile.

Gabriel held their pictures to his chest and wept for the first time in six years.

* * *

O'Connell's was busy, as Finn knew it would be. On a night like this, what else was there to do but head out to drink and gamble? Stay in by the wireless and listen to all the bad news from around the world while your missus heats the iron over the fire and gives you hell for not going out to find work?

Thick smoke filled the air, competing with the reek of sweat, stale booze, spilled beer, and open bottles of whiskey. Damn, but it smelled good. It was the smell of a drinker's den, a refuge from the world where you could sing, play billiards, fight and shout and swear with the best of them.

God love it, Finn had missed this place.

"Howye, folks," said Finn, marching straight to the bar and placing a crisp five dollar bill on the counter next to a collection of shot glasses and a bottle of Bushmills. The bartender, a big auld fella by the name of Fibber McGee glared at him with his one good eye, but didn't make any move to pour Finn a drink.

"Ah, you're not still sore about that hundred dollars I owe ye?"

"Finn Edwards," said McGee, folding his ham-hock arms over his belly. "Now what would a gobshite like you be doing showin' his face around here when he knows there'd be a dozen men at least want to send him straight to Hell."

"Come on now, McGee," said Finn. "Isn't that just Irish diplomacy? Telling a man to go to Hell, then having him look forward to making the trip."

McGee bent to retrieve a blackthorn shillelagh from beneath the bar, a long walking stick, cum cudgel with a smooth, glossy finish. Finn saw the knobbed end had been hollowed out and filled with lead. Anyone hit by that little beauty wasn't getting up in a hurry.

The barman's gaze drifted over Finn's shoulder and he heard the shuffle of feet as a bunch of lads from the billiards tables moved to surround him. He grinned at McGee, earning himself a look of confusion. Men about to get a beating didn't normally grin.

Finn poured himself a large whiskey, which he downed, then a second which he threw straight in McGee's face. The barman's hands flew to his eyes and Finn sent a pistoning jab straight into his nose. McGee yowled in pain. Finn swept up the shillelagh as the man fell and his weapon clattered to the bar. He spun around in time to see a dozen men staring at him with undisguised venom. A few carried billiard cues, but most were just armed with bare knuckles and bad attitudes.

He knew them all, hard lads who loved an Irish lament and the hurly burly of a swinging brawl as much as he did.

"Tell me, fellas," said Finn, pouring another large glass of whiskey. "D'ye know why the Irish are always fighting each other?"

No one answered him, and Finn laughed uproariously as he downed his whiskey.

"It's because we've no other worthy opponents!" roared Finn, charging into battle.

* * *

As far as Henry could tell, Arkham hadn't changed at all in the three years he had been incarcerated at the asylum. The rain made everything crisp, and though he was soaked to the skin, he didn't mind. There was something cleansing in the deluge, as though the accumulation of madness, isolation, and despair was being washed from his flesh.

Henry had the town to himself, a lone traveler along streets that were as familiar to him as those of his boyhood Boston. The moon was obscured behind black rain clouds, but its diffuse glow bathed the buildings to either side of him in a wonderful, fairy tale light. Far from rendering their close-packed roofs and darkened windows threatening, it imparted a light, ethereal splendor to them that Henry found most amenable.

Right now, the people of Arkham would be abed, dreaming of tomorrow's chores and small dramas, unaware there were men and women fighting to give them that tomorrow. The world spun on its axis, with its inhabitants blissfully ignorant of the terrible dangers that surrounded them or the monstrous hands at their throats. Which was as it should be, for no one can live under the threat of extinction.

That a few had to bear the burden of knowledge and risk of madness at their cosmic insignificance was a small price to pay for the continued safety of the world. Which was all very well unless you happened to *be* one of those who capricious fate had decreed should bear such a burden. Henry had already paid a steep price for his involvement in this affair, but what more was there for him to give?

He was under no illusions as to his fate even should they succeed in thwarting Alexander's mad plan to drown the world. His academic career was over, for Miskatonic would surely not take him back, he had no income and only the faint hope that he would not see the inside of a jail cell thanks to his escape from the asylum.

Yet such gloomy thoughts could not keep Henry from enjoying his late night walk.

The baptism of the rain was entirely thorough, seeming to penetrate his skin and bone, to bathe every cell of Henry's body and purge him of such petty concerns. He no longer felt the cold, and nor did any thoughts of earthly concerns trouble him.

Henry turned his face to the heavens and let the rain renew him.

* * *

For the first time ever, Aunt Lucy's was quiet. No cups rattled on tables and no cutlery clattered against flatware as the hungry folk of Arkham devoured their eggs and bacon and muffins. A pretty young waitress lounged at the counter, flicking through a department store catalogue, and a pot of coffee bubbled on the hot plate.

The bell over the door rang as Rex and Minnie came in out of the rain, dripping water to the tiled floor. A cold wind chased them inside, but no one complained, for they had the place to themselves. Minnie sat at a table in the center of the diner as Rex made his way to the diner's pay phone. He slotted in a couple of coins and spoke with quiet urgency for a few moments before hanging up and returning to the table.

Minnie hadn't chosen the booth at the end they'd habitually occupied with Gabriel Stone and the others, knowing that this wasn't a moment for caution or anything other than total honesty. He sat down and the waitress came over with an attentive look that Rex saw was entirely genuine. Her name badge told him that her name was Annabelle and that she was happy to help.

"What can I get you two lovebirds?" said Annabelle.

Rex grinned and said, "Just coffee, thanks."

"And two slices of key lime pie, please," said Minnie.

"Would you like fresh cream on your pie?" asked Annabelle.

"Oh, absolutely," said Minnie.

"Bit late for pie, isn't it?" said Rex as Annabelle scooted off to prepare their pie and coffee.

"It's never too late for pie, Rex," said Minnie. "And it's never too early either."

"Pie in the evening. Could be the start of something, Minnie."

"You and I sharing supper together?" said Minnie with a smile. "People will talk."

Rex took Minnie's hand. "Let them."

* * *

Though it was only a short walk home from the Commercial, Oliver took a cab to Easttown. Unlike Henry, he had no desire to spend the night in a soaking wet suit, and resolved to change as soon as he got in. Even the dash from the curb to his front door was enough to see him drenched.

Oliver shut the door behind him and locked it securely. A wasted gesture perhaps, for which of the diabolical monsters Alexander could summon would be halted by something so prosaic as a lock? But this was Oliver's home, and such routines were a part of what made him who he was. He set a fire in the grate before heading upstairs to strip off his wet suit and dry himself with a fresh towel from his linen closet. Then, wrapped in his dressing gown and slippers, he descended the stairs to his parlor where the heat from the fire had filled the room with drowsy warmth.

Oliver wondered what the others were doing right now. He hoped each of them would find a measure of peace in this last night before they climbed into the hills to face Alexander. The thought of that inevitable confrontation plucked at Oliver's nerves and he found his thoughts restive, jumping from one concern to another as he tried to imagine how they could possibly prevail.

The spell of Nereus-Kai was burned into his mind, and he could feel the unknowable syllables bubbling at the back of his throat, as though eager to be spoken aloud. He had no idea if the wily Atlantean priest's conjuration would be enough to stop the Old One's sunken city from rising and destroying the world. Was there anything else that could be done to augment their only weapon?

What else might he do that might better prepare them for battle?

Oliver poured himself a drink from the last remnants of his bottle of Talisker, and raised his glass in a silent toast to Morley Dean. How he wished Morley and Hillshore were at his side right now. Until this moment, Oliver had not realized how much he had relied on Morley's vast knowledge of such terrible things. Without Morley's febrile store of esoteric craft, Oliver knew he was adrift in a sea of guesswork and hope. There had to be more Oliver could know that would better prepare him for this final fight for the survival of the world.

With drink in hand, Oliver made a slow inspection of his shelves and the books scattered around the room on tables, chairs and piled on the floor. He picked up a copy of Laban Shrewsbury's book, *Investigation into the Myth-Patterns of the Latter-Day Primitives with Especial Reference to the R'lyeh text*, before deciding against it.

Might *The Golden Bough* help?

No, decided Oliver, also discarding *Witch Cults in Western Europe*, the *Malleus Maleficarum, Exiles of Hyboria*, and the poetic stanzas of *People of the Monolith*. Oliver smiled as he saw a copy of the disgraced Prothero Fitzgibbon's *Dreams of Atlantis*. The book had been ridiculed by academics the world over for its ludicrous phantasies of a drowned city and the ancient star god that had seen it sunk to the bottom of the ocean.

How foolish such ridicule seemed now. For the briefest moment, Oliver considered reading this book once more, but he decided against it as his eyes alighted on another behind it. At a stroke, the furrow on his brow was eased, and he understood what Rufus had intended with his last piece of advice.

Taking the book and his scotch, Oliver sat beside the fire and began to read.

"Mr. Phileas Fogg lived, in 1872, at No.7, Saville Row, Burlington Gardens. He was one of the most noticeable members of the Reform Club, though he seemed always to avoid attracting attention..."

CHAPTER TWENTY-TWO

Morning brought no respite from the rain, and Arkham appeared deserted as Oliver drove through the waterlogged streets toward Independence Square. He had read the first few chapters of his book before drowsiness that could not be fought had sent him to bed. Though only a few hours had passed since then, he felt invigorated far beyond what so meager a rest should have allowed. He had dreamed of a Pacific island beach and woke with a sharp pain in his brow that swiftly vanished as he washed and dressed himself.

Henry Cartwright sat in the passenger seat, newly outfitted in stout clothing from Oliver's wardrobe. Both men were clad in noble tweeds and leather boots suitable for a climb into the hills, and both wore heavy coats and hats. Henry had arrived at Oliver's door just as he was preparing a breakfast of coffee and some eggs that had miraculously not gone bad in his absence.

Oliver had not asked about Henry's midnight perambulations, sensing that to do so would spoil whatever boons it had bestowed upon him. Nor did Henry ask him of his own evening, merely accepting Oliver's offer of some dry clothes and a warm breakfast.

Together they drove north through the silent streets of the city, with only the swish of the window wipers and the splash of the wheels through puddles to break the silence. The banks of the Miskatonic were swollen and in imminent danger of bursting. Sandbags had been placed along the lower portions of the river's banks, but were already proving to be wholly inadequate. Many of the streets on both sides of the river were already in danger of flooding and Oliver knew it was only going to get worse.

The sun had not yet risen, nor would it for another couple of hours. Oliver was grateful for the darkness. A venture such as this should not begin in the daylight, it should be kept to the shadows where none but those embarked upon it need know such things were necessary.

Oliver pulled his car to the curb at the entrance to the park, next to a memorial of fallen soldiers and across from the nearest gazebo bandstand. Four figures stood in its shelter, huddled together for comfort and warmth. Amanda Sharpe and Rita Young had clearly not spent the entire night dancing, for they were dressed in sensible clothes and wore laced-up boots, hats, and heavy waxed coats against the rain. Rex Murphy and Minnie Klein stood hand in hand, and Rex waved to them as the car halted.

"That's good to see," said Henry, at last breaking the silence of their journey.

"Indeed," agreed Oliver. "One night of love is better than never to have loved at all."

Both men climbed from the car and ran across to the bandstand. Rex and Minnie smiled in welcome. Rex shook Oliver and Henry's hands and Minnie gave each of them a warm hug and a kiss on each cheek.

"That's how they do it in France," she explained, seeing Oliver's pleasingly bemused smile.

"I like it," said Henry.

"Me, too," said Rex.

Amanda still carried the dagger Minnie had given her, and though she shivered in the cold, Oliver could see her determination to see this through. Rita held Amanda's hand, and gave Oliver a nod of acknowledgement. Both had reserves of courage beyond anything anyone could have expected, and though he baulked at the notion of having members of the fairer sex accompanying them into battle, he knew that nothing he might say would sway them to inaction.

"Girls," said Oliver. "It's good to see you. I wondered if you might reconsider."

"No, we want this finished," said Amanda.

Oliver nodded and said, "Any sign of the others?"

Rex shook his head. "Nothing yet, but we only just got here."

"They'll be here," said Minnie, and Oliver saw she had brought an incredibly compact camera with her, well-protected in a leather case with a waterproof shroud.

"I don't doubt it for a minute," said Oliver. "Though, heaven knows, one would understand if the enormity of everything became too much for them."

"Gabe wouldn't walk away from a fight," said Rex. "Especially not one with the guy that got his little girl killed."

Minnie nodded and said, "Finn's a rogue all right, but I get the feeling he's the kind of man that hates to see the little guy beaten down. And right now the human race is the little guy."

Approaching lights from the east drew everyone's gaze as a pair of trucks drove into the grassy common, though vehicles entering Independence Square was forbidden by a strongly worded local ordinance.

"Trouble?" wondered Henry.

"I don't know," was Oliver's honest answer.

"It's not trouble," said Rex. "It's reinforcements."

"Reinforcements?" said Oliver.

"Yeah, I made a call last night," said Rex with a mischievous grin as a dozen burly men in hard-wearing canvas dungarees disembarked from the trucks. Each carried a solid piece of wood, crowbar or length of scaffold pole. A few even carried axes. Oliver was perplexed until he saw a large man with ruddy cheeks and a wiry mat of coppery hair.

"You remember Donald McCarney," said Rex as the Scottish foreman of the workers building the Wireless station on Kingsport Head greeted Rex with a series of heavily accented expletives.

"Rex told us you could use a few lads that know their way around a fight," said Donald.

"That's right, Mr. McCarney," said Oliver. "Though I don't know if Rex will have explained exactly what we are going up against. You see it's rather—"

Donald held up his hand. "Ah just need to ken one thing. Where they are and how badly you want them busted."

Oliver said, "We are going up into the hills, and the people we hope to stop will, I suspect, kill you if you do not kill them first. But I must warn you, the things we will see are more horrific than you can possibly imagine."

Donald hefted his dented scaffold pole and said, "Aye, Rex telt me that wid be the score, but I've seen some pretty bad stuff masel, ken?"

Oliver didn't, but nodded anyway. "Your aid is most welcome, Mr. McCarney. You and all your men may well swing the balance of this fight."

Donald shrugged and said, "Rex, you owe me big time for this. And ma lads, too."

"Understood," said Rex. "And, Donald, thanks."

"Nae bother," said Donald, retreating back to the trucks as two cars drove into the square from the opposite side.

Both were grey Model Ts, ex-government issue, and Oliver let out a sigh of relief as Gabriel Stone climbed from the first car. Dressed in a long brown storm coat and with a wide-brimmed fedora, he looked every inch the frontier marshal that Rex had first mistaken him for. Gabriel walked over to the bandstand through the rain, his stride purposeful and his face cold. Wyatt Earp or William H. Bonney could not have looked more fearsome or single-minded.

"I brought help," said Gabriel. "Pinkerton help. Only another seven guys, but I reckon we need every scrap we can get. Looks like you thought the same."

"Rex brought some reinforcements, yes," said Oliver, shaking Gabriel's hand.

Last to arrive was Finn Edwards, who strolled through the rain like a man without a care in the world. He carried a long black stick, like the branch of a tree with a solid knob of wood at the end. Only as he climbed the steps to the bandstand did Oliver see the bruises and cuts on his face.

"Ah, don't worry yourselves none about me," said Finn, resting the black cudgel over his shoulder with casual insouciance. "It's the other ten lads you need to be worrying about. Their own ma's wouldn't recognize 'em."

The eight of them stood together under the bandstand in silence, each knowing that this could very well be the last time they shared a moment of peace. The rain fell on the gazebo roof like the drumming of a military tattoo, and Oliver cleared his throat to say something to mark the moment.

"Don't," said Gabriel. "Anything you say now will sound like a goodbye."

Oliver nodded, wishing he had time to get to know these extraordinary people better or that they had met under different circumstances and grown to know and love each other without such terrible danger hanging over their heads. Whatever happened today, Oliver would cherish the memory of these people with whom he had shared this fleeting moment between life and death.

"Then let's go," he said.

* * *

Oliver's car took the lead, with the Pinkertons following them and Donald McCarney's trucks bringing up the rear. Finn rode with Oliver and Henry, Amanda and Rita with Gabriel, and Rex and Minnie climbed into the cab of Donald's truck. The roads of Arkham were wet and treacherous, but Oliver kept his speed moderate as he traveled westwards from the square before making the turn north on Garrison Street. No sooner had they passed the city limits than they were swallowed by bleak forest canopy, and the small illumination provided by starlight was cut off completely.

Flashes of lightning from high in the hills made black scratches of the trees to either side of them, providing Oliver with his only means of navigation. The farther out of town they traveled, the more the quality of the road deteriorated, tarmac quickly giving way to hard-packed earth that was, in many places, little more than a waterlogged track that required deft driving to navigate.

"Be a shame if a flooded road was what stopped us, eh?" said Finn from the back seat.

"That it would, Finn," said Henry, twisting around in his seat. "That's quite some stick you have there. A shillelagh if I'm not mistaken, yes?"

"Aye, a good lump of Kerry-grown blackthorn," said Finn, thumping the weighted end into his palm. "Used to belong to a man who'd stupidly lent me some money. He wasn't needing this anymore so I borrowed it, if you take my meaning."

"I hope you know how to use it."

Finn shrugged. "You swing it, you crack someone's head. What's to know?"

"The man has a point," said Oliver, struggling to see through the downpour and navigate the route to Meadow Hill. The rain made seeing anything through the windshield hellishly difficult, and their bouncing, muddy course made it almost impossible to pick out any landmark with any certainty.

"You sure you know where you're going, Oliver?" asked Finn.

"I think so," said Oliver. "I climbed this hill last year."

"You did? Why?"

"I was keen to see the monolithic white stone atop its summit, so I took a clement day in spring last year to hike to the top. The road winds in a switchback pattern toward a vantage point, and if we can reach that, it should only take an hour or so to reach the dark vales cut around the summit. Well, an hour under normal circumstances, but in this weather...who knows?"

"Climbing a hill when you don't have to?" said Finn, tapping Henry on the shoulder. "You sure he's not already mad as a bucket of frogs?"

"Hard to say for certain," answered Henry with a grin.

Oliver tried to look affronted, but failed miserably.

"Are the others still behind us?" he asked.

Finn peered back through the rain-smeared window in the back of Oliver's car. Its inside surface was fogged with moisture, and he wiped his sleeve across it.

"Aye, still back there," he said.

Oliver gripped the steering wheel tightly as lightning flashed that lasted far longer than any natural meteorological phenomenon ought to last. The strange surge of brilliance revealed the strangely rounded summit of the hill ahead. The actinic brightness began to fade as they emerged from the forest, revealing a lonely and curious country with sparsely scattered houses in various states of disrepair and squalor.

Fields of particularly barren aspect stretched away on either side, like marshland that one instinctively dislikes. Darting lights, like flitting fireflies or will-o'-the-wisps swarmed the sides of the car, and Oliver reduced his speed as their presence made it extremely difficult to discern the edges of the road.

Another flash of light drenched the sky, and Oliver saw the stone wall he had been seeking.

"There," he said, pointing to the overgrown divide in the road, where the rutted track split and the going became truly appalling. The leftmost track led to the town dump and the abandoned Chapman Farm, the site of a notorious fire nearly two decades ago when a medical student by the name of West burned it to the ground. Oliver took the right-hand track, and Henry and Finn bounced about as the rocky road bore them toward a natural ravine carved in the rock by the action of water pouring down from the hills. Here, at least, the ground became more solid, and Oliver felt it rising beneath his wheels as they began their curving ascent.

The car cleaved to the sheer sides of the hill as it cut its lonely way up the eastern slopes of Meadow Hill. He dared not increase their speed, for the higher they climbed, the sharper the drop became. Several times, the tires slipped in the mud, sending the rear of the automobile veering dangerously close to the edge. Finn and Henry clung to their seats as Oliver wrestled with the steering wheel, fighting the slippery ground and his own sense of disorientation.

The flashes of lightning grew ever more frequent, lending the night an air of gothic melodrama, but eventually the road widened out into a sheltered plateau halfway up the mountain. A barrier had been constructed at the edges of the cliff, from which intrepid hikers could enjoy the fruits of their efforts and look out over the entire Miskatonic Valley. Oliver had stopped here on his previous ascent of the hill, and knew the view over to Innsmouth and Ipswich was spectacular indeed.

"This is it," he said, pulling the car to a halt in the lee of a vertical slice of rock, through which was cut a stepped ravine that led to the summit. "This is as far as I can take us."

He climbed out into the rain as the two Pinkerton cars pulled up alongside, quickly followed by the trucks. The men they had brought dropped from the back, and Oliver felt like he was at the head of the Spartan warriors whose coup-de-main had captured the Cadmean citadel of Thebes.

"Ours is a motley assembly of heroes," said Henry as they assembled at the mouth of the ravine. "Thirty brave souls against a monster that seeks to drown the world, but no finer a group of friends than I would wish for at such a moment."

Gabriel removed a heavy valise from the trunk of one his cars and knelt in the mud to open it. He withdrew a handgun and held it out to Henry.

"I'm guessing you know how to use this," he said.

"I do," replied Henry, taking the weapon and a box of shells.

Gabriel offered identical pistols to Rex and Minnie, both of which were accepted. Rita took a pistol after assuring Gabriel that she knew how to use it, but Amanda declined, saying she already had a weapon in the form of the comte's dagger.

"Finn?"

"No, you're grand," said Finn, hefting the shillelagh. "A solid piece of Irish wood'll be fine."

"What about you, Oliver?" asked Gabriel. "You might not be a crack shot, but at least I know you know how to shoot one of these."

Oliver withdrew the greenish soapstone he had been given by the strange old man in Kingsport and shook his head.

"No, I think not," he said. "I think my participation in this fight will be through means other than earthly weapons. I have Nereus-Kai's spell, and that will have to be sufficient."

"Okay," said Gabriel, unholstering his thirty-eight special and checking its load. "So are we all ready?"

"I guess," said Rex.

"Then lay on, Oliver, and damned be him who first cries, *Hold!*" said Henry.

* * *

The climb through the ravine had been challenging the first time Oliver had made this ascent, but with the added difficulties of darkness and the rainwater pouring down its center, it became doubly arduous. Sporadic flashes of bitter lightning split the sky and low reverberatory dissonance made the atmosphere greasy and electric tasting.

Oliver's arms ached from pulling himself up each step, for the wind and rain were conspiring to make it next to impossible to press forward without great effort. On a sheltered ledge, he paused to catch his breath, though the taste on the air was foul. Something out of place caught his eye, and he looked up to his left to see a niche in the rock into which someone had been placed a greenish statue of hideous aspect.

He needed no time to study its loathsome form to recognize the graven image of Cthulhu, and averted his eyes as a bilious nausea churned in his gut.

"At least we know we are in the right place," said Henry.

"I will try and take comfort in that," said Oliver, placing his hands upon the rocks for balance.

He felt a perceptible vibration beneath his fingertips, as though some vast mechanical process was underway somewhere above and was being transmitted through the very bedrock of the hills.

"What do you think that is?" asked Henry.

"I have no idea, but it cannot be anything good."

"And it sounds like it's getting more frequent," said Rex, helping Minnie to climb a deep step in the rock. Oliver paused, looking back down the ravine to see Finn, Amanda, and Rita just behind them. The Pinkerton men climbed together, looking like they were on a liquor bust, which, for all Oliver knew, might be exactly what Gabriel had told them.

He felt momentary guilt at the idea that these men might very well be going to their deaths. Even were they successful today, not all of these men would return to their homes and loved ones. Wives would lose husbands and children would lose fathers. A terrible price to pay for any victory, yet without such aid they would stand little or no chance of stopping Alexander. That did not lessen the remorse he would feel at such losses, but what other choice was there?

"Why we stopping?" asked Finn.

"We're not," said Oliver, turning to keep climbing.

The ravine grew steeper and more convoluted, twisting a crooked route into the heart of the hills, and the higher they climbed, the more of the leering idols they saw in the small reliquary niches. Finn smashed some with his club, while others were simply toppled down the ravine to shatter on the rocks below. Dark and viscous rainwater sluiced down the ravine like stagnant effluent draining from a mountaintop tarn. Oliver noticed a faint, yet unmistakable iridescence to the rocks, a sparkling light that seemed to be emanating from somewhere deep inside. He paused to consult his pocket watch and stared into the east with growing unease.

"It's still dark," he said.

"What?" asked Henry, between breathless gulps of air.

"Look at the time," said Oliver, holding out his watch.

"Half past nine," observed Henry, looking into the sky. "It's dark. It shouldn't be dark. Not now."

"Not by this time," said Oliver. "Whatever Alexander is planning, it's already begun."

The air took on a bitter, salty taste and Oliver saw the tallest reaches of Meadow Hill were illuminated by a crackling artificial glow. He heard a building whine, like an electric motor being pushed beyond its maximum tolerance.

Oliver turned and cupped his hand around his mouth.

"Hurry," he shouted. "There's no time to lose!"

He scrambled upwards with no regard for caution or stealth. The time for such niceties was passed. His boots slipped on the wet stone, and he cut his hands on the sharp edges of rock. Though his body and soul were aching with abuse, Oliver knew this was the last and only chance they would ever have to stop Alexander.

The glow from the hilltop grew ever more intense, and Oliver looked up in time to see a hideous shape silhouetted above him. Its outline was humanoid, but all kinship between it and humanity ended there. Its distended skull was hairless and though its features were impossible to make out against the glow behind it, Oliver knew he was looking at another of the ghoul creatures.

The creature let out a hideous screech that was swiftly cut off as the deafening boom of a gunshot blew out the back of its skull. Oliver turned to see Henry Cartwright with his pistol extended and a thin line of smoke trailing from its barrel.

"Damn, but that felt good," said Henry.

* * *

The *Matilda* rocked and dipped in the mounting swells of the ocean. The currents and tides of the Pacific had grown ever more uneasy over the last ten hours, as though the waters of the Earth sought to dislodge the vessel from its unnatural mooring. The Eye of Infinite Stars blazed like a signal flare atop the steel tower, a miniature sun that twisted the light of the stars above it like a divine watchmaker resetting his timepiece of the heavens.

Had any eye been able to see past its incandescent glare, they would have seen a multitude of impossibly arranged facets, like the latter works of Samuel Jessurun de Mesquita, the man who would later go on to mentor the works of the Dutchman, Escher. The hideous artifact of the Atlantean exile cycled through millions of years of celestial arrangements, its inexorable manipulation of mutant beams of light sending the world's astronomers into paroxysms of incredulity within myriad observatories as they watched their science turned on its head by the nightmarish arrangements of stars and galaxies. Yet for all its untold permutations, not one arrangement had proven to be auspicious.

Until now.

A precise conjunction of stars that had not been seen on Earth for hundreds of millions of years was crafted and shone down on the world, illuminating its deepest, darkest corners. The hellish hue of that light bathed the world in frequencies, wavelengths, and insane geometries that were, to the great, cyclopean prison on the seabed, as a jailer's key was to a cell door.

Uncounted fathoms below the *Matilda*, titanic blocks of seaweed-garlanded stone ground upon one another, and a mountain that had not raised the entirety of its monstrous form to the surface in millions of years shook as the being within stirred from its epochs-long imprisonment.

Suspended above the sunken tomb city, a silver sphere with spines like a metallic urchin began to rotate in the blackness as alien sensory devices registered the activity beneath it. Unknown mechanisms within the sphere clicked into motion, its internal structure sliding, shifting and arranging themselves in ways that should have been out of the question for a solid object.

A maelstrom of light built beneath the silver sphere, a spiral gateway of untenable light and non-Euclidian form that was never meant to exist on this world.

A shrieking sonic chime echoed through the deepest waters of the Pacific.

And on the far side of the world, it was answered.

* * *

The sound rolled across the hilltop and it took Kate a moment to realize what it was. Even over the buzzing reverberations of the active machinery and the roaring winds, it was unmistakably a gunshot. She looked up from the brushed steel and bronze control panel the aliens had manufactured, an operating station built with her size and reach in mind, but subtly and almost imperceptibly *wrong* in its proportions.

Kate listened for another shot, sudden hope flaring in her breast at the idea of rescuers coming to end this terror. As little as she had managed to delay the fabrication of the inter-dimensional anchor gate, perhaps it had been enough. Perhaps a hundred US Marines or Police Officers were even now storming the hilltop to stop Alexander.

One of her readouts fluctuated at her momentary distraction and a sopping gurgle behind her made her quickly return her attention to the displays. Charles Warren took a step toward her, and it took every scrap of Kate's self-control not to recoil at his proximity. His body had deteriorated still further, now little more than a puppet of rotten meat barely hanging onto the skeleton beneath. His skull was draped in skin, but the meat beneath had long since sloughed from the bone.

Charles no longer possessed the power of speech, but his grossly decayed body was still capable of exerting enormous strength and he still ached to hurt her.

Kate swiftly returned her attention to the control panel, but her mind was racing.

Constructed from the dismantled portions of what had once been her prison cell, the panel comprised a dizzying array of dials, levers, scopes, and gem-like buttons. Perched on a flattened portion of rock overlooking the silver spire the alien creatures had raised, the panel allowed her to regulate the motion, speed, and pitch of the tower's looping metallic rings.

The machine dwarfed the white stone monolith, and coruscating fields of energy rippled up and down its length. The air buckled with intersecting dimensions pressing on the invisible skein that separated them, and Kate felt their presence as a painful pressure in her skull.

Alexander Templeton stood with one arm upraised before the silver tower, standing atop the black rock she had earlier taken for a sacrificial altar. Robed in red and screaming words that were snatched away by the wind and thankfully rendered unintelligible, his arm moved in oddly geometric patterns. The monstrous cannibal beasts squatted in fear around him, each braying to the heavens like a pack of deranged wolves, while all but one of the buzzing, insect maggots flitted through the air with nervous, darting motions.

This last creature sat perched on a metallic protrusion next to her, and though it was without any sense organs Kate could readily identify, she knew it was monitoring her actions with a thoroughness that would be impossible to fool. Its ridged, brain-like frontal organ shimmered through the spectrum of colors, and numerous freshly extruded feelers whipped in the high winds filling the valley.

It took all Kate's concentration to maintain the field strength's equilibrium, but she forced herself to consider how she might buy some more time for her rescuers.

* * *

Deep within the blackest, lightless trench of the ocean, a dreaming god stirred as dormant senses that had all but forgotten the world of air and light roused from eternal torpor. In a prison of unnatural angles and concavities that could not exist in a world of sanity, blocks of stone carried from a world that had gone to dust many rotations of the galaxy ago began to move. Carved sigils that could never be broken were obliterated by a conjunction of stars and alignments that no one, neither god nor man, could have foreseen.

A booming heartbeat thundered, and the seabed cracked for hundreds of miles in all directions as the immense shock wave radiated from the sunken mountain. A black fluid arose from the crazed abyssal depths like squid ink, but questing with hidden intelligence. Creatures of jade green scale, like aquatic apes with vaguely piscine skulls, emerged from burrows sealed away within the newly exposed strata, shrieking praise to their ancient master.

A hideous, reedy noise, like insane piping echoed in the depths and the deep-born creatures capered and danced as the mountain shook itself apart. Another pounding heartbeat struck and the force of that great reverberation surged toward the surface.

A portion of the great mountain fell away in a cascading avalanche, as if the side of Everest had detached and taken half the Himalayas with it. A vast maw of a black gateway was revealed, a depthless chasm into the lightless abyss of the planet's heart.

Something *shifted.*

Something *moved.*

A being older than could ever be measured by the minds of Men *stirred.*

In his house at R'lyeh, dead Cthulhu waits dreaming.

Dreaming no longer.

Rising.

Chapter Twenty-Three

O liver and his brave Spartans finally reached the edge of the valley at the top of Meadow Hill, and the sight before him quite took his breath away. Where their route up the hill had been dogged by the constant rainfall, the summit of the hill was utterly dry, as though an invisible umbra shielded it from the deluge.

He instantly saw Alexander standing before an immense silver tower that blazed with whipping arcs of lightning and pulsed like a lighthouse. The metaphor was an apt one, for Oliver knew exactly which infernal monstrosity would be drawn to such a damnable beacon.

Gabriel and Henry appeared at Oliver's side.

"What do you need to do?" asked Gabriel.

"I need to get to that tower," he said. "Any gateway to R'lyeh will be opened there."

"And Alexander?"

"Kill him," said Oliver. "Kill them all."

Gabriel nodded as the Pinkertons and Donald McCarney's men arrived at the hilltop. Though they had been forewarned as to the nature of the foe they should expect to find here, nothing could adequately prepare a man for so hideous a sight. Several of Donald's men turned tail and ran screaming back down the hillside, while one of the Pinkertons simply dropped to his knees and curled into a weeping fetal ball.

Flying creatures that were part insect, part mutant grub buzzed and droned overhead on insubstantial, gelatinous wings, as a host of rabid, hunched monsters loped over the hillside with a mix of guttural barks and slavering howls. Oliver experienced a moment's terrified recall as he relived the moment such creatures had attacked him in his university office.

Despite his earlier words to Gabriel, he suddenly wished he had a firearm about his person.

A volley of gunfire blazed from the edge of the hill and half a dozen of the creatures were felled.

"Keep shooting," shouted Gabriel amid the boom of pistol fire and cracks of lightning.

"Come on," said Finn, pulling Oliver forward. Rex and Minnie came along with them; Rex with his revolver drawn and ready to fire, Minnie with her camera pulled tight to her eye. Rex gave Oliver a wink.

"Hell, Professor, if we live through this, it's going to make a hell of a story."

The Pinkerton men advanced in a steady line, firing as they went, but Oliver immediately saw there were too many of the ghoul creatures to be halted by so few guns. Donald McCarney saw it too and lifting his steel scaffolding bar like a claymore, he charged toward the surging mass of howling beasts.

Oliver watched as the big man's first swing crushed the skull of a beast with grotesquely twisted features that were still damnably human. He head-butted another creature and his backswing broke the arm of another monster as his men waded into the fray like Wallace's Highlanders. They beat back their horror at such creatures with the violence of their attack, but Oliver felt only a crawling revulsion at the nature of this fight when he saw the glazed eyes of one beast.

Whatever these creatures were now, they had once been people.

Donald's men and Gabriel's Pinkertons were making good headway through the bestial host, but the monsters were fast and strong, with yellowed fangs and sharpened claws. A young man in muddy dungarees and a flatcap died with his throat torn out, and another fell with his chest ripped open to the bone. Two of the Pinkertons were dragged from their feet as they paused to reload. Gabriel and Henry fought together, two old soldiers standing shoulder to shoulder in the thick of the heaviest fighting.

Three of the flying grubs descended and unleashed a torrent of alien fire from tined weapons affixed to the undersides of their bulbous thoraxes. Oliver had seen the effects of such weapons before in Ma's Boarding House, and these weapons were—if anything—more lethal. Five men were reduced to ash by blazing gouts of electrical fire, while another two were bifurcated by actinic whips of light.

The swirling melee became a roaring free for all, with clubs of iron and wood rising and falling, claws and teeth tearing. Gunshots boomed and the cannibal beasts were punched from their feet by the force of the bullets. Two of the flying beasts were brought down and trampled in the ferocious brawl. More of the men that had made this nightmare climb were killed or so horribly mangled as to be unrecognizable.

"Here now, Professor," said Finn. "Isn't that the young girl you took me to see about that funny-looking sphere I brought you?"

Oliver looked over to where Finn was pointing, and sure enough, he saw what looked to be Kate Winthrop—though what she was doing here was beyond his ability to fathom just now. He had no more time to think of an answer as a screeching monster flew down at them from a jutting boulder high up on his right. A crackling fire built on the jutting prongs of its forked weapon, but before it could unleash its power, Finn Edwards swung his shillelagh and the sound of weighted wood against the bulbous mass of what appeared to be its head was savage in its intensity. The creature dropped to the ground, and Finn punched the air with his club, as though he'd just hit a home run to win the World Series.

"Away, ye gobshite ye!" shouted the Irishman. "I owed you a doing, ya wee bastard!"

Oliver said nothing, staring up at the man whose mania and perverse sense of hatred for the human race had brought this slaughter about. Alexander Templeton looked down on them from the pulpit of his altar before the electrically charged tower and its leaping bolts of lightning that shot into the sky with the regularity of a heartbeat.

Together, Oliver, Finn, Rex, and Minnie pushed toward the tower.

"Alexander!" shouted Oliver. "You have to stop this, before it's too late!"

"It's already too late!" shouted Alexander with delirious fervor. "Cthulhu wakes! R'lyeh rises!"

* * *

Gabriel ducked behind a jutting platform upon which stood one of the hellish statues of some hideous creature that was part squid, part gorilla and thumbed his speed loader into the breech of his revolver. Henry Cartwright knelt beside him, still firing until the hammer of his revolver snapped down on an empty chamber.

"Reload, Henry," shouted Gabriel, swinging out and, just for good measure, kicking over the abhorrent statue. Sparks flared from the barrel of his gun like corposant and he sighted down its length at a ghoul creature as it reared up behind Henry.

The bullet detonated inside its skull, and Gabriel ducked as a blast of fire seared the air less than a foot overhead.

"Thank you," said Henry, the chambers of his gun now reloaded.

Gabriel didn't answer, sighting at one of the flying monsters as it skimmed the ground toward them, its belly twitching with crackling energies. He and Henry both fired twice, and thick, pinkish ichor burst from its membranous head as it plowed into the earth like a downed plane.

"Agent Stone!" cried a voice to the side. A girl's voice.

Gabriel risked a quick glance to his left and saw a stone platform on which stood what looked like a grand piano made from gleaming sheet steel. Standing next to it was a girl whose face he knew. It took him a moment to figure out where he'd seen her, then it came to him. She was the scientist girl who'd traveled to the other world with Finn and Oliver. Kate…something…

"What the hell…?"

No sooner had she shouted to him than a horror far worse than any of the creatures he and his men were fighting appeared at her side. Both Henry and Gabriel pulled up short as they saw a mangled corpse of a man pull her back from the edge of the platform. This was no man brought low by diabolical powers, but a dead thing kept from death by the most hideous powers imaginable.

Though he knew it was a risk, Gabriel took a moment to brace himself in the classic shooter's pose, legs apart, shoulders braced and gun held in front of him, one hand cupping the other.

"Cover me," he told Henry, and took aim.

Gabriel squeezed the trigger, and right away he knew the shot was a good one. It struck the center of the walking corpse's head and punched a hole through its brain.

And Gabriel's jaw dropped open as he saw his bullet had had no effect. He cursed himself for thinking that a bullet in the head might stop a corpse. Kate screamed as the dead man bent over her neck to take a bite of her flesh, and for the briefest moment, Gabriel saw something of Lydia in her pained features.

"Come on, Henry!" shouted Gabriel.

"What about Alexander?"

"I said *come on*!"

The two men ran toward the rocky platform as the dead man threw Kate's bleeding body aside. The full horror of his mangled flesh now became apparent; this was a *thing* that had died a long time ago, but had yet to lay down. But for all that, his body was still possessed of terrible animation, the flesh had not ceased its slide into decomposition. Only the eyes retained a measure of the man's former incarnation, and as Gabriel scrambled onto the platform, he had a terrible moment of recognition.

He had seen these hateful eyes before, but it was Henry Cartwright who supplied the name.

"Christ!" cried Henry, his advance faltering in the face of this nightmarish apparition from his past. "Warren..."

The dead man gurgled in what might have been pleasure, and hurled himself at Gabriel. He managed two shots before Warren slammed into him with savage force. Neither bullet had any effect, simply tearing rotten meat and passing through the ruined body. Gabriel lost his grip on his gun as they fell to the rocky platform, rolling like street brawlers outside a speakeasy. Warren's hands were bony talons that tore the skin at Gabriel's neck, and his fetid breath was like an open sewer.

Gabriel rabbit-punched up into Warren's side, but the man's lungs had long since emptied themselves of air and his blows simply served to denude the ribs of what little flesh remained. Clawing, skeletal hands fastened on Gabriel's neck and he fought to get his arms up to break the hold. Nothing biological or mortal empowered these dead limbs, and Gabriel couldn't loosen the grip. He brought his knee up into Warren's groin, but whatever harm such a blow might do to a living, breathing soul was meaningless to a dead man.

"Henry!" he managed to gurgle through his constricting throat. "For God's sake..."

Warren's eyes were inches from his own, blazing pools of raw madness and hunger. Something bubbled up from deep within him, words perhaps; a threat or a final parting insult.

Gabriel would never know, for all that emerged from Warren's throat was a wet rattle of decaying vocal chords. Bared teeth, loose in the gums descended to rip the flesh from Gabriel's cheek and droplets of soiled meat fell from his opened jaw.

And then Henry was there.

Henry's fist slammed into the side of Warren's face, a roundhouse the equal of anything Jack Dempsey threw in the ring. The pressure on Gabriel's throat was released and he drew in a deep lungful of air. Warren lashed out at Henry, hurling him back against the rock before rising to his feet in agony.

The dead man clutched his head, where a shard of glassy blue stone was embedded in the bone tissue. From the visible outline, Gabriel saw it was a curved five-pointed star with what might have been an eye at its center. White fire, like burning phosphor, drooled from the wound and meat slid from Warren's skull like molten wax.

And despite the decay within his throat, Warren was still capable of screaming.

Henry lay prone, one arm held close to his lacerated chest, and the same brilliant white light that was devouring Warren's flesh wreathed his fist.

"Quickly, Gabriel!" gasped Henry. "While Ndoto's sign still has power."

Warren lunged at Henry in a rage, but Gabriel scrambled to put himself between them. He tackled Warren like a defensive end taking down a quarterback, and the pair of them slammed into the side of the metallic panel. Gabriel hammered his elbow into Warren's jaw, and the bone snapped with a wet crack. Warren's eyes widened in shock and pain, but his strength wasn't done. He spat a froth of decaying matter into Gabriel's eyes, one clawed hand tearing at his throat. Gabriel slammed his forehead into Warren's face, and the soft bone of his skull caved inwards.

Yet even as Gabriel drew back his fist for a thunderous uppercut, he saw the tissue of Warren's skull knitting together again. He needed a killer blow and he needed it now. His gun was lost in the scramble of the fight, and he had no other weapon left.

Except that wasn't true.

Holding Warren pinned with his left hand, Gabriel reached into his coat pocket and withdrew the venomously green crystal he had brought from the wreckage of the Markham-Hyde collection. He thrust the fragile gem into Warren's sagging jaw.

"You say Hell welcomes men like you?" snarled Gabriel. "Time to find out."

Gabriel's fist slammed forward like a piston into the dead man's mouth.

The Serpent's Fang shattered with a flash of jade light, and Warren staggered at the distilled venom of the world's snakes coursed through his rotten body. The chemicals and abominable reagents that had brought Charles back from death were vastly potent to have sustained his existence for so long, but they were no match for the poisonous breath of Yig.

Warren's flesh and bone disintegrated in a heartbeat, leaving nothing but a smear of bone fragments to fall to the ground. Gabriel stepped away in disgust and turned toward Henry.

"Oh, no…" he said.

* * *

To stand before Alexander after so long and after so much pain and anguish was almost too much for Oliver. In the wake of the Kingsport horror, Oliver had not allowed himself to think on how he might feel at confronting their nemesis, but now that moment was at hand, it took his breath away.

One of Alexander's arms was a twisted ruin, a fused and useless claw after his wounding aboard the *Persephone*. Vile black ropes of decay pulsed at his neck and shoulder, reaching up to vein his face with a spiderweb of degeneration. Now his physical corruption matched that of his soul, and the monster hiding behind Alexander Templeton was hideously revealed.

Oliver had trusted Alexander, and that trust had been cruelly betrayed in the worst possible way.

Alexander had used him to further his own diabolical plans, to hasten the demise of the human race and the destruction of the Earth. He had kept Oliver and his compatriots close to learn of them: their secrets, their strengths, and their weaknesses. Only to then horribly exploit them. He had murdered and destroyed for the sake of his grief and disgust at the human race, and it seemed absurd to see such monstrous evil personified in the face of a mortal man.

"I see you brought your friends," said Alexander, bathed in the searing glow of his infernal tower. "It won't matter now, Oliver. The thing is done."

The machine was like some monstrous orrery in its construction, its multiple spinning discs moving in strange circuits of the tower and intersecting in ways that Oliver's eyes told him should have been impossible. The shimmering space englobed by the arcane arrangement of discs expanded and contracted like a bubble on the verge of explosion, and Oliver felt a dreadful tension in its seething motion.

"I won't let you do this," said Oliver.

"Were you not listening?" said Alexander. "There was never anything you could have done to stop it. The Old One will ascend and this world will drown in his rebirth. The waters will rise and wash away our failed species. All the dirt and desperation, all the pain and fear. The cruelty and the malice of men's blackened souls will be cleansed from the Earth, can't you see that? We don't deserve this world, anyone who saw the horror of the Great War would know that…"

"And what of all the good?" countered Oliver. "What of all the love and compassion? All the capacity for understanding and growth? You would cast aside all that is good in this world for your own grief?"

"What do you know of my grief?" spat Alexander. "I fought and killed for my country. I put aside all notions of humanity in the war only to have the one last, good thing in my life snatched away. All that I was died in Flanders. I saw things there that, had you seen them too, would cause you to realize the absurdity of that which you defend. Humanity? There is no such thing."

"But there is, Alexander," said Oliver. "You must see that? This world can be cruel, yes. It can be awful and uncaring in its indifference to human life, but it can also be beautiful. Grief can swallow a man's soul, but only if he lets it."

"So speaks a man who has not seen the darkest heart of his fellow man," said Alexander.

Oliver met Alexander's gaze and knew his words were wasted. Whatever good had once lived in Alexander Templeton had been extinguished many years ago.

"You're wrong, Alexander," said Oliver. "I see that dark heart now. In you."

A hideous roaring, like an onrushing tsunami built behind Alexander, a titanic rumbling of continents colliding. Alexander lifted his remaining arm to the sky as fresh bolts of lightning arced up from the tip of the mighty silver tower. Dozens of the flying beasts were instantly incinerated as whipping arcs of purple lightning split the sky, and plumes of green light illuminated the valley as the tentacle-faced statues burst into flames.

"He comes…," breathed Alexander.

"Just shoot the bastard, will ye!" yelled Finn, fighting alongside Amanda and Rita as more of the degenerate ghouls closed in. The Irishman's shillelagh cracked skulls and broke bones, while Amanda's dagger killed with even the slightest touch of its silver blade. Rita had long since fired her pistol empty and clutched a long branch in lieu of an actual weapon.

Rex and Minnie took Finn's advice and turned their guns on Alexander, letting fly with a blazing volley of shots. Alexander laughed as the bullets were sucked into the howling vortex behind him.

"It's over," said Alexander, stepping down from the altar stone upon which he had cast his summoning. "It is the end of our world, Oliver. I promise you it will be spectacular."

The roiling chaos at the heart of the madly spinning discs suddenly erupted as the air buckled and tore like someone scrunching a sheet of translucent plastic. Dark water gushed through and a freezing wave poured into the valley.

The tang of salt filled the air as dead water from the depths of the Pacific flooded onto dry land.

* * *

"Come on, Henry," said Gabriel. "Stay with me, damn you."

"I'm not sure I can, Mr. Stone," said Henry, looking down at his bloody chest. "I think Charles has done for me."

Gabriel ripped off his coat, pressing the sodden fabric to Henry's body in a futile attempt to halt the flow of blood from his ruined torso.

"Did you kill him?" asked Henry, his breath coming in wheezing hikes. "Warren, I mean…"

"Yeah," said Gabriel. "He's dead."

Henry nodded. "Oliver told me he was dead. I'd rather hoped he was correct…"

Gabriel glanced over to the stinking pile of decayed matter that was all that remained of the late and unlamented Charles Warren.

"I suppose he was, kind of," said Gabriel. "But he ain't coming back from this one."

"The others…?" managed Henry. "Have we succeeded…?"

Gabriel had no answer for Henry, but he didn't think it looked good. Torrents of water spilled from thin air at the heart of the huge machine Alexander had built, and it looked like most of the men they'd brought with them were either dead or drowned. Here and there a few figures thrashed in the water, but it was impossible to tell friend from foe in the confusion.

"Yeah," he said. "We won. You just gotta stay with me long enough to see it for yourself."

"Ah," said Henry, his eyes easing shut. "I'm not sure I'll manage that. Sorry."

"Mr. Stone," cried Kate Winthrop as she struggled with her panel of instruments. It spat sparks and coruscating tendrils of flame. "Please, I need your help! I can shut the machine off, but I can't do it on my own."

"I'm kind of busy here," shouted Gabriel.

"His death will be for nothing if you don't help me!"

"He's not gonna die," snapped Gabriel.

But Henry was already dead.

* * *

The flood knocked Alexander and Oliver from their feet, sweeping into the valley like a tidal wave. Within seconds it was several feet deep and pouring downhill in an unstoppable river. Oliver fought to regain his footing, but the force of the water was too strong. He scrambled toward one of the horrid statues that had burned with flickering green fire. The water had extinguished the flames, and Oliver grasped its crudely carved pedestal as churning waves buffeted him.

The valley was no longer a battlefield, but a roaring, seething flood plain. Ghouls and men were swept away by the water, spilling downhill in an oceanic avalanche. Oliver wiped seawater from his face, gasping for breath as the cold of the utter deeps chilled him to the bone. He saw Finn swept away, fighting uselessly against the current, but he saw no sign of the others who had stood with him before Alexander. Rex and Minnie were gone, as were Rita and Amanda.

Alexander clung to the altar stone, his face turned in rapt adoration to the expanding flood of ocean spilling from the gate machine. On a raised platform of rock as yet untouched by the rising waters, Oliver saw a pallid Kate Winthrop working furiously at some unknown mechanism. Gabriel Stone stood beside her, holding what appeared to be a binding at her injured neck.

Henry sat slumped with his back to the side of the valley, and even from this distance, Oliver saw that Henry's chest and stomach were red with blood.

Anger filled Oliver, and he pulled himself upright. The power of the water was growing with every passing second, and Oliver knew he would not be able to hold on for long. Quickly he unbuckled his belt and lashed it around the stone statue to anchor himself in place.

Alexander saw him rise from the water and grinned maniacally.

"Isn't it wonderful, Oliver!" shouted Alexander. "Our world is being reborn!"

"No," said Oliver, reaching deep inside to where the completed spell of Nereus-Kai sat like a coiled serpent awaiting its moment to strike. "Nereus-Kai stopped this once, and I will stop it now."

Knowledge won in an earlier age of the world bubbled up into Oliver's throat, and words—the pronunciation of which he was entirely ignorant—formed on his lips. He felt the ancient syllables folding themselves into the fabric of the world and *changing* it. Dimensional harmonics were contained in their arrangements, forbidden sounds conjured into being by those whose understanding of the mathematics and formulae that bound worlds and dimensions together far exceeded contemporary learning.

That learning had been forgotten over the eons, and with good reason, for mere mortals were ill-equipped to dabble in such world-unmaking magics. Every word that left Oliver's lips bore terrible echoes that lingered long after they should have dispersed, sinking down into the invisible matter of the universe and strengthening what Alexander's machine sought to unmake.

Oliver saw that realization in Alexander's face. Terrible rage twisted his features into something hideous and utterly mad. The waters pouring in through the gateway still came in a relentless flood, but its pace was visibly slackening as the rift torn between Meadow Hill and the depths of the Pacific began to close.

Alexander hauled himself to the altar's surface, his red robes plastered to his body by the waterfall rushing over him. He screamed words in response to Oliver's, incantations that stabbed in opposition to those coming from his mouth. Despite the power granted to him by the last revenant of Nereus-Kai, Oliver felt his grip on the spell faltering.

"You have power," shouted Alexander over the pounding flood, "but it is borrowed power."

Oliver knew he was right. The knowledge and energy he had brought from Celaeno was not his own, merely that which had survived the uncounted eons between the sinking of Atlantis and this moment. And second-hand ability could not prevail against singular will and determination to destroy.

The ocean water surged through the gateway once more, and Oliver recoiled as he saw an infinitely vast, amorphous shadow assume potency in the nightmare vortex behind Alexander. Something titanic in scale and unlimited in its potential for evil loomed large above the rock of Meadow Hill, its grotesque outline swelling beyond the confines of the machinery intended to bring it to the surface. Oliver felt every last buttress within his mind crumbling under the assault of so abominable a form—mountainous and impossible to comprehend, yet loathsomely familiar from the pages of the dread *Necronomicon*.

A booming heartbeat thundered over the hillside, a hammer-blow that parted the waters before it and sent those not already on their knees tumbling into the churning ocean as their minds were shattered by so maddening a sight. Oliver slid down the rock, still speaking the words imparted to him by the Atlantean priest, but each one faltering and having to be forced to the surface.

A gigantic, cyclopean shadow fell across the mountainside, vast as a low-slung moon and leprously greenish. Its mass was inconceivable, its bulk vaster than any living being of earthly matter could sustain. Though yet inconstant and not fully manifested, Oliver perceived a writhing forest of tentacles where a terrestrial creature might expect to evolve a mouth, eyes that had extinguished worlds with their gaze and which had beheld the fall of countless galactic civilizations by its clawed hand. Monstrous chanting and damnable piping accompanied the star god's ascension, and hideous words formed in Oliver's mind.

Iä! Iä! Cthulhu! Iä! Iä! Iä! Cthulhu!

His body spasmed at the sound as his mind fought to refuse the existence of this dread apparition from the dawn of time. Yet even as his mind crumbled under the assault of Cthulhu's appearance, he kept up his recitation of the Atlantean spell. He heard Alexander's laughter over the cascading waters, a delirious cacophony of lunatic howls and supreme terror.

Only then did Oliver see that Alexander was not alone on the altar.

A slender shape staggered through the thunderous waterfall, surely too slight and delicate to keep her feet in the face of the water's fury.

Something shone brightly and reflected lightning from its silver steel.

Amanda Sharpe plunged the Comte D'Erlette's dagger between Alexander's shoulder blades.

Alexander fell to his knees in pain, and Oliver felt his former colleague's hold on the gateway's permanence falter. Amanda screamed as she wrenched the dagger from Alexander's back and stabbed it home again.

A primeval, bellowing roar echoed from the sides of the valley like the most deafening peal of thunder, and the white monolith shattered into thousands of fragments. Cracking boulders fell from the valley sides and Alexander's machine swayed as foundations sunk deep into the rock were ripped from their moorings. Amanda fell from the altar and was instantly swept away by the roaring tides, leaving the gleaming silver blade buried in Alexander's back. Wild arcs of lightning lashed the water and Oliver felt the searing power of nameless alien energy course through him. With a hysterical scream, Oliver pushed himself back to his feet as the words he had learned on a far distant planet poured from him with renewed vigor.

So fast it seemed as though his words were tumbling over one another in their haste to be spoken, Oliver yelled the words of Nereus-Kai over and over again. He could feel their potency growing with every repetition, knowing on some protean level that the very act of speaking them again and again gave them power.

The bloated shape of the star god and his attendant ocean pushed at the barrier between its world and this. Dark waters gushed around it, and its screeching roar was that of a monstrous entity denied that which a foolish mortal had promised it. Its incredible anatomy was hideously revealed as portions of its star-formed matter pushed themselves into existence with a howl of violated space-time.

The beat of monstrous wings fanned the water into churning waves and the crash of an impossibly vast paw split the bedrock of the mountain. Oliver spoke the last words of the spell, and fell back into the water, unable to continue as the last of his strength fled his body.

Alexander swayed on his knees atop the altar and his eyes locked with Oliver's as they stood on the precipice of death and the end of the world. Oliver thought he saw anger through Alexander's pain, but perhaps it was sorrow. In the end, he would never know.

The immensity of waving tentacles that served Cthulhu for a maw descended and gathered Alexander up in their thick, fibrous mass. No pain or terror or sorrow, no matter how intense, no matter how profound, could ever compete with the horror of being devoured for all eternity.

Alexander's cries rose to a fevered pitch so terrible, so suffused with the very worst torments imaginable that Oliver screamed at their merest echoes. Cthulhu's bloated and hideous head lifted up as the healing matter of the world finally shut it out. Alexander's machine tore loose from the earth and toppled into the water with a thunderous crash of buckling metal and shrieking electrical discharge.

And with its destruction, the gateway to the waters of R'lyeh were sealed.

Oliver watched the hole in the world seal.

And the eyes of Cthulhu sucked him into their cosmic darkness.

* * *

The quantity of water loosed from the gateway to R'lyeh, though now sealed, was so enormous that its effects could not help but be widely felt. Millions upon millions of gallons of oceanic water flooded the fields and plains at the base of Meadow Hill in a torrential wavefront unlike anything seen before. Scores of homes and farmsteads were washed away in a tsunami of destruction that saw scores dead and many more lost, never to be found. The waters spilled into the Miskatonic and its banks rose by tens of feet, thundering toward Arkham in a spuming tide that crashed into the town with devastating consequences.

For a hundred yards either side of the river, the town was literally wiped out. Raging waters reached up with incredible power to destroy homes and businesses with unstoppable elemental fury. The West Street bridge was smashed to rubble by the force of the wave, and the Garrison Street bridge was closed for two months while repairs were carried out to render it fit for traffic. Thousands of tons of debris was dragged into the river and washed downstream, where much of it was washed up on the beaches of Kingsport.

The floodwaters swirled through the streets of the town like an invading army before morning brought any sign of it receding. The unnaturally delayed onset of sunlight brought with it scenes of utter carnage: a swath of destruction unrivaled during any period of the town's history. The death toll would not be known for months, but initial estimates were in the region of five hundred souls. The majority of those deaths were in the Merchant Town or Northside districts, but buildings as far away as the university campus were collapsed in the terrible flood.

The people of Arkham were stunned by so comprehensive a disaster, unaware of how much worse it could have been. They reacted with typical Massachusetts pluck and began the business of rebuilding with the same fortitude of spirit that had served the inhabitants of San Francisco so well in 1906.

Amid the chaos of the catastrophic freak flooding, no one noticed a lone car that wended its sad and weary way down from the north. It went straight to St. Mary's Hospital before driving to the screaming, wailing corridors of a damnable institution on the very edges of town.

And there it stayed for the rest of the day.

ONE YEAR LATER
1927

Though he had visited Arkham Asylum every day since the horror atop Meadow Hill, Rex had never lost his dislike for its grim facade and claustrophobic hallways. He still walked with a limp after being swept down the rocky gullies and ravines of the hill, and though his broken leg had healed, Rex wouldn't be dancing the Charleston any time soon. He'd also cracked five ribs and fractured both his collarbone and his left wrist.

And he still considered himself one of the lucky ones.

All but three of Donald's men had perished atop the hill, and two of those were also resident here, confined to padded rooms and unable to mix with the rest of the patients. Donald himself had come through the ordeal with little more than cuts and bruises, and was back at work on the rapidly rising wireless station atop Kingsport Head.

Gabriel was waiting for him in the checkerboard-floored vestibule, looking pale and drawn, even after the six months he'd spent recuperating at his family's farm in Vermont. They'd corresponded infrequently, neither man wishing to relive the things they had glimpsed on that blasted hilltop as the gateway to R'lyeh opened.

"Hey, Gabriel," said Rex, holding out his hand. "It's been a while. You okay?"

"Rex," said Gabriel. "As well as can be expected. I'm not sleeping much."

"I know what you mean," said Rex. "I close my eyes and all I see is that—"

"Don't," said Gabriel brusquely. "I know."

"Sure, sorry," said Rex. "I forget sometimes, you know."

"Yeah," said Gabriel, and Rex saw how wretched and thin Gabriel looked beneath his heavy coat.

"How was Vermont?" asked Rex.

"Cold," answered Gabriel. "How's this place been?"

"Wet, like you'd expect after a disaster like this," said Rex. "It's been a year, but people are still scared it might happen again."

"They're right to think that."

"I don't think so," said Rex. "Alexander's gone."

"There'll be someone else who thinks like him," said Gabriel. "You know what I know, more maybe. You think someone isn't going to try and do something like this again? Or something worse?"

"I don't think there could be anything worse than that thing," said Rex, trying to shut out the image of questing tentacles and monstrous bat wings that had woken him screaming every night for the past twelve months.

"Don't bet on it," said Gabriel.

His friend's mood was sour, but Rex couldn't blame him. Gabriel had been fired from the Pinkertons following the deaths of the men he'd brought from New York. He'd returned to Arkham only once, for Henry Cartwright's funeral, and stayed only long enough to see the old soldier's body laid in the ground at Christchurch Cemetery before leaving town.

As other mourners had thrown in handfuls of earth, Finn Edwards had tossed a silver pendant onto the lid of Henry's coffin. When Rex had asked him about it, all he'd said was that it had saved his life when it had snagged on a tree branch and kept him from being swept over a cliff to his death. He'd reeked of whiskey, even before the wake, and spent the evening staring into the depths of a bottle before starting a fight and being ejected from the building.

That was the last time Rex had seen Finn.

Rita and Amanda had come to the funeral, and both had a haunted look that Rex was coming to realize was a hallmark of guilty survivors the world over. He'd seen it in the faces of bystanders and survivors in dozens of different countries, but he'd never expected to see it in the faces of people he knew and loved. Both girls had been badly hurt in the flood that poured from the mountain. They'd suffered broken bones that had healed well and mental scars that only time would reveal how well they had healed.

Rex suspected they might never completely heal.

Despite the flooding that had devastated Arkham (and a great many coastal locations around the globe, according to news coming in from numerous low-lying counties) they had elected to remain in Arkham. Amanda in particular appeared to have weathered the storm well, possessing a decadent confidence and largesse of character that bordered on the remarkable.

Kate Winthrop returned to work in the laboratories of Miskatonic University after a period of convalescence from injuries and trauma she would not describe, even to her personal physician. To ensure continued funding from the Nathaniel Derby Pickman Foundation, work at the university was continuing at a rapid pace on the proposed exploration of the Antarctic wastelands. Every able-bodied scientist was required to ensure this astounding expedition was ready to depart on schedule, a few years hence. Though she had clearly suffered terribly at the hands of Alexander, Kate was only too pleased to be plunged deep into work.

She told Rex it kept the worst of the nightmares at bay.

He could easily understand that sentiment.

Since the deluge that had laid waste to Arkham, he'd been kept busier than he'd ever known. He'd filed hundreds of articles with Harvey Gedney: miraculous stories of survival, harrowing tales of families wiped out, businesses ruined, and the proposed rebuilding work. Rex wrote dutifully and diligently, but could never quite wring his words of the hint that, for all that the flood had wrought terrible damage, the town had escaped a far more terrible fate. He'd made discreet enquiries into the fate of the *Matilda*, and learned that it had been reported lost at sea some weeks after the events of Meadow Hill.

Scarcely six months later, the Warren Mining Company had gone to the wall, its investors suddenly realizing that their money had been plowed into worthless digs and unworkable technology. Its board of directors was facing jail time as scandal after scandal was brought to light, and though no trace could be found of its founder, it was widely believed that he had perished on the *Matilda* when it sank in strange southern latitudes.

"Gentlemen," said Dr. Hardstrom, emerging from his office at the back of the vestibule.

"Doctor," said Gabriel, shaking the man's hand. Rex followed Gabriel's example, though he disliked the man intensely. His grip was limp and wet, and he seemed not to be as concerned with the welfare of his patients as he ought to be.

"Dr. Hillshore is with him just now," said Hardstrom, unable to keep the irritation from his voice at the thought of a practicing physician beyond his control within his walls. "If you'd like to come with me."

Rex and Gabriel followed Hardstrom through the corridors of the asylum, paying no attention to his functional and rote recitations of symptoms and unlikely outcomes. He cautioned them to expect no change, but still Rex hoped that Hillshore might find something Hardstrom had overlooked.

A surly-looking orderly opened the door to the recreation room, and Rex felt his spirits sink as he entered this drab dormitory of the damned. Weak sunlight filled the room, filtered through barred windows and Georgian wired glass, draining every face of life and vitality.

Most of the people in this room didn't even look up as they entered, too stupefied on medication or sunk too deeply into their manias to pay them any mind. Here and there, an orderly maintained a cautious distance from someone who had previously displayed violent tendencies. Rex knew a great many of these people by reputation and had seen plenty of them kick off at the slightest provocation.

There was Kelly, who had been incarcerated after displaying an alarming fondness for leaping off tall buildings and whose manic energy had to be controlled by pacifying drugs. There was Monroe, who had once been an orderly here before suffering a complete psychotic break, and pacing by the far wall was a man with copious tattoos who was known only as the Count. Rex wondered if the man believed himself to be royalty. Or perhaps he thought he might be a relative of Stoker's Dracula.

Rex saw Hillshore seated with Oliver at a table by the window. An untouched chess board sat between them, next to a copy of *Twenty Thousand Leagues Under the Sea*. Hillshore saw them enter and raised a hand in welcome.

"I shall leave you to it," said Hardstrom. "Let Wilkins know when you are ready to leave."

"Sure," said Rex as Hardstrom withdrew.

He and Gabriel picked a careful route through the patients toward Hillshore, exchanging pleasantries as they sat around the table. Gabriel asked after Morley Dean, but a solemn shake of the head was his only answer.

Though it broke his heart every time, Rex looked into Oliver's face.

He saw the same vacant, empty look he'd seen when they had found him strapped to a rock at the top of the mountain a year ago. His expression had remained unchanged ever since, and though his body endured, his mind was no more. Rex felt tears at the corners of his eyes, knowing that, but for this man's willing sacrifice, the world would already be gone.

"Who's winning?" said Rex, gesturing to the chess board.

"Stalemate," answered Hillshore.

* * *

Minnie saw Rex emerge from the asylum, feeling a weight lift from her shoulders at the sight of him, as though she feared that one day he might not come out. He took a breath of crisp air and walked down the worn steps, crossing the short distance to where she stood beside his battered but reliable Model T. Minnie had her long coat pulled tight around her and a thick scarf wrapped around her neck.

Even in the low, bleaching winter sun he was dashing, and her mood lifted at the sight of his face.

She opened her arms and enfolded Rex in a loving embrace.

He held her just as tight and let the emotion of this latest visit drain from him.

"You don't need to do this every day, you know that, right?" she said.

"Yeah," said Rex. "I do. He saved us all."

"I know that, hun," said Minnie. "I was there too, but Oliver wouldn't want this."

"He visited Henry every week."

"Maybe so, but this isn't healthy," said Minnie, opening the passenger door. Ordinarily Rex would sooner cut off a finger than let someone else drive his car, but she had more than earned that right. It had been Minnie that drove Rex's car from the bottom of Meadow Hill back to town and gotten him to the hospital before he'd bled out.

Rex paused before climbing in and looked over the crooked spires of Arkham. He didn't look to the north, where the rounded summit of Meadow Hill dominated the skyline. These days, none of them ever looked to the north.

"It was all worth it, wasn't it?" he asked.

Minnie took his hands and nodded.

"Of course it was," she said. "We're alive aren't we? We've got each other."

"And let me tell you, that's all that gets me through the days," said Rex, gripping her tightly. She saw he was fighting back the urge to cry. "But we lost so much."

"And we would have lost more if it wasn't for Oliver."

"But what's the point of it all? If we're all just specks of insignificant dust in the universe, irrelevant and meaningless to the cosmos…why does it matter if we're alive?"

Minnie released Rex's hands and cupped his chin. She kissed him on the mouth, a long, passionate kiss like she'd seen in the movies.

"What was that for?" he asked with a bemused smile when she finally released him.

"The cosmos might not care about us, but screw the cosmos," said Minnie. "*We* care. *We* matter. It's the connections people make between each other that are the most important thing. People matter to one other, and that's got to be enough. It's all we've got, sweetheart."

Rex nodded and said, "You're smarter than you look, you know that?"

Minnie went around the car and got into the driver's seat.

"Just you remember that," she said as Rex climbed in the opposite side.

"How could I forget?" he replied. "You never stop reminding me."

Minnie leaned over and gave Rex a kiss on the cheek before turning the engine over with a throaty growl. The car protested, threatening to stall, but Minnie feathered the gas pedal and coaxed it back to life.

"You've got the touch," said Rex.

"I know," said Minnie, guiding the car down the long gravel driveway.

The sun was rising in the east as they drove to the offices of the *Arkham Advertiser*.

Another day had dawned and that, thought Minnie, was something to be thankful for.

THE END

About the Author

Hailing from Scotland, Graham was first exposed to the horrors of the uncaring cosmos when he came across the works of H.P. Lovecraft in the sci-fi section of his local library. Haunted by the experience, he narrowly avoided the sanity drain of a career in surveying to join Games Workshop's Games Development team, which, frankly, was a lucky escape. He worked there for six and a half years before taking the plunge to becoming a full-time author. With a *New York Times* bestseller under his belt (and a replica of Snaga, the axe of Druss the Legend, which he received after his novel, *Empire*, won the 2010 David Gemmell Legend Award) and thirty novels in his back catalog, he reckons he chose the right path.

Graham lives and works in Nottingham.
You can keep up with what he's up to by visiting his website at www.graham-mcneill.com.

Facebook: The Fortress of Hera

Twitter: @grahammcneill

ARKHAM HORROR

THE CLASSIC GAME OF LOVECRAFTIAN ADVENTURE

Gather the clues, test your sanity, and face the terrible powers of the Ancient One!

Arkham Horror is a cooperative board game of Lovecraftian terror for one to eight players. Taking on the roles of investigators during the 1920s, players search for the secrets needed to defend the town of Arkham from otherworldly powers.

While the base game provides plenty of frightening adventure, *Arkham Horror's* library of expansions add limitless variety, creating a unique experience every time.

FANTASY FLIGHT GAMES

WWW.FANTASYFLIGHTGAMES.COM

Fantasy Flight Games, the FFG Logo, and *Arkham Horror* are trademarks or registered trademarks of Fantasy Flight Publishing, Inc.